ALSO BY DAVID ROBERTS

*The Pueblo Revolt: The Secret Rebellion That Drove the
Spaniards Out of the Southwest*

Four Against the Arctic: Shipwrecked for Six Years at the Top of the World

Escape from Lucania: An Epic Story of Survival

*True Summit: What Really Happened on the Legendary
Ascent of Annapurna*

*A Newer World: Kit Carson, John C. Frémont, and the
Claiming of the American West*

The Lost Explorer: Finding Mallory on Mount Everest
(with Conrad Anker)

Escape Routes: Further Adventure Writings of David Roberts

In Search of the Old Ones: Exploring the Anasazi World of the Southwest

Once They Moved Like the Wind: Cochise, Geronimo, and the Apache Wars

Mount McKinley: The Conquest of Denali (with Bradford Washburn)

Iceland: Land of the Sagas (with Jon Krakauer)

Jean Stafford: A Biography

Moments of Doubt: And Other Mountaineering Writings

Great Exploration Hoaxes

Deborah: A Wilderness Narrative

The Mountain of My Fear

On the
Ridge
Between
Life
and
Death

A Climbing Life Reexamined

DAVID ROBERTS

Simon & Schuster
NEW YORK LONDON TORONTO SYDNEY

SIMON & SCHUSTER
Rockefeller Center
1230 Avenue of the Americas
New York, NY 10020

Simon & Schuster and colophon are registered trademarks
of Simon & Schuster, Inc.

For information about special discounts for bulk purchases,
please contact Simon & Schuster Special Sales at
1-800-456-6798 or business@simonandschuster.com.

DESIGNED BY PAUL DIPPOLITO

Manufactured in the United States of America

3   5   7   9   10   8   6   4

Library of Congress Cataloging-in-Publication Data
Roberts, David, date.
On the ridge between life and death : a climbing life reexamined / David Roberts.
p.   cm.
Includes index.
1. Roberts, David, date. 2. Mountaineers—United States—Biography. I. Title.
GV199.92R62435 2005
796.52'2'092—dc22
[B]   2005044109
ISBN-13: 978-0-7432-5518-9
ISBN-10:   0-7432-5518-6

In memory of

Gabe Lee
Ed Bernd
Don Jensen

Contents

On the Ridge Between
Life and Death

ONE

Gabe

THE TROUBLE BEGAN ON THE FIFTH PITCH.
I handed Gabe our hardware—half a dozen soft-iron pitons and eight
or nine carabiners dangling from a nylon sling—and said, "On belay."
Once again, I had been unable to drive a single piton for my anchor:
instead, I had found a bucket-shaped hollow in the ruddy sandstone
and sat in it with my back against the right wall, my feet braced
against an opposing bulge.

Gabe started up the inside corner, angling left as the arching dihedral dictated his path. The going looked easy, for he was moving with
that jerky efficiency that had become his forte during the last three
months. My breath escaped in a sigh of well-being. Once again, we
were launched on the flight that turned the neurotic thrum of ordinary life into a staccato pulse of purpose.

But there were no cracks for our pitons. That was the trouble with
the First Flatiron—with all the Flatirons, those massive tilting slabs
that stared east from Green Mountain over the mesas above Boulder.
Eighty feet up, Gabe sidled left around a protruding arête and passed
out of sight. Still he had placed no protection, so as I fed the rope out,
I knew my belay was worthless.

The rope stopped. Gabe's distant voice: "Should I go straight up?
Or traverse left?"

We had been shouting too much on this climb—conferring from
a hundred feet apart, as we had forced our way through the route's
odd intricacies. The elders in the Colorado Mountain Club who had
taught us to climb early that spring had stressed the importance of

economy in our shouted signals: "On belay!," "Climbing!," "Slack!," "Up rope!"—the syllables apportioned so that even over a droning wind one call should never be mistaken for its opposite.

"Try to go straight up!" I yelled back. So the route had seemed to unfold, as I had studied it in binoculars from my home on Blue-bell Avenue. Atop this pitch, I thought, we would have it made, with less than 200 feet of easy scrambling to the notch just below the summit.

The rope inched out again. Ten minutes later came Gabe's call: "Off belay!"

With a sense of relief, I started up. It was a perfect summer day, pine sap wafting on the fickle breeze, warm sun slanting across the cliff, the whole of the First Flatiron to ourselves. Each wrinkle in the sandstone offered a toehold, each knob a handle to seize with my fingers. The rhythm of movement absorbed me.

The burden of my previous winter lifted: in the blue sky at the brow of our universe, an answer hovered. I need only struggle up to find it, turning fear into power, ambivalence into act. After this pitch, we could waltz to the top. Gabe would get back in plenty of time for his cousin's birthday party.

As I climbed, the rope drooped unnaturally to my left. Despite my advice, Gabe must have continued his traverse, rather than heading straight up. Oh, well: I trusted his route-finding.

When I was fifty feet up, the rope began to drag at my waist. I pulled in about ten feet of slack, then moved farther up. Once again, the drag restrained me. This time when I pulled, no slack came. Somewhere the rope must be stuck. I peered left, and noticed, across forty feet of blank purple slab, a downward-pointing prong, beneath which the rope disappeared.

I stepped carefully left, hanging on to a horn with my right hand, to regain a few feet of slack. Taking the rope in my left hand, I swung it vigorously in a counterclockwise turn. A loop spun down the Gold-Line cord, ebbing as it went. At the prong, it died. I tried several more times, but the rope was jammed fast.

On my tongue, I tasted the first trickle of dread.

It was July 9, 1961. I had turned eighteen a little more than a month before, Gabe Lee two months before that. We had taken minimum-wage jobs that summer between high school and college: I planted seedlings in the tundra at 12,000 feet for an alpine research lab, while Gabe peeled potatoes in a kitchen at the University of Colorado. We lived for the weekends, when we could climb together.

I had known Gabe since our kindergarten days at Uni Hill, and yet, how well did I really know him? I could picture him in third grade, hunkered in jeans fraying at the knees on the gravel playground, as he thumbed an aggie toward my vulnerable marble in our endless game of keepsies. I saw him in gym class at Baseline Junior High, gliding deep down the left sideline under a bomb hurled by Steve Green, our sandlot Johnny Unitas. And I saw him the previous fall on our Boulder High tennis team, as he gritted through a pivotal match against Fort Morgan, his lobs sailing astray in a blue wind out of the east, heavy with the sickly-sweet odor of the sugar-beet factories.

Gabe was shy. He kept his private self impermeable, deflecting any questions that veered toward the personal. When he talked, it was in that quick, jerky voice, the complement of the way he climbed—as if each sentence were a burst of weakness that he could not purge soon enough. And we, his classmates, cut him all the slack he needed: for, with his younger brother, Martin, and his sister, Marian, Gabe had grown up without a mother. Why, we had no idea. We never thought to ask.

Then, just three months before our climb on the First Flatiron, in March, driving on a freeway south of Houston, Gabe's father had been hit from behind by a speeding drunk. His car had shot across the divider and collided with an oncoming vehicle. Gabe's father had died in the hospital an hour later.

A week before his eighteenth birthday, Gabe had in effect become the head of his orphaned family. When he resurfaced at Boulder High after his week in purgatory, I mumbled my prepared formula: "I'm really sorry about what happened."

"That's okay," Gabe said in his breathless syllables. "When can we go climbing?"

Gabe was an inch taller than I, at five eleven, with short brown hair swept left, a round face, and heavy eyebrows shielding his brown eyes. He was as thin as I was. He was smart in school, though not the scholar I fancied myself. At first, I had been the better rock climber; but he had improved so rapidly in the last two months that now he routinely took the leads of which I was leery.

On weekends through May and June, Gabe and I had gone after all five Flatirons. The Colorado Mountain Club mentors who had given us our lessons on five successive Saturdays had taken us up the Second Flatiron as our graduation exercise, then turned us loose into the labyrinth of our half-mastered craft. Gabe and I had done the standard routes on the First and Third, at the time the most popular climbs near Boulder. It was the Fourth and Fifth Flatirons that remained obscure, and, as we roped up at their bases, we had no idea where our predecessors had gone, or how hard the climbing might prove. With those forays had come a new, deeper enthusiasm, that of explorers setting out upon uncharted oceans. And on the Fifth Flatiron several weeks before, Gabe had led a dauntingly smooth pitch without placing a single piton—his finest effort yet. I knew that I wouldn't have had the guts to try it myself.

Early that morning in July, I had called Gabe up with my plan. "I want to try the First, but not the standard route," I told him over the phone. "I've been looking at a line on the left. It goes pretty much straight from the bottom of the cliff to the summit. Maybe eight or nine pitches. It's possible nobody's done it."

Gabe had hesitated; I heard talk in the background about a birthday party. "We can get back by five," I exhorted. "We're fast. It'll be a great thing to do."

"The rope's stuck!" I yelled. "Pull!"

Gabe pulled, to no avail. Later I would wonder whether the effort had only jammed the GoldLine tighter under the downward-pointing prong.

The dread on my tongue blossomed in a wave of malaise, which

I tried to swallow down. An obvious course of action loomed. I could try to traverse to the snag, free it, and climb straight up to Gabe. But as I gazed at the frighteningly smooth tract of no-man's-land that lay between me and the prong, I knew that I couldn't climb it. At some point, I would fall, whipping down and then left as forty feet of slack abetted my plunge. The brunt would come in a sudden, wrenching jerk. If it were forceful enough, and if Gabe, like me, had been unable to place an anchor piton, that jerk could pull him off his ledge. Alternatively, if the $\frac{3}{8}$-inch rope were wedged across a sharp edge, there was a chance that it would sever on impact.

My mind raced. I looked hard at the smooth slab, searching for nubbins that would hold the sharp rubber edges of my rock shoes. But there was nothing.

I could think of only one other thing to do. As I contemplated that choice, a gust of pure nausea chilled me. With careful fingers, I untied from the end of the rope. Gathering up as much of the GoldLine as I could, I made three small coils. Then, awkwardly, I hung on with my left hand while I cocked my right arm, like a discus thrower, and flung the coils as hard as I could into the void. "Pull!" I screamed at Gabe.

What I had hoped to accomplish was to snap the line loose from the prong with the force of my throw. If that worked, Gabe could simply pull the rope up to his ledge. Reunited there, we would tie in once more and get on with our crawl toward the summit.

I took two deep breaths, then started climbing, unroped, up to Gabe. For the next eight or ten minutes, I concentrated so hard on the sandstone beneath my feet and hands that the rest of the world vanished. I made each move with an exaggerated, stodgy caution, hesitating before I dared transfer my weight. I could not afford the slightest misstep.

In the myopia of my concentration, however, I must have taken a route different from the one Gabe had followed. A hundred and twenty feet out, I saw no sign of him. At last I stood on a generous, rounded shelf. Above me, the going looked easy. "Where are you?" I called.

"Right here!" His voice was so close it startled me. He must have been only fifteen feet below me and to the left, yet an intervening bulge had eclipsed him from my sight. "It's still stuck!"

The nausea returned. What could we do? Briefly, I toyed with a humiliating scenario. We could call for help, hoping to catch the ear of some hiker on the Mesa Trail below. Then wait for hours, stranded on our separate ledges, as experts from the Rocky Mountain Rescue Group climbed up the back of the First Flatiron and down the face till they could lower us a rope. Yet I knew I could never bring myself to take that course. In the mountains, as all the climbing narratives I had read since I was twelve made clear, you got yourself out of trouble.

"Can you set up a rappel?" I yelled.

"No!" answered Gabe. "I can't get anything in."

What could we do? Then, from the depths of our predicament, Gabe delivered the answer. "I think I can climb down to it!" he yelled.

A tide of relief engulfed me. Gabe would do the hard work, just as he had volunteered to take the scariest leads on the Fourth and Fifth Flatirons. "Be careful," I pleaded, then sat down to wait.

That summer, it was not college that loomed on my horizon. It was the north face of Grand Teton, up in Wyoming—the August test of all that I should have learned about rock and balance and nerve. The Grand scared me, and yet I longed for it with a passion as sharp as first love. Somewhere on that great wall, I might find the signposts that could guide me out of the benightment of myself.

For two years before the Colorado Mountain Club had taught me the rudiments of rope and piton, I had hiked in the Colorado mountains, gradually taking on more and more difficult challenges. The previous August, I had made a solo traverse of the Maroon Bells; that December, a long scramble in a blizzard up the sharp, notched east ridge of Pacific Peak in the Tenmile Range.

I would never, however, have dared approach such a storied wall as the north face of the Grand, had another schoolmate—the most accomplished climber in our Boulder High crowd, with two solid years of rope craft under his belt—not invited me. Though Jock (not his real name) and I had never been friends, he had taken notice of my bold mountain scrambles and had approached me when his regular partner had backed out.

My final exam had come just the month before, in June, when Jock and I climbed the east face of Longs Peak. On that 2,000-foot wall, I had led the hardest pitch, and when, exhausted, only 400 feet below the summit, Jock had started to lose his cool as he kicked steps up a snow couloir that was ready to avalanche, I had talked him back to calm proficiency.

As skillfully as Gabe scaled the cliffs we tackled together, Jock and I never considered including him in our plans for the Grand; for before the previous week, Gabe had had no mountain experience at all. That Sunday, he and I had barged unroped up a dangerous chimney on Mount of the Holy Cross, in the Sawatch Range. Unacclimatized, Gabe had trailed behind all day, pausing to plant a forearm on his knee and gasp for breath. On the summit, he threw up; but only moments later he blurted out an uncharacteristic confession of the overarching joy the climb had brought him.

As we had rested there at 14,000 feet, Gabe said that he had finished the copy of *Annapurna* that I had lent him. I had first read the book some years before. Maurice Herzog's grim tale of frostbitten fingers and toes sacrificed to the first conquest of an 8,000-meter peak had paradoxically infused me with my passion for ascent. In the ecstatic redemption the Frenchman had found as he languished in his hospital bed, I divined a mystic alternative to the dreary plod of Baseline Junior High.

Atop Holy Cross, still dizzy with altitude, Gabe struggled to express a kindred transport. "Those guys," he said, "Terray and Lachenal and the rest—what they did was incredible. The whole thing is just so inspiring." He paused, looking out at other Sawatch summits. "We gotta do more stuff like this, Dave," he said.

For ten minutes, I sat on my shelf, staring east over the straw-colored plains. Lazy cumulus clouds sailed far above, riding the breeze over the crest of the Front Range. It was still a perfect day, warmer than it had been all morning, though the sun had nothing to do with the clammy sweat on my palms. I guessed that it was three o'clock. Still time to get back for the birthday party, if things worked out. . . .

I could not stay silent. "How's it going?" I called, trying to sound calm.

Gabe's voice was much farther away, the words strung even tighter than usual. But the news was joyous. "I've got the rope!"

"Way to go!" I yelled. "Coil it up."

"No, I'll just drape it over my shoulder." Gabe had always been impatient. In the circumstances, I could hardly blame him. "I'm going to go up a different way."

That last remark disturbed me. It was almost always easier to climb up a pitch than down it. Having successfully descended to the snag, why didn't Gabe simply reverse the moves as he climbed back up? Something on that line must have bothered him. *Be careful, Gabe,* I pleaded silently.

Again I waited. Throughout the process, I had caught not a glimpse of my friend: the bulge ten feet beneath me blocked out much of the lower face of the Flatiron. And again, to wait and say nothing was agony. "How's it going?" I yelled for the second time.

Gabe's voice had an unfamiliar, choked urgency. "I just got past a hard place," he said, "but now it's easier." I guessed that he had climbed to within twenty-five feet of my shelf of safety. My brain whispered, *Bring up the rope, Gabe, and we'll be all right.*

I waited and stared. Far out, above the plains, a hawk danced in circles on an updraft, mocking our gravity-bound plight. The sun blazed on my back and neck.

A sound I had never heard before seized my ears, yet I knew at once what it was. It was the sound of cloth sliding against rock.

"Dave!" Gabe screamed.

I lurched upright, holding a knob with one hand, straining forward to peer over the brow of the eclipsing ledge. For the first time in half an hour, I saw Gabe, forty feet below me. He was rolling and sliding down the smooth, steep slab, the rope whirling about his body like an unraveling ball of yarn. "Grab something!" I yelled.

Gabe's cry came up to me, even as his body accelerated away: "No! Oh, no!" He began to bounce, the terrible arc of his trajectory longer after each impact. Four hundred feet below, he sailed upside down through the empty air, hit the cliff headfirst, and was flung into the treetops at the base of the Flatiron.

Only seconds had passed. Silence reclaimed Green Mountain—but my blood was roaring in my ears. I forced myself to breathe.

It was impossible that Gabe had survived such a fall. And yet if there was the slightest chance . . .

The Colorado Mountain Club training came to me unbidden. As loud as I could, I yelled "Help!" in successive bursts of three. After a few repetitions, a voice from below answered me: "Help coming!" It turned out that two observers had watched Gabe's fall, one (the patriarch of the Rocky Mountain Rescue Group) through binoculars from his home on the south edge of Boulder.

Now I knew with absolute certainty what I had to do. I must sit and wait for the rescue that, a few minutes before, had loomed as a humiliation. There was nothing I could do for Gabe. The worst scenario would be to compound the disaster with a fall of my own. I sat down on my ledge.

Within seconds, I was back on my feet, headed up the last 200 feet of the Flatiron. To sit and wait, with the film clip of Gabe's plunge playing over and over before my eyes, was impossible. Adrenaline drove me upward. My scrambling was almost out of control, a scuttling jog from hold to hold.

Minutes later, I stood on the summit of the Flatiron. I had been there before, setting up a rappel off the overhanging back side. I knew there was a tricky down climb somewhere on the south, so I set out to find it.

Now adrenaline served to calm me. I made the moves, traversing right at the crux, muttering under my breath, "Don't blow it here." The moment I reached solid earth, I started running down the gully between the First and Second Flatirons.

I met the first rescuer, who looked as wild-eyed as I felt, near the base. "Where is he?" he cried.

"In the trees!"

For five minutes we searched, as one by one, other rescuers arrived. Our inability to find Gabe seemed to add a cruel insult to the blow the cliff had dealt him. I crashed through downed trees and slipped on moss-covered talus as, fueled by desperation, I sought my friend.

At last I heard a call: "Here he is!"

A rescuer led me to the spot. Gabe lay facedown on a pine-needled slope, his limbs bent in positions no living person could have struck. A big swath of blue jeans had torn away, baring one buttock, scraped and raw with blood.

I could not bring myself to touch Gabe's body. I slumped to the ground, caught my head in my hands, and gave myself up to the sobbing that the last thirty minutes of terror had kept at bay.

TWO

The Vacant Lot

WHAT SEEMED LIKE HOURS LATER—BUT IT CANNOT have been that long, for the sun in the west was still spreading its benediction over the perfect July day—a policeman led me up the front walk on Bluebell Avenue. My mother came to the door, grasped the situation in an instant, and burst into tears.

Shortly before, someone from Gabe's house had called in annoyance, wondering why Gabe was late for the birthday party. Now my father took on the task of telephoning and breaking the news. Years later, he would tell me that it was the hardest thing he had ever done.

The newspapers put the accident on the front page. As was the norm in those days, when the general public had no comprehension of the arcane business of mountain climbing, the reporters garbled everything. The *Rocky Mountain News* quoted the Boulder County coroner, who claimed that I had told him not only that Gabe and I were still roped together as the accident began to unfold, but that we had reached an "overhang" 100 feet below the summit, where (insisted the coroner)

> Roberts said he made his way around the overhanging rock by means of handholds already carved in the sheer cliff and then went on to the summit.
>
> He said Lee called out to him to release the rope. Roberts watched his companion coil the rope over his left shoulder and begin working his way horizontally out from beneath the overhang.
>
> Suddenly, Roberts said, the youth fell without a cry.

(I have no memory of ever speaking to the coroner, who must have gotten this nonsensical account of Gabe's fall thirdhand.)

Boulder's *Daily Camera* published a picture of the Flatiron with a dotted line that fairly accurately traced Gabe's plunge, ending in a Maltese cross in the treetops. In the opposite column Gabe and I appeared in our high school yearbook photos. Crew-cut, neatly dressed in jacket and tie, we sport identical grins as we seem to contemplate our limitless futures. The *Camera*'s version of the accident was as confused as the *News*'s:

> Roberts was above Lee near the top of the 800-foot, steep rock formation. Unable to get the rope untangled, Lee called to Roberts and asked him to "unrope." Roberts untied the rope from himself and threw it down to Lee. It was at this point that Lee fell.

The *Camera* reporter also found a hiker on the Mesa Trail, identified as a Mountain Park patrolman, who claimed "he watched Lee and Roberts climb earlier in the afternoon and heard them chattering back and forth. He said he tried to 'warn the boys to come down about 3 or 3:30.'"

The reason for his warning, this witness declared, was that "experienced mountain climbers usually don't banter back and forth as Lee and Roberts were doing." Whether or not the man had concocted his I-told-you-so story out of thin air, Gabe and I never heard anyone calling to us from the mesa. Our "bantering" had been all about the route and the scarcity of piton cracks.

Perhaps as a corrective to these maledictions and inanities in the public record, my father urged me to put down on paper my own account of what had happened on the First Flatiron. I still have my two-and-a-half-page report, dutifully typed up on my Hermes portable like a term paper, complete with my own "analysis" of what Gabe and I might have done wrong.

There was a memorial service at a Boulder chapel. Of this undoubtedly lugubrious event, I retain not a jot of recollection.

A few days after the accident, Jock came by my house. "The thing you've got to do," he said, squinting with acumen, "is get right back on the rock." He was still counting on me for the north face of the Grand Teton in August.

We drove up Flagstaff Mountain and parked next to the Cookie Jar, a lumpy spike of sandstone some twenty-five feet tall. Jock soloed up the easiest route, then sat on top to belay me from above. The moment I touched the rock, I started trembling. Jock hauled me in with vicious tugs, and I floundered to the top, my moves a lurching travesty of climbing technique. Jock waved away my distress: "That's okay, it'll come back."

At the end of the week, I returned to my job planting seedlings for the alpine lab. To my puzzlement, not one of my colleagues, not even the two or three fellow climbers among the gang, said a word about what had happened. It was as if the very subject were taboo. Faced with their silence, I started to internalize Gabe's death, like a shameful secret.

Yet at the same time, I still planned to go with Jock to the Grand. To back out, I thought, with a logic more emotional than rational, would prove just how pointless Gabe's death had been. I do not remember even discussing the question with my parents.

At this point came a crucial intervention. Although in the spring of 1961, Gabe had become my regular climbing partner, he was not my best friend. For years, I had spent much of my free time with Paul, a witty, athletic prankster—just a month earlier, he had been voted Class Clown at Boulder High—whose dour parents had fled Hitler's Germany just before the outbreak of World War II. Paul and I had in fact been buddies since kindergarten, partners in all sorts of adolescent delinquency, and a two-man touch football team of some aplomb. Yet, although Paul aspired to become a professional race car driver (his hero was the Argentine Grand Prix champion Juan-Manuel Fangio), he thought mountaineering sheer insanity. Clued in as no one else was to the psychic chaos I was keeping beneath the surface, he took me aside one day in late July and pleaded with me not to go to Wyoming. At last he made a deal: if I backed out of the Grand, he would join me on a four-day hiking traverse of the Gore Range in August—even though Paul had never spent a night in a sleeping bag farther afield than his own backyard.

It was the push I needed. I called Jock and invited him over for a talk. We sat on my front porch as I told him I couldn't go to the Grand. "I'm just a mess," I said wretchedly. "I wouldn't be any use on the north face."

He glared at me, stood up and walked away, pausing to spit back, "You rat fink." We never spoke again.

In the end, Jock recruited another partner, but the two of them got weathered off the Grand low on the wall. At the end of August, Paul and I backpacked in from State Highway 9 toward Eagles Nest and Mount Powell. The second day, a freak late-summer storm moved in. We topped out on Powell in a blind fog, the temperature below freezing. By our last day we were stumbling in a blizzard through calf-deep snow down Booth Creek, having slept not a minute in our soaked sleeping bags the night before (we had neglected to bring a rain fly for the tent). Paul thought there was a reasonable chance of perishing, but I felt oddly elated. Mere hypothermia held no terrors comparable to those of the precipice.

In early September, I flew back east to go to college. At Harvard, I planned to major in mathematics and go out for the tennis team. With my new roommates, I pored over the Radcliffe freshman register, wondering how I might get up the nerve to talk to any of the girls whose smug, preppie portraits beamed from the slick pages.

It had been two months since I had spoken to anyone about Gabe. Even during our soggy ordeal in the Gore Range, Paul and I had avoided the subject. In that indelible moment in early July, when I had walked, exhausted, toward the front door on Bluebell Avenue, escorted by the policeman, to unleash my mother's flood of tears, I had forged in my unconscious a deep conviction that something besides tragedy had occurred on the First Flatiron. It was as though I had committed a crime, and been caught in the act.

In the subsequent weeks, the silence of my colleagues at the alpine lab had reinforced that conviction. By September, Gabe was buried deep, a guilty secret I was determined to keep hidden from view. In backing out of the Grand Teton, I had made, I thought, a life-altering choice. Whether or not mountain climbing truly offered the mystic alternative to the dreary plod of daily life I had divined in the pages of Herzog's *Annapurna*, it was not for me. Gabe's last words, shouted to the darkening sky—"No! Oh, no!"—were all the proof I needed.

Then, one evening in September, I made the mistake of dropping by the Lowell House common room. There, shortly after dinner, the school newspaper had informed me, the initial fall meeting of the Harvard Mountaineering Club would take place.

Contrary to my inklings early that autumn of 1961, I have continued to climb cliffs and mountains. Today, past the age of sixty, I would no longer call myself a serious climber: but I *am* a climber, and I've never let more than six or seven months go by without roping up with some comrade and launching out on some route I had never before touched.

For seventeen of those years, climbing was the most important thing in my life. In my twenties and early thirties, I co-led thirteen expeditions in as many years to unclimbed mountains and walls all over Alaska and the Yukon, making dozens of first ascents. During that span, mountaineering anchored my very identity, my sense of self. Far more than as a student, a grad student, or a professor, I thought of myself during those years first and last as a climber. As such, I belonged to a worldwide fraternity of kindred fanatics whom I regarded as supplying an ideal model for friendship and common purpose.

This, despite the fact that by the age of twenty-two I had been the firsthand witness not only of Gabe's death on the First Flatiron, but of two further fatal accidents, costing a total of three more lives. The second came in March 1965, when two experienced veterans, Dan Doody and Craig Merrihue, fell roped together out of Pinnacle Gully on Mount Washington in New Hampshire. As the first potential rescuer to arrive on the scene, I spent a futile hour trying to revive Merrihue with mouth-to-mouth resuscitation. My companions and I then hauled the two bodies down to Pinkham Notch.

The final accident occurred only four months thereafter, on the descent from the west face of Mount Huntington—the finest climb of my life—when, in the dusk of an Alaskan midnight, my partner Ed Bernd got on rappel. Though he was standing next to me, I do not to this day know what went wrong. Somehow the rappel anchor failed, and Ed plunged without a word down a 4,000-foot precipice to the lower Tokositna Glacier. I had to descend solo without a rope to our next camp, then wait through two days of storm before Matt Hale and Don Jensen (whom I had begun to fear dead as well) climbed down to join me and learned about the tragedy. We were never able even to search for Ed's body.

In 1979, when I gave up teaching to write full-time, it was via articles about mountaineering that I first gained entrée to the mainstream magazines. My expertise in climbing served as the pedestal for a career that eventually broadened to embrace archaeology, history, anthropology, biography, exploration, and other forms of adventure.

In 1980, in Outside magazine, I published "Moments of Doubt," which remains today my best known and most anthologized essay. The piece was an attempt to come to grips, fifteen years after Huntington, with those three early fatal accidents, and to explain why I kept climbing after Ed Bernd's death. The essay was in essence an apologia for the climbing life (my tentative title was "Worth the Risk").

Almost twenty years later, I began to have second thoughts about what I wrote in "Moments of Doubt"—in no small part because of various readers' reactions to that piece. As a writer, moreover, I had occasion to interview some of the world's outstanding mountaineers, from Reinhold Messner to Lynn Hill to Ed Viesturs and the like. Pondering their justifications for the extreme risks they routinely took gave me a new perspective on my own trajectory as a climber.

This memoir is thus a reassessment of my 1980 apologia, an attempt de novo to weigh against each other what the great Victorian climber Alfred Mummery called "the pleasures and penalties of mountaineering."

At the heart of my inquiry is an attempt to answer what I consider the two fundamental questions that a passionate pursuit of routes and summits inevitably poses: "Why do we climb mountains?" and "How do we justify the risk and the inevitable tragedy climbing entails?" Oddly enough, it has taken me until now to see that the way climbers (including myself, in "Moments of Doubt") usually grapple with these questions is ultimately solipsistic. Climbers tend to answer those queries solely in reference to themselves, as if the impact of a death in the mountains on those who cared most about the victim were irrelevant, or at most an unfortunate by-product of the tragedy. For such apologists, "Is it worth the risk?" reduces to a much simpler and less interesting question: "Do I get enough rewards from climbing to justify the chance of dying?" ("Do the thrills outweigh the terrors?")

To explain, however, why I didn't turn my back on mountaineering after Gabe's death, I need to go back and figure out just what kind of person I had already become by the age of eighteen—for in the tangles of childhood and adolescence, I am sure, lies the camouflaged answer.

Born in 1943, I spent my first five years not in Boulder, but in Climax, Colorado, where one of the world's richest molybdenum deposits had given birth to a mining camp. At 11,300 feet, Climax was the highest town in the United States. Having completed his Ph.D. work in astronomy at Harvard, my father was delegated in 1940 to cart the first coronagraph ever deployed in the Western Hemisphere to Fremont Pass on the Continental Divide, where he established the High Altitude Observatory. (A coronagraph is a telescope that artificially eclipses the sun, allowing its coronal atmosphere to be observed—a feat previously possible only during rare, brief total eclipses.)

At first, my parents embraced the alien wilderness into which they had so abruptly been plunged. In summertime, they scrambled up several 13,000-foot peaks—Mounts Bartlett, Fletcher, and McNamee—but one day an impetuous companion from the molybdenum mine got far ahead of them on a steep talus slope and accidentally dislodged a boulder. Rolling, then bouncing erratically down the incline, the boulder narrowly missed my mother. She never climbed another mountain.

My father learned to ski and joined the Fremont Pass emergency patrol. Called out in early spring to probe the debris of a nearby avalanche, Dad helped dig out the corpse of a local man who had been caught in the slide. Like my mother's close call, this brush with mortality turned my father away from mountaineering for good.

Knowing no other world than the Mosquito Range, whose soaring ridges enclosed my life, and ignorant of the mementi mori that had so chastened my parents, I heard in my infancy only the siren song of the mountains. An alpine meadow was my front yard, across which scuttled, instead of chipmunks and squirrels, conies and marmots that pierced the thin air with their shrill whistles before they ducked into holes they had burrowed in the tundra. On July afternoons, I lolled among the primrose and forget-me-nots, caressed by the sun whose thermonuclear secrets my father probed with his coronagraph. Safe in my bed, I listened to the tormented howls of timber wolves at dawn, over on Ceresco Ridge. In the morning, I would stare at the sharp summit of 14,142-foot Mount Democrat, impossibly far away, its north face still choked with winter snowfields, and wonder, *What is it like up there? What can you see?*

To his friends, my father was known as Walt, but professionally, he insisted on Walter Orr Roberts, after some early mentor had convinced him that "Walter Roberts" was too common a name to stamp the distinguished scientist he planned to become. I was only two at the time, but my mother later told me that Dad's thirtieth birthday was an occasion of agony for him. He believed in his bones the truth of the old canard that in pure science, if you haven't made your great discovery by the age of thirty, you will never make it. By thirty, Dad had filmed the largest solar prominence ever seen, and he had discovered elusive jets of gas flung from the sun's polar regions, which he named spicules. But these did not amount to the great breakthrough he craved.

My mother, Janet Smock, had wanted to be a writer, publishing well-wrought short stories in the literary magazine at Wheaton College in Massachusetts. Her ambition, however, was no match for my father's. After marrying Walter Orr Roberts, she devoted herself for the next twenty years to raising a family.

In 1948, we moved to Boulder, where Dad allied his observatory with the University of Colorado. By the age of five, I had internalized my father's drive and perfectionism. From kindergarten on, I burned with a fervor to outperform all the other kids in my class in whatever combat lay at hand. Intellectually, in the small pond that was University Hill School, I could nurse the delusion that I might prevail: I got straight As and won all the spelling bees and arithmetic contests our teachers inflicted on us.

The competitive rage that anchored my life was correspondingly grandiose. As soon as I grew aware of the larger world, my cherished ambition was to be the best at something. Not just the best in Boulder—the best in the world. The first realm on which I fastened this dark fantasy was baseball. Pee Wee Reese, the Brooklyn Dodgers' shortstop, became my hero, but my paragon was Ty Cobb, who was at least as real to me as any active player. Cobb's own rage to be best stood as a shining lesson in the will to excel. The trouble was that I wasn't even the best baseball player in second grade—let alone Boulder or the world. Both Donnie Owen and Butch Teegarden could clout a slow-pitch hardball fifty feet farther than my best pokes, and Jim Bartlett was a slicker fielder of hot ground balls. My response to this intolerable truth was characteristic. Though I had played Little League and Pony League, in junior high school I didn't go out for the team. Instead, well into adolescence, I played a different game nearly every day in the vacant lot on the corner of Bluebell and 18th Street. Though weedy and strewn with small boulders, this patch of turf served as Ebbets Field for our neighborhood gang of twelve or fifteen kids. Because I was the oldest of all those kids, I became a tyrant, the organizer of all the games, the arbiter of rules, first-up and first-choose.

The chief rule that I imposed was that any ball hit out of the lot, even on the ground, was an out. I became, like Cobb, a master of the place hit, punching a soft liner down the rightfield line where Kenny Woodward could be counted on not to get it back to the infield fast

enough to keep me from reaching third base. In this absurdly cir-
cumscribed parody of baseball, I became at least the best in the neighborhood.

As a child, I had little talent for comradeship. On a psychological
questionnaire we were given one year in school, I answered the query
"What kinds of friends do you like to have?" by indicating that I
didn't care if I had any friends, as long as I had people to beat in
games. I usually had a best buddy, such as Paul, but never a regular
gang to hang out with. And not until I turned sixteen did I muster the
courage to attempt a girlfriend.

Children are oddly obtuse about what is going on with their parents. My father, at first, had seemed capable of a parental charade. He
had taught my brother Alan, a year younger, and me to fly-fish. At the
age of eight, when I caught my first trout, in the inlet to Twin Lakes
below Independence Pass, I had carried the trophy hidden in a wet
sneaker back to our car camp to present to my mother (who hated
everything to do with camping, even when supplemented by our Plymouth station wagon). Dad had played ball with me in our front yard,
tossing grounders and swatting fungoes. Increasingly, though, after
we moved to Boulder, he was too busy to play.

When I was still very young, my mother turned to me for the intimacy she could not extract from my father. At the age of five, I
endured a frightening morning, when my mother would not stop
weeping. What was the matter, I asked. She stifled her sobs, held me
tight, and said, "Your father's going to Europe for a whole month. I
don't know if I can get through it. You're going to have to be the
daddy while he's gone."

In certain fundamental ways, my parents were incompatible. Dad
loved classical music and wildflowers, both of which left Mom
unmoved; in turn, she could quote Keats and Swinburne and Housman by the yard, while to Dad, literature was a blank.

The most serious incompatibility between my parents had to do
with their feelings about home. My father was at his most alive when
he was dashing around the world talking to scientists. He made many
trips to Russia, and Lake Baikal became his favorite place on the globe.

At the end of each trip, however, as he flew into Denver's Stapleton Airport to be picked up by my mother, Dad would crash hard. The drive home passed in a wordless torpor. Invariably, on his first day home, my father would develop a migraine headache so severe he had to take to his bed. He could gain relief only after six or eight hours, when, sweating with pain, he threw up into the toilet bowl.

For Mom, on the other hand, travel had no appeal. In the late 1950s, she made her first professional foray beyond the circle of our family, getting involved in local politics. Boulder became her universe. Though she spoke and read French well, Mom had no desire ever to take a trip to France—let alone to Lake Baikal.

In a less overt way, my mother conveyed to me the deep-seated fear that to venture out into the world was to risk harm and even death. Home was the only safe place.

I could hardly, then, have been caught in the crossfire of a more profoundly mixed message than the one my parents unwittingly conveyed. For Dad, home was poisonous. For Mom, hiking out the front door was fraught with peril. One day when I was twelve or thirteen, Mom and I locked horns in some bitter dispute. In a fury, I fled our house, walked up Bluebell Avenue and onto a faint path that gained the mesa above town, then headed south on the well-worn Mesa Trail. Dusk turned to dark, but I marched on at a pace that was nearly a jog. In the night I could barely tell where the trail was. A couple of miles out, I blundered headlong into a barbed wire fence, tearing a nasty gash just above my right knee.

Spurting blood, I hobbled home, where my mother, seeing what had happened, gasped in dismay, then took me to a doctor for bandaging and a tetanus shot. My dash into the dangerous night had proved her unspoken point.

Just as, from an early age, I had taken on my father's puritan ambition rather than my mother's craving for intimacy, so in adolescence it was Dad's sense of home as poisonous that infused my spirit. Each evening on Bluebell Avenue came to seem a minor ordeal: the dinner of frozen fish sticks or chicken à la king on toast my mother whipped up, the episodes of I Love Lucy and I Led Three Lives on our new TV, before which Alan and my sister, Jenny (three years younger), and my second brother, Jonny (eight years younger), sat in rapt absorption.

During two junior high years, I devised a nightly escape from that trial by family. Dad had bought me a three-and-a-half-inch reflecting telescope. At first, in deference to his own professional specialty, I charted sunspots with it, but it was the night sky that enthralled me. In those days, the atmosphere was still so clear in Colorado that from my backyard, I could easily make out stars of the sixth magnitude (the faintest that can be seen with the naked eye).

I began spending two hours every clear evening, even in the dead of winter, with my telescope. I decided to specialize in double stars. At first I sought out the pairs extolled in my father's battered old copy of Olcott's *Field Book of the Skies*, but I graduated to "discovering" my own double stars, which I charted on an atlas of the heavens and recorded in a notebook. I invented a diamond-grid symbol for "my" double stars and numbered them in order of discovery. In my notebook I jotted down laconic comments: "Trouble seeing the companion," or, "Main star is blue-white."

Somehow I must have been aware that this collector's mania had nothing to do with real astronomy. With my telescope, there was no way to tell a true double (in which the stars revolve around each other) from an accidental one (in which a pair of stars at vast distances from each other happen to be aligned as seen from Earth). I entered my "project" in a science fair, where, even as he awarded me first prize, a colleague of my father's seemed aghast at the sheer energy I had poured into this theoretically useless fetish.

But after two years I was burned out on double stars. Another passion took the place of backyard astronomy. Recognizing that I had a certain precocity in mathematics, my father arranged for me to be tutored after school by a lecturer in math at the university. Mr. Householder's specialty was number theory, and soon I was happily awash in the half-charted seas of prime numbers and the Fibonacci Series. At Boulder High, in geometry class, we rehashed Euclid's easier theorems, but at 4:00 once a week, in Mr. Householder's cramped office in the Hellems Building at the university, I laid out the conjectures I had spent the previous six days gnawing on. "Mmm," he would say, squinting at my equations, "now how might we go about proving that?"

At home, I sequestered myself in my bedroom with pencil and paper for hours every evening, finding there an escape from family every bit as effective as the backyard telescope. Ty Cobb was no longer my paragon. I brooded instead on Pierre de Fermat, jotting his lightning theorem in the margin of Diophantus; on Leonhard Euler, blindly traversing the seven bridges of Königsberg; on Evariste Galois, staying up all night before the duel that would take his life at twenty, scribbling down the equations that would ensure his immortality.

The staleness that had crept into sandlot baseball and backyard double stars saved me from the kind of narcissistic monomania that might have turned me into a lifelong stamp collector. Somehow I knew that the soft triple eluding Kenny Woodward's grasp, the thirty-fourth "new" double star in Cygnus, were dead ends, that the real games were played in Fenway Park and at Mount Palomar. But the game of number theory that I entered into in Mr. Householder's office was, I sensed, the real thing. After, at age seventeen, I published a paper in the *American Mathematical Monthly* ("A Theorem in the Farey Series"), I could cherish for several more years the illusion that I could play in the big leagues with Galois and Euler.

Thus at age fifteen and sixteen, the life I led most deeply was entirely in my head. As a kid, I had loved sports; at Boulder High, I dreaded gym class. Yet in lieu of sports, a certain physical restlessness disturbed the repose of the number theory sanctum I had built in my bedroom. At fifteen, I would no longer have answered the question on the grade school psychological questionnaire the same way. Now, I would have said that I didn't care if I had any friends, as long as I had interesting ways to be alone.

The solution to that restlessness came on Green Mountain, the graceful, forested peak that towers 2,700 feet above Boulder on the southwest. In ninth grade, I started hiking its trails, almost always alone. Striding among the pines and spruces, with birdsong the only accompaniment to my ragged breathing, I calculated Mersenne primes in my head. To deepen its challenge, I climbed Green Mountain in the winter and at night.

In a sense, I was fetishizing the peak in the same way that I had my double stars and my vacant lot baseball. I kept careful track of the number of my ascents, and set personal record times on various routes. Yet it was not so much a collector's mania that obsessed me on Green Mountain, as the fantasy that I had found a private wilderness where I could be myself as I could not at school or home. I had discovered secret places all over the mountain, where I would sit and drink in the glory and silence of nature.

By tenth grade, I had made some fifty ascents of Green Mountain, with scarcely a foray to another peak. But from the summit, as I sat catching my breath, I stared west at the Indian Peaks, 5,000 feet higher than my lofty perch, often covered with snow, and felt a wild longing to explore. In the classic mountaineering accounts I had checked out of the public library since the age of twelve, I had devoured the exploits and tragedies of Germans on Nanga Parbat and Frenchmen on Annapurna as I had the sleuthing of the Hardy Boys. But of course, I was convinced, I could never go on a real expedition to a real mountain in the remote ranges: only gods such as Hermann Buhl and Lionel Terray were admitted to those Olympian realms.

Still, from the summit of Green Mountain, I could see Longs Peak looming in the northwest. I knew that the blank, vertical upper 1,000 feet of its savage east face, a cliff called the Diamond, had never been climbed. I could almost picture myself standing beneath it, like the French beneath Annapurna, scanning its impassive granite shield with binoculars. And one day, winding down a trailless gully on the side of Green Mountain that faced Boulder, I passed between the First and Second Flatirons. I stopped in my tracks halfway down the gully, to gaze at the giant leaning slab of the First Flatiron on my left. I felt the itch to set hand and foot on it.

For the first time, I tasted the rapture of the abyss, as I tried to imagine the skill and nerve it would take to launch out onto that sea of sandstone.

THREE

Lisa

AND THEN, IN TENTH GRADE, I FELL IN LOVE.

Lisa (not her real name) was a new arrival in Boulder, having emigrated from somewhere in the Midwest. In our "accelerated" geometry class, she soon became part of the group of eggheads—most of us sons and daughters of university professors—with whom I had loosely identified since first grade. Lisa was tall and thin (at five eight, she was only two inches shorter than I), with thin, graceful fingers, pale eyes, and wavy blond hair. She had a geeky insecurity that exploded at odd moments in a quick, nervous laugh; but even so, she was too pretty for me to approach.

Something about my haughty aloofness, however, intrigued her. At the end of one class in February 1959, Lisa handed me a brief note. "What do you really think of Bartók?" she asked. Six or seven of us played in the high school orchestra (I was second-chair cello), and a few weeks before, we had attended the Juilliard String Quartet's performances of the six Bartók quartets in Macky Auditorium, which had electrified a tiny segment of the audience and alienated the remainder.

Surprised to receive the note, I was too cocooned in my proud isolation to entertain the possibility that Lisa might be flirting with me. So, at the end of the next class, I delivered my dutiful, handwritten appraisal of Bartók.

Thus began three solid months of note-passing at the end of geometry class. From a mere several paragraphs each, our missives grew to the length of three or five or even eight pages. For the most part, they were all about books and art and ideas: with relentless solemnity, we evaluated Hindemith and Prokofiev, Lao-tzu and Santayana.

Yet early in the correspondence, Lisa pushed toward the personal, asking such blunt questions as, "What do you believe in, Dave?," and "Who exactly are you, anyway?" She also transcribed poems she had written, full of blue and purple landscapes drenched in rain and wistful solitude.

By April, Lisa's letters had become the most dangerous and exciting thing in my life, and yet I was paralyzed by pride and shame. Her queries pushed closer and closer to the personal. "Oh yes—I must ask you," she wrote in one note, "how many times you've been in love." And in another, she gave vent to her pent-up frustration: "Let me be the first to say this—this 'correspondence' seems rather absurd in a way. It seems more logical to talk."

Indeed: all I need do was offer to walk Lisa home after school; somehow I knew where she lived, only four blocks from Bluebell Avenue. Yet the thought of upping the ante with so bold an act terrified me. It was safer each night to hide in my bedroom, while, neglecting my quadratic residues, I scribbled down weighty *pensées* and attempted overwrought free verse of my own, all the while deflecting Lisa's personal probes.

As the spring bloomed toward summer, however, I dared to fantasize about what it might mean to have a girlfriend. Alone in my bed, I pictured Lisa's shy blue eyes, her willowy hair, the equipoise of her fingers holding a pen. I tried to imagine kissing her. Yet along with intimations of some rapturous freedom I had never before known, Lisa excavated an unhappiness at the center of my being that had become so habitual I had forgotten it was there, like an old, unhealed injury that one limps to compensate for.

Meanwhile, the spring term plodded toward a deadline that began to hang over my spirit like a threat. When school let out at the end of May, there would be no more geometry class. How, and where, would we then exchange our letters?

Suddenly, my parents made an unfathomable decision. My father had been invited to give a commencement speech at Amherst College, his alma mater. Around that occasion, we would construct a family vacation. As soon as school was out, we would drive, all six of us crammed into our Plymouth station wagon, back to Massachusetts, visiting relatives along the way. We would leave on June 2. The trip would take three weeks.

On the evening of June 1, I finally summoned the courage to telephone. "I have to see you, Lisa," I murmured, in the phrase I had practiced for a week. "Come over," she answered, "and we can go for a walk."

To my relief, when I rang the doorbell, only Lisa was home. She grabbed a sweater, and we set off westward through the Boulder streets. As we headed toward the mountains, I struggled to make conversation. It was so much harder than writing a letter. Everything I said sounded both false and banal. The panic in the back of my throat would not go away: I swallowed it down as I composed another insipid utterance. We passed under a streetlight, and I saw our twin shadows leap and elongate ahead of us. If only I could stay as faceless, as two-dimensional as that shadow of myself.

I suggested that we hike up Bluebell Canyon, past the road-end picnic shelter, where we might sit under the pines, away from the streetlights. There, I had planned to try to kiss Lisa. But once we sat down, side by side on the pine needles, the awkwardness only magnified. I stole a look at her. Her blond hair hung loose on either side of her face: the pale blue eyes looked puzzled, her delicate mouth twisted at one corner. I looked away.

I had thought that all I needed to do was step off the edge of the cliff. But this endless free fall was not what I had bargained for. Now I longed for the safety of my sanctum among the prime numbers.

Yet here she sat, on my right, only inches away. The darkness shrouded us: the pines swayed in an easy breeze. She brushed back a strand of hair with her left hand. I felt my nerve endings fire: my own hand started to lift itself to take hers. Then the moment passed.

At last Lisa said she ought to be heading home. I was relieved. We walked down Bluebell Canyon and back through the streets in virtual silence.

We paused not on her porch, but out where her front walkway met the street. Lisa herself was nervous now. "Write me, then, will you, from back east?" she murmured.

"Lisa, will you give me a kiss?"

A half-smile contorted her face. She inclined her head toward mine. Our lips brushed, unopened. It was over. I felt only a crashing disappointment.

The first kiss of my life, the kiss I had planned all evening—all week, all month—had meant nothing. I turned and walked back to the prison on Bluebell Avenue.

The next week's ordeal in our station wagon, as we hurtled east, was the worst possible treatment for my sorry condition. What I needed was to be alone, hiking on Green Mountain, nursing my self-esteem among the spruces. Instead, we sat thigh-to-thigh, my parents and one child in the front seat, the other three in back. For hours I slouched against the right-hand window, staring at the wheat fields or reading *Thus Spake Zarathustra*.

At last we reached Amherst, where we would spend most of a week. The campus was almost deserted, caught in the lull between the end of term and commencement. We were put up in South Hall, one of the older dormitories on the campus's crowning hill. To my relief, I was assigned a room of my own. The window looked out on a lush frieze of beech and maple trees. But the spartan furnishings—bare iron bedstead, khaki army blankets, a battered brown desk, gray walls unadorned except for fire escape instructions—fit the specifications of a cell I would have designed for myself.

Of the commencement ceremony itself, I recall nothing, not even my father's speech. On the drive east across the desolate heartland of America, with the Plymouth in full career, the very throb of the tires on asphalt had minimally distracted me from my quandary. Now, in the stasis of South Hall, I was thrust face-to-face with it. Having had no word from Lisa in two weeks, I sensed her slipping away. I could not even remember precisely what she looked like.

One night in my room I wrote her a halfhearted letter, sealed it, then tried to go to sleep. Instead, I tossed and turned for hours, as my mood grew darker. Sometime in the middle of the night I got up and wrote another letter. It was not a letter to Lisa, however, but one to myself. Only a page long, it ended with the prescription, "so that you know there is no choice but to end it all."

In my letters to Lisa, I had flirted with a romantic idea of suicide. Now, in the darkness of my spartan room, as I lay vigilant through the rest of the sleepless night, the simple fact that to end it all would solve my problems presented itself in all its elegant economy.

The question was how to do it. I could not imagine jumping off a cliff or a building. I knew nothing about guns. I had no access to pills. Slitting my wrists had a certain appeal. I need only take the Gillette Blue Blade out of my razor, lying there on the desktop, and make two sharp swipes across the veins. But there would be blood everywhere. . . .

The next morning we started driving west, headed home. The plan was to take a more northerly route back, crossing New York state, dipping in and out of Canada, retracing the path by which my parents had carried the coronagraph out to Colorado in 1940.

In the afternoon, we stopped to look at Niagara Falls. Exhausted from lack of sleep, still in the grips of my late-night revelation, I wandered away from my family, hiking upstream along the path behind the guardrail. I turned a corner and was suddenly alone. I stopped and stared into the powerful river, a few hundred yards above the roaring cascade.

The surging water beckoned. This was the way to do it. A simple clamber over the guardrail, a leap into the current—then the river would take care of the rest. Since I had never learned how to swim, there would be no risk that some involuntary instinct of survival would take over and deliver me back to shore. The plunge off the falls would be sudden and glorious. There would be no pain—only blessed blankness. If I were lucky, they would never find my body.

A voice in my head said, *Don't even think. Just do it. Now.* I felt my calf muscles twitch. I rocked back on my right heel, preparing my sprint. I visualized myself flying from the guardrail into the black water.

And then the moment passed. I lacked the courage for even this simplest of deeds.

I walked back downstream to rejoin my family. We piled into the Plymouth and headed toward that night's motel.

Why is it that misery embalms itself in the amber of memory, while happiness evaporates like dew? Forty-five years later, the moment on the bank above Niagara Falls remains indelible; but of my first week back in Boulder, I can scarcely recall a single detail. I know that I called Lisa the day we returned, and that that evening we went for another walk. Through the rest of the long summer, we saw each other every day.

At first we walked the streets of Boulder, but on each trek we edged toward the darker wilds on the southern and western outskirts of town. During the first weeks, our physical contact was limited to a chaste good night kiss on her front porch. Unlike our first kiss, however, each of these seemed freighted with promise.

It did not take us long to discover our secret bower. It was Green Mountain Cemetery, at the southern terminus of 20th Street, a grassy, hilly graveyard seamed with granite headstones dating back to Boulder's incarnation as a mining town. Our favorite lair was situated just below its summit hill, where a pair of pretentious sandstone mausoleums stood. Sitting on the cool lawn, we stared north at Boulder's streetlights, secure in the comfort that the town could not see us.

One evening in early July, as we sat in the cemetery, only inches apart, I felt all the strain and anguish of the spring, of the trip back east, come crowding up my spine. I turned toward Lisa. "Lisa, please . . ." I whispered. She took me in her arms. Our kiss lasted and lasted. She held me, and with a kind of desperation I clasped her back, my eyes shut tight.

My parents knew I was out with Lisa every night. But it seemed vital to keep our graveyard intimacy a secret—in a separate universe not only from Mom and Dad and from Lisa's parents, but from everyone else in the world.

By August, we were staying out longer and longer, walking home now only at 2:00 or 3:00 A.M. Then one night we stayed till 5:00, creeping out past the cemetery's front gate as dawn began to break over the plains to the east.

My parents were up when I got home. My mother asked, "Where were you?" I refused to answer. It was none of their business.

To my surprise, it was my father—so habitually aloof, so distracted from his family when he was home—who now assumed the prosecutorial role. It was simply ridiculous, he stated, that a sixteen-year-old boy should stay out till dawn without his parents knowing where he was.

I was not about to give in. Sleep-deprived but self-righteous, I argued bitterly against my father. Locked in an adamantine contest of wills, we turned up the screws of our anger.

I could not say, of course, what I really felt—that Lisa was a secret that it was intolerable to share with my parents. Instead, Dad and I waxed theoretical about the constitutional rights of teenagers. In his puritan way, he began harping on the necessity of rules, of responsibility to others. It was my duty to my parents, he said, to spare them the anguish of wondering whether Lisa and I were in trouble somewhere. I countered that my creativity depended on freedom from such rules and obligations.

"That's ridiculous," Dad said. "Do you think that my own creativity as a scientist is a justification for ignoring society's obligations?"

"You're not a scientist," I said. "You're a fund-raiser."

I could not have struck home more cruelly. Dad's eyes got wild, as he roared a curse at me. It was the angriest I had ever seen him, or would ever see him again.

In that callow stab, I had won the argument. My parents gave up. Never again would they demand to know where I was at night, and from now on, I would set my own hours.

And yet Dad had won a certain victory of his own. Responsibility to others: it seemed that he had held this tenet over my head since I was old enough to think. A rational humanist to the core, he would never stand on a dictum such as "because I said so" or "because that's the way things are done." All moral behavior could be lucidly explicated in terms of responsibility to others.

Dad's anger had scared me, and a worm of doubt crept into the woodwork of my willfulness. Perhaps he was right about responsibility. The concept loomed over me as an impossible burden, a colossal homework assignment I could never complete. In Lisa, I had discovered its opposite. I had tasted escape.

During the summer, I had nursed a fantasy as sweet as it was impossible. Lisa and I were in a car, driving day and night in headlong flight from Boulder, aimed nowhere but away. We would never return. Our parents would vanish. All that mattered was to be together, and to be in motion.

Then, suddenly, a speck on the autumn horizon threatened our idyll. A scientist friend of her parents, his wife, and two children would be spending five months in England, while he labored away on some kind of research. Was Lisa interested in free room and board in exchange for helping take care of the house and kids?

Lisa hesitated, then accepted. I was devastated. Why did she have to go to England, I complained one evening. Five months of separation, after we had barely survived three weeks . . .

In the context of those post-Sputnik times, Lisa's choice made perfect sense. She had never been anywhere abroad. She would attend an English school—an incomparable "learning experience." The family would be lodged in Oxford, a place that had Olympian reverberations for both of us. If she declined, simply to stay in Boulder with me, she might regret the lost opportunity for the rest of her life.

During the last week before Lisa's departure, we varied our routine. We would still head off to the cemetery but spend only a few hours there. Then, once we could be sure that Lisa's parents had gone to bed, we would sneak into her living room and lie in the darkness on her couch. This meant that we had to whisper even more softly than we did outdoors and listen for any creak of floorboard or turn of door handle. But the very illicitness of our cuddling, under her parents' noses, added a piquancy to the act.

Along with my superstition about keeping "us" a secret from the rest of the world, I harbored a deep instinct that our love had nothing to do with sex. Sex was the guilty masturbatory business I had performed since thirteen, fantasizing not about real women but about imaginary goddesses and damsels, creatures out of Arthurian romance. Sex, I felt, would only demean Lisa's purity.

Now, however, at the end of August, the warmth of Lisa's living room was a luxurious alternative to the cemetery. And the cramped dimensions of the couch required us to lie facing each other, our bodies pressed head-to-toe.

One night, as we lay in each other's arms, I realized that I had an erection. Mortified, I shifted my hips on the narrow ledge of sofa cushion so that Lisa might not detect my predicament. Yet she moved in response, pressing her own hips against mine.

The last night was fraught with a bittersweet urgency. We did not talk about our separation, for it seemed imperative to live every minute in the present. Around midnight, as we lay on her couch, I pressed my erection deliberately against Lisa's thigh. My fingertips traced designs on her back.

Yet as always, it was Lisa who had to take the next step. She whispered, "Would you like me to take off my bra?" She got up, went into her bedroom, then returned.

Moments later, I unbuttoned Lisa's blouse. With my fingertips, I caressed her small, soft breasts, my right arm pillowing her head.

Suddenly I was coming. Instead of pulling away, I pressed my orgasm against Lisa's thigh. She held me tighter, acknowledging the event. I gasped, as tears crowded the back of my throat.

I was awash in joy. In that instant, all my notions of the power of sex to wreak havoc with our love faded into the limbo of the obsolete. The spasm of release was part of "us," of why things would turn out all right.

Far-off England hung over the evening like a sentence to be carried out in the morning. For an hour longer, we could lie together, bound by a future free of all responsibilities save our limitless pledge to each other.

In Lisa's absence, I resumed my palship with Paul. He had spent the tenth-grade year in Paris, where his father taught on sabbatical leave from the University of Colorado.

In ninth grade, inclined toward chubbiness, Paul had been content to play the buffoon. Now, upon his return to Boulder in the summer of 1959, I was shocked at his transformation. He had shed his buffoonishness with his baby fat, working out in some Parisian weight room to build the muscles that would turn him into a football player. (Jim Brown, the great Cleveland running back, was now on the same pedestal as Juan-Manuel Fangio.)

Paul had become handsome, in a Teutonic way, with his heavy eyebrows and black crew cut. He took a summer job haying on a ranch just east of Boulder, tossing bales onto truck beds in the 95-degree heat for minimum wage, as he performed the brutal work that the high school football coach had prescribed for all his prospective linemen and halfbacks.

As if ashamed of his European heritage and of the rarefied intellectual climate of his upbringing, Paul was in full revolt against his past and his parents. Only two months back in Boulder, he had picked up a cowboy's drawl, and he got me reading Larry McMurtry (Leaving Cheyenne and Horseman, Pass By).

I had grown to hate gym class at Boulder High, but as the fall term began, I went out for the tennis team. Gradually I worked my way up from the bottom rung to number five, played in matches against Fort Morgan and Greeley and Aurora, and narrowly missed earning a varsity letter. Six months before, I had felt only contempt for the jocks who were the high school heroes; now I stood in awe of the three seniors who were the stars of the tennis team. One day Ted Pannebaker offered me a ride home after practice, and when, as I climbed out of his battered Chevy, he muttered, "Take it easy, Dave," I heard music as heady as Beethoven.

Five thousand miles away, Lisa detected my drift toward a different world, and felt only dismay. She knew that Paul lay at the center of my shift—"What does Paul think about us?" she wrote more than once. I never dared ask him.

Of Lisa's return to Boulder at the end of February 1960, I remember no more than I do of my own reentry the previous June. In her absence, I had gotten my driver's license. Now the Plymouth station wagon abetted our evenings. Often we would drive to the cemetery, park just outside its gates, then steal with our blanket into its darker nooks; other nights, I drove up behind Flagstaff Mountain where we parked on little traveled dirt roads, then crawled into the back, the rear seat flattened so that we could lie full-length on our blanket.

Every kiss, every touch of Lisa's skin, seemed blissful to me. Yet something was wrong. Though she said again and again how much she loved me, she felt frozen to my touch. It took weeks to work our way back to the intimacy of our last night on her couch the previous September. She would loosen her bra, but not take it off; allow me to unbutton her blouse, but not to remove it. When I caressed her breasts underneath her loosened clothes, she lay unresponsive.

I had assumed for months that we would soon make love. Yet I had a raft of doubts about that ultimate act. My sole source of information was a copy of The Encyclopedia of Sexual Knowledge, which now and then I furtively borrowed from the top shelf of my parents' bedroom bookcase. That solemn treatise made it clear that the deflowering of a virgin was a painful, traumatic task, sometimes requiring the assistance of a doctor.

We tried to talk about what was wrong, but we lacked the requisite vocabulary. Instead, to my annoyance, Lisa once more resorted to letters to try to articulate her malaise. In one, she pulled the veil partway off the deep-rooted sorrow that lay at the core of her being. "I still remember what it is like to be badly hurt," she wrote. "For three years in a row, I cried myself to sleep because I had been too clumsy. . . . I am afraid to give in to you, because it will be too painful when you leave."

Meanwhile, I hung out with Paul, who was on a campaign to lose his own virginity with the first available girl he could manage to seduce. His coolness toward Lisa, I would realize decades later, sprang from his feeling that in having a steady girlfriend, I had an unfair advantage in a competition I didn't even realize we were waging—the race to be the first, in Paul's phrase, to "get laid."

One day Paul pulled out his billfold and said, "Look at this." An older friend of his had bought some condoms, two of which he had sold to Paul. I had never seen one before. I held the strange little foil package in my hand, ashamed to voice my bewilderment about how the thing worked. Instead, I asked Paul if his friend could get me a couple, "just in case." "Here," said Paul. "Take one." Then he added, in his best worldly-wise drawl, "You can always go to a drugstore and buy more. Lots of places sell them to minors." From then on, I carried the condom everywhere, tucked inside my own billfold.

The fall tennis matches had reawakened my body to the joys of sport. That spring, I climbed Green Mountain by harder and more obscure routes than I had previously attempted. And now that I could drive, I realized, I could approach the higher mountains I had gazed at in the west. For the summer of 1960, I plotted a campaign among the 13,000-ers of the Front Range. I bought a copy of Robert Ormes's *Guide to the Colorado Mountains.*

Hoping to share my wanderlust with Lisa, and perhaps to disrupt the tension of our evening ritual in the back of the Plymouth, I took her up Green Mountain by one of its easier routes. I set out on the trail up Gregory Canyon at what seemed to me a leisurely pace, only to find Lisa dragging behind. When I stopped to wait for her, she would slowly approach, panting hard. I could not bear to stop and rest, so the moment she caught up with me, I would set off again. Lisa's not being in shape was disappointing, and on the rockier slopes, she had a bad habit of placing her foot gingerly, tentatively, before daring to transfer her weight onto it. If we did more hiking, I told myself, eventually she'd get the hang of it.

Finally, one evening at the end of May, as we lay embracing on our blanket in the darkest corner of the cemetery, beside a quiet stream under the pines, I gathered my resolve. "Lisa," I asked, "would you like to make love?"

She paused, then answered, almost dispiritedly, "All right."

"I have a condom," I said.

"Good."

For the first time, we took off all our clothes. "I love you, Lisa," I murmured, as if afraid that she would change her mind. I got the condom out of my billfold. When I tore open the foil package, however, I was shocked to find that the implement was covered with a slimy gelatin. At least it was obvious how it worked. But by the time I got the condom on, my erection had wilted.

For most of an hour, I struggled to perform, trembling with anxiety. "Dave, relax, relax," Lisa coaxed, as her hands stroked my naked back and shoulders.

Finally we got dressed and walked arm-in-arm out of the cemetery. "I'm sorry," I said miserably, "I don't know what—"

"It doesn't matter," Lisa answered, kissing my cheek. "It's all right."

At home, I washed off the condom and put it back in my billfold. I didn't realize the device was meant to be used only once.

The next night, it was raining, so we drove into the cemetery, taking the chance of having the gates locked behind us, then crawled in back with our blanket. The illicitness worked its aphrodisiac charm. When we were naked once again, I reached for my billfold.

"You don't have to use that," said Lisa. "It's close enough to my period. We're safe."

She had never before talked about sex in such pragmatic terms. Now Lisa lay beneath me, opened her legs, and for the first time, took hold of my penis, which was gloriously erect. She guided it in inside her. "Oh, my God!" I whispered. Nothing had ever felt so good.

My purgative spasm was only seconds away, but The Encyclopedia of Sexual Knowledge had sung the praises of simultaneous orgasm. I delayed, stopping and starting, fighting my own excitement. Sensing what I was doing, Lisa murmured, "Just go ahead."

Afterward, I lay beside her, holding her in my arms, murmuring,

"I love you so much." Then, as we drove out of the cemetery, I exacted a pledge: "I don't want anyone to know about this, not anyone." She looked at me quizzically and said nothing.

Back home on Bluebell Avenue, unable to fall asleep, I was assailed with doubts. Hadn't the *Encyclopedia* insisted that the rhythm method was unreliable? If it hadn't been safe the night before, how could Lisa know it was safe now? Why hadn't I felt her hymen break, and why had there been no blood?

The next week, I launched my campaign among the 13,000-foot peaks of the Front Range. Still hoping to share the mountains with Lisa, I chose as my first objective Mount Audubon, reputed to be the easiest summit among the Indian Peaks. Leaving Boulder at 4:00 A.M., we drove up to Brainerd Lake, then set out at dawn on a well-marked trail.

I was bursting with impatience to reach timberline, as if to rekindle the enchantment of Climax, but in early June, deep, soft snowbanks clogged the trail as it wound through dense groves of limber pine. I postholed across these nuisances, oblivious to the soaking of my boots and jeans, but Lisa found the snow almost impossible to negotiate. More than once I had to backtrack and offer her a hand.

As we broke clear of the forest, my heart sang. I saw the way leading up through bright green tussocks, across trickling rills of meltwater, toward the gray rocks that prefigured the distant summit. I knew that, for a real mountaineer, Audubon was beneath interest. I would soon come myself to disdain such gently inclined high-altitude lumps as "talus heaps." But that day, merely to put one foot in front of the other was to taste joy.

Not, however, for Lisa. As I waited for her to catch up, she would stagger toward me, then bend over, a hand on one knee, gasping for breath in the thin air. As on Green Mountain, the moment she arrived, I set off again. At about 12,000 feet, during one of our brief reconnections, she complained, "Why do we have to hurry like this?" Hurry? We seemed to be plodding like octogenarians.

Somehow, a little before noon, we reached the summit. Lisa sat panting, on the verge of throwing up. I ignored her distress, gazing at the sharp triangle of Mount Toll to the south, at the rugged crest of the Gore Range forty miles to the west. I had not kissed Lisa since picking her up at her house in the early darkness.

Yet that night, back in the cemetery, as we had sex, I told Lisa once more that I loved her. For the third or fourth time, I reused the condom I had washed out at home and reinserted in my billfold. She lay inert beneath me, her hands clutching my back.

So our summer settled into a routine. Only once more did I climb a 13,000-foot peak with Lisa, this time South Arapaho. Her brother, two years younger, joined our expedition (perhaps their parents had assigned him as a chaperon), but he moved as slowly as she did. Vexed, I would wait again and again for the two of them to catch up, then immediately charge off. Above 12,500 feet, they indulged in regular five-minute sit-down rests, finally arriving at the top exhausted. I asked them if they would wait while I traversed the sharp ridge that led to the higher summit of North Arapaho, half a mile away. Lisa was shivering in the stiff wind.

Speeding across that ridge, for the first time I flirted with real mountaineering, as I kicked precise steps below the treacherous cornice but above the precipitous west face. At that moment, I realized that Lisa would never share the high ranges with me. Yet as we trudged that afternoon back down toward the trailhead, I felt exhilarated. My solo traverse had unleashed a freedom I didn't really want to share with an anxious girlfriend.

One night in the cemetery, in the middle of the act, I whispered fiercely, "This is the best thing there is, in the whole universe." Lisa stared up at me, bemused.

Then one night, as I forced the dry, wrinkled condom onto my penis, it broke. I cursed the fallible contraption, even as it dawned on me that perhaps condoms weren't meant to be reused. Lisa lay still for a long time, calculating. Then she said, as she had on our second attempt in late May, "It's all right, it's close enough to my period." I plunged without hesitation into my greedy pleasure. But afterward, I promised Lisa I'd get another condom.

A day or two later, I caught up with Paul. Trying to sound offhand, I muttered, "Hey, do you have any more condoms? I lost mine, and—"

"Lost it, bullshit!" Paul roared, then subsided into rude guffaws. "Congratulations, you bastard!"

Paul wouldn't let it rest. "How was it?" he demanded. "Is she a good piece?"

That same afternoon, I walked into Potter's, where as kids my brother Alan and I had drunk cherry Cokes at the fountain. For long minutes, I pretended to browse. The stern-looking man behind the pharmacy counter wore a white uniform. Circling the shelves, I lost my nerve. I walked out of Potter's with the latest issue of U.S. News and World Report in hand instead of a package of Trojans.

So, for the rest of the summer, Lisa and I abstained during the dangerous days of her fertility, but made love up to eight and then even ten days before her period, as well as five days after. Lisa claimed that she could feel the very moment when the unfertilized egg in her body descended from the ovary to the uterus. I had read in The Encyclopedia of Sexual Knowledge that no woman could be sure of that event, but Lisa's pledge was all I needed to hear. The best thing in the universe was still mine for the taking.

And slowly, during that summer, that is what sex came to be for me—a "thing." I had abandoned the fantasy of running away from the world in some endless automotive flight, with Lisa at my side. Under our blanket in the cemetery, after the act, I lay next to her, aware of her unhappiness, yet squirming with avoidance. Now, in the passion of the act, I felt, Yes, this is the best thing there is, but it would be even better if it could be divorced from the mess of a "relationship."

Throughout the summer of 1960, licensed to explore by the same station wagon in the back of which on rainy nights Lisa and I made love, I pursued summits not only in the Front Range, but in the Sawatch and Mosquito massifs near the center of the state. Instead of Lisa, I chose as partner my next-door neighbor Tom Dugan, a veteran of our vacant lot baseball games. Tom at least could almost keep up with the breakneck hiking pace I favored.

For a while, the novelty and beauty of the alpine world above timberline sufficed. Tom and I ascended quite a few talus heaps, including Colorado's highest peak, 14,433-foot Mount Elbert in the Sawatch—an interminable slog from the trailhead at 9,000 feet up ill-defined humpbacked ridges, across oceans of scree. I might well have turned Colorado's boring 13-ers and 14-ers into another vacant lot, becoming what mountaineers dismiss as a "peak-bagger." But from the start there was a disparity between Tom's ambitions and mine that would lead our paths apart. Tom would never become a climber. He was stamped in the mold of his father, Jim Dugan, an economics professor at the university, a hearty hiker and cross-country skier for whom taking risks in the wilderness was anathema. On the odd occasion when, during our ascents, we veered near a precipice or a sharp ridge, I felt a tingling of temptation, while Tom experienced only a fretful malaise.

Jim joined us for a three-day jaunt to the Mummy Range in the northern Front Range. The first two days we devoted to talus plods: in his mid-forties, Jim let Tom and me bolt ahead, while he paced himself, eventually arriving at the summit on which we had been resting for an hour.

I had been eyeing a beautiful, forked couloir on the east face of Mount Ypsilon—the feature that gave the peak its name. I'd never climbed snow that steep, and it looked challenging. I proposed the route to Tom. "Boy, I don't know," he mused, staring at the couloir. "I'd better ask my dad."

Jim blew up at me. In the thirteen years we had been neighbors, I had never seen him so angry. Evidently, what looked like a feasible proposition to my untrained eye struck Jim as (in climbers' parlance) a death route. For our last hike we tackled another talus heap.

Yet a week or so later, Jim, Tom, and I climbed a far more interesting mountain than the mounds of the Mummy Range: Longs Peak, the cynosure of Rocky Mountain National Park. This bold 14,255-foot summit had been reached by Indians, who built an eagle trap on top, before white men ever came to Colorado. Its first "official" ascent came as early as 1868, by a party that included, among others, the one-armed John Wesley Powell, soon to launch his epic descent of the

Colorado River. Still, Longs was no walk-up like Elbert or Audubon. The easiest route wound from the east around to the north, across the Boulderfield at 12,000 feet, through a sharp notch called the Keyhole, to traverse an airy ledge on the west face before finishing in a steep gully that emerged onto the football-field-sized summit.

I sailed across the traverse, delighting in the clever route, while Tom and Jim moved cautiously from hold to hold, anxiety scrawled on their faces. On the way down, we detoured over to Chasm View, a saddle that gives a sideways view of Longs's dramatic east face. There I stared enthralled at the most ferocious cliff I had ever seen. On its left-hand edge, as early as the 1920s, pioneers such as James Alexander (a Princeton professor) and Joe and Paul Stettner (German-born tradesmiths) had worked out daring routes. But the thousand-foot headwall, a smooth vertical plate of purple granite called the Diamond, had never been touched. By 1960, the best Colorado climbers were divided as to whether the Diamond would ever be conquered. (In fact, only a few weeks later, a pair of aces from Yosemite Valley would snatch its first ascent from under the noses of the Colorado elite. I would climb the Diamond myself fourteen years later.)

One night in late July, Lisa told me that her period was four days overdue. I felt stunned and angry: what had happened to her perfect barometer for gauging the cycles of her ovulation? For the next three nights, as if by sympathetic magic we might kill the homunculus burgeoning into our future, we refrained from sex. Each day, on first seeing her, I asked Lisa, "Has it come yet?" And each day, she murmured a miserable "No."

A few nights later, I took a break from Lisa to camp out in the backyard with Paul, sleeping on the grass in the bulky kapok Sears Roebuck bags my parents had bought a decade earlier for our Twin Lakes outings. Staring up at Cygnus and Lyra, we chatted about his chances of making the football team in the fall, my hopes for the tennis team. By now, however, my predicament had taken on an intolerable weight. I needed someone to confide in. But by the time I had

gathered the nerve to confess, I heard the heavy breathing that signi-
fied Paul had fallen asleep.

I lay awake for hours, watching the stars wheel west. My own stu-
pidity, my cowardice about buying condoms, stared me in the face. At
my elbow yawned an abyss, defined by the simple proposition, *What
do we do if she's pregnant?* Yet it was an abyss into which I could not gaze.

Here, I realized sullenly, was the bogeyman of "responsibility" my
father had terrorized me with since I was a child. I rolled over in my
sleeping bag and begged for sleep, but lay awake until dawn.

The next evening, as I picked up Lisa, I saw a strange look on her
face. As soon as we were alone, she said, "I have something to tell
you." I dared to hope. "I got my period." I clasped her in my arms,
murmuring the formulas of love I no longer fully believed in. Two
nights later, we had sex again. The bogeyman of responsibility had
fled.

However game a hiking pal he was, Tom Dugan, I knew, could never
be my ideal partner in the mountains. By late July, I had performed a
few solo ascents of Colorado 13-ers. These headlong flights above
timberline resuscitated the joys of outdoor solitude I had discovered
on Green Mountain. I could move at my own pace, heedless of the
balky progress of others; I could choose whatever route I fancied.
And, as was not the case on Green Mountain, a modicum of risk now
spiced the enterprise. Descending some obscure gully in the Sawatch
Range, having left no itinerary with my parents, I realized that if I
slipped and broke an ankle, it could be a long time before anyone
found me.

My parents had planned a two-week vacation in mid-August in
Aspen, where Dad would perform certain duties for the Aspen Institute for Humanistic Studies. Dreading another enforced confinement
en famille, I anticipated the trip at the same time as an opportunity. By
now I had virtually memorized Ormes's *Guide to the Colorado Mountains*, a
catalogue of promised delights. The Elk Range, surrounding Aspen on
the west and south, Ormes made it clear, abounded in peaks more

serious than anything in the Sawatch or Mosquito Ranges. I fixed my ambition on the pair of twin 14-ers called the Maroon Bells. I would traverse them solo.

I left the car at Maroon Lake before dawn. By the first gray light, I was picking my way through a boulder-strewn moraine beneath the north face of North Maroon. There was no obvious route. I chose a couloir, kicked steps up its hard 40-degree snow, then, where the couloir pinched closed, traversed right on a ledge. The rock, an igneous intrusion into very old sedimentary strata, was, as Ormes had hinted, terrible: big chunks of it came loose in my hands, and I tossed the debris into the void below.

Yet this was by several orders of magnitude the most challenging scramble I had yet performed in the mountains, and I felt a heady exhilaration. Just below the north summit, the face steepened, verging on technical. An old rope, too weathered to trust, dangled from some out-of-sight anchor. Avoiding it, I worked my way up a rotten chute, then stepped with a gasp onto the summit.

Already, however, dark clouds were amassing in the west. After only two or three minutes on top, as I wolfed down cheese and chocolate and swigged from my canteen, I set off along the knife-edge ridge leading to the higher South Maroon Peak. Almost without recognizing the trap, I found myself stuck on tiny footholds, halfway down a twenty-foot cliff. It would be easier to climb back up than down, but I could not countenance reversing my path to descend the treacherous face on North Maroon I had worked my way up so impetuously. If I fell here, I wouldn't kill myself, but I could easily break a leg or my back. I took a deep breath and moved down and right, desperately clinging to small handholds. At last I stepped onto easier ground. For the first time in the mountains, I felt foolish rather than proud: I had gotten away with a gamble on which I had not planned to bet.

By the time I reached the summit of South Maroon, lightning bolts were forking out of thunderheads only ten miles to the west. In a kind of controlled panic, I set off down the mountain's east face. From the hike in, I had spotted a series of couloirs and snowfields that promised an all-snow descent. Now, in the blind perspective of hovering right above that convex precipice, I had to guess at the right line. The snow in mid-August was almost as hard as ice: I could kick only the edges of my boots into it. But by the time I was less than a thousand feet down, lightning was striking the summit ridge above me.

I didn't have an ice axe—I didn't even own one—but now, terrified by the lightning, I started to glissade, sliding on the rigid edges of my boots, controlling my speed by altering the pitch of my ankles. Later I would learn that I had a natural aptitude for this technique, for (in general) what climbers call "mixed ground"—snow and ice interspersed with rock, not so much difficult as fiendishly dangerous. But the charm of pure luck must also have graced that pell-mell descent. A few years later, on the same slope, a party of four experienced climbers, roped together, wielding axes, would suffer a fatal accident here, when they fell and pulled one another off.

By the time I reached the valley, the storm had descended with a vengeance. Torrential rain swept in curtains down the mountain wall behind me, and the lightning bolts were striking only hundreds of yards away. I crept into a stand of willows, lay supine on the ground, shivering, and waited for the storm to pass.

As if from a bad dream, the skies had completely cleared when I regained the car; late-afternoon sunlight was turning the drenched aspens and spruces into a fairy forest. I had forgotten my fright, as well. Throwing my pack into the back seat, I pulsed with the pride of accomplishment. It was my best day yet in the mountains, and it had been mine alone.

Later, the glow of achievement faded. With my awakening to the high Colorado peaks had come a renewed interest in the literature of mountaineering. Two books that I came upon that year electrified me: Starlight and Storm, by the Chamonix guide Gaston Rébuffat, with its lyrical evocation of the brotherhood of the rope; and Lonely Challenge, by Hermann Buhl, the Austrian genius whose obsession with solo climbing had reached its apotheosis in 1953, when he stood alone atop Nanga Parbat, the ninth-highest mountain in the world, and the only Himalayan giant ever first attained by a solitary climber.

Unlike the expedition accounts I had checked out of the library at twelve or thirteen, Buhl and Rébuffat (whose books I bought in hardback and would cherish for decades) amounted to no mere escape reading, no Hardy Boys. The French guide and the Austrian loner had begun to loom for me as Ty Cobb had when I was eight: they were the best in the world at an endeavor in which I passionately longed to excel. Yet the gulf between me and them yawned unbridgeable. Nothing I had done on the Maroon Bells could be mentioned in the same breath as the Walker Spur on the Grandes Jorasses, the northeast face of the Piz Badile.

By late September, Lisa and I were seeing each other only every third or fourth evening. Sex had become such a dutiful chore for her that she had started bringing a jar of Vaseline to the cemetery, to lubricate herself for my disposal. Yet even the cold-blooded ritual that our lovemaking had become failed to negate the illicit magic of my orgasm. I still believed that if I lost Lisa, there was a good chance I would never have sex with another woman.

Meanwhile, our senior year at Boulder High had begun. For the first time in five semesters, Lisa and I had no classes in common. I spent a lot of time with Paul, hustling two-on-two touch football games after school. Struggling even to make second string on the varsity team, he claimed the coach had formed an inflexible bias against him, as a result of the irrepressible wisecracks with which he tried to enliven practices. Still on a campaign to lose his own virginity, Paul had stopped asking me about Lisa. He seemed to regard us as a boring married couple.

Two other returnees from the previous year and I had taken over the role on the tennis team of savvy veterans, like the seniors I had idolized the fall before. I bounced back and forth between the number two and three spots, but played every match and won my varsity letter. Among the newcomers to the team was my friend since kindergarten, Gabe Lee. Capable of great shots, Gabe had an erratic serve; twice he challenged me for third place on the team, but I beat him both times. This in no way discouraged our growing friendship. Gabe was aware of my mountain scrambling, about which he queried me with relentless curiosity.

Gunning for a conference championship, our team finished a disappointing third, losing to Aurora and, shamefully, to the sugar-beet cowboys of Sterling. My doubles partner and I, however, went all the way to the state finals before losing in three sets. After that mini-triumph, several stars from the football team—the coolest guys at Boulder High—went out of their way to congratulate me.

That fall, Indian summer lingered in the high country, so I seized several weekends to scramble up 13-ers in the Front Range—peaks, such as Navajo, that were more challenging than the talus heaps on which I had cut my teeth in June, but nothing in the league of the Maroon Bells. But at some point, I befriended Jock, one of only two guys in the school who had actually learned to rock climb. When I mentioned my solo traverse of the Maroon Bells, he was impressed. A few days later, he invited me to join him and some older members of the Colorado Mountain Club on a Christmas trip to Mexico. The plan was to climb the three big volcanoes near Mexico City—Popocatépetl, Ixtaccíhuatl, and 18,696-foot Orizaba, the third-highest mountain in North America. Sprawling, extinct volcanoes (though Popo still burst into magma-spewing life every few decades), these peaks were, to be sure, walk-ups, but walk-ups on a quasi-expeditionary scale. Except for a family trip to a resort in British Columbia in junior high, I had never been outside the country. And I had never been higher than 14,433 feet. Thrilled by Jock's invitation, I accepted at once.

I could not remember a time in my life when things seemed to be going so well. I had accommodated to the very school I had once despised, winning the approbation of cheerleaders and fullbacks. In mathematics, I had started to make a mark. I had discovered the mountains, and could dream of the empyrean realms of Buhl and Rébuffat. And even though all was not well on that front, I had a girlfriend, as Paul did not.

One night in early November, Lisa and I drove up past the summit of Green Mountain, all the way to Kosslers Lake. We parked in a dark pullout and climbed in back. It was cold enough outside so that I left the engine running, with the heater on.

Lisa was in a strange mood. She took her own clothes off, then helped me off with mine. She kissed me more passionately than she had in weeks, and her body actually seemed to respond to my touch. She didn't use her Vaseline. After I entered her, I prolonged the act as long as I could, instead of driving toward my orgasm. She murmured in my ear, and her hands lovingly stroked my back.

Afterward, I lay beside her, as the hum of the engine lulled me half-asleep. Then, as if from the end of a long tunnel, I heard her whisper, "Dave, there's something I have to tell you."

Jolted alert, I propped myself on one elbow.

"I think I'm pregnant."

It took me a while to speak again. "How do you know?" I finally demanded. "Maybe it's like July—"

Lisa, propped on her own elbow, the blanket covering her nakedness, shook her head. "It's been almost two months since my last period." *Why didn't you tell me?* I lashed out silently. "I think I can feel it inside me," Lisa went on. "Here, feel my stomach." I touched her skin with my fingertips, then quickly withdrew them. I sat up, turned half away from Lisa, folded my arms across my knees, and laid my forehead against my right wrist. After a long pause, I said, as calmly as I could, "All right. What are we going to do about it?"

Now we sat in the darkness, listening to the throb of the engine. When might she have gotten pregnant? Working backward, we came to light on a night in the cemetery in late September. It had been the fifth day after her period, and Lisa was reluctant, but my impatience had won the day.

So accustomed by now were we to the fortress of our secrecy that not even Lisa suggested going to a doctor to find out for sure if she was pregnant. Now I drove slowly back down the Flagstaff road and dropped Lisa off at her home. We had agreed to wait until her second period was due, some ten days hence, on the remote chance that the whole business could still be a false alarm. During those ten days, we met only to talk about what to do. For me, making love was no longer a temptation. I soldiered through my classes at Boulder High, but at night, alone in my bed on Bluebell Avenue, I stared at the ceiling and begged for sleep.

For weeks, Lisa had been writing me an ongoing letter—a letter she doubted she would ever deliver. Eventually she did give it to me, the last letter I would ever have from her. Its fifteen pages composed a soliloquy veering between abject love and blind rage.

One day she recorded, "The dreams that I keep having. . . . Suddenly I awaken in the darkness, afraid. You are hurt badly, or dead. And then I cry, realizing that it's not real." On another: "Look what I have given to you—my body. I never should have. You didn't love me for it; in fact, you loved me less and less. Maybe it was my fault for being such a bitch." And again, at her most despairing, "I wish this world would die, and I could find myself in a warm, cheery atmosphere of German Christmas cookies."

The ten days came and went with no reprieve. In the third week in November, we agreed to tell our parents.

After school on November 20, I waited for a moment when my siblings happened to be absent. Dad was still at work. My mother stood over the kitchen counter, cutting carrots and tomatoes for our dinner salad. I stood a few feet away, fiddling with the handle of the refrigerator. Two or three times I started to speak, only to swallow my words like bile.

Finally I steeled myself. "Mom," I said hoarsely, "there's something I have to tell you."

The knife fell from her hand as she turned to look at me. "Lisa's pregnant!" she wailed. "Oh, no! That's what we were afraid of!" As she would almost eight months later, when the policeman would lead me up the front sidewalk, my mother burst into tears. Elbows on the counter, she buried her face in her hands and wept. I stood there, paralyzed. Suddenly she turned and put her arms around me. "I love you, David," she pleaded. Only my parents called me David. I bore her embrace as long as I could, then shrugged free.

Later that evening, or the next afternoon, my father arranged a private audience with me. I had expected him to lash out at me with an anger akin to that of the stunned, wounded moment more than a year before when I had accused him of being a fund-raiser rather than a scientist. Instead, he spoke in calm, rational tones, though his voice was leaden with exhaustion. There was no recrimination—only the pragmatic agenda of what to do next. And that amounted to two things. First, Lisa must see a doctor to make sure she was pregnant. Second, assuming she was, we must meet with her parents, all six of us together, to discuss our options. My head bowed, I nodded acquiescence, surprised by his demeanor. Perhaps I had been wrong about Dad after all. Perhaps he cared more about me than he had ever dared let me know.

Over the months, thanks to the logistics of picking Lisa up for our dates, I had gotten to know her mom and dad superficially. Her father was some sort of self-employed inventor, who tinkered away at his own downtown lab. From our first acquaintance, he had made a point of soliciting my views on such questions as the U.S.-Soviet arms race or the novels of C. P. Snow, as if we were colleagues in some rarefied intellectual colloquium. Lisa's petite mother, dizzy and distracted, seemed to have no job other than painting soulfully splotchy watercolors of the flowers in her backyard garden.

Through the mordant vignettes in Lisa's early letters, however, I got to know her parents as she saw them. Her mother's rapid and ready giggle, then, I understood as nervous rather than hearty, her flippant cutesiness as a retreat into a long-lost haven of whimsical adolescence. And I knew that her father drank too much, that in his cups he was wont to rage against a world that had dealt a man with his high ambitions a hand in life as a third-rate engineer.

For her part, Lisa had only traded greetings a few times with my mother. She had never met my father.

The meeting was to be held at Lisa's father's lab. As my parents and I climbed the back stairs and entered the cluttered fluorescent sanctum, to find her family already seated at their posts, I realized that the encounter was going to be even more dreadful than I had imagined.

When we had all taken our places—the three of them toward the back wall, my parents and I nearest the door—my father started talking. Without preamble, he assumed the chairmanship of the conference, as he was accustomed to do at scientific gatherings all over the world. By now a physician had certified Lisa's pregnancy.

In 1960, abortion was still illegal in every state. *Roe v. Wade* was thirteen years in the future. In Colorado, as far as our parents knew, even the proverbial back-alley abortion was an almost unknown phenomenon—and far too risky to contemplate.

There were thus, as Dad now outlined it, three options facing us. Lisa and I could get married and have the child. I would then probably have to get a job to support the family, delaying college. Eventually, perhaps, Lisa could work at a part-time job and raise the baby while I went to college. We would almost surely, Dad went on in his calm, reasonable tones, have to go to inexpensive colleges like the University of Colorado—not the elite eastern schools to which we had applied.

A second option was for Lisa to take a year off and go to a home for unwed mothers. I knew of one or two girls at Boulder High, mysteriously transplanted for a year to Indiana or Wisconsin "to visit a cousin," who were rumored to have chosen such a course—but they were, in the parlance of my peers, sluts from the wrong side of the tracks. In this event, Lisa would have to delay her graduation for a year. And, Dad editorialized, as though he were as au courant on maternal psychology as he was on the technology of the infrared spectrometer, a mother inevitably built up feelings for her unborn child. It might be harder than Lisa thought to give up her baby for adoption after carrying it for nine months.

No one spoke except my father. The tension in the room was excruciating. I sneaked a glance at Lisa: she seemed shrunken within herself, staring at the floor.

Finally Dad unveiled the third option. He had been in touch with scientific colleagues around the world—in particular, with one in Sweden and one in Japan, countries where, for citizens at least, abortion was legal. With the right strings pulled, it might be possible to arrange an abortion for Lisa. There were problems with this solution. The trip and the procedure would be very expensive. And since Lisa was more than two months pregnant already, there would be no time to waste.

My heart leapt at the prospect of this escape route, but I didn't dare sneak another glance at Lisa. Dad finished his presentation. An agonizing silence claimed the laboratory. At last, my mother managed to say, "I think David and Lisa need to discuss this between themselves." The meeting adjourned.

Three or four days passed before the families met again, during which interval Lisa and I procrastinated. On November 27, our quorum of six reassembled at Lisa's home. Dad reported that the Swedish possibility had fallen through, but the Japanese lay open. The parents turned to Lisa and me, surprised to discover that we had not yet had our fateful discussion.

It had to come now. While the grown-ups waited (Lisa's mother served tea), Lisa and I left the living room, went into her bedroom, closed the door, and sat on her bed. We had never before shared that intimacy, never made love in any bed, let alone hers. Now we sat at a distance from each other and tried to speak.

Assuming we would both jump at the Japanese escape, I was stunned to learn that Lisa wasn't sure.

"Well," I managed at last to ask, "do you want to get married?"

She was silent for an eternity. Then, almost in a whisper: "If I knew that you still loved me, then nothing would matter. I would marry you, child or no child. I would do anything for you. But . . ."

She could not finish the sentence. And I could not finish it for her. My own silence dictated the decision for us.

The day after our families' second meeting, Lisa locked herself in a closet at home. For hours, her parents pleaded with her through the door, but she did not respond. At last her father unscrewed the door from the hinges, to find Lisa lying on the floor in a fetal position, covered in an immense pile made of all the coats in the closet.

In Lisa's last letter, I learned of another scene that took place at her house a few days later: "My parents keep going over and over the fact that I ought to force you to marry me. They point out that all I have to do is yell 'rape!' and you go to jail and your father loses his job." (Not likely, since my father was the director of his own observatory— but the scandal might have made the newspapers.)

As I would six months later, when I backed out of the Grand Teton, now I called up Jock and told him that, sadly, I couldn't go to Mexico with him to climb the volcanoes. The trip, I said, was just too expensive.

It was not until the first week in January that Lisa and her father flew to Tokyo. By then, she was more than three months pregnant. The operation succeeded, however, without complications.

Lisa missed almost two weeks of school. When several friends, including Paul, asked me where she was (I mumbled some excuse about a bad case of flu), I realized with a flood of gratitude that now, when it counted most, Lisa and I had kept our whole mess a secret.

During our last five months of senior year, I exchanged not a word with Lisa, not even to ask how things had gone in Japan. We must have crossed paths in the hallways, but if so, I have censored the memory. I do recall, however, the all-school awards assembly at the end of May. Toward the close of that pageant of facile congratulation, I stood center front on the auditorium stage, co-valedictorian of the Class of 1961.

Then the principal asked me to step forward. "And now," he intoned into the microphone, "please everybody join me in honoring the recipient of an Honorary National Scholarship to Harvard—"

All at once everyone in the school was on their feet, cheering and clapping—even the jocks and the cheerleaders. I stared out at the throng of faces, attempting a smile. The principal was pumping my right hand. Bathed in sweaty humiliation, I held my half-smile, while the voice in my head jeered, *If only they knew....*

FOUR

Hard Man

LISA RETURNED FROM JAPAN THE SECOND WEEK
of January 1961. At the beginning of February, I started my course in
rock climbing, on the first of five successive Saturdays, as veterans
from the Colorado Mountain Club taught me and five or six other
beginners (including Gabe Lee) how to belay, rappel, and place pitons.
I bought my first rope, a 150-foot length of ⅜-inch GoldLine that cost
twelve dollars, as well as a handful of carabiners and soft-iron pitons
made in France and Austria.

Ever since those two events in my eighteenth year—Lisa's abortion, and my learning to rock climb—I have been keenly aware that
both were pivot points in my life. But it was not until more than thirty
years after the fact, in an unbidden moment of retrospective clarity,
that I suddenly recognized how inextricably linked those two events
were.

Lisa and I had failed spectacularly, and only a Japanese abortion
had saved us from the tawdry tragedy of premature parenthood. Now,
more than ever, I needed to taste the forbidden wine of escape. In
choosing to learn to rock climb that February, I made in a sense a lasting decision—to seek the meaning of my existence not in the wilderness of love and intimacy, but in the terra incognita of the precipice.

Through the last four months of my senior year, Boulder High
became once more, as it had been in tenth grade, an asylum whose
regimented drills I numbly endured. Now, however, it was not nights
in the cemetery for which I lived, but Saturdays and Sundays on the
sandstone cliffs above Boulder. Back from knocking off the Mexican

volcanoes, Jock welcomed me to the obscure elite of the town's technical climbers. With his best friend, Gerry, the only other high school adept before Gabe and I had taken our CMC lessons, Jock and I climbed some of the classic showpieces of the region: the slender arête on Bear Mountain called the Maiden, with its exhilarating 120-foot free rappel off the back; its cousin pinnacle, the Matron; and the soaring vector at Eldorado Canyon named the Bastille Crack.

In those days, there was no guidebook to the climbs around Boulder. The classic routes were passed on by word of mouth, and the prescriptions were vague, at best: "You start out on the north side, and about a hundred feet up you traverse out to the east face. One tricky move, then it's a piece of cake to the top." In consequence, from the very beginning, rock climbing for me was all about exploration. I was at my happiest standing beneath a cliff with no idea whether anyone had climbed it before, relying only on my wits to solve the puzzle of a possible route.

In retrospect, one might find fault with the way the CMC taught us to climb. Five Saturdays do not a sound apprenticeship make, and yet after our fifth lesson, we were in effect licensed to set off on our own and lead pitches wherever we fancied. (In more conservative programs of the day, a climber might be relegated to seconding, with a tight belay from above, for as long as a whole year before he was allowed to attempt his first lead.) Moreover, the soft-iron pitons manufactured in the workshops of Simond in France and Stubai in the Tirol were devised for the clean granite aiguilles above Chamonix, the gleaming limestone crags of the Dolomites—massifs abounding in deep natural cracks into which pitons could be pounded to the hilt, ringing with the bell-clear tones climbers hear as solid protection. No one in the CMC told us that our European pitons were ill-suited to Boulder sandstone, particularly to the great slabs of the Flatirons, so deficient in natural cracks.

Yet a majority of the world's best mountaineers, from the early nineteenth century to the present, have graduated from climbing kindergartens at least as shaky as our CMC course. An irony of the business is that the most cautious, rule-bound training schools tend to produce only mediocre climbers. A good portion of mountaineering's legendary "tigers" taught themselves to climb, with perhaps a stolen clothesline and an old pair of sneakers or work boots, and only by surviving the follies of headstrong youth did they gain their mastery of the intrinsically treacherous world of rock and ice.

Nowadays, climbing protection—in the form not so much of pitons, as of expansion bolts drilled into the rock and of nuts and stoppers and camming devices slotted into the most ephemeral of natural fissures—has grown so sophisticated that falling has lost virtually all its terrors and consequences. Working out a difficult new route at a voguish crag such as the New River Gorge in West Virginia or Rifle in Colorado, a young rock jock will take fall after leader fall on the "crux" sequence, without risking even a skinned knee.

In 1961 in Boulder, on the other hand, we stood at the tag end of a hoary tradition whose roots sprang from the Victorian Alps, where the boldest pioneers of ascent adhered to an ironclad dictum: *The leader must not fall*. That was the rule by which Whymper had lived, and Mummery, and Mallory—and though by 1960 it was no longer an adamantine commandment (the chief function of a well-driven piton was to render a leader fall less than fatal), we understood that to "come off" on the lead end of the rope was a mistake fraught with potential consequences.

So, above Boulder, Jock and Gerry and Gabe and I learned by simple trial and error just how seldom our pitons were truly effective, and we learned our limits as leaders by pushing close to the point of falling, all the while teaching ourselves how to back off, to reverse the moves that might lead to the trap of an unclimbable patch of cliff. At seventeen, however, we knew nothing about hubris; instead, we drank the heady elixir of our burgeoning competence, as week by week through the spring of 1961 we grew stronger and more skillful, daring now to tackle cliffs that a year earlier we would have deemed impossible.

By late May, Jock had convinced me that we were ready to attempt the east face of Longs Peak. I wasn't so sure, but for some reason Gerry was unavailable, and I was flattered to be Jock's second choice. Already he was plotting his August campaign against the north face of the Grand Teton.

On a Sunday in early June—partly, for me at least, as preparation for Longs—Gerry and I set out to investigate a high, little-known formation on Green Mountain called the Fist. Ever since we had moved to Boulder in 1948, I had gazed at that graceful plug of purple sandstone. From Bluebell Avenue, it rode the skyline, directly above the pointed summit of the Fifth Flatiron. It looked to be about 120 feet tall, the clenched fingers of the right hand forming the solid bulk of the cliff, out of which towered the raised thumb of the summit. No one Gerry had talked to had ever been on the Fist, or knew anything about routes up it.

By the time we had hiked 2,000 feet up steep, trailless slopes, through tangles of spruce and pine, to the foot of the cliff, ominous dark clouds were sailing east over the summit of Green Mountain, close above us. We had come too far, however, to back off at the threat of a storm. In the little climbing that I had done with Gerry, I had learned just how stubborn he could be about decision-making. Now he took one look at the Fist and declared its right-hand (northeast) ridge the logical route. Without a word, he started scrambling up its easy lower moves.

I thought there was a better line up the middle of the east face, but Gerry was already launched on his route. Instead of following him, I scrambled up the equally easy lower slabs of my passageway. Sixty feet up, I arrived at an ample ledge that looked as though it should link our disparate routes. Gerry was out of sight, but judging from his answering call, I guessed that he had reached the same ledge around the corner to the right. I could traverse and join him, or he could traverse to me.

It was absurd to stick to our separate routes. Over my shoulder, I carried a nylon sling from which dangled our hardware: six or eight steel carabiners and as many soft-iron pitons. Gerry was carrying our rope, coiled and slung over his shoulder. From my stance, I glanced up. A slight overhang blocked my way, but a rare crack ran through it.

I thought I could drive a piton into it. I reached up and clasped a pair of solid handholds just above the overhang.

"Hey, Gerry!" I yelled. "I think it'll go here!"

It took a minute for his voice to answer. "There's a way over here! It looks pretty good."

Briefly I pondered giving in and joining my partner. What good were our rope and hardware doing us if we each insisted on soloing his own route? But I had fallen in love with my handholds, and I felt a stubborn defiance of my own.

Suddenly it started to snow—soft, wet flakes drifting down out of the black sky. Snow, in June!

The only sane thing to do was to climb back down. Instead, I seized the handholds, stuck my right toe on a prong half-hidden beneath the overhang, and pulled myself up.

Without warning, my right toe slipped off its hold. My body, which had been arched backward over the sixty-foot abyss, plummeted back to the vertical. My right hand came off its hold . . . but the left hand held. "Shit!" I muttered, as I hung, swaying from one hand.

I didn't think I could find the toehold again and climb back down. Instead, I seized the right handhold once more and, with a brutal effort, pulled myself over the bulge. My feet found sloping ledges on which to stand. I looked up. The crack continued, angling up and right toward the summit. All at once the snowfall intensified.

Driven by mindless adrenaline, I powered my way sloppily up the crack. *God, that was close,* I allowed myself to think. I knew I couldn't go down: up was the only escape. Within minutes, I reached the summit. There was no sign of Gerry. *Now what do I do?* I wondered, as I sat down on the highest ledge and stared at the snowflakes.

Then Gerry's head abruptly appeared, popping up almost on the back side of the whole formation, ten feet below me. His eyes swam in their own adrenaline. "Man, that was wild!" he sang out. "I had to lasso a prong and pull myself up!" I didn't tell him about my own near slip.

Half an hour later, we had rappelled off the back side and regained the safety of the trees. As we stumbled down Green Mountain in the snow, we whooped and hollered, reveling in the privilege of being alive.

A week later, Jock and I drove to Rocky Mountain National Park to pursue our assault on the east face of Longs Peak. Signing in at the trailhead register, we were greeted with unwelcome news. A notice proclaimed in no uncertain terms that the east face was officially closed: it was too early in the season, for snow conditions up high rendered the face unreasonably dangerous.

The park rangers, always a conservative bunch, were (we later learned) acting in response to a cautionary tragedy that had occurred the previous year. Three expert climbers had come to the east face in April to attempt an off-season climb. They were fresh from climbing desert spires in southern Utah, and, it was later suggested, brought with them a cockiness born of their success in warm weather on sandstone pinnacles quite different from the high-altitude granite of Longs, where—despite a balmy spell at the outset of their climb—it was still full-blown winter. In any event, the trio had brought inadequate clothing; one of the men didn't even have a pair of gloves. Halfway up the east face, they got stuck in a snowstorm that lasted two days. Only one of the three survived—the least experienced climber, and the only woman, who, remarkably, made her way off the wall unaided. Rescuers found the two men still on their bivouac ledge, dead of hypothermia.

Now, standing over the trailhead register, Jock and I looked at each other in dismay. What else could we climb, instead of the east face? Then a sly smile twisted Jock's lips. "Fuck the rangers," he said. "We'll do it anyway."

We hiked up to Chasm Lake, at 12,000 feet, directly under the gigantic wall. The snow did look heavy up high, on Lambs Slide and the Notch Couloir, but the weather was holding magnificently. We bivouacked inside the old stone cabin that somebody had built on the lakeshore several decades before, cooking up soup and canned wieners on Jock's stove. I snuggled inside my sleeping bag and lay awake for hours. By 3:00 A.M., I was half hoping a storm would roll in and force us to cancel. The precipice frightened me.

We got up before dawn, however, and clumped off across the scree toward the foot of the face. At first light, we were roping up below Alexander's Chimney. Soon, the ecstasy of action took over. We traded leads, moving fast. Then, on the fifth pitch, I got off route, angling too far along a dead-end ledge toward the right. A kind of desperation took hold of me, as I forged recklessly on. My hands were starting to cramp from hanging on to marginal holds. Then, just as I thought I might fall, I spied a fixed piton pounded by some previous passerby into a thin crack. I slammed a carabiner into it, tied a clove hitch with one hand, and sagged with all my weight onto the saving anchor.

On the next pitch, Jock got us back on route. Things went well through the rest of the day, until, high on Kiener's Route, deep, wet snow started to prove the wisdom of the rangers' injunction. Jock was fifty feet above me, kicking thigh-deep steps in snow he increasingly thought might avalanche. Suddenly he lost his cool. "Hang on, hang on, Dave! This whole slope is about to go!"

"Calm down," I admonished, looking at my worthless belay—a shallow hollow I had packed in anchorless snow. Stupidly, we had not brought an ice axe, thinking the east face in June would be mainly a rock climb. "Just take it slowly. We'll make it." Jock regained his composure, and stumped on toward the brow of the cliff.

At last we pulled ourselves onto the summit, almost sick with relief. Exhausted, we staggered down the Cable Route off the north face, circled arduously back to Chasm Lake, gathered our camping gear, and regained the car in late afternoon.

The next day, the rangers saw our tracks crossing the high snow-fields. They checked the trailhead register and learned our identities (we were so naive we hadn't thought to scratch out our signatures). A few days later, two rangers drove down to Boulder to arrest Jock and me. But when they inquired of Baker Armstrong, the genial elder of the Colorado Mountain Club, as to how to locate the miscreants, he told the rangers to cool their prosecutorial ardor. The boys were good climbers, he swore; they knew what they were doing. It wouldn't do their progress as mountaineers any service, he pointed out, to slap them with a fine.

Back in Boulder, Gerry was suitably impressed by our bold ascent. And so was Gabe, who as yet had still never climbed a real mountain.

That spring and summer of 1961, even more than Jock or Gerry, Gabe was always available at the drop of a hat to go climbing. During several of our Saturday CMC lessons in February, Gabe and I had roped together with a third partner, the instructor who taught us our craft. And the previous fall, we had often played our singles tennis matches, against such schools as Greeley and Fort Collins, on adjoining courts. We had become better friends than we had ever been in the thirteen years since kindergarten.

Yet for a week in early March, I thought I had lost Gabe for good as a climbing partner. It was on the evening of Friday, March 3, that Gabe's father was killed on the freeway near Houston, when his car was rear-ended by a drunk driver. That terrible event came about a week after our fifth and last CMC lesson.

Teenage compassion, however, is choked and inarticulate. I remember thinking, during Gabe's week away from school, as he attended the funeral service in Texas, not, *What is he going through?* so much as *What will I say when I see him again?* Thus when I muttered my formula, "I'm really sorry about what happened," I was first surprised, then selfishly delighted, when Gabe blurted back, "That's okay. When can we go climbing?"

At seventeen, I had no road map to a fellow seventeen-year-old's grief. Nor did it ever occur to me when, upon his return to the rocks, Gabe suddenly started taking the lead on pitches I didn't like the looks of, that his newfound boldness might have anything to do with the loss of his father.

We never talked about the accident. Gabe kept his feelings to himself—I don't think he had a true confidant anywhere in the world—and so his loss, though blazoned on the front page of the *Daily Camera*, came to seem a private secret. I had my own secret, just two months in my past, and it was all I could do to navigate my own route through

the cliffs and summits that promised a way out of my failure and
humiliation.

On July 2, on Mount of the Holy Cross—Gabe's first mountain—
he became, thanks to altitude sickness and the unfamiliarity of alpine
terrain, once more the acolyte. I was now, after all, a graduate of the
east face of Longs. Lagging behind me up a loose and dangerous
chimney on Holy Cross, Gabe plugged gamely on. At the top of the
chute, when I had to spiral out of the chimney and traverse a dubious-
looking bridge that spanned the gap, I never thought of uncoiling the
rope I carried over my shoulder and tossing Gabe an end.

"We gotta do more stuff like this, Dave," said Gabe on the summit. But Holy Cross was the only mountain he would ever climb. It
was the very next Sunday that we went up on the First Flatiron.

Thanks to Paul and our backpack traverse of the Gore Range in late-
August snow, I got through the rest of the summer. By the time I went
off to Harvard in September, however, Gabe had become a second
secret. It would be more than a year before I dared tell anyone what
had happened that day on Green Mountain.

That September, I thought I had made my choice for good to turn
my back on technical climbing. Only the idlest curiosity bent my steps
toward the Lowell House common room and the initial fall meeting
of the Harvard Mountaineering Club. For one thing, I assumed that,
because there were no "real" mountains in New England (its highest
summit, Mount Washington, is a puny 6,288 feet above sea level), the
climbers at Harvard could hardly be serious devotees. I anticipated a
coterie of chummy backpackers in the mold of Jim Dugan, my next-
door-neighbor who was happy to slog up talus heaps. I envisioned
HMC gatherings in the White Mountains as akin to the CMC summer
camps, where members assembled three dozen strong in some bland
cirque every August to sing campfire songs and photograph wildflowers.

It took about five minutes to have all my preconceptions blown away. As soon as I walked into the common room, I saw juniors and seniors greeting each other with slaps on the back and vigorous hand-shakes. Eavesdropping on their chat, I learned how these veterans had spent their summer. Two HMCers, a junior and a senior, had been part of a team that had made the third ascent of the east ridge of Mount Logan, a remote, glaciated giant in the Yukon, at 19,850 feet the sec-ond-highest peak in North America. Seven or eight others were fresh off the club's biennial Climbing Camp. No flower-gazing outing in the Sawatch Range, this HMC foray had unleashed a gang of twenty-one climbers for a month in the Coast Range of British Columbia. Graced by impossibly good weather (only two storm days during the month), they had made fifty ascents of twenty-six different peaks, including Tiedemann, Asperity, the Serra group, Stiletto Needle, and the range's highest summit, Waddington.

Mount Logan! Mount Waddington! These were no Mexican vol-cano walk-ups. I had read about the epic first ascent of Logan in 1925, when a team comprising some of the finest campaigners in the Far North had spent five months, starting in February, horse-packing sup-plies 140 miles up the Chitina River gorge, finally reaching, in June, the summit plateau of what is often called the most massive mountain in the world, where several members got lost in a whiteout and came close to perishing before claiming their prize. And I knew about Waddington—"Mystery Mountain," it was nicknamed, after a half-dozen attempts to climb it failed even to penetrate the fiendish defenses of the Coast Range to reach the base of the peak. It had finally been conquered in 1936 by two blithe experts, the stronger of them the legendary German-American mountaineer Fritz Wiessner.

Intimidated by the European chronicles of the Himalaya I had first read at age twelve, I had never glimpsed the possibility that twenty-year-old Americans might go on real expeditions. But even more than their outsized deeds, what dazzled me now in the company of these upperclassmen was the effulgent joy of their camaraderie, their radi-ant sense of a common purpose in life. That made the laid-back cool of the tennis team lettermen at Boulder High seem minor-league in comparison. Half an hour into the meeting, I ached with envy.

At the onset of the session, we rookies had been asked to fill out index cards itemizing our climbing experience, if any. Now I watched as Ted Carman—six two, sandy-haired, boyishly handsome, returnee from Mount Logan, and the club's vice president—held a card in his hand and called across the room, "Hey, Rick, one of these freshmen has climbed the east face of Longs Peak! Isn't that where the Diamond is?"

No, not the Diamond, I silently editorialized, *just an old, easy route on the left side of the face.* But my shame was trumped by a bursting pride.

I signed up for an afternoon trip to the Quincy Quarries, the local crag nearest Harvard. As we parked on a shoulder of the Southeast Expressway and hiked up the short cart path to the quarry, I was put off by the urban squalor of the place—graffiti painted all over the rock faces, junked autos in the weeds. But here, I quickly learned, was a far better *gymnasium* for rock climbing than the Flatirons. Out west, I had done virtually no top-roping, a technique peculiarly suited to New England, in which the belayer hikes around to the top of a short cliff, ties himself into a tree, then secures his partner from above. Despite decades of dynamiting, the rock in the Quarries was a solid granite. Safeguarded by the top rope, the climber could afford to fall, and thus to push the difficulty to his limit. And the juniors and seniors who instructed us that afternoon, I saw at once, were far better rock climbers than I.

Soon after that outing, I signed up for the first weekend trip to the Shawangunks, near New Paltz, New York. At the time the leading climbing arena in the East, the Gunks looked, at first glimpse from Highway 299, like a nondescript band of gray-brown rock topped by a crest of pine trees. Up close, however, as we walked the old carriage roads that skirted the base of the cliff, the Gunks revealed themselves as a dauntingly steep precipice abounding in huge overhangs, arching inside corners, and sharp-prowed arêtes. The rock, a quartz conglomerate covered with black *Umbilicaria* lichens, proved as solid as any I had ever touched. The secret of the Gunks lay in a tilt of its strata some 15 degrees back from the horizontal, so that the most wildly vertical lines abounded in ledges offering a profusion of sharp-cut, perfect "t.g." ("thank God") holds.

I had done plenty of leading in Colorado, but HMC protocol dictated that the veterans harness us rookies in the role of seconds, while they led every pitch, until they could ascertain just how talented or safe we might be. And at the Gunks that weekend, I was happy to do nothing but second my betters. It took several climbs, each two or three pitches long, for me to begin to trust those t.g. holds, to get used to the severe exposure under my shoes 200 feet off the ground.

Nor, during that first weekend, was I likely to resolve the trauma that had settled under my skin after July 9. I had never before climbed at a crag that was swarming with other climbers. In Colorado, on every route with Gabe or Jock or Gerry, the only other actors in my universe were the partners I was roped to, the only human voices their belay signals. Now, as I sat on a ledge feeding out the rope to an upperclassman who had passed out of sight around a jutting corner above me, every minute or two the silence was pierced by a loud call from some other team: "Off belay!" or "Up rope!" or "Slack!" At each such shout, I jerked involuntarily in fright, then sat there as the jangling in my nerves slowly ebbed away.

By late October, I could not say that I had decided to resume climbing; but I had gone on nearly every HMC trip. The fellowship of the older guys in the club stung me with a fervor to belong. That fall, I also tried out for the freshman tennis team. From the start, however, my heart wasn't in it. The Harvard courts were sand over clay, which favored a dinking, slicing, drop-shot game that was the antithesis of the topspin drives I had learned on asphalt at 5,000 feet above sea level. I dropped out in mid-season.

Nor, that fall, did mathematics rekindle in me the fire that, two years before, had lighted my way through the wilderness of prime numbers. During the next four years, I endured an ultimately oppressive slog through a major in a discipline that, I knew by junior year, would have nothing to do with my eventual career. At Harvard, math was taught in a soulless, hyper-professional fashion. The professor walked into his class, barely acknowledged his charges, turned to the blackboard, and began scribbling equations. We copied them down, then went back to our rooms and tried to decipher the runes.

For me, by late that autumn, Galois and Euler had faded to hollow ghosts. The shining exemplars on the horizon of my dreams were Buhl and Rébuffat—and, to a certain extent, Ted Carman and Rick Millikan.

Rick, shaggy and full-bearded, with gleaming eyes and a soft voice, had knocked off most of the harder summits in the Coast Range during the previous summer's Climbing Camp. Also a junior, he served as the club's cabin chairman (overseeing a ramshackle edifice, built in 1932 halfway up Mount Washington, which served as base camp for the HMC ice climbing season in Huntington Ravine every March and April). At some point that fall, I learned from other club members about Rick's remarkable legacy. He was the grandson of George Leigh Mallory, who had vanished on Mount Everest in 1924. His other grandfather (on his father's side) was Robert Millikan, who had won the 1923 Nobel Prize in physics for his famous oil-drop experiment.

As if this were not enough, I learned that Rick's father, Glenn, had been killed in an absurd climbing accident in the Great Smoky Mountains in 1947, when Rick was only six years old. A small rock dislodged by another climber above had struck Glenn square on the head as, standing at the base of an insignificant cliff, he bent to pick up the end of a rope and start coiling it. Though it would be years before I dared talk to Rick about these matters, I was deeply impressed that autumn to discover that a family that had suffered such losses in the mountains should produce so blithe and ambitious a climber as Rick. A few years later, I met Clare—Rick's mother, Glenn's widow, and the oldest of Mallory's three children (she had been eight when the news came from Everest). It was Clare who had set the mold: in the early 1950s, newly bereft, she had taken her three sons, who had barely entered adolescence, off to the high Sierra Nevada in California, where she taught them to rock climb.

At the end of each January, when Harvard students got a four-day break between finals and the onset of the spring term, the HMC launched its annual Winter Traverse—an attempt to hike the crest of the Presidential Range in New Hampshire from Randolph to Crawford

Notch (or vice versa). So predictably hideous was the weather each January in the White Mountains that the Traverse succeeded, on the average, only once every five years. No matter: it was the best possible training for the great ranges.

I had hiked up two or three 13-ers in Colorado the previous winter. Jock and I had been stormed off Mount Silverheels, a bland peak in the Tenmile Range, though not before both suffering superficial frostbite of the nose. But I had never camped in the mountains in the dead of winter. I was not sure such a feat was possible. As we drove off from Lowell House that Wednesday evening, with most of us beginners huddled in the unheated rear compartment of Ted Carman's hearse (the unofficial HMC carry-all), I was filled with foreboding.

That midnight, as we piled out of the hearse at Randolph, the temperature was a bona fide minus 30 degrees Fahrenheit. Under Ted and Rick's hectoring, we got our tents pitched and ourselves inside before frostbite could claim any digits. Cocooned inside a pair of army surplus mummy bags, however, I shivered for three hours before I started to get warm. Then, on the verge of sleep, I heard the scream of a train whistle. The angry chuffing of the engine grew louder and louder: the behemoth seemed to be coming straight at us. Only at the last minute did the obscene noise bend in a Doppler wail. In the morning, we discovered that we had pitched our tents six feet from the snow-covered railroad tracks.

On Thursday we attacked the Howker Ridge on Mount Madison, soon losing the trail as we floundered in bearpaw snowshoes across the snow-encrusted tops of thickets of krummholz. In places Ted or Rick had to chop steps for the snowshoes, to prevent our sliding back on the crust; if we took off the bearpaws, we sank chest-deep into air pockets trapped by tangled evergreen boughs. It was by far the worst bushwhacking I had ever undertaken. I was amazed at the prowess of our leaders, who could each break trail for an hour at a time before succumbing to fatigue.

On Friday we got to timberline, changed to crampons, and struggled to the col between Mounts Madison and Adams for a second camp. Eventually we bagged the summits of both Adams and Madison before the inevitable storm raged in from the north, forcing us to retreat back to Randolph down a more hospitable ridge on Madison.

As we drove back to Cambridge in the hearse, a throb of happiness had replaced the dull anxiety I had felt on the trip north. On the second day of the Traverse, Rick had waved his ice axe at the trackless snow ahead and murmured, "Why don't you break trail for a ways, Dave?" And on the last evening, as we were ensconced in the relative comfort of a cabin at Crag Camp, Ted, with other chores to perform, handed me the ingredients and asked me to cook glop for our group of eight. Stirring the big pot full of Minute rice, Lipton powdered soup, cheese, and canned corn beef, I was suffused with pride. Entrusted to break trail and to make dinner, I had passed, it seemed to me, from merely "one of the freshmen" to a candidate for meaningful identity in the HMC. Someday I might become a mountaineer.

Despite the HMC, I did not manage to cultivate a new best friend my freshman year. The two roommates I had been arbitrarily assigned were not kindred souls. One would eventually become a small-time doctor, like his father; the other, a professor of economics.

Instead, I stayed in touch with Paul, who was at Amherst College, ninety miles west of Cambridge. On some weekends, one of us would hitchhike via the Mass Pike to visit the other. Whenever we could, we hustled two-on-two touch football games against strangers. On three halcyon occasions in the autumn, we hitched to New York City, where we got into Yankee Stadium on Sunday afternoon during the last season the football Giants still sold unreserved day-of-game tickets for bleachers in the north end zone. Unfortunately for Paul, we did not catch the Cleveland Browns, when he could have paid homage to his hero, Jim Brown. But we got to see, live, the great Giants squad of Charley Conerly, Kyle Rote, Sam Huff, Rosey Grier, Jim Katcavage, and Jimmy Patton, who that year won the Eastern Conference championship but lost the NFL title to the Green Bay Packers.

During our time together, I minimized for Paul's ears my enthusiasm for the HMC. It was as though I had lapsed from a New Year's pledge I had made in his presence.

Instead, we talked about girls. In the spring of his senior year at Boulder High, Paul had at last gotten laid, in a one-night stand that seemed rather to dismay than to gratify him. Now he was trying to figure out how to finesse dates at Mount Holyoke or Sarah Lawrence. Smith girls, Paul told me, were uniformly stuck-up and frigid.

For my own part, I was scarcely trying to construct a social life. At Radcliffe, I attended a single "jolly-up"—a ghastly afternoon tea during which the "ladies" of Barnard House received the "men" of Lionel. Under the stern gaze of resident chaperones, I fled before attempting conversation. At several other colleges, I ventured into mixers, only to wander aimlessly on the edges, afraid to ask a girl to dance.

Harvard's parietal rules allowed us to entertain the opposite sex in our rooms only from 1:00 to 5:00 P.M. on weekdays, from 6:00 to 10:00 P.M. on Saturdays. In loco parentis was the catchphrase of the day, by which the administration justified its policing of our romantic lives. What if a girl got pregnant in a Harvard dorm? one official speculated for the Crimson. The university itself might bear the brunt of a messy lawsuit. Several classmates of mine got expelled for a full year for the first infraction of having a girlfriend spend the night.

By the spring of 1962, however, I had yet to exercise my 6:00 to 10:00 Saturday option. Trips to the Gunks, among their other rewards, freed us climbers from the opprobrium of hanging around Harvard Yard dateless on a beautiful April weekend.

As western boys from public high school, Paul and I had started college at a certain social disadvantage compared to the preppies who had learned the dating system at Andover and Groton. For Paul, his frustrations at Smith and Sarah Lawrence merged with homesickness for Boulder, issuing in a Larry McMurtry–fueled rant about how "phony" and "effete" everything in the East was. Paul's classmates, amused by his affected drawl, quickly typed him as a cowboy from the prairie.

Under Paul's sway, I agreed to spend the summer of 1962 in Boulder. We would get "real" jobs working construction, he rhapsodized, build up our muscles, play two-on-two touch every day after work, and date the girls we had lusted after in high school, who weren't too stuck-up to cap an evening drinking 3.2 beer at Tulagi's with making out in a pullout on Flagstaff Mountain.

Through the spring, I continued to go on HMC trips. In March, Ted Carman taught me to ice climb in Huntington Ravine. On Colorado mountains, so dry is the climate, I had never run into hard ice—only snow into which I could kick steps. I had never worn crampons before the Winter Traverse. Now, for my first lesson on ice, Ted headed for Pinnacle Gully, a four-pitch couloir that at the time was the hardest ice climb in the East. In those days, still almost a decade before rigid crampon front-points would transform ice climbing, the only way to get up such a gully was laboriously to chop a ladder of steps— just as Mallory had, half a century before.

On that gray, cold day on Mount Washington, I was thrilled to watch Ted balance on 70-degree ice while he dexterously carved the next steps in just the right places. A hundred and twenty feet out, he chopped a ledge to stand on, twisted in a Marwa "coat-hanger" ice screw for belay, and brought me up. Seconding the chopped steps was easy, but I was further thrilled that Ted had chosen me among all the freshmen to initiate on this classic test piece of a route.

On my last climbing weekend in May, Charlie Bickel, another veteran of the Coast Range Climbing Camp, took me up the Old Man route on Cannon Cliff in New Hampshire, at a thousand feet from bottom to top the tallest precipice in the East. Charlie let me lead two of the easier pitches. As we sat picnicking on the summit, he said, "You should keep it up, Dave. You could be good."

In retrospect, the summer of 1962 in Boulder seems like a wasted season. Paul and I found work the first day we looked, on the University of Colorado grounds crew, at minimum wage. The daily chores were tedious—hauling office furniture about, tearing down the "temporary buildings" erected on campus during World War II—but we went at them as if we were trying out for the varsity. One 90-degree day, as we sat sweating through lunch, a fellow crew member, a Hispanic guy in his thirties, eyed us and said softly, "Hey, *compañeros*, doan work so hard. You doan make no more moaney. Make the rest of us look bad."

Nonetheless, Paul and I did our best to turn our crewmates into characters out of McMurtry, or at least Steinbeck. Out of his earshot, we joked about "old Ralph" (he was probably forty), our sour, phlegmatic boss, who never had a kind word for either of us. We reveled in *Schadenfreude* when the number-two guy fucked up (in Ralph's succinct judgment), causing a grand piano to get dropped down a stairwell.

After a few weeks, Paul landed a better-paying gig with a private construction firm, which had no opening for me. We spent the rest of the summer in separate workplaces, the 5:00 P.M. touch football games our only shared pleasure. I asked Jane McPhetres and Barb Hall out on dates—pretty former classmates from Boulder High who had spent the year at CU, and who were perhaps flattered to go out with a Harvard man. But no quantities of 3.2 Coors seemed to put them or me in a romantic mood, and the evenings ended with snacks at the Twinburger drive-in out east on Arapahoe Avenue.

There was something regressive about living again in my bedroom on Bluebell Avenue. Years later, my mother told me that when I had gone off to college in September 1961, I had seemed so alienated that she thought she might never see me again. Now, in the summer of 1962, I tried to maintain a fortress of privacy, but it was still my parents' station wagon that I had to borrow to go out on dates.

Out of the twin debacles of my senior year in high school—Lisa's pregnancy and Gabe's death—I had absorbed, like the doom-saying formulas of medieval parables, the lessons that sex and climbing unleashed calamity on the world. Away from Boulder, I could ignore those dark imprecations for weeks at a time, as I sought the kind of escape that might define for me a new identity. But from Bluebell Avenue, no such escape was possible.

It was for that reason, I think, that my dates with Jane and Barb remained so chaste, and for the same reason that during the summer of 1962, I did no climbing. I spent a few weekends in the mountains, bagging 13-ers and 14-ers that were challenging scrambles, not mere talus heaps. But not once that summer did I tie in to a rope or drive a piton.

I had gone off to Harvard for my freshman year reeling with disorientation, uncertain what to do next in life. A year later, in September 1962, I returned to Cambridge eager to become a sophomore. And the first station at which I disembarked was the Mountaineering Club.

At the last meeting the previous spring, I had been elected equipment manager. My duties were not inconsiderable: at a club gathering, I took orders for climbing rope, then made my way to Harrington King, the Boston cordage firm, and surveyed the process as they lopped off custom-made 150-foot lengths of $7/_{16}$-inch GoldLine. With my pocket full of HMC dues, I hiked down Mass Avenue to Central Surplus to buy used mummy bags to replace the ones from which sodden down had begun irremediably to leak.

That fall, the HMC was anchored by four returning seniors: Ted Carman, Rick Millikan, Charlie Bickel, and Hank Abrons. Hank was a mercurial climber, brilliant when he was on his game, but given to funks that left him stranded in his inertia. He had grown up privileged, the son of a Scarsdale lawyer, and though part of him reveled in the persona of an unwashed climbing bum, at the same time he was majoring in classics and seeing an expensive psychotherapist once a week (the first person I had ever met who had resorted to such treatment).

Among the four, Hank was the most thoughtful and empathic, and it was to him, late one night that autumn, as we lay in our sleeping bags on the carriage road below the Gunks, that I unburdened the secret of Gabe's fall from the First Flatiron.

The previous summer, club members had done great things once more in the mountains. Hank had been the only HMC undergraduate on an expedition that made the first ascent of the Southeast Spur on Mount McKinley—though he was sorely disappointed not to be chosen to join the team leader as the only pair who would actually stand on the summit.

From its founding in 1924 by Henry Hall, a member of the path-breaking party that made the first ascent of Mount Logan, the HMC had squarely oriented itself toward expeditions in the great ranges. Rock climbing had always been viewed not as an end in itself, but as training for big mountains.

That autumn, however, Rick Millikan and Pete Carman (Ted's younger brother, an iconoclastic junior) came back from the Tetons, where they had spent many weeks hanging out in a campground scene that included such already legendary Yosemite big-wall rats as Yvon Chouinard and Chuck Pratt. There, Pete and Rick had penetrated beyond the 5.8 level of difficulty that had formed an HMC ceiling for several years at the Gunks, entering the empyrean realms of 5.9, and daring to contemplate 5.10 (at the time, the highest grade rating in the country—see glossary). They had become indisputably the finest rock climbers in HMC history, and that fall, they comported themselves with a swagger that let the rest of us know they knew it.

I had become friends with the four seniors and Pete, but I stood in renewed awe of them—especially after my own wasted summer with no new notches in my climbing belt. That fall, along with seconding Rick or Hank on hard climbs at the Gunks, I led my own routes, training in turn the beginners among the incoming crop of freshmen.

For the first time in my life, I was firmly ensconced in a gang of cronies whose values and ambitions sang a siren song of the future. Yet I was still casting about for a regular climbing partner, a best friend to replace Paul, whose own values were causing him at last to drift away from me.

On the first outing of the fall, I had lugged my gear over to Lowell House to wait for Ted's hearse. A heavyset, muscular, dark-haired fellow who had already arrived stepped forward, thrust out his hand, and with awkward formality, said, "Hi. I'm Don Jensen." It turned out that we were both sophomores, both lodged in Dunster House. Doubtless I had met Don the previous year (at the end of which he was elected club librarian), but somehow we had managed never to spend the same weekend at the Gunks or Huntington Ravine.

Don was from Walnut Creek, California, a public high school boy from out west like me. A loner by instinct, he had, at the age of seventeen, undertaken a twenty-day solo traverse of the Sierra Nevada. He missed his home mountains as much as I still longed for the Colorado Rockies.

We hit it off from that first meeting. Soon we were eating our Dunster House dinners together regularly, and each invited the other up to his room to riffle through black-and-white snapshots of the Gore Range or the Palisades. At the Gunks, or in New Hampshire at Cathedral Ledge or Joe English, we tried to rope up together whenever we could.

The climbing trips ended in late November, and soon after we settled in to prepare for January finals. But Don had come up with a plan. Instead of simply heading home for Christmas, why didn't we organize a climbing trip, either in Colorado or California—a kind of Winter Traverse of our own, among sharper and higher peaks than the Presidentials?

We thought we needed at least three actors for so bold a drama, so we invited a third sophomore, Bert Redmayne. Two days after Christmas, the three of us hiked up South Colony Creek toward the Crestone group in Colorado's Sangre de Cristo Mountains. The second day, we reached timberline, where we set up a base camp on the frozen streambed just below South Colony Lake. The weather held perfect throughout our trip. On successive days, we climbed two 14-ers—the steep, nearly technical Crestone Needle, and a walk-up, Humboldt Peak—before having to turn back short of the summit of a third, Kit Carson Peak, when Bert got sick.

Hiking out on the sixth day, I felt a glow of satisfaction. But Don expressed his regret that we hadn't planned a longer trip. There had been other mountains looming above our camp—most notably, the difficult, seldom-climbed Crestone Peak—that he longed to tackle. For Don, the end of a trip would always spell disappointment, the uneasy return to a life more ambivalent than the simple existence he crafted for himself in the mountains. It was a temperamental difference that would come to bedevil our friendship.

School was hard on Don. Socially, he was even more of a misfit than I in the smug, arch-critical milieu that was Harvard in the early 1960s. He was incapable of the cutting quip, the cool witticism that passed for conversational currency at the Dunster House dining table. Like me, Don was majoring in math. Potentially, he was a much deeper mathematician than I, but while I managed to coast through courses in topology and calculus, earning a gentleman's B minus, he suffered Sisyphean agonies over his textbooks and exams.

That January, facing finals, Don reached a new nadir. He took NoDoz tablets to stay awake and study, but found he couldn't concentrate on the equations before him. I had never met anyone so psychosomatically vulnerable as Don. Now, during Reading Period, he gained weight and looked more haggard every day. He managed to get through his final exams, but he knew he had performed poorly. As the spring semester began, Don was mired in a deep funk.

One day in February, Hank Abrons and Rick Millikan invited me up to Rick's room in Leverett House. As I sat down facing them, I saw that both seniors had a certain gleam in the eye. Rick spoke first, in his usual offhand way: "We're planning an expedition to McKinley next summer. You wanna come?"

I was stunned. Despite the evidence of Waddington, Logan, and Hank's own venture to McKinley the previous summer, I still believed that some nearly insuperable barrier loomed between me and a true expedition. And I was further stunned to learn that I was the sixth and last teammate to be invited, the only sophomore. Ted and Rick had chosen me over not only Bert Redmayne, but over Don Jensen—who, I thought in my heart of hearts, was really the more deserving candidate.

In the moment before I could answer, I felt a wave of sheer terror. McKinley . . . that was the real thing. I was not at all sure I was up to the challenge. And if I accepted, I would be turning my back on the resolve that had gotten me through the rest of the haunted summer of 1961, after Gabe's death. I could no longer pretend that climbing was a pastime in which I was dabbling. I would be committing myself for good to becoming a mountaineer. I would take the first timid steps on the Olympus explored by Buhl and Rébuffat.

Of course there was no way I could say no. "Sure," I murmured, as conflicting feelings played havoc with my nerves. "Wow. Hey, thanks, you guys."

Don magnanimously congratulated me on my invitation to McKinley, but he could not hide his disappointment at having been passed over himself. Shortly after that, he decided to drop out of school for the spring semester. He came up with a wonderful rationalization for defecting: in the coming fall, he planned to take Professor David Riesman's famous course on social structures in America, based on his best-seller, *The Lonely Crowd*. As field study for the course, Don would hang out in the tiny town of Big Pine, California, gateway to his beloved Palisades. Buying groceries in Big Pine before many a jaunt into the High Sierra, he had observed the intricate network of cliques and prejudices that ruled its social life. Like Malinowski in the Trobriand Islands, Don would plop himself down among the natives as a participant-observer.

By April, of course, Don was established not in Big Pine, but in his one-man camp at timberline in the Palisades. He sent me a few letters, mailed during his infrequent trips into town to resupply. Instead of untangling the social webs of Big Pine, he was reading Goethe, he wrote, and learning far more in his self-devised alpine tutorial than he could have in an eastern classroom. He had discovered an echoing rock near camp, with which he carried on shouted conversations for fifteen minutes at a time. He was in the best shape of his life.

Meanwhile, at Harvard, preparing for McKinley began to overwhelm our curricular duties. Our initial plan was to make the second ascent of the mountain's Southeast Spur, thereby avenging Hank's failure to make the summit in 1962. But Bradford Washburn, who had been one of the leaders of an extraordinary bunch of HMC climbers in the 1930s, got wind of our plans and invited us over to his house on Sparks Street.

Fifty-two years old that spring, Washburn had stopped climbing about a decade earlier, but in his heyday he had been the finest mountaineer in Alaskan history (the author of three ascents of McKinley and of more than half a dozen first ascents of other subarctic giants). In his retirement, he loved nothing more than to push the younger generation toward objectives he had discovered during his twenty years of exploring the Far North.

"You don't want to make just the second ascent of the Southeast Spur," Brad said dismissively that evening on Sparks Street. "Here, take a look at this." He had laid a pair of large-format photos he had taken from an airplane side-by-side on his kitchen table. Now he slapped a stereo viewer on top of the pictures. One by one, we peered through the viewer and saw the massive north face, or Wickersham Wall, of McKinley leap into three dimensions. At 14,000 feet from bottom to top, the Wickersham was one of the two or three tallest precipices in the world. It had never been climbed, or even seriously attempted.

"You get the most god-awful avalanches off the Wickersham," Brad said. Then, tracing a line on one of the photos with the eraser end of a pencil, he added, "But look how this rib divides 'em right and left." He waited till each of us had stared through the viewer, then commanded our attention. "I guarantee you it's a safe route. You fellows are up to it. And you damned well better grab it before somebody else does."

I have no recollection of telling my parents that in the summer of 1963 I would not be working construction in Boulder, but launching out on an attempt, way up in Alaska, to climb the biggest mountain face in North America. I am sure that I presented the expedition as a fait accompli—I was not asking their permission—though a guilty memory prods me now to suspect that Mom and Dad ponied up the $400 that my share in the expedition cost.

Besides Rick, Hank, and myself, our six comprised the brilliant rock climber Pete Carman; his fellow junior, the solid but less talented John Graham; and a grad student named Chris Goetze, whose gear-making genius dictated the customized production of our three "bomb shelter" tents, whose sleeve doors could be rolled into one another to form a cozy end-to-end indoor colony during storms. Then, in early May, for reasons I no longer recall, Pete abruptly dropped out.

The whole conception of our trip was based on the number six: three roped pairs, three tents of two men each. In dismay at losing Pete, we set out to find his replacement. Hank and Rick asked me about Bert Redmayne. Without hesitation, I urged them to consider Don Jensen instead. Don was, I insisted, really the strongest of all us sophomores. His twenty-day solo Sierra trip in high school had been like an expedition in its own right.

But how to get hold of Don? After fruitless phone calls to his parents, we sent a telegram to General Delivery in Big Pine. Coming out for supplies a few days later, Don happened upon our missive. He wired back an immediate acceptance. In early June, he would meet the rest of us at McKinley Park headquarters.

Then, as abruptly as he had dropped out, Pete changed his mind and asked back in. We couldn't disinvite Don. The rest of us held a meeting to decide what to do. A certain faction was inclined to turn Pete down. Then Hank proposed what seemed at the time a radical idea: "What the hell," he said, "let's just go as a team of seven." In the end, Pete's addition immensely strengthened our party, and all our fears about uneven numbers mucking up the logistics proved groundless.

As soon as school got out, we adjourned to Hank's house in Scarsdale for several days of frantic gear and food packing. Then we drove the VW Microbus we had bought for the trip nonstop to Alaska, taking six days for the passage.

Lying in the back of the bus, as mile after dreary mile of the unpaved Alaska Highway crept past the windows in an endless blur of dwarf spruce and muskeg, I surrendered to the vague fears and misgivings that had clouded my spirits all spring. It was not simply the audacity of our route on the Wickersham Wall that troubled me. It was the whole psychological weight of an expedition. The longest stretch of time I had ever spent in the mountains was our six days in the Sangre de Cristos at Christmas. On McKinley, we would need more than a month in the wilderness to come to grips with our challenge. At low moments during the drive north, I would happily have traded pounding nails in Boulder for our mission into the unknown.

Yet meeting Don at McKinley Park headquarters instantly restored my equanimity. He looked indeed in terrific shape, his earnest face chiseled rather than haggard. Don seemed to have no ambivalence at all about plunging into the climb of our young lives.

Groaning under seventy-pound packs, we set out at midnight on June 19 from the Denali Highway near Wonder Lake. Three days and thirty-five miles later, we set up base camp at 5,300 feet on the Peters Glacier, directly beneath our route. There we waited four days for the precision airdrop that our bush pilot, the legendary Don Sheldon, ultimately delivered. During those days, we watched in shuddering awe as the most gigantic avalanches any of us would ever see peeled off the north face, rumbling 12,000 feet down to the glacier: several times a cloud of spindrift, driven before the tons of avalanche debris, swept over base camp, blinding us in a thirty-second snowstorm. But Washburn seemed to be right: the rib we hoped to climb did indeed divide the snowslides right and left.

Though we were ostensibly equals, there was a half-spoken understanding among the seven of us that separated the acolytes—Don, John Graham, and me—from the veterans (Hank, Rick, Pete Carman, and Chris Goetze). Thus we regularly permutated our rope teams, but always so that I, for instance, was paired with Hank, Rick, or Chris. Throughout most of the expedition, then, I never got to rope up with Don.

A raucous camaraderie prevailed in camp. Though hauling enough supplies up the monstrously long route to allow us to traverse over the north summit would require a tremendous outpouring of effort, we threw ourselves at the task. And in the zest of hard days and deep-sleeping nights, my vague fears fell away. On the seventh day, for the first time, paired with Hank, I got to pioneer several rope-lengths of new route. As we climbed the icefall that led to the foot of the rib in the ghostly light of 1:00 A.M., I was filled with a penetrating joy. On the Fourth and Fifth Flatirons, two years earlier, it was barely possible that Gabe and I had climbed pitches no one had ever touched before—but if so, those lines lay only some forty or fifty feet away from known itineraries. Here, as I wove my way between crevasses up the icefall, I dwelt, incredulous, on a novel realization: *In the whole history of the world, no one has ever been here before.*

For the most part, the route went like clockwork. A hard pitch led by Pete or Rick became, with the fixing of a rope to use as handline, negotiable with a forty-five-pound pack. Steadily we moved a series of camps up the rib. Our timing was perfect, for just as the heat of the waxing summer began to collapse the séracs and slopes on the lower part of the route, we moved up into colder, safer realms.

In retrospect, after thirteen seasons of Alaskan climbing, I can see that the Wickersham Wall was far more dangerous than we realized. One interim camp that we set up at the top of the icefall, beneath the foot of the rib, was a piece of pure folly, for it lay smack in the path of a chute down which rotten rock spilled regularly off the rib. During the single night we spent there, tiny stones drilled holes in our nylon "bomb shelters," and one boulder bounced right over John Graham's head as he sorted gear beside his tent.

Like twenty-year-olds the world over, we greeted such hazards with blithe bravado. Pete, in particular, treated the whole expedition like a summer camp. At one point, halfway up the face, he returned from a load carry not by our willow-wand-marked path, but by jumping, in his snowshoes, ten feet off a sérac, like a townie diving off a cliff into some swimming hole. Had he broken his ankle, our expedition would have ended there, but for Pete, tempting fate was a recreational drug.

By July 11, earlier than we had dared hope, we had established Camp IX on a shallow shelf we carved out of hard snow at 17,400 feet—only 2,000 feet below the north summit. The route, we thought, was in the bag. But then a five-day storm descended upon Mount McKinley. We lay in our sleeping bags, struggling to stay warm. On July 14, our thermometer recorded 8 degrees Fahrenheit, our wind gauge a steady forty-four-mile-an-hour gale out of the west. We cut our rations to two meals a day.

During those days, unbeknownst to us, a drama started playing itself out in the outside world. We had carried with us no two-way radio. During the five-day storm, as he flew other parties in and out from the West Buttress (McKinley's easiest route), Don Sheldon tried to check on our progress. Aware of our projected timetable, he pushed his Cessna in and out of the billowing clouds that shrouded the Wickersham Wall, probing our route around the 12,000-foot level. Finally, on one gutsy flyby, he caught sight of our tracks. What he saw deeply alarmed him, for those tracks disappeared into a blank sheet of bare ice, where a huge avalanche had cut loose from the face.

The finest bush pilot in Alaska, with decades of mountain flying under his belt, Sheldon was by temperament the last person in the world to cry wolf. But he felt he had to report his darkest fears. There was no way for him to know that the avalanche had wiped out our tracks several days after we had printed them—no way of knowing that we were camped safely on the mountain 5,000 feet above the scene of his ominous discovery.

The news spread nationwide. On the Huntley-Brinkley evening report on television, the whole Harvard team was declared missing and feared dead. In Denver, the Rocky Mountain News's banner front-page headline for July 14 screamed, "Coloradan, 6 Others Lost on Mt. McKinley." The subhead, in bold italics above the main headline, announced, "Walter Orr Roberts' Son Missing." Inside the paper, a reporter offered a lurid account of his interview with my father on Bluebell Avenue. "Dr. Walter Orr Roberts," the piece began, "whose intellectual prowess has brought the secrets of the Sun within the reach of Man, reacted like any other father and husband to a family crisis here Saturday." On "this terrifying night in the peaceful campus town of Boulder, Colo.," Dad spoke "quietly in the shadow of this news" before "hurr[ying] back to comfort his frantic wife." "I'm an old mountain climber myself," the reporter quoted Dad as saying, "And I know it—McKinley is a formidable mountain."

Among all the parents of the seven of us, only Clare Millikan (the one genuine climber in the lot) pooh-poohed the news as premature. Brad Washburn was similarly skeptical. As he told the Boston Globe, "I can't see what all the excitement is about. . . . Three or four days of bad weather is no problem."

Meanwhile, several other pilots joined Sheldon in a further search for the missing Harvard party. Then, on July 15—two days after he had raised the alarm—Sheldon and one other aviator spotted us in our tents at 17,400 feet. That day, our fifth in a row in our chilly camp, as the clouds began to thin, we heard the whine of plane engines in the sky. At last, a patch of clearing allowed us to spot Sheldon's Cessna. He waggled his wings as we waved a cheery hello. "Must be a bunch of tourists out on scenic flights around the mountain," Hank speculated. "Don likes to show off his climbers."

On July 16, we trudged up to the north summit, as a day of good weather once more deteriorated into storm. That night we camped on the first shelf below the top on the far side, hunkering down in a fifty-five-mile-an-hour wind, with temperatures down to 25 below Fahrenheit. Two days later, we climbed the south (true) summit at 20,320 feet, becoming the first party to traverse both summits of McKinley, then, in one exhausting twenty-four-hour push, descended the West Buttress, passed over Kahiltna Pass, flew down the Peters Glacier, and arrived back at base camp.

Despite our inexperience, we had formed a very strong team on McKinley. With seven climbers working on the route, there was always someone else to pick up the slack, after you exhausted yourself on a double-load carry or a tough pitch. Forty-two years later, it is gratifying to know that no one has repeated our route.

It was only after we staggered out to the Denali Highway in the wee morning hours of July 24 that we ran into tourists who told us that we had been reported missing, touching off an intensive aerial search. For several days, we were feted at park headquarters like celebrities, treated to expensive dinners and besought for our autographs. When I returned to Boulder, the *Rocky Mountain News* and *Daily Camera* interviewed me about "conquering the treacherous mountain." "I'd love to go again," I babbled to the *News*. "It's an impressive mountain. You just can't fail to be attracted by it."

Neither article mentioned the last time I had made the pages of the *Camera* and the *News*, twenty-five months before.

After a few days in Boulder, I headed off to Marble, where the Colorado Outward Bound School was in its second year of operation. I had wangled a job as an assistant instructor for the month of August. At twenty, I was the youngest patrol leader in the organization (I was in fact younger than several of the students I taught in Boone Patrol), but the McKinley fuss had preceded me, and a number of senior instructors congratulated me on the climb. Among them was Paul Petzoldt, the legendary Wyoming cowboy who way back in 1936 had made the first ascent of the north face of the Grand Teton (the route on which Jock and I had set our sights two years before). Resurfaced after a lost decade, during which it was rumored he had hit the bottle hard, Petzoldt was bushy-tailed and full of mischief at fifty-six. His measured approbation vis-à-vis the Wickersham Wall was some of the sweetest music I had ever heard.

The month at Outward Bound was halcyon. I hit it off with my senior instructor in Boone Patrol, a grizzled Brit named Ralph Clough, master of all kinds of outdoor skills besides climbing. And for the first time, the skills of my own that I took for granted bore dividends in terms of hero worship among the youths I chaperoned through the Elk Range, as I grabbed the backpack of a worn-out seventeen-year-old and humped it up to camp along with my own, or clung to a dangerous precipice with one hand while I caught stones my clumsy charges dislodged with the other.

At twenty, teaching scared kids to rappel, I felt like a grizzled veteran myself. I had become what I had only dreamed of being, since reading those expedition books checked out of the library at twelve: a mountaineer. Around the students, in camp and on the trail, I wore my nonchalance like a uniform.

The psyche, however, has a life of its own. One night, Boone Patrol was camped in a rainstorm above timberline. Each of us had crawled under the willows and pitched a poncho over himself in lieu of a tent. In the middle of the night, I dreamed about Gabe, for the first time since his death. In the dream, he was trapped in a metal cage, falling headlong through endless reaches of black space, as I screamed his name.

I woke with a sudden jolt, then sat shivering as the dream slowly dissolved. I crawled out of my shelter and dragged my sleeping bag far from the others. It had stopped raining, but I lay awake through the rest of the long night.

In the morning, I found Clough blowing the previous night's campfire back to life. "Did you hear the screams?" he asked. "One of the poor lads must have had a nightmare."

Back at Harvard, classmates congratulated us on McKinley. Hank and Rick had graduated, and Pete was taking the year off. Don and I— and John Graham and Bert Redmayne—thus became the HMC veterans whom the younger climbers looked up to, just as, in my freshman year, I had adulated Ted Carman and Rick Millikan. I was now the club's vice president, while Don (despite his sabbatical in the Palisades the previous spring) had been elected treasurer.

That fall, whenever we could, Don and I escaped our instructional duties at the Gunks or Cathedral Ledge to tackle hard routes together. During the last hours of our expedition, he and I had roped up to cross the McKinley River, swollen to an angry brown flood by mid-summer snowmelt. We managed the ford without incident, while, tied to other partners, both Pete Carman and John Graham got knocked off their feet in the river, dragging their belayers along the shore before they managed to eddy out. It was the closest we had come to a serious accident during the whole expedition.

In that last deed of comradeship, Don and I felt that we had solidified the pledge to each other we had first made in the Sangre de Cristo Range the previous Christmas. There was no doubt that Don had become my best friend; by junior year, I was seeing very little of Paul, out in Amherst. There was also no doubt that climbing had become the most important thing in my life.

That fall, it was too soon to evaluate the incoming freshmen who joined the HMC. We had been disappointed at the relatively weak crop produced by the previous year's freshman class (now sophomores).

Only one, a thin, wiry athlete named Matt Hale, showed much promise on the harder routes we tried to stump him with at the Gunks. Meanwhile, Don and I and Bert reveled in the way, at HMC meetings or on climbing weekends, the beginners hung on our every word.

Don and I had already started to build our own private collection of tag phrases, which we used in a kind of ironic banter. Most of these sayings were culled from the more gruesome episodes in canonical mountaineering books both of us had read. Thus, scrambling up an ice gully on Mount Washington in a snowstorm, Don would cry, "*Fame! Freddo!*" ("Hungry! Cold!")—Stefano Longhi's last words, wafted on the wind, before he froze to death on the north face of the Eiger in 1957, as reported in Heinrich Harrer's *The White Spider*. Or, waking in a tent I shared with Don, I would swipe at the ceiling with an imaginary knife, muttering, "I'm a doctor. I know about these things"—the words a delirious Charlie Houston had spoken, after a nearly fatal fall on K2 in 1953, as he tried to cut open his tent, in the grips of a conviction that he was suffocating.

My mother had made me a scrapbook of McKinley clippings. That fall, I passed it around among my HMC cronies. Seizing upon the melodramatic interview with my father in the *Rocky Mountain News*, Bert nicknamed my dad the Sun King. And my father's purported claim— "I'm an old mountain climber myself. And I know it—McKinley is a formidable mountain"—became one of Don's and my choice tags.

In that fashion, I managed to ignore the genuine anguish my parents had undergone during those two days of waiting for news in July. Rereading the clippings forty years later (and thirteen years after my father's death to melanoma), I am smitten with shame. The *News* piece was indeed riddled with maudlin clichés, but it is easy to see past them to the suffering they bespoke. In another quotation in that article, Dad said, "I know how people during the war felt. I went through the same kind of anxiety with a brother who was in the service."

In that semi-revelation, my father spoke with a certain reticence. Even in 1963, I knew the family story well. During World War II, Dad's younger brother—the Uncle Stuart whom I never knew, but from whom I received my middle name—had been an ace bomber pilot in the Pacific theater. In June 1944, Stuart's plane did not return from a mission over Guam. Fellow pilots had seen two planes go down but could not be sure whose they were. In Climax, my parents got a phone call notifying them that Stuart was missing—and then they sat down to wait, hoping against hope that Stuart had merely been taken prisoner by the Japanese. It was not until four months later that the Navy Department informed Dad's family that the wreckage of Stuart's plane, with his charred body inside, had been found on a remote Guam peninsula.

Stuart had been the charmed one, the natural, in the family—the star quarterback in high school and college (Dad had lettered in the high hurdles at Amherst), the handsome rake with a woman always on his arm. During the war, Dad had been exempted from the service because his astronomy was deemed crucial to the defense effort (for the simple reason that solar flares were a reliable predictor of magnetic storms in the earth's atmosphere a few days later, which wreaked havoc with radio transmissions all over the globe). After Stuart's death, I think, Dad never fully exorcised a sense of guilt about having seen no combat in the war.

In the fall of 1963, however, there was a good reason why I could not empathize with the pain my being reported missing on McKinley had caused my parents. Out of the British climbing scene in the 1950s, dominated for the first time by blue-collar blokes from the north of England (many were plumbers), a new piece of mountaineering vocabulary had emerged. Devotees such as Joe Brown and Don Whillans, who would go on from the gritstone crags of their apprenticeship to perform great deeds on Kangchenjunga, Annapurna, and Everest, were "hard men." As used by climbers, "hard man" was a term of wholehearted approval, without an ounce of undercutting irony. The mind-set involved is epitomized in a delicious exchange recorded by the Scottish climber and satirist Tom Patey, in a piece called "A Short Walk with Whillans." In a bar in Alpiglen the night before an attempt on the Eiger Nordwand—the North Face— the congenitally fatalistic Whillans philosophizes, apropos of nothing, "Ay, it's a good life, providing you don't weaken."

"What happens if you do?" wonders Patey.

"They bury you," growls Whillans, finishing his pint.

For various reasons, a hard man makes a good climber. And that is what I was starting to become in 1963, turning my father's anguish into a quip to trade with Don.

Over Christmas vacation, Don and I planned another trip to Colorado. This time we would assault the Needle Mountains in the San Juan Range: the state's ruggedest peaks, they had never been attempted in winter. And we would allot a full eleven days to our trip, not a mere six, to ensure that Don would not have to hike out with unfinished business on his plate. For our team of six, we recruited Bert Redmayne, two other solid juniors, and Matt Hale, the most talented of the sophomores.

Two days before Christmas, we rendezvoused in the moribund mining town of Silverton, where the locals, aghast at our ambitions, told us eastern boys that we were all going to die in avalanches. The hike in—six miles down the narrow gauge railroad tracks, then up Elk Creek—was brutal, requiring steep snowshoe bushwhacking not unlike what I'd encountered on the Howker Ridge on my first Winter Traverse. Not until the third day did we establish camp in a gloomy, north-facing cirque at 12,200 feet under soaring Vestal Peak.

On December 28, climbing as three ropes of two, we knocked off a pair of prizes, Vestal and Arrow Peaks. But by the next morning, which dawned on a storm, there were signs of "crump" among our companions.

Don and I had told ourselves that, as the most experienced climbers, in the Needles we would need to split up each day and choose partners from among the other four, just as the veterans on McKinley had divvied themselves up among us acolytes. On the 29th, however, neither Don nor I could bear to waste a day lying in a sleeping bag. We packed up and headed out in full storm, intending to traverse over a high pass, descend to the Tenmile Creek drainage, and climb to a lake at 12,000 feet under the Trinity Peaks. The others would follow us a day later.

As it turned out, we never saw our companions the rest of the trip. As he had the year before, Bert fell ill, then persuaded another disheartened junior to bag the outing and hike out early down Elk Creek. On December 30, Matt (who all his life would suffer extreme altitude sickness above 11,000 feet) and the other junior followed Don's and my tracks, but exhausted themselves well short of our camp. During the following two days, they hiked out Tenmile Creek and back up the tracks to Silverton.

Though alarmed by the absence of our comrades, Don and I wasted not a minute of the next three days, as we enjoyed the finest mountain campaign we had yet shared outside Alaska. In perfect weather, we climbed East Trinity, Storm King, and Peak 8, all by technical routes. The latter, it turned out, was a first ascent for any season, one of the very few remaining virgin summits anywhere in Colorado.

Clumping back into Silverton on January 3, we found our teammates sequestered like invalids in a pair of dingy rooms in an old hotel called the Benson Arms. Their terrible moods were not improved by Don's and my gloating about all the great climbing we had done. Only Matt, still recovering from altitude sickness, offered us anything like a congratulatory word.

From the Needles trip was born the conviction that Don and I had formed that rarest of things, a perfect partnership in the mountains. We even gave a kind of instinctive credence to the notion that we were invincible. There were unclimbed mountains all over the world awaiting our efforts. Whatever we set out to do, we believed we could achieve.

There was never any doubt that we would plan another Alaskan expedition for the summer of 1964. The only question was which mountain to choose as our goal. Throughout the winter months, Don and I ransacked old journals in the HMC club room, looking for an objective.

Thus by my junior year in college, my life had developed the structure that would sustain it for more than a decade. Everything else was subordinated to the coming summer's expedition. All the climbing I did on weekends was training for Alaska. School itself was a necessary evil, a plod through the off-season. By 1964, I had lost all interest in mathematics, but I plugged on with my major (earning, my senior year, a pair of Ds in advanced classes) as a less disruptive course than switching to English, music, or anthropology.

During four years at Harvard, I never came close to having a girl-friend. Yet after my lonely freshman year, that failure bothered me not at all. My passion for the mountains had entirely sublimated whatever sexual or romantic impulses I might have had. My bridge-playing roommates dated pretty girls at Endicott Junior College and Pine Manor. I envied them not at all.

One day in the club room, I said, "Hey, Don, look at this." I handed him an old copy of the *American Alpine Journal*. The photo, by Bradford Washburn, shot from an airplane from the north, showed the soaring ridges and stern faces of Mount Deborah, a 12,339-foot peak in the Hayes Range. The article recounted Deborah's first and only ascent, by a trio in 1954 that included two legendary mountaineers, the American Fred Beckey and the Austrian Heinrich Harrer. "It was our unanimous conclusion," wrote Beckey, "that Deborah was the most sensational ice climb any of us had ever undertaken."

Beckey's team had tackled the mountain's only "reasonable" aspect, the west face. The whole east side of Deborah, plunging 6,000 feet from the summit ridge to the West Fork Glacier, remained unexplored. Within minutes, Don and I chose the east ridge for our objective. It would take a devious climb just to circle around and reach the col at 9,000 feet separating Deborah from its neighbor, Mount Hess. From that col, as we saw in profile in the Washburn photo, a serpentine ridge, inclined at an average angle of 60 degrees, rose like an arrow to the summit.

Deborah was, to be sure, a much smaller mountain than McKinley. But it was obvious that the east ridge would be far more difficult than anything we had climbed on the Wickersham Wall.

The only remaining problem was the composition of the team. None of our cronies from McKinley was available for the summer of 1964. Having twice fallen ill on our Christmas trips, Bert Redmayne did not seem like the kind of partner we wanted on Deborah. Don and I pondered inviting Matt Hale, but, game though he might be, our promising sophomore simply had too little experience in the mountains (before Harvard, Matt had done little but bag summits in the Adirondacks).

One day in March, Don said, "Dave, I've been thinking this over." He paused to make sure he had my full attention. "What do you think about just the two of us—a two-man expedition?"

The moment Don proposed it, I was won over to his radical idea. A two-man assault on Deborah would be the perfect fulfillment of our pledge to each other, the test of our invincibility.

In the first decade of the twenty-first century, a two-man expedition is no longer a radical proposition. In the 1960s, however, it went against all the tenets of mountaineering. Once they learned about our plan, several of our HMC mentors tried to talk us out of it. Adams Carter, editor of the *American Alpine Journal*, who was still, in his fifties, leading expeditions to the Andes, took me aside to say, "It's not a wise idea. If one fellow falls in a crevasse, you have the devil of a time getting him out."

Don and I turned a deaf ear to all such admonitions. At once Don plunged into planning for Deborah. And almost as soon as we had committed ourselves to that ultimate expression of our partnership, the cracks began to show.

As Don immersed himself in his preparations, studying maps by the hour, making a finicky catalogue of unclimbed summits in the Hayes Range, he began to neglect his schoolwork. As he had the previous spring, before he dropped out of Harvard, Don started sliding into a psychological torpor. He could not both keep up with his mathematics and obsess about Deborah—and Deborah prevailed. Once more, he started to gain weight, and his face took on the haggard look I remembered from the previous February.

To plan for Deborah, Don actually stayed in Cambridge over several prime climbing weekends. That spring I roped up a lot with Matt and came to delight in our fast, efficient teamwork. One unfortunate Saturday at the Gunks, I led a tough 5.9 pitch, which Matt seconded smoothly. Third on the rope, Don cursed and made excuses as he struggled with the awkward holds. I had to give him tension twice before he floundered onto the belay ledge.

Never before in our partnership had I been in conspicuously better climbing shape than Don. I began to worry about his poor condition: Deborah would obviously require rock and ice climbing of an extreme difficulty. At the same time, Don wore on his sleeve an air of constant reproach for the fact that I seemed less involved in the logistics of our upcoming expedition than he.

By the beginning of May, we were seriously on each other's nerves. Don's roommates noticed the tension and begged him to back out of the trip. Instead, Don wrote me a letter.

As I read this earnest entreaty, I heard discomforting echoes of the long missive Lisa had written three and a half years earlier, while our relationship was falling apart as she feared she was pregnant. For Don's phrases were akin to those of an unhappy lover, pleading for reconciliation. "We are undefeatable," he wrote, in part. "It is immensely important that we understand and respect each other. . . . Fruitless arguments must be eliminated. . . . I am sure we have sufficient experience in this sort of climbing."

By mid-May, both of us were dreading Deborah as much as we were looking forward to it. Yet we could not change our plans. We had absorbed the puritan ethic of our pastime: hard men do not crump.

On June 4, we drank a beer at Cronin's, then climbed, exhausted, into a pickup truck we had contracted to drive north, and headed off toward Alaska.

If McKinley, at its best, had resembled the summer camp lark through which Pete Carman had blithely led our way, Deborah would unfold as a relentless nightmare. On June 18, hoisting heavy packs, we set off across the tundra from the Denali Highway. Four days and forty miles later, we arrived at the swath of scattered packages Don had pushed out of our bush pilot's plane five days before. We tore open the double boxes, then organized our supplies in a neat cache. In theory, at least, we had food for forty-four days. We also had 3,000 feet of fixed rope to string out on our pitches, eighty pitons, a number of ice daggers Don had crafted out of L-bar aluminum, and a pint of "victory brandy."

In two days of hard load-ferrying, we got everything except eight days' worth of food up to a higher camp, at the head of the West Fork Glacier. The cirque felt like a glaciated box canyon, as our tent sat dwarfed on three sides by towering cliffs of snow and rock. "It is a gloomy spot," I wrote in my diary, "a place we would call dismal if we had to spend too much time in it." After enduring the next three days there in a storm, we dubbed this way station Dismal Camp.

To get to the col 3,000 feet above, where the true east ridge began, we would have to climb most of the way up South Hess, as we called the unnamed satellite peak that loomed above us, then circle around to the ridge that connected it to Deborah, and descend a thousand feet to the col. Once we got ourselves established there, the real challenge would begin.

We had hoped to perform this shuttle in two or three days, but on Deborah, nothing would go as planned. On our first effort to climb above Dismal Camp, I got an ominous confirmation of my qualms about Don's poor condition. We were roped together, but climbing "continuously," without a belay, as, in the lead, I chopped steps up low-angle ice. When I paused to bring Don up to my stance, I was alarmed to see that he slipped and caught himself twice on easy terrain. When he joined me, I asked, "Is there anything the matter? How do you feel?"

He looked exhausted. "Out of it," he answered listlessly. "Sleepy . . . and cold."

"We better go down." Don seemed to agree. I started building a platform of rocks on which to leave our loads.

Suddenly Don grabbed my arm, blurting out, "We can't go down, Dave! We've got to get to the col! I've got to drive myself!"

My alarm escalated. Don was acting crazy. Even as he urged us onward, I could see that he was shivering with cold—and it wasn't really that cold out. Patiently, I talked Don out of pushing on. Then, all the way back to Dismal Camp, I belayed him from above. Even on easy moves, he took forever.

The gear shuttle to the col that we had hoped to pull off in two or three days ended up taking a full two weeks. The long loop via South Hess was not technically difficult, but it was very dangerous, as we traversed in all kinds of different conditions steep slopes that were ready to avalanche. Since we could not make the full 4,000-foot climb and 1,000-foot descent in one push, we had to establish a cache halfway. The only available depot was a precarious rock ledge threatened by avalanches.

Though Don had recovered from his out-of-it first climbing day, something seemed to go wrong with every shuttle load. One day the rope trailing behind me dislodged a hefty rock that rolled down the slope and struck Don in the elbow. He cried out in pain and clutched his arm, which, fortunately, was only bruised. We had brought no willow wands to mark our route, so we had to plant snow pickets and ice daggers to indicate the trail to the midway cache. On July 7, on our last trip to the cache, we found the marking stakes buried under new snow. When we got to where we thought the rock ledge ought to be, it seemed to have vanished. There was no sign of our precious gear and food, which, we realized, must have been buried under a small avalanche. Only after an hour of probing with our ice axes did I manage, purely by accident, to hit the soft, yielding surface of a food box, still anchored to a piton under three feet of snow.

Worse, however, than the balkiest gear shuttles were the storm days when we were confined to our tent. It was during those endless hours of lying in our sleeping bags, staring at the orange ripstop fabric of the tent roof, listening to the snow fall, that the tension between us fanned into full-blown cabin fever. The soggy paperback books we had brought seemed irrelevant. Don could lie for hours, thinking about nothing more than how many pounds and ounces a given load might weigh, but I needed conversation and escape. If I tried to engage him in chat about the outside world, far from Deborah, he discouraged me with monosyllabic answers. I laid out a paper chess set in the back cover of my diary. We played a few games, but Don's novice skills and lack of interest kept the matches from dispelling our boredom.

Having left all the crucial logistical decisions up to Don, now I had to live under the tyranny of his ascetic style. Just to save a few ounces, we had chosen to use the tent Don had made for himself, rather than the one I had commissioned our McKinley pal Chris Goetze to construct for me. Don's tent was noticeably smaller than mine—smaller, in fact, than any two-man tent on the market. During storms, we pulled a food box inside the tent, rather than have to open the door every few hours and admit a flurry of blowing snow. But this meant that neither of us could stretch out full-length. With our knees bent, each of us frequently impinged on the other's space. Seething inside at Don's having stolen a few inches of my Ensolite pad, I would finally voice a polite complaint: "Can you move over a little? I'm right against the wall."

After the first week, we noticed that, despite three hearty meals a day, we were constantly hungry. It took weeks, however, for either of us to acknowledge that fact to the other. In the menu planning, Don's parsimony, it turned out, had worked us a real hardship. Eventually we figured out that while we were each consuming more than 4,000 calories per day, we were regularly burning more than 5,000. Slowly we lost weight, and with it, reserves of energy.

Meanwhile the mealtimes between which we counted the hours and minutes took on an absurd routine founded on mutual distrust. One of us would pour out the cereal into our two plastic bowls, then let the other choose the portion he craved. Even within a single lunch or dinner, we alternated the jobs of dividing and choosing. What drove me to distraction was that Don, slow and methodical as he was about everything (by now I was convinced that it took him two or three times as long to climb a given pitch as it did me), could always make his glop or porridge last longer than mine.

As a safety factor, we had rented an expensive radio in Fairbanks. Because it worked only by line-of-sight, we had to wait until we were camped on the col, looking out across the tundra to the north, to try it. On July 2, shortly after we first arrived at the col, I turned on the radio, which linked us directly to the telephone system. It worked perfectly. The voice of the operator in Fairbanks sounded as clear as if she were camped in an adjoining tent. Amazingly, she could patch us through to long distance. Within minutes, Don was gabbing away with his parents in Walnut Creek.

The radio promised us huge dividends not only in safety, but in terms of dissipating our cabin fever. The second time we tried it, however, the radio was dead. We had a spare battery, but it made no difference. Mechanically incompetent, I threw up my hands in despair, but Don spent many a storm hour over the next two weeks with the back off the radio, fiddling with wires, trying to follow the circuit diagram. We never again raised even a burst of static. In the end, because it was too valuable to chuck, I had to lug the radio's six worthless pounds in my pack throughout the rest of the expedition.

The storms continued almost without respite. On the col, as had not been the case down at Dismal Camp, the tent, sticking out of an otherwise smooth plain of snow, had the fiendish propensity of attracting drifts. During the night of July 5–6, in a particularly intense blizzard, it took only four hours for snow to drift halfway up the tent walls. At 2:30 P.M. on the 5th, Don went out to shovel the drift away. It was my turn at 6:30 P.M., and Don's again at 10:30.

Then we both fell asleep. When I awakened, it was 9:30 in the morning. The world was strangely silent and dark, and I almost succumbed to the temptation to drift back to sleep before I came to my senses. "Don!" I cried. "Wake up! The tent's buried."

Only a strip of faint orange light, a couple of inches deep, illuminated the ridgepole. The walls were sagging against our faces. Don managed to get dressed, then lunged against the door like the football lineman he had been in high school, slowly packing the drift back from the sleeve that was our only exit. At last he was able to slither out, locate the shovel, and dig out the tent. Later he described the terrifying sight of a uniform blear of snow, out of which protruded, like a stick laid on the ground, the horizontal crest of the nylon-encased ridgepole. (Over the years, a number of experienced climbers on expeditions in various ranges have suffocated in their tents in conditions identical to ours.)

It was not until July 9—the twenty-second day of the expedition—that we finally came to grips with the east ridge itself. We were so far behind the schedule we had mapped out for ourselves in Cambridge that a dark fatalism had descended upon our spirits. As early as July 4, I had written in my diary, "We like to think others would have quit by now."

Late on the 9th, in clear, cold weather, we traversed the col till it narrowed into a ribbon of corniced knife-edge, reaching at last the base of the ridge. As soon as we laid our hands on the first cliff, our gloomiest premonition, formed on the intermittent rock bands of South Hess, was confirmed. The rock was terrible—a black, fractured schist that came loose in our fingers, and into which it was almost impossible to drive a good piton.

The weather, however, had taken a turn for the good. During four all-out efforts stretched over the next six days, we made painfully slow inroads on the east ridge, returning each afternoon to camp on the col. It often took two hours to lead a single, 100-foot pitch; but once a line was fixed and our chopped steps had frozen solid, we could repeat the pitch in ten or fifteen minutes. We found that wearing our crampons on ice and rock alike gave us the best purchase. Even so, thanks to crumbly schist and hollow ice, the going was constantly nerve-racking, by far the most dangerous climbing Don or I had ever undertaken.

Just before noon on July 14, I led the last pitch to the top of a plume of rime ice, a thousand feet above the col, one-third of the way up the east ridge. Since first studying the Washburn photos back in Cambridge, we had known that the plume was a key to the climb. Behind it stretched a tiny gap of a col, the only interruption in the 3,000-foot sweep of the ridge. The steepest part of the whole route was a 600-foot headwall above that gap. If the gap offered a decent shelf where we could pitch the tent, we might camp here and work out the rest of the route in one 2,000-foot push.

As I pulled myself to the top of the plume, I knew in an instant's glance that our attempt on Deborah was over. Instead of a shelf, the thirty-foot col proved to be a wispy curl of double-cornice froth. The headwall above, brown and evil-looking, was only a few degrees less than vertical. A thousand feet above us, at the brow of the world, huge ice masses clung to the rock. As I watched, one broke loose, fell most of the thousand feet free, and smashed to pieces on a ledge to my left.

I scuttled over the plume and down to the start of the double-cornice, stomped a shaky platform in honeycomb-like snow, and belayed Don up. As his head popped over the plume, I shouted, "Don't come any farther! It isn't safe." The plume itself was our only protection: the rope running over it might hold us on the mountain if one of us broke out his steps and fell. Don stared upward. I could read in his anguished look the same realization that had dawned on me half an hour before.

We were back at camp on the col by 4:30 P.M. During the last six days of frenzied action, we had gotten along better than ever before on the expedition. Now we drank our misnamed victory brandy, then packed up our loads in preparation for the descent.

The nightmare had only begun.

By 1:00 P.M. on July 18, we had regained base camp. During the last twenty-seven days, I had never been farther than a rope-length away from Don. I had had enough of Deborah, and enough of Don. I was ready to hike out and get on with life. But that was not our plan.

Way back on June 17, after Don had pushed the packages out of the plane to deliver our airdrop under Deborah, he had flown with the pilot fifteen miles east, to a cirque beneath Mount Hayes, where he had performed a second airdrop. On the trackless snows at the head of the Gillam Glacier, twenty-eight days of double-boxed food, as well as more fixed ropes and hardware, lay waiting for us.

The whole scheme had been Don's, for whom no expedition was ever long enough. After we had knocked off the east ridge, we would cross low passes, traversing the heads of three glaciers—West Fork, Susitna, and Gillam—to alight in a cirque full of handsome, virtually unknown peaks. After sixty days or so, we would hike out of the Hayes Range not only with Deborah under our belts, but with first ascents of several mountains no one had ever bothered to name, let alone climb.

After the storms of the previous month, I thought there was a better than even chance the second airdrop would be buried under many
feet of new snow. We had eight days of food here at base camp (plus
two days' worth we had carried down from the col), but if it took us
six or seven days to get to the new cirque, and then if we failed to find
the airdrop, we could be in real trouble.

It was obvious, however, that Don had no such qualms. With our
failure in Deborah lodged in his craw, only first ascents above the
Gillam would begin to make things right. Out of pride, I kept my
doubts to myself. To crump at this point would be not only to succumb to failure on our chosen mountain, but to the failure of the perfect partnership that, only six months before, had seemed to bind our
lives in a common purpose stretching limitless into the future.

The next five days passed in a miasma of lethargy. After the climbing we had done on Deborah, mere snowshoe trudging across gentle
glaciers ought to have been a piece of cake. Yet each day one of us, and
sometimes both, felt completely played out after only two or three
hours of work. We were double-packing loads of about forty-five
pounds, always disheartening work, as one traveled twelve miles
(ahead, back, and ahead again) to accomplish a gain of only four.
Some nights we couldn't sleep, even after taking sleeping pills. Then,
on July 22–23, we both slept for twenty-two hours straight—a lifetime record for each of us.

Something was clearly wrong with us physically. At the time, I
wondered whether, in this apparently germ-free environment, we had
managed to catch some kind of disease. In retrospect, it is obvious that
the inadequacy of our food had caught up with us. We were often not
merely hungry, but ravenous, and even when we cheated and gave
ourselves four meals instead of three over a twenty-four-hour period,
the largess did little to soothe the pangs. On July 23, our thirty-sixth
day, I realized that we had exceeded the span of our whole McKinley
expedition, from start to finish. Thinking about McKinley, I felt a
sharp longing for the companionship of other friends. How a third
person—anyone—would have changed the dynamics on Deborah! As
it was, we had spent more than a month trapped in the hall of mirrors

of our two-headed relativity. Was I reckless, or was Don overcautious? Did he really take three times as long to get up a pitch as I did? Had he tricked me into accepting the smaller portion of glop by spooning it into my yellow bowl rather than his green one?

On the morning of July 24, under fair skies, we set out from our camp on a west branch of the Gillam Glacier. Only a last pass, a mere three miles away, stood between us and our phantom airdrop.

Don went first. A mere hundred yards from camp, he slumped abruptly up to his waist in a crevasse. At the other end of the rope, I plunged my axe into the snow to give Don a static belay.

Earlier, high on South Hess, on separate days, we had each fallen fifteen feet into a hidden crevasse—scary plunges, but not life-threatening ones. Impatient to get moving again on this sunny day, I waited for Don to crawl out of his hole and get back on his feet, but he seemed unable to move. As his arms thrashed on the surface, he called out, "I'm choking!"

In my irritation at Don—it was so like him, I thought, to turn a little crevasse into a melodrama—I failed to take the situation seriously enough. If his pack straps or the crevasse lip were starting to choke him, I thought, maybe I could come up and give him a hand. I plunged my axe in deeper to set it as an anchor, got our spare axe from my pack and planted it as backup, untied from the rope, tied its end to the heads of both axes, then waddled on my snowshoes up to my partner.

Don had grasped his predicament instantly. He was stuck like a cork in the small hole he had plunged through, his pack and arms the only things holding him on the surface. His feet, in snowshoes, dangled free in space. He could not see into the black depths of the crevasse, but he sensed that it was huge.

I knelt, reached forward, seized the back of Don's pack, and started to pull. "Stop!" Don screamed. "It's the only thing holding me up!" He had sunk almost to his neck in the little hole.

"Dave!" Don called, his voice rising in panic. "Get away from the crevasse!" I backed up five feet, then stood there, helpless.

All at once the plug broke, and Don disappeared from sight. The

rope ripped the anchoring axes free from the glacier like toothpicks
out of butter. I grabbed the rope, but it whipped violently through my
hands. I heard Don's yell, sharp at first, trail away as he fell.

When the rope stopped, sixty feet of it had disappeared into the
hole after Don. An excruciating silence engulfed me. "Don!" I yelled.
"Are you all right?"

Perhaps a minute passed before I heard a weak, distant answer:
"I . . . I'm alive." Then, "I hit my head, and it's bleeding! My right leg
is hurt, and I think I broke my thumb!" As I stood staring at the hole
in the gleaming snow, I heard Adams Carter's sober words, back in
Cambridge, predicting the mess we now found ourselves in.

Falling free, Don had had the sensation of bouncing against ice
and of breaking through ice. He kept expecting the rope to stop him,
and when it didn't, he glimpsed the possibility that I had been pulled
into the crevasse with him. At last he came to a crushing stop, wedged
between walls of hard ice. As he lay there, piles of snow and ice landed
on top of him in the darkness.

Now I hurried back to my pack, got the shovel free, and dug a pit
in the soft glacial snow. I planted the two axes at the bottom of the pit,
with the rope still tied to their heads, shoveled snow back in, stomped
it down, and waited for the anchor to freeze. Only when I thought it
was solid did I dare approach the crevasse once more. When I shouted
down to Don again, he called out, with great presence of mind, "Dave!
Be careful! Don't come too near!"

Gradually Don's eyes had adjusted to the darkness, until he could
see the interior of his icy chamber. The sight was petrifying. The crevasse gaped to a huge width some thirty feet above his head, then
arched in overhanging walls that closed in at the tiny hole, the only
source of light, sixty feet up. All the edges of the crevasse near the hole
overhung, ready to break loose like the plug he had taken with him.

Had I ventured too near the edge and fallen in myself, I know
today, we would both have died of hypothermia inside the crevasse. I
doubt that anyone would ever have figured out what happened to us,
for by the time our families had raised an alarm and the bush pilot
started a search, my pack—the only vestige of our expedition left on

the surface—might have melted into the glacier or been covered with new snow.

In a party of four or more, the partners of the victim of a crevasse fall can do much to aid in his rescue, hauling from different angles with different ropes. Alone, I was powerless to help Don get out. With our only rope cutting into the edge of the crevasse, with Don weighing thirty pounds more than I, I could not begin to boost him upward with even the strongest pull I could muster. Don would have to get himself out.

But I knew now what I had to do. I returned to my pack and dug out the skein of nylon parachute cord in our repair kit. Not nearly long enough. Fortunately, I was carrying our hardware: I retrieved the eight or ten nylon slings we had attached to our pitons as we led pitches on the east ridge, untied each one, and tied them end to end with the parachute cord. Finally I augmented this makeshift line with a spare pair of boot laces.

The first thing we had to do was get Don's pack to the surface. We couldn't leave it in the crevasse, and Don couldn't carry it out with him. I would have to haul it out, in small pieces. Nor could we afford to use the climbing rope to haul: once Don had untied from it, it might be impossible to fish the loose end back down to him.

I returned to the crevasse and tossed in one end of my jury-rigged line. Moments later, Don yelled that it reached. He tied his sleeping bag to the cord, and I pulled it up. The line, however, had cut a groove into the soft snow that hovered on the lip of the crevasse, beneath which the sleeping bag hung up.

Now I yanked hard on the climbing rope, to make sure my buried two-axe anchor had frozen solid. Then I unknotted a spare sling, tied it around my waist, and tied the other end to the climbing rope with a prusik—a clever knot, invented more than half a century before, that could be loosened to slide along the climbing rope, but which held fast under a tight pull. With my prusik self-belay, now I dared to scuttle close to the crevasse edge, where I used the shovel to dig away at the soft snow that had trapped the sleeping bag. At last I had carved a channel in the corniced lip back to bare ice.

After that, the hauling went quickly, the seventy-pound load divided into five or six bundles. Finally I lowered Don our two stir-rups—nylon ladders used for aid climbing. He would have to attach these to the climbing rope with his own prusik knots, then, slowly and laboriously, inch his way up the rope to the surface. In the mean-time, he had changed from snowshoes to crampons.

There was nothing I could do but wait. Just in case, I went back and sat down on top of my buried anchor, to add my own weight to its frozen inertia.

Inside the crevasse, Don's bleeding had stopped, and he found that his thumb was only badly sprained, not broken. He was soaking wet, however, and starting to shiver, in the first stages of hypothermia. He fumbled with the prusik knots, eventually having to add an extra loop to each, because the slings were so wet they didn't grip properly on the smooth sheath of the climbing rope. Then he began to claw his way toward the surface.

I stared at the sun, which had moved far to the west. In the low-angled light, now I could see one faint blue crease of shadow after another running athwart the route we had hoped to take to the last pass—each one indicating a hidden crevasse like the abyss that had swallowed Don. Four hours had passed since his plunge. Now, from time to time, he called out to report his progress, and each time, his voice rang louder and closer. At last his head popped out of the hole. I uttered a cheer. A few minutes later, Don rolled onto firm snow, then sat there gasping for breath, completely spent. I walked up to him and put my arm around his shoulders. "Hey, you did a great job," I said. Don didn't answer.

We decided simply to backtrack the hundred yards to the site of the previous night's camp. I pitched the tent, then retrieved the debris from Don's pack. Don got inside his sleeping bag. After half an hour the shivering stopped. We assessed the damage. He had bad bruises on his head and his right thigh, and fully half his fingers were sprained, along with the thumb. When I handed him dinner, he could barely hold the bowl and spoon.

Despite our near catastrophe, I was awash in an odd sense of relief. It was obvious now that we had to abandon the Gillam and hike out. We had barely escaped the trap of a single crevasse fall. It would be insane to court disaster among the blue creases that stretched beyond Don's hole. We were down to five days of food, and the hike out could easily take five or six.

I assumed Don saw the logic as clearly as I. But to my astonishment, after dinner, he blurted out, "Tomorrow, we can go up to the edge of the glacier and skirt around those crevasses."

I stared at him in disbelief. "You've got to be kidding. We have no choice but to hike out."

We argued on for an hour. I had resolved not to give in. Don's fanaticism alarmed me. To push on toward our lost airdrop might well, I thought, amount to a death sentence. At one point, Don said plaintively, "I'd almost rather starve here than go out now." Slowly, I dismantled his rationalizations, attacking with the crystalline logic that seemed to hang over our fate. At last Don gave in. "All right," he sighed, in a hoarse whisper.

We each took a sleeping pill. Exhausted myself, on the verge of nodding off, I felt a surge of grudging admiration for my battered comrade, framed in the sleepy thought, *He's a harder man than I am.*

It took us five days to hike out, during which the wilderness threw at us everything we could handle. Crossing back over a pass to the Susitna Glacier, then trudging down that ice stream toward the névé line, I led virtually all the next day, probing nervously with my axe at any discoloration in the snow. After hours of this, we passed onto an apparently safe plateau, where Don offered to take the lead.

Only minutes later, he disappeared into another crevasse. I plunged my axe in and held on, thinking I must have stopped Don's fall after five or ten feet. But thanks to stretch in the rope and the angle of the crevasse (which slanted back toward us), Don fell thirty feet unchecked. This time the crevasse was only three or four feet wide, but in consequence, as he fell, Don's face smashed hard against one ice ledge after another.

"There's blood all over in here!" Don yelled, once we had established contact. "I've got to get out quick!" In a panic, he abandoned his pack and chimneyed to the surface. I pulled him in like a deep sea trophy, then, with Don's token belay, chimneyed down into the crevasse myself to retrieve his pack. There was indeed blood splattered everywhere, and I felt a panic of my own to get back to the surface.

Once more, we set up camp on the spot and surveyed the damage. I wiped the blood off Don's face, revealing several nasty cuts on his chin, one of which had gouged a hole clean through his cheek. Don had resprained all the fingers on his left hand, which now he could barely use. I gave him two codeine tablets, then, later, a sleeping pill. This second fall seemed to have knocked the stuffing out of him. He lay in a wordless stupor as I cooked dinner, then fed him glop spoonful by tiny spoonful.

On July 26, we finally got off the glaciers for good—only to find that, on this unanticipated escape route, we had walked off the edge of the map we carried. Here all of Don's fussy planning in the HMC club room paid off, for he remembered a shortcut pass through low foothills that ended up saving us many hours.

The east fork of the Susitna River nearly stopped us. In flood every bit as angry as that of the McKinley River the year before, the east fork repulsed our first three attempts to wade it. At last, we came upon a braided maze of sandbars and channels, where we managed the ford, barely in balance, through hip-deep, numbing glacial water. During subsequent days, there followed one vexing mini-ordeal after another: the worst mosquitoes we had ever seen, hideous bushwhacking through a mile of tangled alders, a relentless spongy sidehill that slowly sprained our ankles as they rolled in our soggy boots.

We ate our last scrap of food at noon on July 29. Eleven hours later, in the dusk approaching midnight, we staggered out to the Denali Highway, then plodded a mile east to the hunting lodge where we had left our pickup truck forty-two days before.

The previous year on McKinley, once we had regained base camp after two weeks on reduced rations, we had gorged on cans of fruit cocktail and loaves of Logan bread until we all got sick. Mindful of that lesson, Don and I resolved to eat temperately when we hit Fairbanks. But a friend invited us to dinner our first evening back—a feast of wild game he had hunted himself. A month and a half of semi-starvation overcame our best resolutions. We pigged out on moose and bear and caribou and homemade cranberry sauce and ice cream. A day later, having flown to Seattle, as we limped across downtown toward the Greyhound bus depot, diarrhea drove us every few blocks to the refuge of a café restroom. We felt as feeble as octogenarians.

What Don and I needed above all else was to get away from each other. Foolishly, we had agreed to spend a week together at Don's home in Walnut Creek. After his wretched spring semester, Don had decided to drop out of Harvard for good. He didn't know what he'd be doing in the fall (one reason, I am sure, for his fanatic reluctance to abandon the Hayes Range), but he planned to stay in California.

In Walnut Creek, Don's parents greeted us warmly: for almost a month after their ebullient phone conversation with Don via radio on July 2, they had had no word from us. Don's brother was there, too, with his new wife, who was seven months pregnant.

The gouges in Don's chin and cheeks had become infected. I was with him when he went to a doctor in Fairbanks, who groaned in disgust as he cleaned the pus and dirt and matted blood out of the wounds. By the time we reached California, Don was on antibiotics, to which he developed a strange reaction that stiffened his joints like a bad case of arthritis. (Later, Don would get cysts in the healed wounds, which it took several operations to remove.)

In Walnut Creek, we had no obligations, no chores any more to ensure our survival, nothing to do but loaf and enjoy Don's mother's generous cooking. This was, of course, the worst possible regimen. The tension between us was there every waking moment. I had lost all sympathy for Don's medical ailments: the Frankenstein's monster he resembled as he climbed jerkily out of bed in the morning seemed like a psychosomatic caricature. In Don's darkroom, as he tried to develop large-format pictures he had taken on Deborah, he fumbled fixer and negatives with his sprained, arthritic fingers. But when I tried to take over, he screamed at my incompetence.

In the evenings, as I prattled on glibly to Don's parents, I sensed him sitting there in silent disapproval, red-penciling my fulsome assertions in his mind. Our pathetic comedy reached a head on my last night in Walnut Creek. Having drunk too much wine, I started flirting with Don's pregnant sister-in-law. Neither she nor Don's laid-back brother seemed to mind, but my cavalier play drove Don into a rage.

At midnight, with everyone else asleep, Don confronted me on the patio. We traded harsh words; then suddenly Don grabbed me in his arms as he had tackled many a fullback in high school. Holding on tight, he drove me from one end of the patio to the other, slamming me against the walls, breaking wicker chairs. Startled, still drunk, I did not try to fight back. This seemed to be something Don needed to do.

In the morning, he drove me to the bus station. We shook hands, but couldn't look each other in the eye.

In the broken patio furniture, we had left the wreckage of our perfect partnership. As the bus rolled out of Walnut Creek, I did not expect ever to see Don again.

FIVE

Ed

THAT FALL, AS I BEGAN MY SENIOR YEAR OF COL-
lege, I was, in several senses, at sea without a compass. Mathematics,
which in high school had glimmered on the horizon with Hes-
peridean inklings, had proved instead a sterile backwater. To complete
my math major, I scraped by in torturous courses in algebraic topology and theory and functions of a complex variable. With vague
hopes of becoming a writer, I had decided to go to grad school in
English literature. Now I took as many English courses as I could,
including English C, the beginning writing course that had become a
canonic rite of passage for aspiring Harvard novelists.

A useful response to the kind of anomie that had descended upon
my spirits is to plunge into work and play—which is what I did that
autumn of 1964. Thanks to the Harvard intramural program, which
in those days was nearly as competitive as the varsity teams, I had
rediscovered the childhood joys of sport. That fall and winter and
spring, I played a full schedule of intramural tennis, touch football,
soccer, track, squash, and softball, and when, in May, I was voted Dunster House intramural athlete of the year (my name engraved on a
pewter trophy that sat under glass in the dining hall), I was as proud
as a Little Leaguer.

My roommates were dating regularly by now; one was engaged to
his Endicott Junior College sweetheart. For me, girls remained as
unfathomable as the topology theorems I blinked at in my textbook.
During four years at Harvard, I never once "got laid," as Paul would
have phrased it. The fact that Paul himself, out at Amherst, was having

little better luck with women, despite trying a lot harder, was faint gratification.

Nor did I lose much sleep over the absence of a girlfriend in my life. I had climbing. That fall, having been elected president of the HMC, I took on the organizing of our fall and spring climbing trips, the Winter Traverse, the biweekly club meetings with invited speakers, the raising of funds for the biennial journal the HMC published, the fall and spring banquets, and even the purchase of the bottle of Duff Gordon amontillado sherry that Henry Hall—who had founded the club in 1924 and who still, in his seventies, attended every meeting—demanded to lubricate the Advisory Council meetings, during which the club's august mentors pondered such weighty questions as whether to buy a new stove for the HMC cabin.

As much as I could that year, I climbed with Matt Hale, the junior whom Don and I had contemplated inviting to Mount Deborah. Before the fall term, Matt and I had met in Colorado in early September for eight days of climbing in the Needle Mountains. Around our campfire on Ruby Creek, I had recounted the severities of Deborah, and though he never said so in so many words, Matt made it clear that he was heartily glad not to have participated in Don's and my ordeal by cabin fever.

Now, at the Gunks and Cathedral Ledge and Cannon Cliff, whenever we could free ourselves from the duties of teaching the rookies, Matt and I climbed hard routes together. A year before, I had thought that Don and I made up the perfect team, but it was soon evident that Matt and I were better matched. Unlike the methodical Don, Matt was a fast and impulsive climber, as I was, too. Matt's wry, sharp-witted humor was a breath of fresh air after Don's ponderous sincerity. And Matt's performance on rock and ice maintained an even keel of excellence. There were none of the manic spurts and depressive funks that made Don's efforts so unpredictable. Even physically, the two were opposites. Thin as a waif, Matt moved on rock with a catlike, sinewy grace. Strong and stocky, Don approached a pitch like a chess problem, all logic and no intuition.

No matter how active I stayed that senior year, leading such test piece routes as the ConnCourse and Broken Sling, playing squash and soccer all out, pouring my guts into pretentious short stories for English C, the crushing failure of Deborah hung over me. Those forty-two days in the Hayes Range had been the most intense experience of my life—more intense even than the heights and depths that had measured out the moribund course of that other failure in my past, my affair with Lisa. Mount Deborah had lodged in my spirit as a guilty, incessant ache, and I took little comfort in the knowledge that Don and I had given it our best, that indeed, we had been lucky to get out alive. The fact was that we had failed badly on a route we originally thought we were good enough to climb. Failed 2,000 feet below the summit, without even having come to grips with the hardest part of the east ridge. We were not, after all, in anything like the league of Hermann Buhl and Gaston Rébuffat.

From the leaden dismay that settled upon me certain nights as I lay in my bed in Dunster House trying to sleep, only a single answer emerged. Another expedition. The chance of revenge. A deed to make up for Deborah.

By now, however, I had only a single friend with whom I wished to share such an enterprise. I wasn't sure that Matt would be up for a serious expedition, and I knew that I did not want to repeat the folly of attacking an Alaskan mountain as a two-man team. Each of the other five or six leading HMC climbers had his virtues and talents, but none of them except Matt seemed right for a project on the scale of Deborah.

Late in the autumn—was it December?—Don and I finally broke our glacial chill and traded a few perfunctory notes. They began with housekeeping details—sending each other duplicate slides from Deborah, tidying up the odds and ends of our expenses. Out in California, Don had taken a construction job. The next year, quits with Harvard for good, he would enroll at Fresno State College, from which he graduated in 1967 with a BA in math.

The notes slowly thawed our impasse, and stung us with nostalgia for the sense of linked invincibility we had first discovered in the Needle Mountains over Christmas 1963. In a letter I wrote sometime in January 1965, I stammered out a few lines of remorse about how we had parted in Walnut Creek. And Don wrote back, "Let me say then . . . I wish to apologize for my asininity at the summer's end (I guess I was sick enough to give everyone shit)." For twenty-one-year-old hard men, these were difficult sentences to write.

Whatever Don's and my incompatibilities, which had wreaked such havoc on Deborah, we shared one critical trait: a fanatic passion for unclimbed routes, preferably in Alaska. By the beginning of February, we were committed to another expedition together in the summer of 1965.

In our letters to each other, we mulled over possible objectives. I proposed the peaks in the Hayes Range to which we had been heading when Don fell sixty feet into the crevasse on the Gillam Glacier. Don argued briefly for a return to Deborah. We considered the Peruvian Andes, then rejected the idea; as Don wrote, Peru "may not necessarily add anything much to total mountaineering experience over Alaskan climbs." By 1965, many mountaineers, some of them international celebrities, had done great things in the Andes. Alaska, in contrast, seemed almost untouched, a half-secret wilderness where we could make a lasting mark as pioneers.

About once a week, I headed off to the Boston Museum of Science, where in a storeroom accessible only through his skytop director's office, Bradford Washburn housed his magnificent collection of thirty years of aerial photographs of peaks in Alaska and the Yukon. It was Washburn who had talked us into our Wickersham Wall route on McKinley in 1963, and a Washburn photograph had pushed us to Deborah's east ridge the following year. Now I toyed with a new route on Mount Foraker, second-highest peak in the Alaska Range. But then I saw some recent photos Brad had shot of Mount Huntington.

Though only 12,240 feet high, Huntington, a slender triangular pyramid rising out of the Ruth and Tokositna Glaciers some nine miles southeast of McKinley's summit, had been called by more than one observer "the most beautiful mountain in Alaska." By 1964, its first ascent had become a sought-after prize, but that May—just a month before Don and I had hefted our eighty-pound packs and started the hike in to Mount Deborah—Huntington had been climbed by a crack eight-man French team under the leadership of Lionel Terray.

Then forty-two years old, Terray had become perhaps the greatest expeditionary mountaineer of the twentieth century. On the legendary first ascent of Annapurna in 1950, Terray, the strongest climber, had sacrificed his chance to go to the summit so that his best friend, Louis Lachenal, and the team leader, Maurice Herzog, could reach the top. After 1950, Terray had led small expeditions that succeeded brilliantly on some of the world's most striking mountains: Fitzroy in Patagonia, Chacraraju and Taulliraju in the Peruvian Andes, Makalu in Nepal (the world's fifth-highest peak), the Himalayan cynosure Jannu, and now Huntington.

In 1961, moreover, Terray had published what I still consider the finest climbing autobiography ever written, Les Conquérants de l'Inutile. Two years later, Don and I had come upon its English translation, Conquistadors of the Useless, read and reread it, and committed long passages to memory. For me, Terray at once superseded Buhl and Rébuffat as a paragon. Don and I so immersed ourselves in the Terray mystique that we began jocularly calling each other "Lionel" and "Louis." I "was" Lachenal, mercurial, thin and wiry, impatient with the plod of life; Don, the solid, stocky workhorse, the planner and brooder, "was" Terray.

As I first perused Brad's Huntington photos, therefore, it was with the conviction that the French had beaten us to the prize. Washburn himself had lured the great French mountaineer to Alaska with pictures of Huntington. The team badly underestimated the mountain, intending to knock it off as a warm-up for new routes on McKinley and Foraker. In the end, the French spent nearly a month in a desperate battle on Huntington's northwest ridge before reaching the top in late May. On the climb, Terray suffered the closest call of his life in the great ranges, slipping on ice, avoiding a fatal plunge only by his flukey attachment to a fixed rope, and badly spraining his elbow. Yet he had struggled to the top himself, climbing virtually one-handed.

Huntington would be Terray's last hurrah. Only four months later, on an easy climb in the Vercors, his home cliff near Grenoble, he and Huntington partner Marc Martinetti fell, roped together, a thousand feet to their deaths, in an accident that still baffles experts.

All over the world, the history of mountaineering has followed a more or less inevitable progress. The goal of the first wave of climbers is to make first ascents, usually by the easiest routes the mountains afford. In the Alps, this era closed with the epochal and tragic first ascent of the Matterhorn in 1865. On the descent, with the team of seven all roped together, one man slipped, pulling off his companions one by one; the rope broke below the fifth climber, sending four men to their deaths.

Once its summit has been claimed, climbers turn their attention to a peak's various ridges, which offer more difficult alternatives to the *voie normale* that the first ascent route rapidly becomes. Only after the ridges have been climbed do mountaineers focus on the much steeper and usually more dangerous faces between the ridges. In the Alps, the "last great problems" of the 1930s were two of its most daunting faces—the north face, or Walker Spur, on the Grandes Jorasses in France and the Eiger Nordwand in Switzerland.

By 1965, Alaska was still in its ridge phase. Not a single true face on any of its major peaks had been climbed. The Cassin route on McKinley's south face, a landmark 1961 Italian triumph led by one of the greatest mountaineers in history, Ricardo Cassin (who had spear-headed the first ascent of the Walker Spur on the Grandes Jorasses way back in 1938), actually followed a prominent rib that protruded from the otherwise sweeping wall.

Contemplating the triangular pyramid of Huntington, I scruti-nized its two unclimbed ridges. The east ridge didn't appeal to me: it looked more dangerous than difficult, with bulging séracs teetering over avalanche-prone snow slopes. The south ridge, on the other hand, looked like a monstrous proposition—four sharp, serrated tow-ers leading from a base far down on the lower Tokositna Glacier to a wildly exposed summit icefield. (Although the final stretch has been ascended, the south ridge in its entirety remains unclimbed today.)

I was about to put away Washburn's Huntington photos when my eye caught some new pictures of the mountain's west face. It looked appallingly steep, but there was an obvious line, a serpentine curl of ridge leading into a shallow rib that, halfway up, blended seamlessly into the face itself. Splitting the face down the middle, a vector arrowing straight to the summit, it was a line so pure it made my heart soar.

Brad had shot a stereo pair of the face. I didn't need a viewer: Don had taught me how to cross my eyes but focus at a distance, thereby merging the pictures in a single image. Suddenly the mountain leapt out, a three-dimensional tabletop model of the real thing.

What a route! The stereo view convinced me that the ridge and rib might offer a reasonably safe passage into the headwall, only 1,500 feet below the summit. The rock looked like the clean brownish orange granite we had seen near the south summit of McKinley, not the hideous fractured black schist of Deborah. I wrote Don and sent him some Washburn prints.

His return letter, at the end of February, started off by scolding me: "I could say some awfully nasty things about Huntington W. face"—except, he added, "for the fact that the route really attracts me." He went on to enumerate eight objections to the line, including several ominous ones: the headwall was "probably subject to objective hazards [i.e., falling rock and ice] so severe that no hard hat could cure. . . . Summit slope is dangerous looking . . . also an avalanche threat to much below."

We vacillated for several more weeks, but we were already hooked. Agonizing over our chances on such a bold route, we tried to estimate the odds of success; in one letter, Don weighed them at 10 percent. But on the eve of our third Alaskan expedition, Don and I were at the zenith of our fanaticism. Our letters bandied about the notion of "setting a new standard." We wanted not just to accomplish a fine new route like our climb on the Wickersham Wall. We wanted to complete an ascent that would be unarguably the hardest thing yet done in Alaska.

By early March, we were committed to Huntington. There were only two problems. We still lacked a fourth member of our expedition—for we had decided that four was the optimal number. And our third, Matt Hale, who had never been on an expedition of any kind, was not nearly so sure about Huntington as Don and I were. Though he came nowhere near to backing out of the expedition, the west face daunted him. Reticent by nature, fully aware of the disdain that Don and I had felt for other HMC colleagues who had crumped on our Christmas outings in Colorado, Matt kept a glum but loyal silence. In the myopia of my zeal, I was disappointed.

On Sunday, March 14, Matt and I, on separate ropes, were each leading a relatively inexperienced HMC partner up Odell's Gully, a moderate ice climb in Huntington Ravine on New Hampshire's Mount Washington. It was a nasty day, overcast and cold, with strong gusts of wind alternating with eerie lulls. It was the day before Matt's twenty-first birthday. He had just reached a stance two pitches up, placed an anchor in the ice, and started to belay his second. A pitch below, I had chopped a ledge in the gully, anchored with a single Marwa coat-hanger ice screw, and brought up my partner. I was about to lead the second pitch, on a different line from Matt's chopped steps.

Over the wind, I heard a faint cry from far below, in the catch basin at the foot of the ravine. I pricked my ears and held my breath. "Help!" came the cry. "Help!"

"Matt!" I yelled upward. "Somebody's calling for help." We both listened.

"Help! . . . Help!"

I squinted down through a flurry of blowing snow. A solitary figure seemed to be wandering in aimless circles across the floor of the ravine. I had no idea what had happened, but I knew what I had to do.

Having driven from Cambridge up to Pinkham Notch on Mount Washington after classes on Friday, our HMC contingent had hiked up the Fire Trail and arrived in the night to find the cabin, nestled among the spruces halfway between Tuckerman and Huntington Ravines, already crowded. That weekend would be our last ice climbing outing of the year, and I was determined to use it to hone my technique on the hardest ice route in the East, Pinnacle Gully. With other good climbers among the cabin throng, I resolved on an early start on Saturday morning to beat any potential rivals to the foot of the gully.

My second, the most accomplished among our small group of protégés, and I skipped breakfast and set off at dawn. I led all the pitches in Pinnacle, chopping steps deftly and moving as fast as I knew how. The weather was identical to what we would face the next day— cold and gray, with sudden, violent gusts of wind coming from all directions. Balancing on the minimal steps I had nicked in the 70-degree funnel of ice, I tried to anticipate the wind and make sure my axe was planted firmly when a gust tore across the gully. On the third pitch, however, a burst of wind caught me by surprise. I teetered on the edge of losing my balance, then reclaimed it with a quick stab of the pick.

Topping out before noon, I felt nothing but exhilaration. I was in the best climbing shape of my life, and Pinnacle had been valuable practice for Mount Huntington.

That evening, with the stove roaring in the cabin, Matt and I chatted over dinner with two well-known veteran climbers. Craig Merrihue, thirty-one years old, had himself been president of the HMC in the 1950s. After college he had climbed all over the world, making first ascents in the Karakoram of Pakistan and the Peruvian Andes. Fresh off a Ph.D. from Berkeley, he had taken his first job at Harvard's Smithsonian Astrophysical Observatory. A genial, modest man, Craig would never have told us what others had—that he was currently on the short list of NASA's candidates for astronauts to go to the moon.

His friend Dan Doody, also thirty-one, was of a different temperament, private and dour. He had been a member of the ballyhooed 1963 expedition that made the first American ascent of Everest. Ill most of the trip, Doody had come back utterly disillusioned with the logistical overkill of the assault—twenty "sahibs," thirty-seven Sherpas, 909 porters, and twenty-nine tons of food and gear. In Matt's and my eyes, Doody's purist disdain for the Everest extravaganza was a badge of merit. Dan had also been the co-author of perhaps the finest route yet done in the Canadian Rockies, a 1961 ascent of the north face of Mount Edith Cavell, with two of the legends of American mountaineering, Yvon Chouinard and Fred Beckey. A graduate of the University of Wyoming, Dan had launched a career as a documentary filmmaker.

Matt and I told Dan and Craig about Huntington. They were impressed, and their approbation was music to our ears. For their own part, the summer of 1965 would be devoted to a laid-back trip, with wives and girlfriends, to the Hindu Kush in Afghanistan. Craig had married in 1957, and now had a six-year-old son, so mellowing out was a reasonable option at thirty-one. His wife, Sandy, was in the cabin that Saturday night, but she was so pretty I found it difficult to talk to her. She planned only to hike around the base of the ravine while Dan and Craig did some ice climbing. Although I would not have wanted to squander my summer on moderate ascents in the Hindu Kush, it was impossible not to envy Craig his limitless future and his evident happiness.

On Saturday, Matt had led Damnation Gully, the second-hardest route in the ravine. As HMC leaders, we endorsed a tacit agreement—the same code the veterans had observed when they had trained us novices, a few years before—not to spend more than one out of two weekend days pursuing our own ambitions. Odell's Gully, our Sunday objective, would be a piece of cake for Matt and me, but a good chance to impart some lessons to the seconds on our ropes. We got a leisurely start. Earlier, Doody and Merrihue had left the cabin, bound for Pinnacle Gully.

Then, in mid-morning, came the faint cry for help from below.

Galvanized, I turned to my second, who was clipped in to our Marwa one-screw anchor. "You know how to rappel, right?" I asked. He nodded dubiously. "As soon as I'm off, come on down. Leave the rope."

Without hesitation, I unroped, tied my end into the eye of the screw, wrapped the cord in the S-shaped configuration of a body rappel, and zipped down the rope. As soon as I was free, I started running, crampons still attached to my feet, down the snow skirt toward the basin where all five Huntington gullies eddied out.

Two pitches up, with a single rope, Matt could not afford to rappel. Instead he led his second on a traversing dash to the edge of Odell's Gully, then soloed down its snowy margin, spotting his addled partner on a few rocky stretches. Once they were on safe terrain, he ran as I had down to the basin. So efficiently did Matt perform this escape trick that he arrived only fifteen minutes after I did.

The man who had called for help was nicknamed B.J. A casual and unambitious climber, he had been out for a stroll in the basin, when, suddenly, what he at first thought was "a bundle of rags" came sliding and bouncing past him. He approached the debris. It was the bodies of Doody and Merrihue, still roped together. They were his good friends.

Now B.J. was still wandering in circles, moaning and wailing. He had been unable to bring himself even to touch the bodies. I felt a sharp stab of annoyance at B.J.'s uselessness, then knelt down next to Doody, who lay sprawled, face up, head downward.

In the days before CPR was taught, Matt and I had taken a Red Cross first aid course, where we had learned mouth-to-mouth resuscitation. I reached under Doody's mitten and felt for a pulse, finding none. Looking at his head, I could guess why. A deep hole had been gouged in his skull, leaking blood. I thought I could see exposed brain tissue.

I moved to Merrihue's body. B.J. was still wailing, hugging himself with his arms. I stifled the urge to tell him to shut up. Craig's body, though also bloody, looked less severely damaged, and I thought I detected the faintest of pulses. Without hesitation, I tried to stanch the bleeding, then pinched his nose, pried apart his lips, covered his mouth with mine, and forced air rhythmically into the cavity I had opened. The stubble of Craig's beard scratched my cheeks. I felt his lips slowly go cold, and I tasted a stale exhalation from his lungs, but I kept up the effort for an hour. Meanwhile, Matt had arrived and started to work, however hopelessly, on Doody.

Other men had fallen out of the gullies in Huntington Ravine and lived. Three years before, Don Jensen had been avalanched out of Damnation, fallen 800 feet, and only broken a shoulder blade. It all depended on the snow accumulation in the basin. The year of Don's fall, the snow had been heavy, covering the protruding boulders. But in March 1965, the snow cover was light. Falling out of Pinnacle, Dan and Craig had whipped down the approach slopes, caroming from one exposed rock to another. It was those stones that had done all the damage.

Gradually, other hikers and climbers, including Matt's and my seconds, arrived. Those with first aid training offered to spell Matt and me, but we stuck to our grim posts. Others headed for the cabin to organize what they hoped might still be a rescue. Yet others simply stood around. A weekend climber from MIT arrived, took one look, threw up, and vanished.

I knew after ten or fifteen minutes that my resuscitation efforts were futile, but we had been taught never to give up. That hour passed in a numb miasma, pierced by a single moment of searing pain. The crowd stirred; someone said, "She's coming"; someone else said, "Keep her away." It was Sandy Merrihue, hiking into the basin from below. Glancing up, I saw her face in the moment that she discovered what had happened. I cannot remember if she cried out, or turned away, but I knew in that instant that there were depths of loss that I had never previously guessed.

Doody, I am sure, had been dead from the moment I reached his body. We could not give up on Merrihue, however. Improvising a litter, we carried Merrihue's body back the long mile to the HMC cabin, while one or another of us kept up resuscitation every step of the way.

Once inside the cabin, I collapsed on the floor, leaning against the wall. It was not a sense of tragedy that had drained me so completely, however, but the frustration of failure.

Late into the night, traveling by headlamp, after we had bundled the two bodies into shrouds made of parkas and blankets, Matt and I and the others sledged them down the Fire Trail to Pinkham Notch.

We attended Craig's memorial service. And someone organized a gathering of climbers to discuss the accident. We had found Dan and Craig roped together, with a single, bent Marwa ice screw, clipped in by a carabiner, sliding loose on the rope between them. There was no sign of anchor slings or hardware attached to either man's tie-in. We could not even tell which of them had been leading.

My best guess today is that the leader had either tried to stretch a long pitch to reach an anchor point, asking his second to go off belay (a not unprecedented gambit among experienced climbers), or that in the wind, the men's signals had gotten confused and one had gone off anchor and off belay while the other was still climbing. (A dynamite accident in his youth had left Doody deaf in one ear.) Then one man, probably the leader, had slipped or been blown off his steps by a sudden gust of wind (as had almost happened to me the day before). He had fallen; the Marwa screw—the leader's only point of protection—had ripped out of the ice; and the rope had pulled the second off his feet, sending both men on their fatal ride.

Our gathering sought a rational, mechanical explanation of the tragedy, so we ended by condemning the infamous Marwa "coat-hanger" design. Within a few years, the piece of gear would be removed from the market. Yet Doody and Merrihue had known better than to trust their lives, falling together, to a single ice screw, no matter how solid. (I should have known better than to rappel off a single Marwa to go to their aid.) In the end, all we could really know for sure was that something had gone wrong. In mountaineering, that was all it took.

I lost no sleep over Doody and Merrihue. By the spring of 1965, I had become hard man enough to make a tidy disjunction between the horror of March 14 and anything to do with my own future. In climbing terms, I was the equivalent of the sort of battle-tested foot soldier, so beloved of generals, who can see his comrade shot down beside him, pick up the dead man's rifle, and charge on toward the enemy.

In a well-guarded private recess, I rationalized Doody and Merrihue's deaths. Yes, they were far more experienced mountaineers than I, but that spring I was in better shape than they were. That edge was the difference, I told myself, between getting blown out of my steps by a gust of wind in Pinnacle and hanging on with the pick of my axe.

I never told my parents about the accident, but I wrote to Don. In his next letter, after a two-page discussion of bush pilot logistics and expenses on Mount Huntington, he appended a dutiful note: "If the club is planning to do anything for Doody's and Merrihue's families let us out here know."

The weekend on Mount Washington quickly receded, like a nightmare that had dissolved upon waking. It would not be until twenty or twenty-five years later that, thinking back on the accident, I had a small, unbidden revelation. I had always remembered B.J.'s performance as useless, calling for help but unable to approach the bodies, wailing and walking in circles while the rest of us gave first aid, epitomizing incompetence in the pinch.

Now, decades later, I saw it in a different light. My own ruthlessly efficient descent, my tireless mouth-to-mouth resuscitation, had served to cut off any deeper feelings that might have troubled me. B.J., no hard man himself, but a loving friend, had glimpsed tragedy the moment it had occurred. He knew as surely as I did that Craig and Dan could not survive, and the terrible event had triggered in him a more genuine response than mine. While I was executing my Red Cross training, B.J. was already in the throes of grief.

In California, Don had finally approached an experienced climber whom we had met on McKinley in 1963 about being our fourth for Huntington. The man declined. His response ought to have given us pause. "He was very disturbed about the difficulty of things," Don wrote. "He is afraid to take such a big step."

Meanwhile, Don was climbing hard in Yosemite and the Sierra, had lost fifteen pounds, and reported that he was in the best shape in years. By mid-April, he had flung himself into the planning for Huntington with his characteristic obsessiveness. He wrote me for pages at a time about gear improvements he planned to make (Don was a born tinker and tailor, who ended up inventing several pieces of mountaineering equipment that proved revolutionary). He could go on and on about the nutritional pros and cons of various breakfast foods. A sample passage, about his own efforts to duplicate the formula for a muesli cereal marketed under the Swiss brand name of Familia: "Last night I devoted to numerous attempts to synthesize Familia. As yet I seem to be stumped by the special pulverized shredded wheat in Familia which gives it its mushy swelling up capacity. Hence I think we will get Familia from Richter—Dave would you do that—ask Hank whether we can get it for 45¢/box, 50¢/box, 55¢ or 60¢—Get 60 boxes."

I, too, had plunged into the planning. The last two months of my senior year passed in a blur of academic getting-by. Come June, I would not waste time hanging around to attend my own graduation. All that mattered was Huntington.

But we still needed a fourth member, and meanwhile, Matt was showing signs of a far less total commitment to our project than Don and I thought healthy. Behind Matt's back, Don and I discussed the problem. Our obtuseness about Matt's qualms stuns me today. With no expedition experience of his own, having just turned twenty-one, Matt was being invited on the most ambitious climb yet attempted in Alaska. On top of that, he had just participated in the trauma on Mount Washington. Matt had spent his own hour giving mouth-to-mouth resuscitation to a dead man whose head had been gouged open to the brain. He had come away from that exercise covered with Doody's blood. Unlike myself, Matt had not yet perfected the hard man's defenses against disaster.

"It must be as you suggest," Don wrote me in late April, "that he is just very, very anxious—and in fact so nervous . . . that he literally blows a fuse and cannot start anywhere. . . . I only wish he could transform some of that great nervous anxiety into even the most trivial (though meaningful) type of involvement—like counting calories/man-day like I'm doing and calories/Familia-ounce."

With the code we had developed over the past three years of symbiotic "commitment"—based on Don's truly neurotic fussiness about detail, but also on an inchoate love for and loyalty to each other that could find its expression only in climbing—Don and I were like a secret society taunting Matt, the acolyte, because he didn't know the password or the encrypted handshake. Admiring our passion, while at the same time daunted by our ambition, Matt longed to join, but was afraid to take the pledge.

By May, however, Matt had stepped over the line. Though at times he still seemed mired in his anxious funk, at last he threw himself into the planning. We bought thousands of feet of fixed rope, negotiated at length with our bush pilot, and used the Washburn photos to draw an elaborate topo of the west face route, visualizing pitches and camp-sites on a mountain wall we had yet to see with our own eyes.

And at last, in early May, we chose our fourth member for the expedition. During the previous several weeks, Don and I had each, separately, felt out veterans with good reputations, but with whom we had never climbed. Mindful of the personality clashes that had bedev-iled our Deborah trip, we were reluctant to sign up for a project as serious as Huntington someone with whom we had never shared a tent or a belay ledge.

The far-fetched idea was mine. Among the other HMC under-graduates, one had shown promise that made him stand out from the gang. Like Matt the year before him, Ed Bernd had, from the first Gunks trip in the fall of his freshman year on, displayed a precocious knack for absorbing the rudiments of piton and ice axe. By now, in the spring of his sophomore year, he was a solid leader on 5.7 and the occasional 5.8. Ed had, moreover, a thoroughly winning personality: open, warmhearted, guilelessly enthusiastic, if a trifle naive (Matt and I would tease him unmercifully about his devotion to the works of Ayn Rand).

Ed had grown up lower-middle-class in north Philadelphia, but he had been a shining star among his crowd since grade school. In high school, six two, solidly built, with rugged good looks, he had been a football hero and president of his class three years running. He was the first person in his extended family to go to college, and the first from his high school ever to attend Harvard, which he could afford only thanks to a patchwork of five different scholarships.

At Harvard Ed embraced a number of new activities, including jazz, intramural sports, and the college radio station, WHRB. He was planning to major in philosophy (whence the passion for Ayn Rand). But the mountaineering club held a special fascination for this natu-ral athlete. Unlike Don, Matt, and me, before college Ed had had no

experience whatsoever of mountains. The farthest afield family vaca-
tions had taken him was Jones Beach. But after Ed's freshman year, he
had hitchhiked out to the Canadian Rockies. Unable to find a climbing partner, he had hiked solo among the soaring massifs west of
Banff and Jasper. Matt and I were impressed by the spunk this pil-
grimage betokened.

On the face of it, inviting Ed to Huntington was a crazy idea. He
had performed well on three-pitch climbs at the Gunks, on the storm-
lashed ordeal of the Winter Traverse, but he was only twenty years
old, and he had never climbed a "real" mountain anywhere, let alone
in Alaska.

I wrote Don, outlining my thoughts about Ed, adding a firm
imprimatur as to his character. Having dropped out of Harvard in
1964, Don had overlapped with Ed only on a few trips Ed's freshman
year. I fully expected Don to veto the choice on the grounds of Ed's
inexperience. Instead, he wrote back, "I may surprise you, but I am
quite enthusiastic about the possibility of him going. Why? I must
admit I don't know him very well, yet it is an in-Harvard choice,
apparently a very compatible character. . . . I would very much like to
give Bernd the chance—if he could rise to the occasion—which is
demanding a lot—a lot more than was demanded of us on WWE [the
Wickersham Wall expedition]. We would be banking his potential
greatness or 'inner strength' against his inexperience."

At the end of my own sophomore year, when Hank and Rick had
invited me to Mount McKinley, my first reaction had been sheer terror. Yet there was no way I could have said no. Now Matt and I lured
Ed up to Matt's room in Quincy House and popped the question. Ed
did not even hesitate. Whatever summer plans he had, he dropped
them in an instant. The expedition would be hard for him to finance,
but he would find a way. At last, our team was whole.

Through the end of May, orchestrated by Don's increasingly frantic letters, all four of us flung ourselves into expedition preparations.
The plan was to meet at my parents' house in Boulder, buy food and
pack it into sixteen-man-day allotments stuffed into four-gallon pickle
cans, then drive up the Alaska Highway to Talkeetna, where the leg-

endary pilot Don Sheldon (who had delivered our airdrop and reported us missing, then found, on McKinley) would fly us in to the upper Tokositna Glacier.

Ed, Matt, and I bought a used VW Microbus and set out for Colorado in early June, planning to drive straight through. We made only one stop, at Ed's house in Upper Darby, a Philadelphia suburb. We arrived at 3:00 A.M.

In their twenties, my parents had scrambled up 13,000-foot peaks in the Mosquito Range of Colorado. Don's parents had taken him hiking in the Sierra foothills when he was a toddler. Matt's parents had likewise led him along trails in the Adirondacks. But Ed's had absolutely no conception of mountains. For all they knew, technical climbing was just another sport, like football. Yet they sensed that it was dangerous, and Alaska was farther from home than Ed had ever ventured.

The single hour we spent in Ed's living room was fraught with awkwardness. Ed's mother made us sandwiches, which we chewed self-consciously. All we wanted to do—even Ed—was get back on the road, but duty seemed to decree a stay of a certain length. Ed had brought home a few duffels full of belongings. We talked about school, but not about Huntington.

At last it was time to go. On the porch, in the darkness, the air was cool: a fresh rain had brought out the scent of azaleas in the yard. Ed's parents hugged him and said goodbye.

At first, everything seemed to go well. Sheldon made a brilliant landing on the upper Tokositna, depositing us beneath Mount Hunter, four miles away from Huntington but in plain sight of the west face. His was the first airplane landing ever made on the glacier. The great ice streams immediately east and west of the Tokositna—the Ruth and the Kahiltna—were relatively well known; each had been hiked by several parties from headwall cirque to lowland snout. But the Tokositna, a mammoth glacier with nine branches spilling from savage walls on Hunter and Huntington, was unexplored. Except for a

1906 reconnaissance party, which had camped for one night on the terminus of the glacier, twenty-three miles southeast of our high perch, no one, as far as we could ascertain, had ever set foot on the Tokositna.

We spent the first week ferrying our mammoth pile of gear and food those four miles over to the base of Huntington. Roped together, hiking in our homemade aluminum snowshoes, we were at first extremely leery of crevasses. The last glaciers Don and I had traveled, the Gillam and the Susitna the previous summer, had been the scenes of Don's two brutal crevasse falls. (Matt and Ed had never been on a glacier before.) The Tokositna, however, proved benign, and we established base camp beneath the west face without incident.

Don was transformed from the year before. His once haggard face had a chiseled, youthful look. He was obviously in fantastic shape, and proved a glutton for hard work. Best of all, from the first moment, he and I got along perfectly. There was not a trace left of the grinding antagonisms that had turned Deborah into an interpersonal nightmare.

During that first week, however, Matt and Ed both seemed subdued, even depressed. Don and I arranged for them to share a tent, hoping that chores like melting snow and cooking dinner would boost their morale. Imbued with our Platonic ideal of commitment, Don and I were obtuse to the simple truth that Matt and Ed were overawed by our surroundings and by the ferocity of our route.

Gradually, our junior members got into the spirit of the expedition. On the drive north, Ed had bought a bag of firecrackers in Wyoming; now, on July 4, he set some off at base camp, yelping with each report as he encouraged the explosions to trigger avalanches on the surrounding walls. The slopes needed no help from Ed's pyrotechnics: loosened up in the heat of early July, tons of winter snow and ice were spontaneously sloughing off every couloir in sight, and the cirque was loud with the rumble of nearly nonstop avalanches.

On July 5, Matt tunneled through a cornice and emerged on the col between the serpentine ridge that hung from the face and an unnamed minor summit to the west. He kicked steps forty feet farther up the ridge, reached a rock pillar, and drove a piton. Watching from just below the col, the other three of us cheered out loud at the clear, ringing peal of the piton thrusting home inside the crack. We had officially begun our route, and the rock of the west face, we now knew, was granite as solid as in our fondest dreams.

Just below the col, in a 15-degree slope, we dug a snow cave to serve as advance base camp. Eventually enlarged to accommodate an entrance vestibule giving onto twin elevated "bedroom" shelves, the cave, in which we spent many a day and night, would prove a gloomy place. Outside, in the sun, the temperature often rose into the mid-40s, but inside the cave, it was always 16 degrees Fahrenheit, thanks to the eternal cold of the subarctic.

Then, after such a promising start, everything went wrong. In our Washburn photos, the bottom 900 feet of ridge had been invisible, eclipsed by a cloud. Don and I had blithely assumed that that section of the route, because it was less steep than the face to which it led, would be easy climbing. Instead, the Stegosaur, as we named it, turned out to be a fiendish gauntlet of rock towers and alarmingly steep scallops of hard snow-ice. The Stegosaur was continuously corniced on the left, or north, side, overhanging the basin of our approach route. Thus on every step of the route, we had to climb below the cornice on the right, where a terrifying precipice plunged beneath us 3,000 feet sheer to the lower Tokositna. Day after day, we advanced the route on the Stegosaur, but so devious was the climbing that sometimes, after eight or nine hours of work, we managed to add only one or two new pitches to our progress.

Then the storms came. In Alaska, the worst weather arrives not in gales of cold snow, but when the temperature is around the freezing point. Throughout the first two weeks of July, one day after another was swallowed up in tempests of drizzle, sleet, and lashing rain. More than once, we got dressed in our snow cave, packed up, and started toward the route, only to give up in the face of the miserable weather and return to our chilly biers. Even if we could climb in such conditions, the wet and the warmth had turned every patch of snow and ice into a potential avalanche trap. We had brought a Monopoly set to kill the idle hours; now, in the snow cave, we played so many games that never again after that summer would I be able to countenance little red hotels plunked down on Park Place or Marvin Gardens.

From the start, rather than coddling them, Don and I gave Matt and Ed their full share of the leads. It was a wise decision, for as they immersed themselves in the technical challenges of chopping steps up ice runnels and climbing short rock pitches with their crampons on, our younger teammates shrugged off their glum inertia and entered Don's and my brave new world of commitment.

By July 16, we had led and fixed ropes on eighteen pitches, most of them at least 130 feet in length. Thanks to the insidious warmth of the storms, however, the steps we so laboriously chopped in ice and steep snow melted out in a day or two. With fixed ropes and frozen steps, we could have flown over this conquered ground; now, instead, we had to rechop the steps almost every time we climbed back to our high point.

So circuitous was the Stegosaur that among those eighteen pitches, we had done 2,200 feet of climbing only to gain a paltry 900 feet of altitude on our route. As we peered up at the wall above us during rare clearings, we could see that nothing we had yet tackled was in the same category of difficulty as the true west face looming over us.

Even more problematic than the weather was the fact that, in eighteen pitches, we had passed not a single spot that would serve as a campsite. Without at least two camps on the face itself, we had no chance of reaching the summit. At the top of the eighteenth pitch, Ed and I had reached the foot of a narrow ice chute that connected two long, steeply tilting snowfields that we called the Lower and Upper Parks. I nicknamed the ice chute the Alley. Here, I thought, with a heroic job of excavation, one might just be able to pitch a two-man tent sideways, on a platform made of a wedge carved out of the 50-degree slope. Yet such a campsite would be a last-ditch solution, at best.

In quiet moments inside our snow cave, Don and I each wrestled with the demon of despair. Despite the incalculable head start flying in to Huntington had given us over our launch on Deborah, where we had hiked forty miles just to reach the base of the mountain, we were actually behind our pace of the previous year. After twenty days on Deborah, we had been halfway up the route. After twenty days on Huntington, we had tamed only the lower third—and indubitably the easiest third—of our route on the west face. In my diary, on July 22, I wrote, "Chances on Huntington seem about nil."

There was nothing to do but plug on. By July 16, Matt had led only four, Ed a mere three, of our eighteen pitches, so that day we sent them up the route carrying a two-man tent and four days of food. Their charge was to establish a campsite somewhere and to push on across the Upper Park. The usual storm blew back in, and for the next three days, Don and I stewed in the snow cave, growing increasingly worried about our friends above. For all we knew, they had been unable to pitch the tent anywhere, and were stranded on some ledge in a hypothermic bivouac.

On July 19, Don and I forced our way up the route in wretched conditions. Finding Ed and Matt ensconced in the little orange tent at the foot of the Alley, we were immensely heartened. On July 16, they had dumped their loads here and pushed on above. Matt had led the near-vertical ice groove of the Alley. Then the climbing got easier as they sailed across the Upper Park. But in six more pitches, they found not a single possible campsite. Stringing fixed lines as they descended, they regained the foot of the Alley. There they spent five hours hacking a platform out of the ice. The tent, pitched narrower than normal, was anchored to pitons pounded into the rock pillar above. A fixed line with overhand loops tied in it served as security when one had to wriggle out the sleeve door to relieve himself.

At midnight, after nineteen straight hours of effort, Matt and Ed had finally collapsed inside the tent. Theirs was the finest performance yet on the expedition, and proof that despite their inexperience, Matt and Ed were fully equal to the challenge of the west face. As Don and I saw at once on the 19th, the Alley Camp was by far the most spectacular mountain perch any of us had ever inhabited. The tent door stared out over 4,000 feet of empty space. Anything dropped here (Matt and Ed lost a cook pot in this fashion) plunged all the way to the lower Tokositna Glacier.

We rotated partners: Don and Ed stayed on in the Alley Camp, while Matt and I descended to base, hoping to bring up loads the next morning. Instead, another three-day storm paralyzed us. During those days, Don and Ed managed to get two new pitches led, as they left any trace of the west rib behind and entered the vertiginous wilderness of the wall itself. Those pitches were far more difficult than anything we had climbed below. Don's 26th pitch, in particular, was a dazzling piece of work: a vertical inside corner, full-on 5.8 in difficulty in the best conditions, even harder than that as Don solved it in crampons, kicking front points into verglas slicks, sweeping frost feathers from the handholds.

Only two more pitches in four days, however . . . On July 23, as Matt and I climbed up to the Alley Camp to trade places with Don and Ed, I trudged along in a fog of pessimism. The west face, I had decided, was simply too hard for us.

As we arrived, Don and Ed had just finished cooking a hearty glop for dinner. Magnanimously, they surrendered the meal to Matt and me and started down. Sensing my low spirits, Ed surprised me. "The climbing's beautiful up there," he said, just before leaving camp. "We'll make it, Dave. You wait and see." At the time, I attributed Ed's encouraging words to sheer naïveté.

July 24, another storm day, kept Matt and me confined in our cramped tent. But the 25th dawned utterly clear. And though we could scarcely believe our luck, every one of the next five days turned out to be cloudless and calm, as well.

Matt and I seized the moment. On the 25th, we got heavy loads up to Don's and Ed's high point and tacked another half-pitch onto our route. Then, on July 26, in what would quickly turn into the best day of climbing that either Matt or I had yet enjoyed in our brief careers, we led six new pitches through the heart of the west face. The last of them was a big overhanging roof of brown granite that Matt expertly solved. The Nose, as we named the overhang, was, we believed, the first true ceiling ever climbed in Alaska. It would prove to be the crux of our route: not only the hardest single pitch, but the turning point, after which we could glimpse the ecstatic prospect of success.

On July 27, we ceded the lead back to Ed and Don. Aided by the fixed ropes Matt and I had strung, they swarmed up our pitches, then, working past midnight, hacked a narrow platform out of the ice beneath the Nose. There they pitched our other two-man tent, tied off once more to pitons, in an even dizzier setting than the Alley Camp.

By the morning of July 29, they were ready to probe new ground. The Nose lay about three fifths of the way up the west face, so there was a chance that Don's and Ed's push might take them all the way to the summit. That same morning, camped sixteen pitches and more than a thousand feet lower on the wall, Matt and I hoped only to carry a vital load of food and climbing gear (Don and Ed had only a handful of pitons and ice screws) up to the Nose to support their effort. With no inter-camp radio, we were well out of sight and earshot of our companions above.

Matt and I had reconciled ourselves to the possibility that Don and Ed might get our only chance to go for the top. As I wrote in my diary, "To succeed on this fantastic route, when we'd all but given up hope in the miserable storms down in the cave, would be reward enough, no matter who gets to the summit."

As we set out that morning from our low camp, however, with the weather still perfect—blue sky to the horizon, not a hint of wind—I suggested adding our down jackets and an extra lunch to our heavy loads, just in case our supply relay turned into something more than that. And indeed, a kind of magical efficiency—the fruit of all those days of balky progress during the previous four weeks—took hold. Matt and I climbed those sixteen pitches in only three and a half hours.

There was no question, then, of merely dumping our loads at the camp and heading back down. Instead, we would leave the food boxes at the Nose, but carry our hardware up the fixed ropes above. With great good luck, we might catch up to Don and Ed. At the very least, we could use our pitons, ice screws, and fixed ropes to improve the route behind them and safeguard their descent.

As we sorted out our packs below the Nose, though, we noticed a puzzling and disturbing thing. Ed's ice axe stood planted in the hard snow beside the tent. We could not imagine any reason that he might have deliberately left it behind. On the soaring summit snowfield, the axe would be a climber's single most vital tool. The anomaly of its standing there beside the tent hung over Matt's and my otherwise jubilant mood like an omen.

It would only be hours later that we learned what had happened. Preoccupied with the arduous struggle to get up the overhang, even aided by the fixed rope, Ed had simply forgotten his axe, realizing his error only when he reached the snow slope at the top of the pitch, where Don belayed him.

The oversight was, after all, the fruit of Ed's inexperience. "What a dumb thing to do," he muttered to Don. "You think we should go back for it?"

Don's intense ambition vetoed that suggestion. "No," he said. "It would take too much time. We can make do with an icelite." This was Don's name for the sharp, barbed aluminum dagger he had invented and manufactured himself, a piece of gear halfway between a snow picket and an ice screw, ideally suited to Alaskan conditions. But to use an icelite as a substitute for an axe on the summit icefield would be extremely risky.

As a vote of confidence, Don handed Ed his own axe and bade him lead the steep snow-and-ice pitch above, our 36th overall, the first stretch of new terrain either of them had ventured onto in nine days.

Down below the Nose, Matt added Ed's axe to his load, then monkeyed his way up the fixed rope. By 3:00 P.M., we stood together at the bottom of the 36th pitch—new ground for us. There was no sign of Ed and Don above, but a fixed rope stretched up and left, indicating the route, as did the line of steps Ed had chopped in the icy snow. Matt started up.

With the fixed rope as a handline, the climbing was easy enough, but the afternoon sun had begun to melt the once hard snow. Matt paused now and again to chop at the fragile steps and enlarge them.

I led the 37th pitch, once more following the fixed rope. The ground grew a bit steeper, perhaps 50 or 55 degrees, and the snow grew sloppier as I climbed. A hundred feet up, with no icelites or pitons in place for protection, Don had had to traverse right to a shattered block of granite to set up a belay. It had been a gutsy lead, I realized as I followed Don's marginal steps, hanging on to the fixed rope he had left in place.

We knew that Don and Ed had only about a dozen pitons with them. When I saw the anchor Don had placed at the top of the 37th pitch, I thought at first that their paucity of hardware had driven him to an almost insane parsimony. The sole anchor on this steep and tricky ground was a single piton Don had been unable to drive more than halfway home in the shattered granite. He had taken a short ring of nylon webbing, called a hero loop, cinched it around the blade of the piton where it entered the crack, then clipped his carabiner into the loop rather than the eye of the piton. It was standard practice, resulting in less torque on the piton should it have to bear the brunt of a fall. But it was a dicey gambit to use a tied-off piton for protection on a single move in the middle of a pitch. To use it as the sole attachment anchoring two men on a 50-degree slope was bold beyond belief.

Carrying another twenty pitons myself, I tried, before bringing Matt up, to improve the anchor by pounding a second piton into the block. Nothing held in the decomposed granite, however, and after a few minutes I gave up.

Then I made a mistake of my own—a small one, which came close to having extreme consequences.

Both early and late in my mountaineering career, my greatest failing has stemmed from an apparently innate mechanical incompetence. Gear of all kinds baffles and infuriates me, and I am incapable of repairing the simplest device of any sort, let alone comprehending how it works. (There is faint comfort in knowing that I share this trait with several legendary mountaineers—most notably, George Leigh Mallory.)

Without thinking twice about it, I now clipped my carabiner to the eye of the piton rather than to the hero loop. I shouted "On belay!" Matt climbed the pitch quickly. On arriving at the platform of snow I had stamped beneath the granite block, he might have glanced at the anchor and recognized my mistake, but a sense of urgency turned our eyes only upward, toward the steps and fixed rope above. I handed Matt our rack of pitons and carabiners. He started up the 38th pitch.

Only four feet above me, Matt paused, his feet planted in shallow steps in the snow-ice. The straps on his right crampon had come loose. He took off his mittens, then awkwardly reached down to tighten the straps. As he pulled on the intransigent leather binding, the snow broke loose beneath his right foot, and he fell.

Keeping Matt on belay with my left hand, I held up my right to break his fall. He landed on top of me, but I thought I had caught him successfully: the effort was not unlike spotting a climber on a boulder problem four feet off the ground.

In that instant, however, I felt the snow platform on which I stood collapse beneath my feet. I still expected my tight tie-in to the anchor to hold us both. Yet something had gone wrong. All at once we were falling together, Matt riding me as we gathered speed.

It was my mistake in clipping in to the anchor that had caused the trouble. Don had tied the fixed ropes left on the 37th and 38th pitches to the hero loop cinched around the blade of the piton, not to its eye. When my snow ledge broke, all of Matt's and my weight came onto the piton, yanking it easily out of its inadequate purchase in the shattered rock. The piton, still uselessly connected to me, slid loose from the hero loop. Had I clipped in to the hero loop instead of the eye, there was a chance the fixed rope strung over the 38th pitch, itself anchored far above, would have held us. Because of my error, we were falling together, completely unattached to the mountain.

In that moment, I knew none of this. There was only time to realize that something had gone drastically wrong. "Oh, shit!" I muttered. We slid faster and faster down the 50-degree slope, then started to bounce. I caught a glimpse of the void below. *This is it*, I thought. *This is how it ends.*

Suddenly we came to a wrenching stop. We dangled on our sides against a steep patch of rock and ice, Matt still sprawled on top of me.

"Don't move yet!" I shouted to Matt. "We could start going again!"

I could not figure out why we had stopped. Our climbing rope stretched tight above us, holding us in place, but it was not an easy matter even to get back onto our feet. "We've got to get a piton in immediately," I said, searching the rock for a crack.

During our fall, there had been no time to feel fear: only a detached anticipation of doom. Now a giddy panic seized us both. I frantically hammered home a pair of poor pitons, then tied Matt and me off to them.

We took stock. Matt had lost his right crampon and his mittens. My own right crampon had been knocked off, but it still dangled from my right ankle. My glasses had been knocked off, too, only to fetch up on the toe of my boot—a good thing, for I was so near-sighted that without them the world was a blur.

Riding beneath Matt's body, I had taken the brunt of the impact of our bounces. I felt myself for broken bones, relieved to discover nothing worse than bad bruises.

Now, as I stared upward, I divined the cause of our miraculous deliverance. As Matt and I had fallen, the 150-foot-long climbing rope that bound us together slid down the slope after us. Seventy-five feet above, it had caught on a prong of rock, and held, jerking the two of us to a halt.

The logical course of action now lay before us. We needed to traverse back left to the line of the route, then climb and rappel back down to the safety of the camp below the Nose. We had come as close as you could come in the mountains to dying: we need not tempt fate further.

But it was now that my fanaticism took charge. After a month on the west face—four weeks haunted with the prospect of another failure as debilitating as Deborah—Huntington meant too much to me. We could still climb up to Don and Ed, I insisted. At first, Matt demurred. He was badly shaken—as was I, though the panic produced in me a set of imperatives different from Matt's.

I had an extra pair of mittens in my pack to replace the ones Matt had lost. His missing right crampon would mean a serious handicap, but I promised him that I would lead all the pitches and enlarge the right footsteps in the snow and ice so that he could climb them with his cramponless boot. At last, with trepidation, Matt agreed to go up rather than down.

As I led back up the steep slope toward the failed anchor 75 feet above us, chopping new steps in the snow, I was driven by adrenaline. When I came to the prong that had snagged our rope and saved our lives, I gasped. Prong was too generous a word. It was a mere nubbin, a rounded protrusion of rock the size of a knuckle on my hand.

Through the late afternoon, adrenaline drove me onward, though I felt that, reprieved from certain death, I was climbing as well as I ever had in my life. Because Don and Ed had carried only five or six fixed ropes, they had left blank sections between fixed pitches. Matt and I strung lines on these steep but relatively easy slopes, laying a continuous thread in our comrades' wake, to secure our descent. Assiduously I chopped buckets for Matt's cramponless right foot. He followed with a mute efficiency.

On Pitch 41, we faced the last rock band on the west face, a nearly vertical 140-foot cliff, the crux of the upper third of the route. As I followed the fixed rope, I was impressed with Don's boldness: he had led the difficult pitch with only three pitons, from one of which he had dangled a stirrup to make a delicate aid move, far above his last piece of protection. The rock was superb, however, and I felt exhilarated as I reled the pitch, improving it with five additional pitons.

Abruptly I emerged onto the sweeping summit icefield. At the anchor, I belayed Matt up. Suddenly a yell came from above: Ed had heard our belay signals. We stared up the featureless sweep of 50-degree snow, but could see no one.

"Where are you?" I called.

"In the rock outcrop!"

We could see this tiny island, the only piece of granite between us and the summit, but still could not spot our friends. It was 8:00 P.M. Without the benefit of fixed ropes, I swarmed up the slope. The snow was in the worst condition yet, possibly ready to avalanche. Twice I hammered rock pitons into the ice to give myself an illusion of security. The adrenaline had still not worn off.

At last we joined Don and Ed. They had pitched a minuscule bivouac tent, also of Don's invention, on the narrow, sloping ledge of the outcrop. It was their plan to wait for the semidark of night, hoping the icefield would refreeze, then go for the summit. They had not expected us to catch up to them.

The first thing Ed said was, "You didn't happen to bring up my ice axe, did you?" Then he saw the implement stuffed in the top of Matt's pack. He crowed with gratitude. "What a couple of buddies!"

Downplaying the incident, lest we jinx the euphoria of our reunion, we told Ed and Don about our fall on the 38th pitch. Don said little, retreating behind the stoic reserve I had come to know so well during our three years of climbing together. But Ed was visibly upset.

We ate a few candy bars as the sun set behind Mount Hunter in the west. At 10:30 P.M., we roped all four together and started upward. The summit lay only 500 vertical feet above us. For the first time in a month, I believed we were going to make it.

We climbed through the night, which by now, at the end of July, grew ghostly—if not pitch—dark for two hours around midnight. Don led five pitches up the scary, steep summit snowfield, until we reached the crest of the northwest ridge. For the first time, we were on the route the French had pioneered the year before. Yet the difficulty never relented. A huge cornice hung over the north face: climbing too near it, Don punched a hole with his left foot, then lurched instinctively backward—not before catching a glimpse of the Ruth Glacier, more than 5,000 feet below.

Exhausted, Don turned the lead over to me. I labored on, almost swimming my way up treacherous plumes of hollow snow that had crusted into frozen pillars. My third lead, our 53rd overall, was the hardest snow pitch on the whole climb. Using my axe in one hand, an icelite dagger in the other, I excavated a trough up the short cliff of airy meringue. After that, the ridge leveled again. The sun was about to rise in the northeast. There was still not a breath of wind. I trudged on—and then, all at once, I stood on the summit. One by one, I belayed my partners to the top.

It was 3:30 A.M. on July 30. The sun stood a degree or two above the horizon. Staring off to the northeast, I suddenly recognized the sharp outline of Mount Deborah, 130 miles away. Don had seen it, too. "This makes up for a lot," I said.

We sat down and ate a few bites of lunch, then sipped from our water bottles. Ed had brought a couple of firecrackers all the way from base camp. Now he wanted to set one off, but Don and I talked him out of it, for fear the explosion would knock loose the summit cornice. We spent about forty minutes on top, hardly speaking. I would have liked to spend hours there—I sensed already that a spell of grace such as the one in which we now basked, on the ragged edge of fatigue, was among the rarest of events in life. But we knew that the sun would begin to soften the summit slopes. Better to get down while the snow was still partly frozen.

All too soon, we turned to begin the descent. Coming last, I took a final glance at the top. We had left nothing there, except for our tracks.

Erring on the side of caution, we fixed ropes to aid the descent of the two steepest plumes on the summit ridge. Then we climbed gingerly down the 55-degree snowfield at the top of the west face. Since we had only two climbing ropes for the four of us, we had to tie in at ninety-foot intervals, instead of the normal 150, and our progress was correspondingly awkward. When we reached the bivouac tent Don and Ed had pitched on the only patch of rock in the 800-foot sweep of the snowfield, we split into pairs. Ed and I headed down first, while Don and Matt packed up the minimal camp and followed us.

Ed went first, as I watched him carefully, ready to hold him with an improvised belay if, in his extreme tiredness, he might slip. The fixed ropes we had placed on the way up gave us an immeasurable boost in terms of safety. At last we stood at the anchor above the Nose. It was late morning, already too warm. Ed rappelled over the overhang; I followed; then Matt and Don came right after us.

At noon, we piled, all four, inside the small tent pitched narrow on the icy ledge beneath the sheltering brow of the Nose. We had been climbing for twenty-five hours straight.

Now, finally, we could collapse into giddy celebration. We cheered raucously, then giggled with relief. Out of his pack, Ed pulled our victory brandy, which I had forgotten we had—a pint of blackberry-flavored Hiram Walker. We passed the bottle, spinning manic toasts out of thin air.

There was no way to get comfortable. We were literally lying on top of each other, and though each of us dozed off for half an hour at a time, it was only to wake up to the jab of someone else's elbow in one's face. In mid-afternoon, with sun pouring straight down on the Nose Camp from the south, it grew unbearably hot and stuffy inside the tent. By 6:00 P.M., it had started to cool off, and we could see clouds moving in from the west. Our six days of perfect weather, without which we would never have reached the summit, seemed at last to be coming to an end.

A single exchange, in the middle of our celebration, would haunt me for years afterward. "Man," I crowed, "that's the best day of climbing I've ever had!"

"Mine, too," said Ed, "but I don't know if I'd do the whole thing again."

I was puzzled, even disappointed. "Is it—you know, about Matt's and my near-accident?" I asked.

Ed thought for a while before answering. "No, it's not only that."

We didn't pursue the subject. In late afternoon, we managed to cook dinner. It was clear, however, that we couldn't linger indefinitely in the Nose Camp. We had only two sleeping bags for the four of us, and the cramped discomfort would soon become oppressive—especially if a storm moved in and stalled our further descent.

Around 9:00 P.M., Ed suggested that he and I head down through the night to the Alley Camp. Once there, we could stretch out in ease, a sleeping bag apiece, leaving Matt and Don to come down at their leisure. I agreed. We were packed and off by 9:40 P.M.

Hauling loads during the previous week, I had climbed the pitches below the Nose Camp five times to Ed's one. I knew the moves by heart. So I sent Ed down first, belaying him on the tricky parts, shouting advice. On one pitch, Ed pulled loose a handhold and started to fall, but I held him easily.

On the summit ridge the night before, with a clear view to the northern horizon, the darkness had been merely penumbral. Now we were toiling in the mountain's shadow, and it grew darker than at any time so far on the expedition. It was still too warm, the steps wet and sloppy—a sure sign of coming storm. I could no longer see Ed at the far end of a pitch, but our signals rang clear in the night.

At 11:45 P.M., we stood side-by-side on the ledge above the 26th pitch, the vertical inside corner Don had led so brilliantly on July 20. We clipped our waist harnesses in to the anchor, untied the climbing rope, doubled it, and set up a rappel. A single carabiner attached the rope to the knotted fixed lines strung through the eyes of several pitons.

Hyper-vigilant because of the darkness, I noticed that Ed had clipped the rappel 'biner into only a single strand of tied-off fixed rope. "Clip through two strands," I urged. "It's safer."

Ed adjusted the 'biner. "Like this?" he asked.

I peered at his setup. "Yeah."

Ed wrapped the rope around his body and started to lean back.

"Just this tough pitch," I said, "and we've got it easy."

There was a scraping sound, and a spark in the night. Suddenly Ed was flying backward away from me through the air. He uttered not a word. I saw him fall forty feet free, then smash on the slope below the steepest part of the 26th pitch.

"Grab something, Ed!" I yelled—just as I had to Gabe, on the First Flatiron—knowing at once that it was a useless command. Ed slid and bounced away, vanishing in the darkness. I heard his body falling for several seconds after I lost sight of it. I knew that there was not the slightest chance of his plunge coming to an end above the lower Tokositna Glacier, 4,500 feet below.

Now there was silence. "Ed! Ed! Ed!" I screamed, hearing my shouts dissipate into the darkness. I did not expect an answer.

I stared at the anchor. The knotted fixed ropes were still in place. The carabiner was gone with the rope and Ed. What had happened? What was the scraping noise, what was the spark?

And what could I do now? Perhaps a minute passed as I stood there, my mind racing. I heard the drip from an icicle splashing on the ledge next to me.

"Don!" I screamed as loud as I could. "Matt!" But I was eight pitches below the Nose Camp, 800 vertical feet replete with rock prows and snow slopes that would muffle any sound. There was no way they could hear my calls.

My first impulse was to try to climb back up to Don and Matt. Slowly, I recognized the pointlessness—indeed, the exacerbation of risk—that effort would mean. The three of us had, sooner or later, to get off the mountain. The only thing I could do was to climb down solo to the Alley Camp.

The rope was gone with Ed, so I could not rappel the 26th pitch. Thank God for the fixed lines! Without them, I knew, I could never have down-climbed, solo and unprotected, Don's 5.8 lead in the dark. But with a combination of climbing and hanging from the fixed rope, I might be able to thrutch my way down the vertical inside corner.

I cut off a short section of fixed rope from the anchor, tied it in to my waist harness, then made a loop with the other end. With two carabiners, I attached this makeshift sling to the upper few feet of the fixed line strung on Pitch 26. If I fell, this sliding safety loop might just catch me. Then I unclipped from my anchor, swung over the lip of the ledge, and started down-climbing. For the second time in two days, an uncontrollable surge of adrenaline drove my body. I was moving jerkily, not smoothly, and in the darkness I could barely see the holds. The down-climbing felt desperate. "Slow down, slow down," I muttered to myself, unable to obey my own advice.

All at once I was at the base of the vertical corner. *It's easy from here*, I exhorted myself, clipping my pair of 'biners into the next fixed rope. *Slow down, do it safely*. But I could not slow down. Dashing along the fixed line, feeling for the steps in the snow as much as seeing them, I moved recklessly, at a pace that was almost a jog.

It was the third time in my life that I had responded thus to an accident. The first, after Gabe's fall, when, having told myself to sit still and wait for a rescue, instead I scrambled frantically to the top of the cliff and down the back side. The second, just four months earlier, when I had zipped off the rappel in Odell's Gully and run down to the basin to administer first aid. And now, on Huntington, when there was absolutely no need for haste, except that my body could frame no other response.

Almost four decades after that terrible night, I learned that there was a neurophysiological explanation for my compulsive hurry—one formulated by researchers long after 1965. When one's internal map of the world suddenly fails to correspond with reality, as happens in the midst of a disaster, the part of the brain called the amygdala, scientists say, causes the secretion of chemicals known as catecholamines (what I had always thought of as adrenaline). A mechanism evolved over millions of years to promote survival produces a kind of panic that dictates flight. The hiker, lost in the woods, who starts running in different directions to find his way, is in the grips of such a chemical short circuit. An extreme example is the man on the New Jersey shore who, seeing the first hijacked airplane crash into the World Trade Center on September 11, 2001, jumped fully clothed into the Hudson and started swimming toward Manhattan.

The panic response triggered by runaway catecholamines can serve vital ends, as in the proverbial superhuman feats of strength performed by men and women who lift cars off victims trapped beneath the wheels. On the whole, however, the panic is more dangerous than helpful. Thus survival experts teach their students to "stay calm," to "avoid compulsive behavior and don't hurry." They stand by acronyms such as STOP—"stop, think, observe, plan."

In my three cases, however, the panic response produced useful results—or perhaps I was just lucky to survive my own excesses. In the minutes after Ed's fall, there was no way that haste could do me any good. And yet in retrospect, as I dashed across the Upper Park, I had the feeling that I had never moved more efficiently on mountain terrain. Two or three times my steps in the snow broke loose beneath me, and my weight came full on the fixed lines, but they held. At last I came to the top of the Alley, shinnied down the runnel, gripping the rope tight, and reached the tent. I looked at my watch. I had down-climbed seven pitches in eighteen minutes.

Panting with exhaustion, I unclipped from the fixed rope, took off my crampons, and crawled inside the tent—only to find a pool of water covering the floor. Somehow, on the morning of July 29, Matt and I had left the tent door open. In the warmth of the last two days, snow had melted all around the ledge and trickled into the tent. I sponged up the water as best I could, crawled into my soaked sleeping bag, and begged for sleep I knew would not come.

What could have happened? my mind hammered away as I lay in the darkness. *What went wrong?*

The scraping sound must have been the carabiner raking across rock as it came loose. The spark, I thought, was struck by Ed's crampons skittering across the granite cliff as he started to fall.

The obvious explanation for the accident had to do with the carabiner. Perhaps, as Ed put his weight on the rappel rope, the 'biner had flipped, pressing the gate against the rock, opening it, and coming loose. Or perhaps the 'biner had simply broken. (For a year or two after Huntington, I would conduct my own investigation of the particular brand of carabiner we had used on the 26th pitch, trying to gather other stories of gear failure so that I could blame Ed's death on faulty design—just as our inquest after Doody's and Merrihue's deaths had sought to condemn the Marwa ice screw.)

Today, no one would use a single carabiner to anchor a rappel, for those useful but risky snap-links have indeed been known to flip open and fail. Yet it was far from an unknown practice in 1965, and our need to save gear for the descent meant that we could ill afford to leave behind two 'biners per rappel.

It would not be until several years later, in a moment of sudden clarity, that another explanation occurred to me. When we tied our fixed ropes to the eyes of our anchor pitons, we routinely backed up the knot with a half-hitch or two. Sometimes, to keep the rope tight, we fed a doubled hank of fixed line through the eye of the piton, rather than the single strand of its end. We had likewise tied off these knots with double-strand half-hitches.

When I had urged Ed to change his clip-in, to secure his 'biner to two strands of rope rather than one, had he unwittingly clipped himself through one of our doubled half-hitches? If so, his weight on the rope would easily have pulled loose the half-hitch—the mere over-and-under first half of a miserable granny knot. When I had certified Ed's adjusted clip-in, had I failed to notice this deadly mistake?

Had my mechanical incompetence cost Ed his life? Even those several years after, when this new theory of the accident had suddenly burst upon my brain, I felt a wave of pure nausea. Today, forty years later, there is still a dull ache in my heart whenever I contemplate the possibility of this explanation.

In the wee hours of the morning of July 31, alone in the Alley Camp, I took two sleeping pills. The powerful drugs, combined with my exhaustion, allowed me to lapse into fitful sleep. When I woke in the morning of July 31, it was with no new shock of knowledge. I could hear snow falling softly on the tent. I poked my head out the door and saw that a gray miasma smeared the universe.

There were several of Ed's firecrackers in the tent. We had agreed to set them off as an emergency distress signal, but now I refrained. Strictly speaking, there was no emergency. In the unlikely event Don and Matt could hear the report of the firecracker, it might only cause them to descend too fast and too recklessly themselves. My job was simply to wait.

I took inventory. There was enough food at the Alley Camp for one man for twenty days. At the Nose Camp, Don and Matt had at most five days' food. So they would have to descend long before I would run out of supplies. But they were unlikely to set out in the storm that was now wreathing the mountain. All I need do was wait.

Without a rope, it was out of the question for me to think of trying to descend the lower face to look for Ed's body. Even after Don and Matt joined me, there would be no hope of making that search—a blind descent of 4,000 feet of precipice at least as difficult and dangerous as the west face we had just climbed.

At 1:15 P.M., hoping the act would help keep me sane, I started to write down everything that had happened in my diary. My semi-lucid narrative kept dissolving into howls of existential pain. "Why? Why did it have to happen?" I wrote. And: "It isn't fair. I had a twinge of feeling in the night that I wish it had been me that fell. . . . But that twinge of feeling is dishonest. I don't wish it had been me. . . . Wishing is stupid besides. What I regret and feel guilty for is that I asked Ed on the expedition."

And, grasping at the clichés that try to blunt the sting of untimely death: "We made the summit. We climbed this beautiful route and had the best climbing day of any of our lives, and perhaps that is good, that Ed's last day was his best."

Even as I wrote in my diary, I grew aware that I was holding my breath, listening acutely for some sound that would herald Don's and Matt's arrival. Several times a ball of snow rolled up against the tent from above; each time I jerked my head out the door, sure that Don or Matt had kicked the snowball loose, only to search the blank whiteness in vain for a sign of something moving. Worried that my sleeping pill hangover had affected my balance, each time I went out to relieve myself I clipped in to the fixed rope, rather than just hanging from the overhand loops we had tied in it.

Late that afternoon, I noticed that my watch had stopped. This trivial event hit me with stunning force. As I wrote in my diary the next morning, "Normally it would have been a minor nuisance. Last night it was almost like losing another friend." I set the watch arbitrarily and shook it to get it started again.

I needed another pill to get to sleep on the evening of July 31. A few hours later, as I tossed in my sleeping bag, I was assailed by a nightmare. In it, Ed had stumbled up to the Alley Camp, his body broken and bloody. In the darkness, he yelled out, "Why didn't you come look for me?" I woke up with a jolt, sat up, drank some water, and tried to dispel the horror of the dream. Somehow, eventually I fell back asleep.

On the morning of August 1, it had stopped snowing. For a few minutes, the sun bathed the Alley Camp. Surely, I thought, Don and Matt would arrive today. But the minutes dragged by at their agonizing pace, and nothing happened. The skies clouded up once more. It could mean the beginning of another storm.

By mid-afternoon, I had begun to think that something bad had happened to Matt and Don as well. Surely they were as eager to get off the face as I was. Why had they not descended? Maybe one of them had fallen ill. Or they had started down, and one had fallen? For a long while, I could not get out of my head the fantasy that I might be the only one of our four still alive. And if so, then what?

I would wait at the Alley Camp until August 4, then try to descend alone. If Don and Matt had not arrived by that date, surely that would mean they had come to grief. We had planned to hike out from Huntington, but if I could regain the snow cave by myself, I would stamp out a sign in the snow, pleading for Sheldon to pick me up. And if Sheldon never showed, eventually I would start the seventy-mile hike out the Tokositna Glacier, across plains of tundra and rivers in flood, alone. I would come back to tell the world what had happened.

At 10:00 P.M., I lay in my bag, craving sleep. I had given up hope of my teammates' appearance that evening, when I heard what I thought was a faint shout. I poked my head out of the tent and saw nothing. The sound must have been inanimate, a piece of ice breaking off somewhere, a rock falling. Then Matt abruptly came into view at the top of the Alley. He let out a cheery yell, but I couldn't answer. A new dread had settled into my shoulders.

Now Don appeared just behind Matt. "How are things down there?" he called out. I pretended I couldn't hear him.

Matt said later that he and Don had seen our tracks from above leading down to the Alley Camp but not below, indicating that Ed and I could not have completed the descent to the snow cave. A malaise had thus hung over their own onerous descent—gripping fixed ropes coated with ice, belaying in a waterfall that had frozen their parkas stiff. But then Matt had reached the top of the Alley, seen my head sticking out of the tent, and cast aside his fears. Yet I knelt there, mute, as he approached. A few yards above the tent, he noticed that only one pack stood beside it. At that moment, I spoke: "Matt, I'm alone."

Matt belayed Don down to the camp before either of us said a word. "Ed's dead," I finally managed.

Don stared at the snow in front of him for a long moment, then took a deep breath. "All right," he said, his voice hoarse. "Let's get inside the tent."

We spent a crowded, uncomfortable night, three men in a two-man tent pitched too small. By morning it was snowing hard, with a stiff wind. We resolved to wait for good weather before finishing the descent. All day long, we talked and talked about the accident, trying to understand what had happened. By late afternoon, we could bear the vigil no longer. We decided to go on down, storm or no storm.

I had estimated that the climb down to base camp would take us two hours. In the end, it took eight. To this day, that descent remains the most frightening and miserable I have ever accomplished in the mountains.

With only one rope, we had to tie Matt, still missing a crampon for his right foot, somewhere in the middle, but this wreaked havoc with the 130-foot pitches that stretched between anchors on the Stegosaur. The snow and ice conditions were hideous, with as much as a foot of new powder snow hiding our steps, the fixed lines coated with rime. It grew dim, then almost pitch dark. In the fierce wind, we had trouble hearing each other's belay signals. First Don, then Matt, took a fall on a slick patch of ice, catching themselves only by holding on to the fixed rope with a death-grip. Our belays seemed almost useless. I remember thinking that at times we were only inches away from losing it altogether.

Finally we reached the top of the last pitch and rappelled back into our basin on the Tokositna. We regained the snow cave at 3:30 in the morning.

The storm raged on for three more days, during which we ran out of conversation in our stagnant, slumping cave. At last, when the snow had stopped falling, we used our snowshoes to stamp a big FLY OUT sign in the slope just below the cave.

On August 6, the sun came out again. Sitting on our Ensolite pads beside the cave, we basked in its healing warmth, straining our ears for the sound of an airplane. On Matt's and Don's last day in the Nose Camp, Sheldon had flown by the mountain, seeming to spot them in their airy perch. They had waved at the Cessna as it sped past the upper part of the mountain.

But Sheldon didn't fly by on August 6. Discouraged, we returned to our glacial cell to sleep another night. If ten days passed with no sign of our pilot, we would hike out.

I was awakened at 4:30 A.M. on August 7 by the whine of a plane, barely audible inside the cave. I ran out into the morning shadows and waved my arms. Sheldon's silver plane circled overhead. He had seen our FLY OUT sign, for now a note tied to a stone fluttered down, coming to rest beside a crevasse. We roped up and retrieved it. "Move to pickup site," Sheldon had written, "or mark out nearby spot."

Frantic with haste, we packed up everything of value and hurried down the icefall. On the broad shelf that had served for several days, more than a month before, as temporary base camp and gear depot, before we had moved everything up to the snow cave, we started to mark out a landing strip. Abruptly, Sheldon appeared over the ridge leading to Mount Hunter, on his way back from depositing McKinley climbers on the Kahiltna. He circled, then made one of the perfect, feather-soft landings for which he was famous.

As we shuffled toward the plane on snowshoes, lugging our heavy packs, Sheldon jumped out of the cockpit. The boyish grin we had gotten to know in Talkeetna covered his face. On August 1, he had not only seen Don and Matt at the Nose Camp, he had seen our tracks leading all the way to the summit.

Suddenly the grin vanished. "Where's the fourth guy?" Sheldon blurted out.

For a few moments, none of us could speak. Then Don mumbled an explanation.

Matt and I threw our packs inside the Super Cub and climbed aboard. Sheldon would return for Don and the rest of the gear on a second trip.

On the flight out, Sheldon made four or five slow loops over the lower Tokositna, peering out the left-hand window. "Boy, that's rough," he murmured more than once. In the co-pilot's seat, I peered out the windshield myself, with little hope. Somewhere down there, in that chaos of ice blocks and crevasses, lay Ed's body, covered already, I suspected, by the heavy snows of the last week. It was as good a place as any, I thought, in which to spend eternity.

SIX

Worth the Risk

IN TALKEETNA, I VOLUNTEERED TO CALL ED'S parents. It seemed only fair that I take on this dolorous task: it was I, after all, who had come up with the idea of inviting Ed on the expedition.

From Don Sheldon's living room, I placed the call to Pennsylvania. "Mr. Bernd," I said, reciting the formula I had practiced for half an hour, "I'm afraid I have terrible news." I took a deep breath. "Ed was killed on Mount Huntington."

There was a staticky silence on the line. Then, in a voice already thick with shock: "Is this some kind of joke?"

I tried to explain what had happened on the night of July 30. The connection was bad. Mr. Bernd had to keep asking me to repeat myself. I told him the bare facts of the accident. I added that there was no hope of finding or retrieving Ed's body. I promised to telephone again in a few days, from Colorado.

As soon as I had hung up, I fled the house, walked out across Sheldon's airstrip, then circled to the back of his hangar. It was a warm, beautiful day, with fireweed rioting in the lot. At last, the dam of feelings inside me broke. I slumped to the ground, put my head in my hands, and began to weep. It had been four years since I had cried—since that other perfect summer day, when we had found Gabe's body at the base of the First Flatiron. Hearing me, Don and Matt came around back of the hangar. Don put his hand on my shoulder, saying, "Thanks for making the call."

Later, each of us phoned his own parents to break the news. So lacerating had the call to Mr. Bernd been, however, that I have no memory today of how my parents absorbed the grim tidings.

The next day, Don, Matt, and I drove to Anchorage. We sold the Microbus to a used car dealer; then Don and I booked flights to California and Colorado, respectively. Matt had accepted a job as a handyman for the bush pilot who ran Susitna Lodge, the solitary outpost on the Denali Highway where Don and I had left our pickup in 1964 when we had hiked in to Mount Deborah. Matt spent a stressful and lonely August at the lodge, which was run in a fashion best described as barely contained chaos. The pilot and his wife were in the throes of marital doldrums, and she, a short-tempered harridan, was given to blaming everyone in sight—Matt, as often as not—for each disaster that was built into the routines of their gas station–cum–guiding service.

Only an hour after Matt had phoned his parents from Talkeetna, they received another call, from Matt's mother's sister, telling them that Matt's cousin had just been struck by lightning and killed as he worked building a house in Vermont. It took some weeks for his parents to get the news to Matt, but by the end of August, as he repaired flat tires at Susitna Lodge and backpacked moose meat to remote landing strips, all the while ducking the tirades of the pilot's wife, Matt brooded upon the twin losses of the summer. A sense of doom seemed to hang over that last month in Alaska, and Matt began to have forebodings about his return to school, where, now president himself of the Mountaineering Club, he would be in charge of the weakest aggregation of undergraduate climbers at Harvard in almost a decade.

We were all three in debt after Huntington. Because Ed had not yet paid his share of the expenses, the expedition had ended up costing Matt, Don, and me an ungodly $800 apiece. (McKinley and Deborah had cost no more than $500 per man, round-trip from Cambridge, including food, gear, transportation, and the bush pilot.) In August, I took a job at Holubar Mountaineering, a climbing shop in Boulder run by an eccentric couple of Austro-German heritage. For minimum wage—$1.25 an hour—I used a reversible vacuum cleaner to blow goose down into the baffles of Holubar sleeping bags, or sold copies of *Summit* magazine (now defunct) to those rare customers who not only climbed but were eager to read about our sport. And I spent many an idle moment suspiciously handling carabiners of the make Ed had used for his rappel, trying to find ones with loose or sticky gates.

Only a week after returning to Boulder, however, I signed up, with dread and reluctance, for a mission that seemed on the face of it a good idea, but which in the end may have done more harm than good. At my father's suggestion, I called Ed's parents and offered to come to Philadelphia to explain what had happened on Mount Huntington.

I was met at the airport by a librarian who was a close friend of the family. Her first words were, "Is there any chance he's still alive?" The question stunned me. The jumble of the lower Tokositna, as I had seen it from the front seat of Sheldon's slow-looping plane, with the 4,500-foot vector of Ed's fall line, flashed before my eyes. Here was an inkling of just how unfathomable to the Bernds were the scale and severity of the Alaska wilderness.

With the temperature in the low 90s, Philadelphia was humid, gritty, and hazy. The librarian drove me to the house in Upper Darby where Ed, Matt, and I had eaten sandwiches at 3:00 A.M. Foolishly, I had not offered to stay in a motel, so the Bernds gave me their living room couch to sleep on.

I had volunteered for a three-day visit. To face what I knew would be an ordeal of guilt and recrimination, I had steeled myself to a single purpose. It would be worth the whole trip if I could simply explain to his parents what climbing had meant to Ed, how well he had done on Huntington, what a great deed we had accomplished together. I was itching to explain.

But for two days, the Bernds steered rigidly clear of all talk about Alaska. We barely talked, for that matter, about Ed—even about their Ed, the high school hero, the pride of the family. Yet the accoutrements of mourning pervaded the small, drab house. The Bernds had left Ed's bedroom just as it was the June night we had escaped back onto the road west; I recognized the duffels Ed had dropped off, still sitting, unopened, on the floor. The harbinger was obvious: his parents would no doubt preserve that chamber untouched for years to come, a shrine to their lost son. From time to time, I heard Mrs. Bernd weeping from the distance of her own bedroom, while her husband tried to shush her, for fear of disturbing their guest.

So, in the un-air-conditioned swelter of Philadelphia in August, we sat and made awkward small talk for two days straight. I tried to wait out this storm of avoidance, but the nastiest tent-bound gales I had endured in Alaska seemed preferable to this trial by tedium. Twice, the librarian took me out for lunch, providing blessed interludes in the living room impasse. Back on the couch, I picked up a book now and then, a specimen of Ed's summer reading, then laid it guiltily back down. One morning, at breakfast in the kitchen, as I stared out the window at the small side yard fronting a brick wall, Mrs. Bernd suddenly burst out, "Oh, you look just like Ed! He used to sit right there and look out the window, just like you're doing." I smiled wanly, imagining Ed's own longing for flight.

Finally, on Sunday afternoon, with only two hours left before I had to head to the airport, the Bernds asked me to tell them about Mount Huntington. All my pent-up frustration came out in a recitation of the credo by which I had come to live. Despite his inexperience, I told the Bernds, Ed had performed brilliantly in Alaska. His lead on the fifth pitch was the hardest ice climbing we had done on the whole expedition. The accident was a complete fluke. It was not some mistake of Ed's—it was a mechanical failure, whose true nature I could not divine and probably never would.

We had done the hardest route yet climbed in Alaska, I ranted on. Within the world of mountaineering, it would win notice the world over. What we had done together on the west face was a great accomplishment. Huntington was, in this sense, a noble memorial to Ed's courage and talent.

Mr. and Mrs. Bernd stared at me in incomprehension. There had to be, they felt, some overarching meaning to Ed's death. It was part of God's plan, but how could God have wanted Ed dead? At one point Mrs. Bernd wondered out loud whether Ed had been spared a worse end, perhaps on some battlefield in Vietnam.

They asked me why we had been unable to retrieve Ed's body. I tried to explain the landscape of the west face, the immensity of the Tokositna Glacier. I may have drawn a diagram. For the Bernds, the absence of Ed's body was the cruelest twist of all. As I described the basin to which Ed had fallen, Mrs. Bernd suddenly wailed, "My poor baby! He must be so cold!"

Despite my undergraduate major in math, the University of Denver had accepted me as a full-fledged graduate student in English. In September, I rented a cheap basement apartment on Humboldt Street, a short bike ride from campus. That gloomy garret came to seem something of a dungeon. Almost no sunlight trickled through the small, head-high windows above my bookcase, a sore deprivation in what was then, before smog became a Denver fact of life, one of the sunniest cities in the country. The landlady, who lived upstairs, was a widow addicted to soap operas. All afternoon, every afternoon, I tried to shut out the bass quaver of organ music filtered through the ceiling, punctuated at regular intervals by the woman's ghoulish cackle. Then, once *Days of Our Lives* was over, she started boiling her nightly stew, and the reek of overcooked carrots and cabbages seeped down into my precincts.

The prospect of living close to my family again was not high among my priorities in applying to DU. The proximity of the mountains among which I had become a climber was much higher. But the bottom line was that DU was then the only university in the country that offered a Ph.D. in creative writing. By now I knew that I wanted to be a writer. Though at the time I did not recognize the connection, it was proof of how thoroughly steeped I was in my father's notions of the value of academe that it never occurred to me simply to hang out my shingle and start writing—as Hemingway, Faulkner, and Fitzgerald had. Instead, I assumed the best way to learn how to write was to go to graduate school.

In English C during my senior year at Harvard, thanks to the teacher, a novelist *manqué* and acute critic of the Romantic poets named

Jim Rieger, I served a solid apprenticeship in the craft of fiction. During the next five years at DU, I took seven or eight courses in writing without learning much at all. Yet at the same time, I discovered the glories of the richest modern literature in the world. Before 1965, I had never read Spenser or Pope, never opened *Paradise Lost*, never committed to heart Herrick and Donne and Keats and Browning and Housman. At DU, I flung myself into literature, gradually learning what I did learn about how to write by reading great writers—a course, I would have thought, some teacher might have recommended to me in the eighth or ninth grade and saved me from what I now think of as the fourteen-year detour that lay across my path.

Word of our Huntington climb had indeed traveled across the mountaineering world. Don and I were invited to speak at the annual dinner of the American Alpine Club in Seattle, where we shared the prized Saturday evening stage with California veterans Allen Steck and Dick Long, who had led a six-man team that made the gutsy first ascent of the long and tortuous Hummingbird Ridge on Mount Logan in the Yukon. And the article I wrote about Huntington for the *American Alpine Journal* led off the 1966 issue.

The honor we most craved, however, was snatched out of our grasp by a twist of fate. News of our ascent had filtered all the way to France. An incredulous Lionel Terray wrote to Brad Washburn, wondering whether the west face climb was a hoax. For Terray, it was inconceivable that four unknown college kids could have succeeded on a route that was harder than the ridge that had taken the stuffing out of his superb eight-man team in 1964. Washburn wrote him back, vouching for our deed, but before Terray, our hero, could read the letter, he was killed on the easy climb in the Vercors.

I had weathered the deaths of Merrihue and Doody with hard man rationalizations and an unwavering focus on Huntington. But Ed's death had shaken me as badly as Gabe's had four years before. Despite my obtuse determination to impress upon the Bernds the magnitude of Ed's accomplishment in Alaska, I came back from Upper Darby knowing that I had spent three days in the presence of a grief whose depth was matched, in my limited experience, only by Sandy

Merrihue's as she had hiked into the ravine on Mount Washington the previous March. And Sandy's pain had come home to me only in a flickering glimpse.

I harbored no guilt over Doody's and Merrihue's demise. But during quiet moments in my basement apartment in Denver, guilt over Ed throbbed like an old war wound. I had dwelt at length on Ed's comment as we cheered our victory in the Nose Camp—"I don't know if I'd do the whole thing again." It was obvious to me now that, in the normal course of affairs, Ed would probably have climbed at a moderate level for a few years, then quit to take up some other hobby. The blind commitment with which Don and I had learned to fend off the vexing ambiguities of life was not a pledge to which Ed would have lastingly subscribed.

That fall in Denver, there was no gang of climbers to keep me in the fold, no weekend trips to the Gunks or Cannon to restore my equanimity. The school had an outing club, but its members were more interested in ski trips to Winter Park and A-Basin than in climbing routes at Eldorado Canyon. I went out once or twice with acquaintances from Boulder, but I felt shaky and out of practice, overprotecting 5.7 leads I would have danced up the previous spring.

In Cambridge, Matt was going through a kindred tribulation. On even the mellowest weekends at the Gunks, he was seized with the premonition that some terrible accident was about to happen. None of the other HMCers was solid leading anything harder than 5.6, so at Cathedral Ledge, as he watched his colleagues head off in pairs for routes at the very limit of their abilities, Matt suppressed the urge to steer them away from impending catastrophe.

On top of his fears, Matt was climbing poorly himself. In one letter to me, he wrote self-deprecatingly, "At Cathedral, I was in the worst shape of my life. In my Limmers [mountain boots] I diddled and backed off and overprotected and floundered all up the regular route. I even took a short fall onto the big dirty ledge below the cave."

Only a few years later, Matt would come into his element. For several consecutive seasons, he ranked as one of the best rock climbers in the East. At Seneca Rock in West Virginia, Matt put up several routes that were harder than anything else at the cliff. More than three decades later, those lines are revered as classic test pieces. Matt's prowess on rock during those years far exceeded any skill that I ever attained. But in the fall of 1965, nervous and uncertain, he plunged to the nadir of the four-year career he had so far devoted to climbing.

Hoping that a stern bout of winter mountaineering would round us back into form, Don and I hiked over Christmas into the Palisades, the most challenging high peaks in the Sierra Nevada. It took us two days to reach timberline, where we set up camp on a frozen lake beneath the north face of North Palisade, which was coated smooth with rime ice. Then a storm blew in that lasted for four days. As we had on the col below the east ridge of Deborah a year and a half before, we fought simply to keep the drifts from burying the tent. On the seventh day, disgusted, we hiked out.

After Gabe's death, I had pretty much decided to give up climbing. Now, in the fall of 1965 and the spring of 1966, I was not about to quit—I had too much invested in the passion that had, for three years now, been by far the most important thing in my life. But by February 1966, I had pretty much decided not to go on an expedition the next summer. Don and I had talked much about a virtually unknown range called the Cathedral or Kichatna Spires. Although none of its summits reached even 9,000 feet, we could see from the topo maps that the peaks rose, sheer and startling, as high as 3,000 and even 4,000 feet straight out of the diminutive glaciers that hemmed them in. None of the twenty-odd major peaks in the Spires appeared to have a single easy route on it.

Seventy miles southwest of McKinley, the Kichatnas were unknown to Brad Washburn. As far as Don and I could find out, only a single photo of the Spires had ever been published. When I asked Brad why he had never turned his aerial camera on these evidently majestic peaks, he answered pithily, alluding to the terrible weather, "They call that the asshole of the Alaska Range."

In a spell of blithe optimism, Don and I had tentatively planned to head for the Kichatnas in August 1965, after we had finished climbing Mount Huntington. Instead, that summer, a group of eastern climbers who were more at home in the Gunks than in the great ranges flew in, landed on an unnamed glacier, and spent nearly a month in a state of slack-jawed intimidation among the Kichatna Spires. They managed to climb only three minor peaks.

Now, in the fall and winter of 1965, Don and I traded listless communiqués about the Spires. In the wake of Huntington, our fanaticism had dissolved. We gave up the idea of going to the Kichatnas before we had really formulated it. As of February, I had no idea what I would do with myself during the coming summer.

As compensation for the muddle of my feelings about climbing, I plunged wholeheartedly into graduate school. I took courses in Chaucer, Shakespearean textual criticism, eighteenth-century satire, Melville, and the literature of the American South. Only in brief spurts had I ever been a good student at Harvard, but now I slaved over my textbooks long into the night and every weekend. The perfection of "La Belle Dame sans Merci" and "Lycidas" left me as breathless as the proofs of Euler and Pascal had when I was sixteen. Even the crude insipidities of Restoration comedy seemed well worth a term paper.

In my creative writing courses, I was manufacturing not only short stories, but sonnets, villanelles, and sestinas. For subject matter, I sometimes turned to my beloved wilderness, trying to express in nebulous effusions the absolute truths of beauty and terror I had beheld in Alaska. Yet for school, I felt that I had to couch my passion in statements that aspired to some kind of universal "importance." One of my prouder efforts, for instance, was a rondeau that eventually got published—to my joy and astonishment—in the *South Dakota Review*.

In my spare time, I wrote three different articles about Huntington, one for the *American Alpine Journal*, one for the French magazine *La Montagne*, and one for our biennial Harvard Mountaineering Club journal. Producing these pieces only scratched an itch that was eating away at me from inside. From September through February, I felt haunted by our Huntington experience. Neither in my soliloquy in the Bernds' living room, nor in letters to Matt and Don, nor in the too short compass of the journal articles could I quell an inarticulate but ravenous urge to convey the wonder and agony of our six weeks above the Tokositna Glacier. Sometime in the winter, I realized that I needed to write a book about Huntington.

I was taking my classes so seriously, however, that I was loath to steal time from studying to work on this compulsive but (I thought) professionally useless project. Then a simple solution presented itself.

DU let us out for a week of spring break in March. With reluctance, I turned down an invitation from some Colorado climbers to go to the Wind River Range in Wyoming during that week. Instead, I bicycled up to Boulder, installed myself in the bedroom in my parents' house in which I had grown up, and wrote for eight to ten hours each day. (The basement apartment in Denver, I must have felt, was too redolent of cabbage and soap opera to be conducive to serious work.)

Before I began, I made an outline. Two weekends and a school week long, the vacation stretched over nine days, so my book would have nine chapters. Writing in longhand on ledger pads, I turned out a chapter a day. Except for the number theory proofs I had labored over at age fifteen and sixteen, this was the most intense intellectual effort I had ever made. The book came out of me in one torrential flood.

I emerged from my sanctum late on the second Sunday afternoon to announce that I had finished. Bemused by my effort (for he had planned for years to write a book of his own, but had never gotten around to it), my father said, "So what are you going to do next?"

"Type it up and send it off," I answered flippantly.

"You can't do that," he snapped. For Dad, writing had always been drudgery in the extreme. Only after four or five drafts over many days of hard work could he get a paper in shape to submit to the *American Scientist* or the *Astrophysical Journal*. No publisher, Dad scolded me now, would take seriously what would surely amount to a rough first draft.

I ignored my father's advice. With my right forefinger, on my Hermes portable, I typed up *The Mountain of My Fear* (the title from a W. H. Auden poem), making only a few changes here and there. Two publishers recommended by my Harvard mentor, Jim Rieger, rejected the book before I alighted on a small but venerable New York house called Vanguard Press. According to the *Writer's Market,* Vanguard was constantly looking for new authors. Later I would learn that the press had a reputation for discovering major talents, including James T. Farrell and Joyce Carol Oates, only to lose them, once they started to become famous, to bigger houses with deeper pockets.

Since the spring of 1966, I have written eighteen books, including two novels and a memoir that (mercifully) went unpublished, as well as hundreds of magazine articles. Never again, however, have I labored in the grips of a purgative catharsis of the sort that held me in thrall during those nine days in my bedroom on Bluebell Avenue.

It was not until early in 1967 that I received a letter from Vanguard accepting my book. I read the short note over and over again, incredulous at my good fortune. On top of the fact that my narrative would actually be published, bound in hard covers and sold in bookstores, Vanguard offered me the princely advance of $500. In my grad student naïveté, I had no idea just how long the odds were, even in the 1960s, of a manuscript being rescued from the slush pile of a New York publisher. On the other hand, unlike most first-time novelists, I had been handed, thanks to Huntington, a plot as dramatic as any memoirist could ask for.

Until that letter of acceptance arrived, I had not even told my DU professors that I had written a book. It was not false pride that kept me from doing so: I assumed that the story of a mountaineering expedition had nothing to do with "creative writing." When he learned about my imminent publication, the founder and director of the DU writing program, an alcoholic novelist named John Williams, who would later win the National Book Award for *Augustus,* was more miffed than pleased. "Why didn't you tell me you were writing this book?" he berated me. "I could have helped you with it."

.*The Mountain of My Fear* finally came out in the spring of 1968. Since my manuscript was less than 35,000 words long, Vanguard had to print the text in large type, with generous margins, and pad the book with maps, photos, and appendices to produce a slender volume of

157 pages. Among the promotional coups the press scored was to land me an appearance on the TV show *To Tell the Truth*, where three out of the four canny panelists guessed that I was "the real David Roberts" because my two handsome impostors looked so much more like mountain climbers than I did.

Thirty-six years later, the book is still in print, and I am gratified to know that *The Mountain of My Fear* is regarded as a mountaineering classic. But I can never reread its more overwrought passages without wincing at my twenty-two-year-old pretensions. In the grips of Faulkner, I spun out long, adjectivally dense, barely punctuated sentences that tried to mirror the intensity of our climb, and I wandered off for pages at a time on woolly metaphysical digressions that had little to do with piton- or ropecraft. If the cathartic frenzy of those nine days on Bluebell Avenue allowed me to get down on the page the bare bones of the dramatic story of our forty days on Huntington—a canonic tale, as the blurb writer's cliché might have it, of triumph and tragedy—it also produced an abundance of rhetorical excess.

The best thing for me about getting a book I had written at twenty-two published, however, was that it kept me from giving up the ambition to become a writer through more than a decade of discouragement and failure that succeeded the appearance of *The Mountain of My Fear*.

That first year at DU there were other pleasures besides the discovery of Swift and Samuel Johnson. With a former high school friend who was now attending the University of Colorado Medical School in Denver, I struck up a touch football partnership. Just as Paul and I had up in Boulder in twelfth grade, now Bill and I cruised the DU playing fields, looking for victims upon whom to inflict our Zigzag Left and Blind Lateral and H Right.

And somehow the change of milieu, from up-tight Cambridge to the laid-back West, allowed me to tame the anxiety of the dating game and summon up the nerve to ask women out. That year I had three brief affairs (one a mere one-night stand), but while sex still seemed as magical as it had during the first months with Lisa, the intimacy that women seemed to demand scared me. From the edge of the dark hole of emotions, I shrank back toward safer ground. With a climbing partner, there was a real granite cliff, a couloir of ice and snow, upon which to unleash the passion that bound us soul-to-soul. In the hazy wilderness of romance, where was the mountain? Could one belay a lover with a rope made only of flickering desire?

In May, I formed a crush on a slender, petite, dark-haired senior in my writing class. Sharon Morris turned out wry, wispy short stories, the antithesis of my heavy meditations on the meaning of existence. She had grown up in Denver, the oldest of four children of a telegrapher for the D&RG Railroad. Like Ed Bernd, I soon learned, Sharon had been the first person in her extended family to go to college.

We started hanging out together after class rather than actually dating. Sharon was in the midst of a painful disentanglement from a boyfriend of three years, a charming, good-looking sociopath who had fooled her throughout that span with the charade that he was an army veteran turned grad student. The truth was that he had never finished high school; homeless, he lived in a basement storage locker on campus. A DU policeman had recently caught him returning to his lair, blowing his cover.

As Sharon pulled away from the relationship, the man turned into a stalker, hiding for hours at a time outside the drawn shades of her first-floor off-campus apartment. During some of those first afternoons together, I sat on the grass in front of the library listening in fascination as Sharon and her best friend, the editor of the undergraduate literary magazine, talked in their half-secret code about him, and about how to escape his creepy pursuit.

Then one evening, after margaritas at Tico's, the cheap but good Mexican restaurant that Sharon had introduced me to, we ended up in bed. The stalker soon found out about our affair. At one point, he threatened to kill both of us.

A few weeks earlier, I had solved the dilemma of the upcoming summer. A friend of a friend told me that a job in Anchorage had suddenly come open. The University of Alaska operated extension schools on the military outposts of Fort Richardson and Elmendorf Air Force Base. Thanks to the sudden departure of an English teacher, there was a vacancy at Elmendorf. So desperate was the base to fill this gap, that they quickly hired me—a first-year grad student without even an MA on my vita—to teach GIs expository writing and introduction to literature. For back-to-back two-hour courses four evenings a week, from June through August, I would earn the astounding sum of $2,700. Even with the inflated cost of living under which Alaskans suffered, this seemed a small fortune.

Impulsively, I invited Sharon to come up to Anchorage and spend the summer with me. Just as impulsively, she accepted. But for a pair of car trips in early childhood, she had never traveled outside the state of Colorado, so Alaska promised an adventure. And the forty-ninth state also seemed to offer an escape from the stalker—though there were times that summer when we believed he had made his way north and was lurking in ambush, behind some fence or abandoned building, ready to mete out his vengeance.

During that tumultuous spring of 1966, a chance encounter further complicated my life. A Denver climber whom I knew only by reputation, Gregg Blomberg, invited me, along with several other mountaineers, over to his apartment. Meeting the stringy, wild-eyed gear manufacturer (his main claim to fame was an all-metal ice axe he had invented), I was sworn to secrecy the moment I entered his front door. When the four or five of us had gathered in his living room, Blomberg unveiled his clandestine project—an attempt, the next March, to make the first winter ascent of Mount McKinley.

I did not hesitate before declining. In July of 1963, McKinley had seemed quite cold enough, with temperatures on our summit day reaching minus 25 degrees Fahrenheit. Ambivalent as I felt about expeditions of any kind after Huntington, the last trip I would have signed up for was a plod up the West Buttress in conditions that seemed to guarantee frostbite. Don and I had reveled in the fanaticism that drove us to Deborah and Huntington, but Blomberg's fanaticism seemed of a different sort—the paranoia of the mad scientist, sure that rivals were about to steal his great idea. As if these were not reasons enough, I also turned down the invitation because I believed that a winter attempt on McKinley stood about one chance in twenty of succeeding.

In the living room that evening, there was another climber whom I knew only by reputation. Though born in Colorado, Art Davidson lived in Anchorage. Roughly the same age as I, he had already notched some impressive deeds in Alaska. Only a few weeks before, with a single companion, Art had made the second ascent of Mount Marcus Baker, the highest peak in the Chugach Range, first climbed by Brad Washburn way back in 1938.

Without a qualm, Art accepted Blomberg's winter McKinley invitation. But that epic campaign lay ten months in the future: there were things to be accomplished in the meantime. The night after our living room séance, Art invited me out for beers. We met at the Stadium Inn, a venerable watering hole near the DU campus.

Art was wearing what I would come to know as his uniform—shapeless khaki trousers, a plaid lumberjack shirt with holes in the elbows. With his flaming red beard and bushy white eyebrows, he looked like the descendant of Icelandic warriors who had intermarried with Irish slaves. Now Art started talking about Alaska and couldn't stop. His monologue, an extended paean to the tundra wastes, the dancing northern lights, the gleaming limitless ranges of his adopted state, was like a Dylan Thomas riff spun out of the fizz of his fourth Miller draft. I listened, stupefied and fascinated, as the poetry awakened my own dormant love of Alaska.

Suddenly Art said, "Hey, you want to go to the Spires?"

Of course I did, I thought, my own drunkenness mingling with alarm. But I answered, "I can't. I've taken this job." I explained to Art about my Elmendorf gig.

"That's okay," he rejoined. "We'll go in September."

In that impulsive moment, my life took another 180-degree turn. Instead of skipping climbing for the summer of 1966, and so, I would guess now, beginning to drift away for good from the consuming passion of my last few years, I would go on my fourth expedition, to the magnificent and still little-explored Kichatna Spires. Thanks to Art, I would keep my string of expeditions in the Far North alive, in a sequence that would eventually number thirteen straight years.

As soon as school got out at the end of May, I flew up to Anchorage. Sharon followed a week later. I rented a dingy one-room shack of an apartment in Spenard, the tacky suburb that had started to sprawl across the bluffs southwest of Anchorage's old railroad depot downtown. The bed took up most of our living room–cum–kitchen; a cubicle partitioned next to the sink—little better than a glorified indoor outhouse—served as our very un-private bathroom.

It is a wonder that my relationship with Sharon survived that summer. Despite the steadiness of her three-year alliance with the stalker, Sharon had never lived with him. I, of course, had had almost no experience with women since the end of things with Lisa in early 1961. If intimacy was full of lurking terrors for me, I could hardly have signed up for a more rigorous course of aversion therapy.

Within the first week, Sharon got a job as a sales clerk at J. C. Penney. Her hours were from 8:00 to 5:00, while my Elmendorf classes lasted from 6:30 to 10:30 P.M. Monday through Thursday. Insomnia wreaked havoc with my diurnal round: coming home from four straight hours of teaching, I was usually too wired to sleep. I would read in bed in the dim light of midsummer nights in June and July, with Sharon asleep next to me. Often I nodded off just as Sharon was waking up to head downtown to J. C. Penney. It was no doubt a blessing that our schedules were so out of sync.

Yet still, we made love every day or night, and sex seemed at first to offer a reasonable facsimile of intimacy. Sharon was taking birth control pills, so the gnawing tension that had hung over Lisa's and my furtive nights in the cemetery was wholly absent in Spenard.

I had entered my first classroom on the air force base with some trepidation. What business had a twenty-three-year-old teaching grammar and literature to men twice his age? Indeed, a number of my students could not hide their shock at the first appearance of their absurdly young teacher, and several harbored an unspoken grudge through the long summer. Having worked full day jobs before heading over to night school, some of my students were so weary they could not help falling asleep in the second hour of diagramming sentences. Yet I was impressed with how seriously these men took their classes—especially when I compared them, two years later, to some of the bored, rich DU kids to whom I taught freshman English.

In my lit course, one of the books on the reading list was *Catch-22*. I was daunted at the prospect of pontificating about Yossarian's take on the armed services to men who had served in Korea, and sure that most of these air force lifers would deeply resent the book. Instead, to the last man, they loved Heller's mad travesty of military life so heartily that more than one of them wept with laughter as he discussed the novel.

When he was not off in the mountains, Art became Sharon's and my constant companion. A true climbing bum, he squandered no money on rent, but lived in the back of his pickup truck—named Bucephalus, after Alexander the Great's horse—in the bed of which he had carpentered a doghouse-like sleeping hut. We made a deal: in exchange for the occasional shower or dinner cooked by Sharon in our Spenard shack, Art lent me Bucephalus to commute to Elmendorf.

Spenard abounded in neighborhood bars, several of which became our regular hangouts, and on weekends we sometimes went, all three, to topless joints (the first I had ever visited) where the strippers bantered good-naturedly with patrons who hooted their approval of each inch of newly exposed flesh. And on exceptionally clear nights, we took the elevator to the top floor of the Westward Hotel, then the city's tallest building. Splurging on overpriced drinks, we watched the sun set in the northwest, then stared for long minutes at the jagged crest of far-off mountains silhouetted in the alpenglow. It was the Kichatna Spires. "We'll be there in a little over a month!" Art would chortle, raising his glass. He and I never got over the astounding fact that this compact range of virtually unknown mountains could be seen, 130 miles away, from Anchorage—though only from the top of the Westward. A mere three peaks in the Spires were officially named, the legacy of a government explorer who had glimpsed them from a hill to the south on his way through Rainy Pass in 1899.

So the summer waxed and waned. With Art I made the third or

fourth ascent of a middling-hard peak in the Chugach, the range that backs Anchorage on the east—three days of drizzle and whiteout among some of the ugliest mountains in Alaska. With Sharon, I did an easy hike up Flattop, the most accessible Chugach peak. It was the first summit she had ever reached.

A self-taught musician, Art had formed the habit of crawling through the window of a locked building on the campus of Alaska Methodist University, where late at night he would thump out blues and jazz on an out-of-tune piano stranded in some student lounge. The cops must have put out an all-points bulletin, for one night, after Art had picked me up at Elmendorf and we were searching for a midnight diner, a trooper pulled Bucephalus over. The nervous young policeman emerged from his squad car with his hand on his gun. Legs spread, palms planted on the hood of Art's truck, we were frisked before the trooper took Art away in handcuffs. I bailed him out the next morning.

When Sharon flew back to Denver at the end of August, we seemed to have little idea what the shared summer had meant. We had not talked very much about our future. To fit the Spires expedition into the academic year, I had originally planned to take the fall term off from DU, but a meeting with my draft board made it clear that such truancy would buy me an instant ticket to the armed forces. In the end, I simply skipped the first three weeks of my second year of grad school, a self-indulgence two or three of my professors were slow to forgive. (During five years at DU, I never thought to question the social wisdom of that elitist boondoggle of the day, the student deferment—even after two of my friends who had chosen the other path ended up dead in Vietnam.)

At the airport, as I hugged Sharon goodbye, I whispered, "I'll miss you." With tears in her eyes, at first she couldn't answer. We kissed once more. As she turned to go, she said, "Be careful in the Spires."

That farewell sent needles of disturbance racing through my veins. Not since Lisa had headed off to England in the fall of 1959 had I known the bittersweet anguish of parting, so perfectly captured in Emily Dickinson's famous lines—"all we know of Heaven, / And all we need of Hell." But this time, there was a wholly novel element, which darkened my feelings with the acid taste of dread. At the airport, as Sharon walked down the concourse toward her gate, I glimpsed a truth that would trouble the next decade of my life. The clean love of mountaineering, the passionate pursuit of new routes and unclimbed summits, the most important thing in my life, was fundamentally incompatible with that other kind of love, the bond between a man and a woman who, no matter how they have hedged their promises, hope to share a life together.

On September 2, we flew into the Spires. Art and I had assembled a team of five, including Rick Millikan, the HMCer who had taught me so much when I was a freshman and sophomore, and with whom I had climbed the Wickersham Wall in 1963.

On McKinley, Deborah, and Huntington, we had tackled unclimbed routes on peaks whose summits had been previously reached—the latter two, to be sure, only once apiece. And on those three trips, we had devoted the whole expedition to a single objective. With the Spires, I made a shift in mountaineering aesthetic, one that would last through the next decade. From 1966 on, with a single exception, all my expeditions would be quests for unclimbed mountains, for first ascents of difficult peaks that, often as not, had not even been named by the few explorers who might have passed nearby.

In the Spires, we hoped to revel in an embarrassment of riches, for every peak we turned our attention to had never before been tried. But from the start, we had agreed to focus our best efforts on the range's highest peak, an intimidating tower of granite known only as Peak 8985, in honor of its altitude above sea level. Just months before, in the *American Alpine Journal*, the team of eastern climbers who had been virtually shut out in the Spires in 1965 had saluted Peak 8985: "We all considered this mountain—from a mountaineering as well as esthetic viewpoint—to be one of the outstanding peaks of North America." I had figured out from the topo maps that a glacier on its northeast flank ought to give the best possible access to this monolith.

We flew in not with Don Sheldon, but with Eric Barnes, a friend of Art's, a veterinarian and former climber who ran a bush flying company as a sideline. Eric made a smooth landing on the virgin glacier, taxied to near its head, and deposited me with a small pile of gear. Three more flights got the rest of the party and the remainder of our supplies in. We had food for forty days. In early October, at the end of the expedition, rather than have Eric pick us up, we would hike out to Rainy Pass, thirty miles to the south, via a circuitous reconnaissance of several of the range's other glaciers.

In the warmth and drizzle of July on Huntington, Don Jensen had more than once vowed, "I'm beginning to think the best time for a climb like this would be September." Now, in the Spires, we learned firsthand the rewards and penalties of an autumnal campaign in the Alaska Range, a gambit that virtually no teams had ever previously attempted.

We named our home the Shadows Glacier, in homage to the perpetual gloom that reigned over our northern-exposure base camp. After the first two weeks, in fact, the sun swung so low in the southern sky that, eclipsed by the soaring walls at the head of the glacier, it never rose on camp. Twice during the expedition, we had to hike more than a mile north and erect a clothesline between planted ice axes, to dry out our sodden sleeping bags in the two or three hours of sunshine that obliquely swept this lower surface of the Shadows Glacier. After the equinox, on September 21, we got a solid twelve hours of darkness each night, a dispiriting condition of life I had never before experienced in Alaska. At base camp, we built a fifty-foot-long multiroom igloo in which to cook and occasionally sleep. After a few weeks, it turned into a virtual cave, so much snow had fallen and drifted up against its walls.

For the first nine days, we had decent weather. We bagged two easy, lower summits, and discovered a remarkable hidden couloir—we called it the Secret Passage—that climbed an alarmingly steep but technically easy 1,600 feet to a dizzy notch on Peak 8985's north ridge. From the col at the top of the Passage, the summit of Kichatna Spire, as we had renamed the range's highest peak, lay only 2,300 feet above.

Yet out of that col, the climbing immediately turned severe. Because our route lay on the dead-north ridge of the mountain, it got no sun in September. Every patch of granite that we came to grips with was plastered with frost feathers, sometimes with sheets of rime ice.

Then a storm blew in that did not relent for twelve straight days. On the only climbing effort we made during that spell, as Rick and I clumped upward only fifty feet below the summit of a minor peak to the north, a windslab broke loose beneath our feet. "Keep out of it!" I yelled, as the avalanche carried us, tumbling helplessly, toward the basin below. We flailed like infants learning to swim. Rick lost his ice axe; mine, knocked out of my hand, stayed attached to me by the wrist loop, and banged me about the head and shoulders as I fell. But we managed to stay atop the cascading debris, eddying out at last 350 feet below the fracture line, bruised but glad to be alive.

Slowly thereafter, during breaks in the consistently bad weather, we added a pitch or two per day to our route on Kichatna Spire. I led some of the hardest pitches, whose starkness was intensified by the wintry cold. We left quarter-inch fixed ropes strung along our route, then, on subsequent forays, used mechanical devices called Jumars, which had just come on the American market, to reascend each pitch. (Today, Jumaring on quarter-inch fixed ropes would be considered the height of lunacy, for the gales that prevail in ranges like the Spires cause the nylon lines to rub and abrade against the rock. Good climbers have died Jumaring frayed fixed lines when thicker ropes than ours broke under their weight.)

Kichatna Spire was a glorious challenge, as hard a climb as we could have asked for. But my mood that September was far from what it had been on Huntington. Now, when the other guys were off climbing, I worried about their safety as I seldom had about partners in the past. And after Rick's and my escape from the avalanche, I never climbed the Secret Passage without premonitions of the whole couloir's cutting loose and carrying us to a snowy grave.

As early as September 10, I wrote in my diary, "I have enjoyed the first nine days of this trip . . . but I wonder if something is missing. I worry a lot, but I always have. I am not sure always if the risk is worth it, as I was sure the last two years. Perhaps I have only in the last year found other things that mean (or that could eventually mean) as much, possibly more, than climbing does to me." In that stodgy entry, even in the privacy of my diary, I had to euphemize the impact of the summer spent with Sharon. And at the time, I thought that writing *The Mountain of My Fear* had served as a catharsis of the nightmarish denouement of our Huntington expedition, but now I can see that, fourteen months afterward, the shadow of Ed's death still hung heavy upon my spirit.

As had been the problem on Huntington, to stand any chance of getting to the summit of Kichatna Spire, we had to establish at least one and possibly two camps along the route. On September 9, we got a two-man tent precariously pitched on the only possible site in the first 2,000 feet, directly beneath a prong of rock that jutted anomalously out of the Secret Passage, just 200 feet below the knife-edged col. A week later, before anyone had been able to occupy the tent, we had to retrieve it, because we had left our only butane stove there and we feared that the tempests might have torn the shelter to shreds.

As it would turn out, it snowed on twenty-five of the last twenty-six days of the expedition. More than once I recalled Brad Washburn's epithet, "the asshole of the Alaska Range." In the Spires, we came close to being shut out as thoroughly as the overawed 1965 party had been on the next glacier to the west. Especially in September conditions, the savagery of the range's wildly sculpted peaks awed us as well. As I would rave in the next year's *American Alpine Journal*, "Nowhere else had any of us seen such remarkable sights as huge ceilings interrupting knife-edged ridges, mushroom-shaped towers of rock, or rime ice coating overhanging walls." Yet in the end, we succeeded on Kichatna Spire, thanks to a bit of logistical luck and some brilliant climbing.

In the Spires, though I was the co-leader, I was not the driving force. Art Davidson was. Art, in fact, was in the middle of a span of seventeen months during which he participated in six successful trips to the great ranges of Alaska and the Yukon—still the most intense spate of expeditionary mountaineering I have ever heard of. Only five months after the Spires, Art and his two partners would survive a six-day-long tentless bivouac at 18,200 feet on McKinley, an ordeal that began only hours after they had succeeded in making the first winter ascent of the highest mountain in North America. By all odds, the trio should have perished; their teammates in camps below, unable to mount a rescue attempt in the hurricane winds, in fact gave them up for dead. Instead, the three men rescued themselves, eventually suffering only the amputation of several toes apiece.

Art would go on to write a book about that expedition, *Minus 148°* (the title alludes to the windchill at the peak of the storm), which is justly hailed as a mountaineering classic. The next August, he would join me for yet another trip to an unexplored range in Alaska. And then, still only twenty-three years old, having burnt his candle at both ends, he would effectively quit climbing for good.

Our luck in September 1966 consisted in the fact that we got two climbers poised for a try at the summit on the eve of the only sunny, perfect day among the last twenty-six. On the 21st, Art and Rick headed up the Secret Passage, planning to repitch the tent under the prong, spend the night there, then push the next day toward a possible bivouac site at the top of our fixed ropes. I walked with them to the foot of the great couloir, wished them well, and gave them each a clap on the back.

My feelings were riddled with ambivalence. Had I been in the frame of mind I was on Huntington, I would certainly have maneuvered my way into the summit party. But now, I was more than half-glad not to be pushing up the Secret Passage with Rick and Art into the desert of cold and danger that hung above. Back in base camp, I wrote in my diary, "So it looks as if three of us won't make the summit; but we have shared with them the necessary effort, and though we too could have done it, let the thrill be theirs and the victory all of ours."

Mine was a time-honored formula of mountaineering magnanimity. Sometimes, especially in the Himalaya, a team of ten or twelve or fifteen strong climbers ends up launching only two toward the summit. The very success of such enterprises depends on the willingness of the team members to sacrifice their own ambitions to the support of others. Yet I suspect that the formula never rings true in the depths of a climber's heart. To this day, I feel a keen regret that I could not push through the risky ordeal up high and claim the summit of Kichatna Spire with Rick and Art.

They pitched the tent that evening below the rock prong, then reached our previous high point in only three and a half hours on September 22. The ledge looked adequate for a bivouac, so they dropped their packs there and put in three more pitches, making a nasty traverse left on bad snow clinging to steep rock.

September 23 dawned clear and windless—the one great day in our last twenty-six. Art and Rick were off at first light. Way below, at base camp, the other three of us tried to follow their progress with a monocular. We would see them silhouetted against the skyline for half an hour; then they would blend into the rock and snow and we would lose track of them for another hour.

What we would only later learn is that Rick and Art had dropped part of the stove the night before as they sat huddled on the ledge, trying to cook dinner on their laps. This meant that they were unable to melt snow, let alone prepare oatmeal or glop. In the end, they went forty hours straight without water, sixty-four without a hot meal.

The day was too perfect to dawdle, however. They climbed without a pause, tackling wildly exposed pitches on a skin of snow barely adhering to steep slabs. It was hard to hammer in pitons anywhere, so they could not afford to fall. At last they gained the summit ridge and marched toward the highest point.

Rick said later that the climbing was so unnerving that if it had been up to him, he would probably have retreated. Art had no such qualms. At the zenith of his short-lived mountaineering genius, he drove his partner onward, barking out peals of joy at the beauty of the frozen world stretching in all directions. The summit itself—a forty-foot block that overhung all but one of its sides—nearly stopped them, but Art swarmed to the top, then belayed Rick up.

It was 4:30 P.M., only two hours before dark. They accomplished the treacherous descent to the bivouac ledge partly by headlamp. The next day, as another storm crept in, the three of us who had waited below climbed up the Passage to help Art and Rick down. We met them near the top of the couloir, exhausted and desperately dehydrated, but as happy as drunken lords.

We had enough time left to attempt another major climb, Peak 8520 just north of Kichatna Spire, but four days of wretched weather kept us from even setting foot on its lower slopes. At last, during the first week of October, we hiked forty-five miles on our roundabout loop out to a hunting lodge at Rainy Pass. Along the way, we traversed the lengths of three glaciers no one had ever before set foot on, passing beneath the sheer, iced-up walls of a dozen peaks whose first ascents would preoccupy some of the world's best mountaineers during the next twenty years. It was too cold to think of climbing anything, but the October Traverse lingers on in my memory as an utterly charmed week of exploration through one of the most convoluted wildernesses in North America. Once off the last glacier, we staggered, soaked to the bone, through alder and willow thickets, then forded two rivers that had nearly drowned previous explorers. Late on the afternoon of October 6, with all five of us on the verge of hypothermia, we stepped onto the porch of the lodge, to be greeted by a band of very startled big-game hunters from Germany who had spent the last week cursing the weather and the scarcity of Dall sheep and grizzly bear to shoot at. Ten minutes later, in dry, borrowed clothes, we stood barefoot on a bearskin rug before a roaring indoor fire, drinking the owner's excellent Scotch.

The next morning, in my last diary entry, I summed up my mixed feelings: "A good expedition, a successful one, and, for the most part, pleasant. Not an ordeal. . . . We never became a tight-knit group, but we remained friends." Thirty-eight years later, in the rosy glow of nostalgia, I remember the Kichatna Spires as a far better trip than that. There, we had been genuine pioneers, and in thirty-five days, the only close call any of us had suffered was Rick's and my avalanche. Perhaps it was possible to do great climbs without taunting the Furies as we had on Deborah and Huntington.

Starting in the late 1980s, the vogue of the Seven Summits took hold among a certain coterie of climbers—the effort by a single alpinist to reach the highest point on all seven continents. And it did not take long for purists to voice a chorus of disdain, for while Everest and McKinley and the Vinson Massif in Antarctica are genuine mountaineering challenges, Kilimanjaro in Africa is a mere walk-up, and Aconcagua in South America not much more than one.

As part of this backlash, in 2003 Climbing magazine (one of the two hard-core American journals of our pastime) published a special issue called "The Real Seven Summits." The magazine's panel of experts spent months determining not the highest peak in each continent, but the hardest—that is, the hardest to ascend by its easiest route. For more than three decades, I had been unable to dislodge that pang of regret that I hadn't been along with Art and Rick on their brave trek to the summit. But now, reading that Climbing had deemed Kichatna Spire the most difficult peak in North America, I felt a burst of pride that I fully expect will last through the remainder of my days. It was music to my ears to read the encomium offered us by one of the experts, a superb mountaineer who made the peak's second ascent (by a different route) thirteen years after our climb. "The 1966 route on Kichatna is a full-on Grade VI," the man was quoted as saying, "a long and treacherous ridge on top of a big wall that took a strong team almost a month to climb. Kichatna Spire is definitely North America's hardest."

The best thing about returning to Denver that October was not the chance to plunge back into Spenser and Milton. It was seeing Sharon again. That year, we rented separate apartments, but we spent virtually every night together. Soon we were acknowledged around the English Department to be a steady couple. And to our relief, the stalker seemed to have left.

Sharon had enlisted for a first year of graduate school, so we shared a class or two, but she was uncertain about her future. Innately restless, having never been abroad, she toyed with the idea of joining the Peace Corps.

Thanks to the Spires, I had settled into a yearly pattern that, however neurotic at the core, would serve for me as a stabilizing gyro-scope through most of the next decade. Serious about school, with no HMC gang to tempt me into weekends at the Gunks or Cathedral, I did relatively little climbing during the fall and spring terms. But I lived for the next summer's expedition. I found that, with a quick June trip to lesser mountains such as the Wind Rivers or the Buga-boos, I could quickly get back into shape for another campaign among the great ranges. I was a mountaineer first and foremost, not a rock climber. Some of my friends—as Matt Hale would do at Seneca Rock a few years later—bent their best efforts toward putting up the hardest new one- and two-pitch climbs at local crags. I had neither the interest nor the aptitude for such gymnastics. What spoke to my soul was the lure of a northern wilderness, of virgin mountains in unex-plored ranges.

The school year, to be sure, took its toll. Every clear day in Denver, as I stared west at the Front Range, its crest dusted with new snow from Pikes Peak in the south to Longs Peak in the north, I felt a wild longing to be clambering past timberline, my steps bringing some distant summit near. Although Vanguard Press accepted my first book that winter, I did not yet really think of myself as a writer. Grad school, as I wrote without intentional irony in a contributor's note for the South Dakota Review, was what I did in the off-season. A few years later, Sharon would point out that I seemed to carry a constant, hectic impatience with me wherever I went, from September through May. Only in summer, in the mountains, did I truly relax.

I would have liked, in some fashion, to share my passion with Sharon. In those days, very few women climbed anywhere in the country. During four HMC years only one Cliffie (as we called Rad-cliffe women, who, though they shared all our classes, were not yet officially deemed Harvard students) went on our climbing trips, and because of Henry Hall's conservatism, she was not allowed to join the club.

In May or June of 1967, I took Sharon on a hike in the Indian Peaks of the Front Range. As our objective, I had chosen Arikaree Peak, an easy 13,000-er, a true talus heap. Sharon did fine until we took a rest break at 12,500 feet. For the first time, she looked around her, instead of concentrating on the uneven ground in front of her boots. A sudden wave of agoraphobia seized her, a panic that she could barely subdue. With much coaxing on my part, we made the summit, but for Sharon those last 500 feet were an ordeal, as she scuttled along, almost on hands and knees.

In subsequent years, she tamed her agoraphobia, but though she eventually did some easy technical routes on "real" mountains (not talus heaps), Sharon never reached the state of alpine equanimity in which good climbers bask. And I never quite got over my disappointment at that fact.

In the winter of 1966–67, it did not take me long to hatch a scheme for the next summer. From high on Kichatna Spire, I had glimpsed a proud peak far to the southwest, standing shoulders above all its neighbors. A little map research revealed it to be North Buttress, at 9,828 feet nearly a thousand feet higher than Kichatna Spire. Named by some soulless U.S. Geological Survey hand, who had seen it from afar in 1958, the peak soared an astounding 7,500 feet above the glacier that flowed beneath it on the west.

The maps further revealed that the mountains stretching south and west from North Buttress looked a lot like the Spires. If they were ever so slightly less compact or steep (and we know today that no other range in the continent is as consistently steep as the Kichatnas), this range was more extensive. And to my wonder and delight, none of the other peaks was named, except a prominent companion summit, labeled by the same surveyor (with bureaucratic logic) South Buttress. No peak within forty miles of North Buttress in any direction had ever been climbed, or, as far as I could tell, even attempted. The range itself, spiraling out from the hub of North and South Buttress, was unnamed!

Here, I thought greedily, lay one of the last challenges of its kind in North America—difficult first ascents of unnamed peaks in an unnamed range, weeks of prowling across terrain that no humans had ever explored. By January, I had decided. The only trick was to scare up a team.

I wrote Art Davidson, chortling over my find. It looked like the best approach would be to land a plane near the head of the biggest glacier, a ten-mile-long ice stream above whose terminus North Buttress towered. "The finest-looking peak," I wrote Art, staring in a trance at the contour lines on the map, "spreads these perfect ridges over the head of the glacier, just like the wings of an angel."

"Does the Angel have a reasonable route?" Art wrote back, thereby naming our first peak before we even saw it. The Angel, though 600 feet lower than North Buttress, proved far more handsome, and turned out to be made of clean granite, while North Buttress, uniquely in the range, was composed almost entirely of loose black schist of the sort Don and I had struggled with on Deborah. From our first day on the glacier in 1967, we made the Angel our prime objective.

In the frenzied midst of preparing for winter McKinley, Art nonetheless signed on the dotted line for the upcoming summer. In subsequent weeks, I talked Rick Millikan and Matt Hale into joining us, promising them good weather on the (as it turned out, specious) pretext that mountains on the northwest edge of the Alaska Range were sheltered from the storms that brewed over the Gulf of Alaska and grew nastier as they drifted north. Eventually two other HMCers came aboard—Rick's older and less ambitious brother, George, and Ned Fetcher, who had been a junior when Matt, as president, had supervised the relatively weak gang that made up the club in 1965–66. During the last year and a half, Ned had radically improved.

Our six-man team—my largest since McKinley in 1963—would also amount to one of the strongest I ever organized in Alaska. Collectively, we had something like fifteen previous expeditions under our belts. And in the end, we would need every ounce of our strength and experience just to survive in the unnamed range.

Despite my happiness with Sharon, the fanaticism that had carried me to Deborah and Huntington was surging back into my veins. I could not wait for classes to end so that I could head off to Alaska. The pall of Ed's death, which had still hung over me, however unconsciously, in the Spires, had faded. For about a year after my visit to Upper Darby, I had kept up a desultory correspondence with Mr.

Bernd. Most of his short notes had to do with insurance companies that were balking, because Ed's body had never been found, at paying off the meager policies his parents had taken out on their son. How could I prove to their satisfaction, Mr. Bernd wrote me plaintively and miserably, that Ed had really died on Mount Huntington?

During the first days in the Spires, afloat in my ambivalence, I had finally framed in words what I would come to think of as the critical question about mountaineering—and framed that question in doubt, rather than affirmation: "I am not sure always if the risk is worth it." By the spring of 1967, I was once again as sure as I had been before Huntington. No matter what might go wrong, climbing was so glorious an enterprise that it was worth the risk.

As token of my fanaticism, I wanted to spend more time in this unknown range than we had spent on Deborah or Huntington. In the end, three of us would live on the ten-mile-long glacier for fifty-two days, the longest span of all my expeditions. The plan was for Matt, Ned, and me to fly in three weeks before the other trio, mainly to make a reconnaissance of the peaks we might later hope to climb.

At 3:30 in the morning of July 11, I took off from Anchorage in a Super Cub, with a load of gear piled all around me. The pilot was Jim Cassady, a young, relatively green aviator Eric Barnes had taken on as his partner. As we flew west past Chakachamna Lake and the big dormant volcano of Mount Spurr, then glided over a labyrinth of peaks neither he nor I had ever seen before, I realized that the pilot was not only nervous, he was almost lost. I had studied the maps carefully, so now I navigated.

Don Sheldon and Eric Barnes, the two pilots I had flown with before, had exuded calm self-confidence. Cassady's apprehension, which emerged in a babbling commentary on the fierceness of the ranges we soared past, was disconcerting. I realized that he might even refuse to land on the ten-mile glacier, the logistical crux of all our plans.

But at last we were coasting at 10,000 feet, just south of North Buttress. "There it is!" I crowed, as the glacier came in sight. For the first time, I saw the Angel, spreading its granite wings just as it had on the map. "As close to the head as you can manage," I exhorted Cassady. He made two slow loops, losing altitude, as he peered anxiously out the side window. There was plenty of snow, no evident crevasses. The landing, I thought, should be a piece of cake.

Cassady straightened out the Super Cub and came in for touchdown. He made a bumpy landing, then gunned the plane toward the head of the glacier. I hopped out and started pulling gear from the fuselage. "Wow!" exclaimed Cassady. "What a place!"

He was not back with Ned for another nine hours. Exhausted after packing supplies all night, I spread out my Ensolite pad on the snow and fell asleep in the sun. When I woke up suddenly, an hour or two later, it was with as profound a sense of disorientation as I had ever known. The silence was oppressive. The surging granite walls on all sides seemed threatening, not beautiful. Where was Cassady? What if he couldn't find the glacier on his second flight? Ned, who had played almost no part in the planning, wouldn't be able to help.

I realized that I was stuck in the most remote place I had ever been. The nearest outpost of civilization was seventy miles away to the north—Farewell, a mere shack or two and a landing strip. The hike out, if we had to make it, would verge on the impossible, with two big rivers in the way that might be too deep and swift to ford. Assailed by a strange despair, I stared at the alien rock and snow around me. Because of possible hidden crevasses, I could not afford even to get up and walk around. I was stranded on my Ensolite pad, with only a meager pile of gear as company.

By late afternoon, however, Cassady had made two more landings to bring in Ned and Matt, and the gloomy funk of my solitary vigil abruptly evaporated. We got our tents pitched, the gear stacked in a tidy cache, and set out to explore.

It had been a winter of heavy snowfall, and now, in the heat of July, avalanches were coming down everywhere, just as they had during our first days on the Tokositna Glacier under Huntington. It was not even safe to climb the easy snow slope to the col south of the Angel, from which the beautiful knife-edged ridge that we had chosen for our route rose 2,500 feet to the pointed summit.

As compensation for this temporary setback, on the third day I talked Matt and Ned into starting up a steep rock wall on another nearby peak. We did not expect to climb the whole of this 2,000-foot precipice, which would have been a major undertaking, but just to go a few pitches up and check out the quality of the rock. And here, we found at once, the granite was looser and crumblier than we had hoped—much looser than anything in the Kichatna Spires. This discovery boded ill for our ambitions. (It would be weeks before we laid hands on the anomalously perfect rock of the Angel.)

Matt was in the process of leading the second pitch when we heard a distant rumbling noise. I craned my neck to look up, and saw a terrifying sight. The sky directly above us was dark with debris, tons of granite blocks falling from more than 1,000 feet above. (The warm sun had probably set loose an avalanche on the summit snowfield, which, as it hit the top of the cliff, pried loose the poorly bonded stones.)

"Rock!" I screamed, involuntarily folding my right arm over my head. Matt, fifty feet to our left, was sheltered by a small overhanging, but Ned and I, standing side-by-side on the belay ledge, had nowhere to hide. We shrank as tight as we could to the wall and waited for the impact.

Rocks falling through the air make an angry whirring noise—a sound that every climber dreads in his guts. Now boulders smashed on our ledge only a few feet away, bursting like bombs, exuding an acrid gunpowder smell. I plastered myself as flat as I could against the cliff. Both Ned and I were struck by small, harmless pieces of rock. By sheer luck, all the big stones missed us.

Once the fusillade ended, Ned and I scrambled unbelayed over to Matt's perch, where he was frantically pounding in pitons for a rappel. One by one, we zipped down the rope, even as more debris came flying out of the sky, like the aftershocks of an earthquake. Once back on the glacier, we literally ran down the approach slope until we were out of range of the bombardment. Panting, I cursed, "Man, that was stupid!" All three of us stared up at the evil wall.

The next day, still in sunny weather, we started the Butterfly Traverse. I had planned this grand reconnaissance of the unknown range months before, perusing the maps in Denver. We would descend the ten-mile glacier at whose head we had established base camp, round the corner beneath North Buttress, head up the braided channels of the Big River, angle off south to cross two passes between three small glaciers, round another lowland corner at the head of the Swift Fork valley, then close the forty-mile loop by climbing back to the head of our base camp glacier. The only question mark, it seemed, was that 1,000-foot ascent to the col at the head of the main glacier, only a mile from camp. On July 12, however, Matt and I had roped up and climbed seven pitches down that precipice, finding it easier than we expected. Even with heavy packs, we expected to be able to get up it at the end of the traverse.

Among the paraphernalia in our fifty-five-pound loads, we carried a six-foot-long butterfly net. From the American Alpine Club, I had wangled a research grant (all of $150, I believe), by promising to collect bugs blown in storms up onto the glaciers—in particular, butterflies, the passion of the Fairbanks entomologist whose program we were carrying out. As we headed down the glacier on July 14, we expected a strenuous lark. In our darkest premonitions, we would never have foreseen the struggle for survival that would ensue.

For three days, things went according to plan. The stupendous tower of North Buttress loomed over us on the right, inspiring no urges to climb it—"a huge and ugly agglomeration of schist, waterfalls, and moss," I described it in my diary. On the banks of the Big River, surging channels forced us up into seemingly limitless thickets of alder—the worst bushwhacking in Alaska, as Don and I had learned coming out from Deborah. With our packs snagging on every limb, crawling and squirming through root tangles, we covered only one mile in three and a half hours of dogged toil. In the lowlands, there were fresh grizzly tracks everywhere. On two nights, we camped next to big boulders up which we thought, in a pinch, we could scramble even barefoot, if a bear decided to investigate our belongings.

On the fourth day, it started to rain and blow—nasty, chilling rain at about 35 degrees Fahrenheit. For three straight days, it did not let up for a single hour. The gear available in 1967, crafted for cold, high mountains, was almost useless in these conditions. Gore-Tex had yet to be invented, as did fiberfill sleeping bags. Our outer jackets were far from waterproof, our tent flies mere sheets of plastic. Our down jackets were soon soaked through, and eventually our down sleeping bags as well.

By now we had collected about eight insects, including two butterflies. Eventually, rain washed the labels off the pill bottles we stored our catches in. The American Alpine Club's research grant, I am ashamed to say, did nothing to advance alpine entomology.

To save weight, I had gone super-light, leaving my sleeping bag at base camp, counting on my down jacket and a thin half-bag covering my waist and legs for nocturnal comfort. The fourth night, I could not sleep at all. At 2:00 A.M., I was shivering inside my cocoon of soggy down. I sat up and lit the stove to try to get warm, but it made only a small difference. I yelled my complaints to Matt and Ned, in the other tent. They were beginning to feel hypothermic as well. We decided the only remedy was to pack up and push on, counting on exertion to warm our bodies.

The insidious wind and rain continued through the next two days. In a lowland camp, the willows were so soaked we couldn't get a campfire started. We were now just a mile or two short of the 1,000-foot cliff that separated us from base camp. If we couldn't ascend that cliff, we would have to backtrack almost forty miles, reversing the loop of the Butterfly Traverse, but I doubted we would make it before succumbing to hypothermia.

At 1:00 P.M. on July 19, we started up the cliff. Since Matt was in better technical shape than Ned or I, we gave him a lighter pack and asked him to lead all the pitches. Coming second, I belayed Matt with one hand and one rope, Ned with the other at the same time. With our gear soaked through, Ned and I were probably carrying seventy pounds apiece, a hideous burden on easy technical ground in dry conditions, a nightmare now. As we gained altitude, the rain turned to sleety snow, and small avalanches spilled around us. To make matters worse, a blind fog had swallowed the mountain, making route-finding tricky. As I later wrote in my diary, "I could literally wring pints of water out of my down jacket, and feel my toes floating in water. . . . Once our chests and backs got wet, we shivered violently, and I began to feel the beginning of a desperation."

Ned seemed out of it, dopey and sluggish, signs of advancing hypothermia. Sometimes I simply hauled him bodily with the rope, rather than belaying. If one of us slipped, I thought, and did nothing more than sprain an ankle, the others would have to leave him behind.

Matt climbed with utter brilliance, leading ten pitches one after the other. We barely spoke, limiting our communication to belay signals shouted over the wind. At last, we topped out on the col. My fingers were so clumsy that I found it almost impossible to coil the ropes. We set out for base camp at a pace that was almost a jog, yet not even that dash could warm our bodies. We found our once tidy gear cache slumped in the snow, a pitiful collection of soggy cardboard boxes, food spilling out of them. With the last of our energy, we got the tents pitched, ourselves inside, what few dry clothes we had left in camp on to replace our soaking outfits, and the stoves going. Gradually the shivering subsided.

To this day, the Butterfly Traverse remains by far the closest brush I have had with death by hypothermia. It was, I think in retrospect, about as close as you can come and still pull out of it with your own unaided efforts, as opposed to those of a rescue team.

At base camp, the storm raged on unabated. With a dry sleeping bag to replace my soaked half-bag, I slept in relative comfort, but for several days Matt and Ned, sharing a single tent, barely held their own. Ned spent much of the time sitting up, claiming that that position allowed less contact with his wet clothes; he also fired up the stove to warm the tent and cook midnight soups. Matt devised a soggy straitjacket in which to sleep. Having donned his only pair of dry socks, he inserted each foot in a plastic bag, then pulled his slimy rucksack over his legs. A scrap of Ensolite pad served as midriff insulation. Last, he stuffed his body into his all but useless sleeping bag, then covered himself with his dish rag of a down jacket. The arrangement was so cramped that he couldn't even turn over, but he claimed it was the only way he could come close to getting warm. Matt started to have a recurring dream, in which he abandoned base camp and headed down our glacier, just as we had on the first day of the Butterfly Traverse. On the gravel bar below the terminus, he strode toward a solid log cabin. He could smell smoke from the fire roaring in the stove inside. But just as he touched the door handle, the cabin vanished and he woke up.

On August 2, Cassady flew the rest of our team in. By that date, after twenty-three days in the range, Matt, Ned, and I had managed to climb only two distinctly minor peaks, arriving on the summit of the second in whiteout and heavy drizzle. The advent of Rick and George Millikan and Art Davidson felt like the canonic scene in a 1950s western, when the beleaguered platoon, about to be wiped out by Comanches or Apaches, hears the cavalry bugle and sees a fresh regiment come galloping over a nearby ridge.

From our new partners we learned sobering news. During the same days that we had stumbled through the Butterfly Traverse, a large party had been trapped in a storm high on Mount McKinley, 140 miles to the northeast. In the end, seven climbers had frozen to death—still the worst disaster in the mountain's history.

Only four months earlier, Art and two companions had survived a six-day storm in an open bivouac at 18,000 feet on McKinley. On that expedition he had lost thirty-five pounds; afterward, he was confined to a wheelchair for eight weeks and to crutches for another six. In Minus 148°, Art would later describe what could only ironically be called his recuperation:

> To observe how the body would heal the frostbite naturally, the doctors left the blackened skin and flesh in place to see what would happen. After 14 weeks the decaying parts of my feet were beginning to smell pretty bad. So late one night, I took out a razor blade, sterilized it over a match and cut off the dead and rotting pieces. After this bit of midnight surgery, the doctors relented and finished up the operation.

In August 1967, the last thing Art needed, both physically and psychologically, was to be back on an Alaskan glacier. Such was his commitment to Rick and me, born in the Kichatna Spires, and to his love of climbing, that he insisted on joining us in this unexplored range, although he planned only a two-week stay, with Cassady picking him up a week or so before he flew the rest of us out.

At first, Art's primary doctor had forbidden him to go back into the mountains so soon after his tribulation, but he was no match for Art's will. Finally the physician consented, as long as Art guaranteed that he would keep his feet dry. To that end, he had brought along a special pair of coated overboots. They proved as worthless as the rest of our footgear. Within days, Art's feet were soaked day and night, just as ours were—especially after he insisted on joining us in many a round of a vicious base camp game of my invention, called Hole Ball—a cross between lacrosse and touch football, with a real leather football as missile (heavy as a rock once it got soaked like our boots) and two pits dug in the slushy glacier as goals. By the end of the trip, all of us but me were suffering from a painful alpine version of trench foot, which eventually took months to heal.

The weather was no better in August than it had been in July. For ten days, from August 11 to 20, we were imprisoned near base camp by a virtually nonstop storm. Some of the most violent winds any of us had ever endured flattened our tents and blew cooking pots and even hard hats as far as a mile down-glacier. I had never before experienced (and never would again) conditions in which our very survival was threatened at base camp, as opposed to high on some route.

Poor Art! As the winds shrieked through the high notches, plastering the granite walls with rime ice, he would stagger around camp in his saturated overboots, staring at the sky and muttering, "God, Dave, this is a foreboding place!" During his stay in the range, Art never reached a single summit. And that expedition, his sixth in the last seventeen months, would be the last he ever went on.

In camp, along with potboiler novels and William Shirer's history of the Third Reich (a mammoth paperback we tore into pieces so that

four of us could read it at once), I was browsing through the Bible—
not in search of divine enlightenment but as part of my grad school
education in literature. The book that vividly matched the gloom and
fury of our surroundings was of course Revelation, and I could not
help reading out loud St. John the Divine's evocations of the angel of
the bottomless pit or the sea of glass mingled with fire, nor sharing
with my teammates his promises of "a woman clothed with the sun"
and "silence in heaven about the space of half an hour."

As the first explorers of this remote range, we knew that we had
earned the right to name it. It was George Millikan, in response to my
biblical recitations, who suggested calling the place the Revelation
Mountains. (So the range is now officially named.) We were already
referring to our prime objective as the Angel; now, giddy with logo-
logical hubris, we bestowed on the more fearsome peaks bordering
our glacier such names as the Four Horsemen, Apocalypse, and Golgotha. (The names have stuck, at least among climbers. Far worse cog-
nomens have been affixed to far more prominent mountains in the
Great North, including McKinley, named for a president who never
went near Alaska nor showed any interest in the territory, and Foraker,
named for an Ohio senator whose career ended in disgrace after he
took bribes from Standard Oil.)

During the odd decent day before and after the ten-day storm, we
launched our effort on the south ridge of the Angel. Elsewhere in the
range we had found indifferent rock, as crumbly as brown sugar at its
worst, but the Angel was made of the kind of clean, sharp-cut granite
climbers dream of. The south ridge, though immensely complicated,
festooned with slabs, notches, and knife-edged arêtes, proved a garden of alpine delights. "You can't believe it," Rick said, as he got back
to camp after our first serious probe of the route. "Everything just
works out."

By 1967, the bolder climbers in Alaska and the Andes (though not
yet in the Himalaya) were starting to apply the tactics of alpine-style
climbing to expeditionary mountains. On the Angel, for the first time,
we ourselves embraced this vogue. On Huntington two years before,
we had fixed lines tediously over virtually every pitch, ferried heavy

loads, and established tent camps to support our final assault. Now, on the Angel, we fixed only a few ropes on pitches otherwise perilous to reverse (a slanting slab covered with a skin of ice over a 2,000-foot drop, a thirty-foot rappel on the way up required to circumvent a wild pinnacle), planned to bivouac rather than sleep in tents, and ferried no depots of supplies. Ideally, the peak could be conquered alpine-style in one two- or three-day push in good weather. At the same time, given the medieval state of our clothing and sleeping bags, getting caught in a storm high on the mountain could mean a true life-or-death struggle.

Between August 3 and August 25, climbing in pairs and trios, we made five separate alpine-style forays on the south ridge of the Angel. Every one was defeated by bad weather. The bravest push was performed by Rick and George, those stalwart grandsons of Mallory, who, climbing fast, not even bothering to rope up on the easier but frightfully exposed pitches, reached a level platform at 7,900 feet, only 1,300 feet below the summit, where they pitched our bivouac tent—a nylon sack supported with a single low arc of tentpole. The rain came in in the night and turned to snow before dawn. After a sleepless night, the brothers Millikan fought a grim battle just to get down to base camp. The rock, soaked by the storm, turned so treacherous that in places Rick and George had to rappel nearly horizontal pitches.

It was during the ten-day storm after August 10 that our morale—not to mention our standard of living—reached its nadir. Weeks of wind and lashing rain had eaten away the glacier. We found to our alarm that the bare ice of permanent glacier—many feet below our tents when we had first pitched them on July 11—was now only a few inches underneath. Among other things, this development meant that the runway for Cassady's landings had radically shortened. We built an igloo, but the wind tore holes in it faster than we could patch them. Finally, in an arduous half-day effort, we moved base camp 100 feet higher on the glacier, tucked under the frowning brow of Golgotha, the most forbidding of all the Revelation peaks.

By August 16, everything we owned was soaked through. The fierce winds blew horizontal rain underneath our tent flies, drilling a fine spray through the ripstop nylon. We joked about our predicament, but simply getting through each tent- and igloo-bound day was a marathon. Though he never complained, Art was sick at heart about the state of his feet. An entry from my diary on the 16th captures the misery:

> Matt and George . . . really had a night of it. Their tent collapsed, they got wet, they spilled a pot of soup into their [sleeping] bags. Matt ran out with only his boots on his bare feet and ran over toward the rocks to look for something to hold the tent down, but his feet got too cold and he stopped short of the ice. Finally, the Primus [stove] seemed to stop working. George spent another miserable night, and emerged in the morning in worse spirits than he'd been in the whole trip. He was beginning to talk about survival and saying to hell with the trip.

Before the expedition, perusing the maps, I had counted thirty-four 8,000-foot peaks and twelve 9,000-foot peaks in what we would name the Revelation Range (including the easterly cirques we had blindly reconnoitered during the Butterfly Traverse). They culminated in 9,828-foot North Buttress, which, despite its modest elevation in absolute terms, was, I reckoned, higher than any peak so far west in the Western Hemisphere.

By August 20, when the long storm at last let up, we had climbed not a single 8,000-er or 9,000-er—even though Matt, Ned, and I had now spent forty-three days in the range. We had seven summits under our belt, none of them a major climb, the highest a mere 7,800 feet. Topping out on the Angel would make the expedition an unqualified success, but after five setbacks, we had begun to despair of our chances on that magnificent peak.

Cassady was due in to pick up Art on August 15. It was no surprise that he had not tried to fly through the worst of the long storm, but as day after day passed without our hearing the blissful buzz of the Super Cub, we grew puzzled, and Art—by now fed up with the Revelations, and frantic to get out—started cursing our tardy pilot. If the plane never came, we started musing, only half in jest, we would have to launch that perhaps impossible seventy-mile hike out to Farewell.

Our ultimate fly-out date had been fixed as August 30. With only nine days left in the expedition, I was eager to bag at least one major summit. On the 21st, in improving weather, Matt and I packed up four days' gear and food and hiked down-glacier toward the next tributary ice stream to the north, above which junction soared a handsome but apparently moderate 9,000-er, made mostly of snow and ice rather than rock. After camping at its foot, the two of us efficiently solved the peak's defenses in a glorious but exhausting nine-hour push. Climbing 4,700 feet from base to summit, we needed to rope up for only a few ice pitches, a few rope-lengths on mixed rock and ice, and a punch through the summit cornice. The only disappointment was that we climbed all day in whiteout, and got a view of nothing from the summit. We named the peak Patmos, after the island to which St. John was exiled and where he received his Revelation.

At 9:30 A.M. on the 22nd, as we toiled up the lower slopes on Patmos, we had heard at last the welcome drone of Cassady's plane— heard him land, then take off an hour and a half later. Because of the whiteout, we never saw the Super Cub, but it was reassuring to know that our pilot had come through, and that Art was finally delivered from alpine purgatory back to his erratic recuperation. It was only when Matt and I trudged back to base camp on August 24 that we got the shocking news.

On August 15, the day scheduled for Art's pickup, Cassady, knowing he could never get in to the Revelations, had taken a hunter up on a short flight over the western Chugach Range. Even there the weather was marginal. Flying low, as his client tried to spot Dall sheep, Cassady was caught in a sudden downdraft. The plane crashed, killing both pilot and hunter.

In those days, bush fliers kept their business mostly in their heads. Eric Barnes, Cassady's senior partner, who had flown us in to the Kichatnas the year before, knew only that we were somewhere in the far southwestern Alaska Range. He had no idea even of when we were supposed to fly out.

On a wall map of Alaska in the office, Barnes found a single tiny
X penned by Cassady. Climbing into a borrowed plane he had never
flown before, Barnes set out on August 22, the first flyable day, to look
for us. Navigating cannily on his solo flight, he found our glacier. The
four guys at base camp started scampering up and down the runway
we had stomped out, but Barnes thought the landing strip offered
such a short stretch of snow-covered glacier between bare ice and the
Golgotha headwall that he would never have dared touch down without those human markers to give the place scale (and, though he was
too modest to say so, without knowing full well the desperate alternative to flying out such a failure would force upon the six of us). On
takeoff with Art, Barnes barely got airborne before hitting bare ice,
which would have torn his ski-wheels apart and possibly caused a
crash.

Back on July 11, coming in on the first flight, I had been mildly
irked by Cassady's nervous anxiety as he prepared for the toughest
landing of his short career. Now I felt a guilty sorrow, knowing that,
still in his twenties, the game aviator had etched his name in the long
and dolorous roster of martyrs to the parlous economics of bush flying in Alaska. Today, thirty-seven years later, I doubt that there are
many men within the close-knit fraternity of northern pilots who
remember Jim Cassady, or even recognize the name.

During those last days in the Revelations, I pondered the lessons
of what would turn out to be the longest expedition I would ever go
on. There was no getting around the nonstop drudgery of our ordeal
by rain, sleet, snow, and wind. Of the six of us, in fact, only I would
ever again go on an expedition to the greater ranges. Yet even as we
had shivered inside our disintegrating igloo, we had mocked our
plight by regaling each other with baroque fancies and hoary anec-
dotes. I have never laughed so much on an expedition, and seldom in
my life have I laughed as hard—rolling on the igloo floor, crying for
relief, pounding my fists on the ice, along with my cronies—while
George, an absentminded ornithologist in the making, told with a
straight face the saga of forgetfully locking his professor at Duke
inside a walk-in bird cage.

The six of us formed the most congenial gang with whom I would ever go into the mountains. During fifty-two days (thirty for Rick and George, twenty-one for Art), we never had a real argument, and scarcely even a sharp word for the sluggard who failed to do his share of the dirty dishes. Of all the pleasures of mountaineering, friendship of this sort is one of the keenest.

At the same time, the illusion I had begun to cherish after the Kichatnas, that one could climb hard with minimal risk in the great ranges, was thoroughly debunked in the Revelations. Besides the two truly close calls Matt, Ned, and I had undergone—the bombardment by tons of falling rock on the third day of the expedition, the reckless flirtation with hypothermia at the end of the Butterfly Traverse—we had suffered other calls not quite so close. Near the top of a 2,500-foot ice-and-snow couloir that we hoped would lead to the summit of a mountain we called Dike Peak, Matt and I were jolted to our senses when the whole huge gully uttered several sharp reports and shifted under our feet—a glacial gesture just preliminary to collapsing. We dashed back down the couloir as fast as we could. On another day, five of us went on an exploratory hike, leaving Ned contentedly reading a book in his tent at base camp. In the afternoon, he heard a sudden explosion. Severely myopic, Ned scrabbled unsuccessfully for his glasses, poked his head out of the tent, and saw a white blur heading straight for him from above to the south. A huge sérac had broken off the shoulder of Golgotha, launching a major avalanche. We thought the new location to which we had shifted base camp was safe from all such cascades, but now that proposition seemed in doubt. Ned got one boot on and was starting to run for it when the slide, full of house-sized ice blocks, plowed to a stop only eighty yards short of camp. The usual avalanche-driven wind cloud bowed the tents and pelted Ned with its mini-hurricane of spindrift before the world returned to normal.

Throughout the history of alpinism, hard men have earnestly concocted rationalizations by which they believe they can outsmart the mountains. The inescapable fact is, however, that in the remote ranges there is no avoiding what climbers dryly call objective danger—avalanches, rock fall, storms, hidden crevasses, and the like, the booby traps laid by the mountain gods that we mortal boobies are helpless to control.

We had given up on the Angel. But now, for the first time since the initial days of the expedition, the weather turned good and held. On August 27, Rick, George, and Ned set off down-glacier to try to bag South Buttress, another 9,000-er (in fact the fourth-highest peak in the range), on which Matt and I had scouted a reasonable route a week before. The next day they succeeded in reaching the summit after an effort comparable to Matt's and mine on Patmos.

For Matt and me, there remained only a salvage operation: a last jaunt up the south ridge of the Angel to retrieve the gear we had left on the route, principally the bivvy tent at 7,900 feet and as many pitons as we could extract on the way down. Having slept poorly, I had to be cajoled out of bed on the morning of the 28th by Matt, who had woken to the finest day of our whole expedition. We were off at 7:30 in the morning.

On this dry, windless, halcyon day, having climbed most of the pitches before in far worse conditions, we flew up the route. By mid-morning we were cavorting in shirtsleeves, traveling continuously or unroped on most of the pitches. It took us only four hours to reach the bivvy tent at Rick's and George's high point—a stretch of intricate climbing that had demanded a full day from our colleagues on August 8. We decided to push on a little farther, seduced by the lure of untrodden ground. We climbed seven or eight more rope lengths on moderate terrain. By mid-afternoon we had reached the foot of a steep snow ramp that bisected a pair of cliffs. Once up that, we thought, and only a sharp, possibly corniced ridge would stand between us and the summit, a mere 700 feet above.

We stopped to confer. The damning fact was that we had only five pitons, one ice axe, and no crampons between us. Without ice gear, the summit ridge could prove dangerous. By now, in late August, it was pitch dark by 7:00 P.M., and we had brought no headlamps. And yet the weather was perfect. . . .

At last we agreed to turn around and descend. We were back at base camp shortly before dark, after an eleven-hour day. We had cleaned the route admirably, leaving only a few scraps of fixed rope and a few rappel pitons in place.

The Angel was finally climbed only in 1985. The pair of strong young Americans who succeeded eighteen years after our attempt apparently tackled a different route. They were repulsed three times before they claimed the summit. Along the way, as they reported in the *American Alpine Journal*, they encountered "a difficult and poorly protected slab (5.9+)," "nerve-wracking crampon-clad free climbing," and a *gendarme* they named Terror Tower—"a two-pitch horror of vertical loose blocks."

Quite a few times since 1967, Matt and I have reminisced about that moment when we turned back on the Angel. In some cozy pub, after three or four beers, in the safe harbor of retrospect, our conversation goes something like this:

"You know, we probably should have gone for it," I venture.

"Of course we should have gone for it. What's the worst that could have happened? A forced bivouac?"

"Remember those storms, what they took out of us . . ."

The worst that could have happened, to be realistic, is that we could have gotten stuck in another storm, above the bivvy tent—and indeed, on the morning of August 29, the usual rain and wind came back in to smother the Revelations. We could have died of hypothermia in the bivouac, or, in a ragged effort to descend without ice gear, one of us could have slipped and pulled the other off. If we had plunged off the west face, away from base camp, our bodies might lie there still, as unfindable as Ed Bernd's on the Tokositna Glacier.

But from the vantage point of middle-aged nostalgia for meteoric youth, it is hard to congratulate yourself for prudence rather than for boldness. I still think Matt and I made the right decision on August 28, 1967. Yet of all the regrets I have about my years in the mountains, in terms of sheer, simple "what-might-have-been"—even more than the pang of not accompanying Rick and Art to the top of Kichatna Spire— letting the Angel slip through our fingers when we were within 700 feet of the summit on a perfect day still stings the sharpest.

Sharon was waiting for me in Anchorage, having flown up to Alaska on impulse with Rick and George at the beginning of August. It was wonderful to see her again. By now, I knew that I was in love with her: I had even dared admit as much to my diary, albeit in hedged circumlocutions. But for some reason, during my first hour in that sprawling town, Sharon had to run an errand at J.C. Penney, the store where she had worked the previous summer. I went with her. Muzak, shopping announcements, matrons wheeling carts, fluorescent lights, children screaming, piles of unnecessary goodies on sale—suddenly I felt overwhelmed. Dizzy and nauseated, I had to find a chair to sit down in to avoid fainting. After fifty-two days in the Revelations, I was not ready for civilization.

Art had wangled Sharon a semi-invitation to spend the month of August on the homestead of a legendary immigrant family near Homer. The setting was heartbreakingly idyllic, sleek, rolling greenswards looking south over Kachemak Bay. But the ménage was so weird as to be oppressive. The family, who had come over from Switzerland in the early 1950s, the vanguard of a utopian colony the rest of whose members chickened out, had clung to their new Alaskan turf with bitter tenacity. Subsistence was hard in this subarctic wilderness, and it had taken its toll on the whole family. Over the years, they had developed an unspoken code of rules and territories that no outsider could hope to fathom. Sharon had discovered this in her first hours on the homestead. Pausing on the long driveway on the way in, she and the eldest daughter had spent several hours picking ripe, juicy raspberries, filling a generous bowl—which the daughter, in response to a harsh word, had suddenly flung in the face of her mother upon arrival in the homestead kitchen. It turned out that that particular raspberry patch belonged to the matriarch, whose daughters were forbidden to pick from it.

Sharon spent one of the loneliest and most awkward months of her life there, sleeping in the barn, living on Coca-Cola and bread that she ran into town to buy, exchanging stillborn conversations with the homesteaders who came and went without apparent pattern. During that month she read Victorian novels, went for walks on the seashore, and waited for me, trying not to worry, just as she had waited through the previous September while I was in the Kichatna Spires.

In early September, we drove at a leisurely pace down the Alaska Highway in the quaint two-stroke Saab (you poured a pint of oil into the gas tank every time you filled it up) that my father had bequeathed to me my first year at the University of Denver. My head was full of literature, but I was not at all sure I wanted to be back in grad school. Each day as we drove south and the nights grew darker and longer, I felt Alaska slipping away behind me. There was nothing to look forward to but another off-season, another nine months of waiting before the next expedition, so far away in the summer of 1968.

That year I began teaching freshman English, while Sharon worked toward the MA she would earn the following year. But she was restless. Sometime during the first weeks of school, a dilemma emerged. It was not that Sharon presented me with an ultimatum. She simply wanted to know what my long-term intentions were. Had we become a couple? If not, or if not lastingly, she wanted to get on with her life. The Peace Corps still had its appeal.

In one sense, the idea of marriage terrified me. I was only twenty-four, Sharon a year younger. But in another sense, it seemed a logical next step. During the latter weeks of September, I spent many an intense hour trying to concentrate on the path bifurcating ahead of me in the woods. It was so much harder than trying to figure out which mountains to climb the next summer.

In the end, a simple realization pushed me over the edge. I was in love, and I somehow knew that Sharon was a good person. That ought to be enough for a lifetime. And if not—well, it was still worth the risk. We set our wedding date for October 29.

SEVEN

Hostage to Fortune

I APPROACHED OUR WEDDING AS THOUGH IT were a shameful, or at least an embarrassing deed. At my insistence, Sharon and I invited only our siblings and parents: for decades thereafter, certain aunts never quite forgave us. The brief ceremony took place on Bluebell Avenue. We said our vows and cut the cake, I tipped the judge (friend of the family) twenty dollars, and we sped off in the Saab amidst a hail of rice flung by our siblings. We spent our wedding night in a motel in Leadville, just down the Arkansas River from Climax, where I had passed my first five years. On Monday, we hiked near the ghost towns of Vicksburg and Winfield, on a perfect Indian summer day, before returning to our grad school duties.

I had told my freshman English class only that I wouldn't be able to meet with them on Monday. On Wednesday, I began our session with a mumbled apology for delaying our discussion of Faulkner's "The Bear." A clutch of sorority girls in the front seats, however, was not about to let me off so easily. Giggling and whispering, they pierced me with their pretty eyes. The thin gold band that had sprouted on my left third finger had given me away. "We know, Mr. Roberts," the boldest of the girls blurted out. "You got married, didn't you?" The class cheered as I blushed and opened our textbook.

For Sharon, getting married had an altogether different significance. Five years earlier, by becoming the first person in her extended family to go to college, and then by defying her father, who had demanded that she live at home her freshman year, she had set her sights unwaveringly on a world larger than the claustrophobic Denver neighborhoods in which she had grown up. She had first discovered that larger world as a thespian at Abraham Lincoln High School. Playing Anne Frank in the play made from the famous diary, Sharon had glimpsed a wilderness of experience to explore, in much the same fashion as the Dutch teenager hiding in the attic had a decade and a half before. By allying herself with me and my highly educated family, Sharon had instinctively taken the first steps toward that wilderness of unguessed experience.

Yet on the evening of October 28, which we spent apart, she could not sleep, plagued with the conviction that she might die before morning. This had little to do with me, I suspect, and everything to do with the fear that she, like Anne Frank, would never be allowed to escape the attic.

My own chagrin at acknowledging Sharon, and love, and marriage had its roots in the trauma Lisa and I had endured during the winter of 1960–61. Yet I see now that it also had much to do with mountain climbing. Thanks to Harvard and Alaska, I had metamorphosed in half a decade from an insecure teenager into a hard man. Having fantasized since childhood about playing shortstop for the Dodgers or solving Fermat's Last Theorem, I had finally, on the west face of Mount Huntington, made a mark that stood up creditably among the best things being done by my peers worldwide. The dream in which Don Jensen and I had wrapped ourselves at twenty, of a limitless future full of unclimbed mountains up which we might dance on the razor edge between glory and extinction, still held me in thrall.

Love and marriage threatened all that. Intimacy—as I had first glimpsed with Lisa, hiking 13,000-foot talus heaps, while she dragged behind, rested too often, and begged for less ambitious treks—was fraught with the pitfalls that could turn a hard man soft. Because I loved Sharon, I discovered with alarm, I worried about her. If she was a mere half an hour late returning from a trip to the grocery store, I began conjuring up car accidents. And while I was off in the Kichatnas and the Revelations, I knew, Sharon had worried incessantly about my safety. In weak moments on the glacier, I caught myself worrying about Sharon's worrying about me.

Yet during my Harvard years without a girlfriend, dateless virtually every Saturday night, I had been starved for affection, for the bliss of touch, even for the comfort of a woman's arm around my shoulders. All kinds of deprivation pass unnoticed—until whatever it is that one has blithely done without abruptly becomes available. In the musty club room in the basement of Lowell House, as Don and I had plotted with our lists and diagrams against Mount Deborah, I would have said that the last thing I needed was a girlfriend. But since the beginning of the summer of 1966, when we had cohabited in the squalid shack in Spenard, Sharon had become first an exciting, then a necessary part of my life. I could not let the Peace Corps snatch her away.

The challenge was how to blend marriage with mountaineering. Through the fall and winter of 1967–68, I struggled with my dilemma. The quandary was hardly unique to me. Don himself—who had been furious after my Dunster House roommates had once fixed him up with a blind date from Endicott Junior College that he somehow construed as a cruel practical joke—would get married in 1968, to a fellow ascetic and nature lover named Joan Vyvyerberg. When Sharon and I first met them as a couple, they seemed perfect soul mates. Yet as I would come to see, Don's own feelings about climbing after marriage veered from his old fanatic commitment to a sometimes paralyzing ambivalence.

Looking back on four decades of observation of my comrades of the rope, I would say that few serious climbers handle this transition well. Many a hard man who marries ends up wretchedly neglecting wife (and children) in order to stay on the cutting edge. Conversely, many an ambitious climber who, through marriage and/or parenthood, discovers the essential fragility of life ends up backing off from the sterner demands of the great ranges. It would be one thing if such a convert could accept the change with equanimity—could say, in effect, "Okay, I did all that crazy stuff when I was young and out for myself, but now I have responsibilities." Instead, all too often the former hard man rationalizes his defection from what Lionel Terray (hard to the end) called *grand alpinisme*, as he pretends that hunting meteorites in Morocco or hiking among the hill tribes of Bhutan offers all the thrills that he used to find on *direttissimas* in the Karakoram.

(The gender-specific formulation of the above paragraph, historically appropriate to the 1960s, can be revised to apply to today's climbing scene. I know of a number of recent hard women who have treated their husbands and children as badly as the vainest of the alpine tigers of my day. And though one can identify a handful of equal partnerships in the mountains—couples who climb together at the same level—most of them seem to suffer the kinds of cabin fever and petty jealousies that afflict husbands and wives who share an office or a kitchen-tabletop business together.)

Yet another development complicated my life that year. By late 1967, Vanguard Press's publication of *The Mountain of My Fear* was well under way. The *Saturday Evening Post* excerpted the story, paying me the unimaginable fortune of $5,000—ten times my book advance. With that windfall, Sharon and I would finance the next two and a half summers of mountain vacations. Meanwhile, I had started work on an MA thesis. John Williams, the director of the DU writing program, had convinced me that an account of one of my own expeditions need not after all lie beyond the pale of "creative writing." For subject, I turned back to Don's and my forty-two-day ordeal on Mount Deborah. By now under the spartan sway of Williams's own aesthetic—an insistence on prose stripped to the bone—I discarded the metaphysical flights and Faulknerian dithyrambs of my first book in favor of plain, short sentences that tried to tell only what had happened to my best friend and me in the Hayes Range.

Deborah: A Wilderness Narrative was published by Vanguard in 1970. Of my first two books, it remains the one I prefer, though few of my friends or readers seem to agree. The story of a grinding failure, unfurling in a fog of mutual paranoia, cannot after all perhaps compete with the formula of "triumph and tragedy" that Huntington had handed me. Or, as a fellow who would become a close climbing buddy ten years later, and who had read *Deborah* when it was published, told me, "Man, was I glad I didn't go on that expedition."

In 1967, climbing was the most important thing in my life. But wanting to be a writer competed with the advent of Sharon as a close second or third. In those days, there was no way to make a living as a climber in the United States, except as a guide in the Tetons or on Mount Rainier—surefire recipes, we "real climbers" thought, for burnout by mediocre repetition. Having had two books accepted for publication by the age of twenty-five, however, ought to have convinced me that it was possible to make a living as a writer.

For reasons I still do not fully understand, I veered away from the path that thus so clearly lay open before me. I would go ahead and get my Ph.D., I decided, become a professor somewhere, and write in my spare time. Such a regimen should be manageable: I had written *The Mountain of My Fear* in nine days, after all, *Deborah* in less than two months. It would take more than a decade for me to realize how wrong I was about all this. Not until the age of thirty-six would I dare at last to try to become a full-time writer.

In the fall of 1967, a month before our wedding, Sharon had moved into the tiny house, converted from a garage, that I had rented on York Street, in a leafy neighborhood some dozen blocks north of the DU campus. For months and even years thereafter, the novelty of living together as husband and wife would retain its charm. We were playing house together, but for keeps. Around the English Department, we were accepted as a "cute couple," invited to dinner parties by our professors.

I had only my ill-starred affair with Lisa with which to compare this new arrangement. In the melodrama I had made of my adolescence, I had felt that it was essential to keep Lisa a secret. No one had ever invited her and me to a dinner party. The passion of our furtive nights in Green Mountain Cemetery had had a doomed urgency about it that was, I now realized, the antithesis of marriage. The horror of the domestic that had always lurked just beneath my skin was still there, at age twenty-four, and during Sharon's and my Denver years, on humdrum evenings when I was too tired or drunk to concentrate on *The Faerie Queene* or *Samson Agonistes*, I felt the dull throb of quiet desperation.

It was to Alaska that I turned for a solution. By the spring of 1968, I thought, I had come up with the perfect recipe to integrate marriage with mountaineering. It was called the Brooks Range.

Stretching 700 miles across Alaska north of the Arctic Circle, the Brooks Range then comprised the last great roadless tract in the United States. Though it lay a solid 300 miles north of the Alaska Range, a climatic fluke had spared these mountains the bad weather and heavy glaciation that smothered all the other massifs in the forty-ninth state. Ranging between latitudes 67° and 69° N., the Brooks lay almost completely beyond the northern limit of treeline. It was an empty wilderness of tundra, rushing rivers, and unnamed peaks. Huge swaths of the range had scarcely been explored, even by government surveyors.

Until the 1890s, the Brooks Range had been the homeland for nomadic bands of Inupiaq, inland Eskimos. With the dwindling of the caribou herds and the advent of miners, whalers, and missionaries, however, the headwaters of such great rivers as the Colville, the Noatak, the Koyukuk, and the Chandalar were swiftly depopulated. No longer self-sufficient, the natives began to settle into symbiotic squalor with white traders in such bleak coastal villages as Barrow, Kotzebue, and Shishmaref. By 1968, only a handful of lonely outposts, some of them derelict mining towns, crept toward the range from the south: Bettles, Wiseman, Ambler, and the like. The single town within the Brooks Range proper was Anaktuvuk Pass, near the headwaters of the John River, a Nunamiut village whose 1968 population was about thirty-five men, women, and children.

The highest peak in the Brooks Range is Mount Isto, at 9,060 feet, way over on the eastern edge of the mountain chain, not far from the Canadian border. Yet that diminutive altitude meant little by itself: Kichatna Spire, after all, stood only 8,985 feet high, the Angel 9,265. I might have turned my attention to the Brooks sooner, except that the word was out that the great range was a jumble of talus heaps, offering little more than walk-up first ascents.

In 1962, however, a small gang of eastern climbers (some of them friends of mine) had made a startling discovery. In a little-noticed book called *Arctic Wilderness*, written by the then obscure explorer and forester Robert Marshall, published posthumously by Marshall's brother in 1956, a single photo heralded the Arrigetch Peaks—a Nunamiut word for "fingers of the hand outstretched." These were self-evidently no talus heaps, but swooping spires of what looked like clean granite.

At the height of the Great Depression, in the early 1930s, Marshall and an assortment of friends had tramped happily over vast, previously unexplored sectors of the Brooks Range. Marshall was not a trained climber, but he made a number of daring first ascents of semi-technical peaks. The book, republished today as *Alaska Wilderness*, has become a classic, for Marshall's hearty prose sings an extended hymn of praise to one of the great remaining wild places in North America. (The Bob Marshall Wilderness Area in Montana is named after this vagabond pioneer, and Gates of the Arctic, a national park established in 1980 that includes the Arrigetch, was named after Marshall's epithet for the headwaters of the Alatna and John Rivers.)

In his rambles, Marshall only skirted the Arrigetch, but the few sentences he devoted to this anomalous pocket of spiky towers and smooth headwalls would have made any mountaineer's mouth water:

> Since neither Ernie nor I belonged to the human-fly category, we did not try to climb the Arrigetch peaks. . . . We wondered what queer geological history was responsible for this one range of granite pinnacles in the world of metamorphic and sedimentary rocks.

That was all it took for my eastern friends to launch an expedition to the Alaskan Arctic in the summer of 1963. Four of them hired a pilot out of Bettles, who flew them to Takahula Lake, a twenty-mile bushwhack from their proposed base camp. To supply the team for a month of climbing, the pilot air-dropped supplies above an idyllic-looking valley in the heart of the Arrigetch three days before the Takahula drop-off (just as Don and our pilot would do on the West Fork Glacier below Deborah the following year). Evidently the aviator was little practiced in the art of air-dropping. Two team members went along for the ride. As Jeanne Bergen later described the process in the *American Alpine Journal*:

> They could see what appeared to be fine scree cascading down from the granite faces to a high, level moraine rising above the valley floor. . . . Andy [the pilot] felt that the boxes, if dropped onto the scree, would roll and bounce down to the moss-covered plateau. They made a pass over the slope, Andy opened the bomb bay, and the boxes tumbled toward earth. They seemed to drop for a long time before disappearing.

Six days later the team arrived at the drop site from Takahula, after a fifty-hour thrash through mosquitoes, willows, and alder, to find no trace of their precious supplies. The pilot (along with his passengers) had completely misjudged the scale of the landscape. Thinking he was fifty or a hundred feet above the ground when he cut loose the boxes, he must have been at least a thousand. The "fine scree" turned out to be a massive boulder field, with stones ranging up to the size of small houses. For three solid days, the party scoured the boulder field and never found a single belonging. (In 1971, on my second trip to the Arrigetch, I would stumble upon one of the 1963 party's lost packages. The debris still bore witness to the violence of impact: bleached white food boxes wrapped like Dali's melted watches around the boulders on which they had smashed, the contents long gone to the scavenging birds; a piton hammer, its handle broken clean in two; and, incongruously, an intact plastic lemon.)

Out of food, plunged into a plight of survival, the quartet hiked back to Takahula Lake. From there they still faced a 150-mile trek to the nearest outpost of civilization, the Indian village of Allakaket, and in those days you could easily go a month in the Brooks Range without seeing a plane. It was the party's good fortune, however, after five foodless days at Takahula, to have their pilot fly by on another mission, see the frantic signals they flashed with the bottom of a cooking pot, and land to rescue the Arctic refugees.

Undaunted, the four returned in 1964 with four more friends. This time they did it right, with an advance party landing at Takahula and hiking in to base camp *before* the pilot attempted his airdrop, which he now performed from a reasonable height. During the next month, the climbers made seven first ascents, including that of a peak they called Wichmann Tower, which would prove to be one of the prizes of the range. My friends came back from the Arrigetch raving about the quality of the granite and the pristine splendor of their surroundings.

Yet four more years passed without any other climbers going to the Arrigetch. In the winter of 1967–68 I ordered the 1:250,000 Survey Pass quadrangle and the aerial photos from which it had been made. Crossing my eyes over an adjoining pair of photos, I saw the peaks pop up in three dimensions. Almost immediately, I was distracted from the jagged ridges of the compact Arrigetch peaks by a towering monolith twenty-five miles to the west. It was Mount Igikpak, at 8,510 feet the highest peak in all the western Brooks Range. It was, in fact, as I later calculated, the highest peak for 285 miles in any direction.

Though the mountains between the Arrigetch and Igikpak reverted to the usual Brooks Range talus piles, Igikpak itself looked like it must be made of the same good granite as my friends had found in 1964. And, as the contour lines made clear, it was a far more major peak than anything in the Arrigetch, with unbroken faces sweeping 3,000 feet from base to top.

Without hesitation, I started planning my sixth expedition. After five straight years in the Alaska and Hayes Ranges, camping on chilly glaciers, waiting out interminable storms, living in daily fear of avalanches and crevasses, I was ready for the benignity of the Brooks Range. Best of all, it solved my personal dilemma, for here was an expedition on which Sharon could accompany me. I had no thought of her climbing Igikpak, but it seemed reasonable to ask her to hang out at base camp, surrounded not by crevasse fields but by mossy, harmless tundra, while my accomplices and I did battle with the main objective. Afterward, no doubt, she and I could bag the first ascents of several of the much lower talus heaps that bordered Igikpak on the west.

I plunged into the planning—a welcome routine that by now I had down pat—as I recruited teammates. In the end, we were six, five climbers and Sharon. My teammates were not close friends from the Harvard Mountaineering Club, but acquaintances from the East and Alaska with whom I had never before roped up. One of them, a shy, gentle schoolteacher named Chuck Loucks, had made five of the Arrigetch first ascents in 1964, including Wichmann Tower.

Yet even as I plotted for Igikpak, I must have recognized that it promised a less ambitious summer than I had recently spent in the Kichatnas or Revelations. To compensate, I planned a trip to the Wind Rivers in Wyoming with Matt Hale for June, then a jaunt to the Bugaboos in British Columbia with Matt and Sharon, before we pointed the Saab north toward Alaska at the end of July.

Matt and I had the Cirque of the Towers—thronged today by hikers, climbers, and fishermen every week of the summer—to ourselves for eight days. We made some decent climbs, including a new route on Watchtower Peak. The Bugaboos, by contrast, seemed as sociable as the Gunks, as we hung out beside the prefab base camp huts just east of the handsome granite monoliths of Snowpatch and Bugaboo Spires with assorted Germans, Canadians, and friends from the East whom we bumped into. A sudden lightning storm chased Matt and me off our one serious attempt, on the east ridge of Bugaboo. Sharon and I got to the summits of a pair of easy peaks—easy for me, that is, but terrifying for her. On Mount Wallace, Al De Maria, a grizzled gnome who taught math in New Paltz, at the doorstep of the Gunks, and who would go on with us to Igikpak, kicked an impetuous staircase up a dangerously steep snow slope to reach the summit ridge. Unwilling to slow down our caravan by stopping to rope Sharon up, as I absolutely should have, I had her go second up the steps, while I, following a few feet below her, promised to spot her if she fell off. (Of such idiocies are disasters born.)

By the time we got to Alaska, then, I felt vaguely disappointed with my summer so far. Only getting up Igikpak would save the season. On July 27, Sharon and I, plus Al and Chuck, flew in from Bettles with a canny young pilot named Daryl Morris, who landed us on a gravel bar at the headwaters of the Noatak River, only fifteen miles west of our base camp meadow. (The other two members of our expedition, Vin and Grace Hoeman, would join us two weeks later.) Because Sharon had done little backpacking before that summer, and because she tended to come unstrung in the face of hordes of mosquitoes or thickets of willow, we dawdled on the hike in, taking four days to cover those fifteen miles.

The Brooks Range was grizzly bear country. I had borrowed a 30.06 rifle, which Sharon and I had practiced firing at a Denver range. Neither of us had ever before wielded a gun that used ammunition much heftier than BBs, and as the kick slammed the butt of the rifle into my shoulder and my shot wildly missed the target, I had my doubts whether either of us would have the skill to stop an *Ursus horribilis* in full charge. (The 1964 Arrigetch party had had to shoot a bear at base camp, more or less in the manner of a cold-blooded murder, for the bear, rather than charging, simply hung around the party's food cache, undeterred by the banging of pots or by shots fired over its head.)

On the third night of our hike in, as we camped near Angiaak Pass, both Sharon and Al heard a coughing noise. Each thought it was produced by one of our teammates, until in the morning a fresh pile of excrement revealed that a bear had walked right through camp without summoning the curiosity to gobble up any of the exotic goodies (including ourselves) strewn about our tundra shelf. The next day Chuck spotted a huge grizzly across the stream we were hiking along, browsing among the flowers; fortunately, the beast was upwind from us and never noticed our intrusion. Later on the expedition, a bear would break into a food cache we had left near Angiaak Pass. On his second bite, he penetrated a can of compressed butane, which must have shot a super-cooled jet of fuel into his face at point-blank range, saving the rest of our groceries from his depredations.

On July 30 Daryl Morris delivered our airdrop, slowing his plane to ninety miles an hour and pushing our packages out from a mere forty feet up. The taped-up cardboard boxes bounced on the spongy tundra and rolled to a stop. We lost only a jar of coffee, a bag of cookies, and a box of crackers.

We were camped a mere three miles from the base of Igikpak. We could see the bulk of the mountain soaring into the sky east of us, but during the first week its summit stayed hidden in cloud cap. Chuck thought the granite looked identical to that of the Arrigetch. Throughout the month we spent in the Brooks Range, big forest fires raged out of control more than fifty miles to the south. Though we were well north of treeline, a haze of sweet-smelling smoke carried by the winds bleared our universe, turning everything pale and muted. Sunsets and moonrises were drenched in ruddy orange.

At last the clouds cleared from the top of Igikpak. We saw, with nervous excitement, that from the summit ridge sprouted four sharp towers. In Inupiaq, the name Igikpak means "two big towers," evidently an allusion to this summit ridge as seen by caribou hunters more than a century before. From almost 6,000 feet below, we could not tell which tower was the highest, but we began to suspect that the wildest of the four—a slender pinnacle topped with a mushroom-shaped overhanging capstone—was the true summit.

On August 6, Al, Chuck, and I set off at 6:15 A.M. on an all-out attempt on Igikpak. I had thought that having Sharon at base camp would tame the jittery angst that worrying about her worrying about me had inflicted on my spirit. Instead, her presence only made it worse. A diary entry, mildly self-censored as usual, reflects my pain on leaving base camp that morning: "Sharon got up to say goodbye to us. Both of us felt sad, even reluctant: I didn't want to leave her at camp alone; she didn't want us to go."

Once in motion, I felt less ambivalent. By now, all three of us were in great shape. It took us only four hours to scramble unroped up the full 5,300 feet of a shallow arête on Igikpak's southwest face, all the way to the summit ridge. The granite was as clean and solid as the Wind Rivers or Bugaboos at their best. We were starting to congratulate ourselves on the first ascent, when we clambered over the westernmost of the four summit towers and ran smack into what I would come to nickname the Hinterstoisser Elevator Shaft.

A sheer gash had been punched into the summit ridge, like the space left by a tooth knocked out of a lower jaw. Vertical cliffs on our side and the far side of the gash framed a knife-edge far below, an inverted guillotine blade. On either side of that blade, the precipice fell 3,000 feet sheer. We spent four hours trying to solve this granite lacuna, only to turn back in the face of an insidious potential trap. (In 1936, in an early attempt on the north face of the Eiger in Switzerland, the German climber Andreas Hinterstoisser had brilliantly led a delicate leftward traverse about a third of the way up the wall. But he failed to recognize the necessity of fixing a rope on the traverse to safeguard a retreat. When a storm turned the team of four back, Hinterstoisser, unable to reverse the tricky moves, fell to his death trying. His three teammates also died: the last man, hanging from a jammed rappel rope, froze to death just as a rescue party got within reach.)

To cross the guillotine blade, we would have to rappel off the west-side cliff, then pull our rope down for use on the terrain ahead. If we could not climb the nasty-looking cliff on the east side of the gap, we would be stuck in a fix even more hopeless than Hinterstoisser's, with no rescue party afoot anywhere in northern Alaska.

We got back to camp after a fourteen-hour day, exhausted and dispirited. Unable to see us, Sharon had assumed from our long absence that we must have climbed the mountain. She was as disappointed as we were, for our failure meant that she would have to go through another solitary vigil like the one she had just endured.

Three days later, we got another chance, this time tackling a different line on the east edge of the mountain's huge south face. Once more we reached the summit ridge without roping up, though some of the moves were tricky enough that, had the rock not been so solid, we would have stopped and belayed. And our route zigzagged so deviously that we built little cairns every few hundred yards to help us find the way down.

By now we knew that the needle—a 200-foot-tall golf tee, its thirty-foot summit block overhanging all sides—was the true summit of Igikpak. I felt strong, and without a word, Al and Chuck handed me the hardware. Two strenuous pitches later, we were crouched under the summit block, which was plainly unscalable from the west side. I had begun to think that we were on the verge of climbing more than 5,000 feet of this splendid mountain, only to be stumped thirty feet short of the top.

There was but one hope. I skittered on a ledge around the north face and onto the east. Here, the summit block overhung by a full 30 degrees beyond the vertical, but a pair of horizontal cracks split the block. Beneath my feet, the east face, which we had never before beheld, plunged so steeply that I could see no part of it above the glacier 3,000 feet below. I started to aid-climb, pounding pitons into the cracks, dangling nylon stirrups from them, and moving crablike up the foot loops as I searched for the next piton placement. One pin jangled loose under the hammer and fell into the void. Another disappeared inside the crack: I could hear it clatter as it slid to a stop somewhere deep beneath the summit mushroom. I realized with a shiver that the whole capstone block was precariously balanced in place, and through my mind flashed the macabre scenario of pulling the whole thing loose as my body weight destabilized it.

My progress was agonizingly slow. On the opposite side of the tower, Chuck and Al could see none of my flailings, which they had to divine from the maddeningly incremental inching out of the rope. At last I got my fingers on the lip of the summit, but my arm strength was giving out. I pulled myself out of the top steps of the stirrups, hung there for an unnerving few seconds, then found the top horizontal crack with my right toe. I planted my elbows on the ledge, then with a grunt of effort, muscled my way onto the summit. It was a flat island of rock, a little bigger than a pool table, floating in the sky. I let out a cheer of joy, then brought Al and Chuck up.

The top of Igikpak was, as Al put it, the "most summit-like summit" I would ever have the privilege to visit. It was all the sweeter as the culmination of the first ascent of the highest peak in the western Brooks Range.

We got back to camp only in the twilight gloom, an hour before midnight, at the end of seventeen hours of nonstop climbing. Sharon rejoiced with us. During the whole day, as on August 6, she had ventured scarcely a dozen yards from the tent. In the back of her mind was a half-spoken terror: *What do I do if they don't come back?* The solitude had ratcheted up her fear of bears. Stray sounds took on ominous meanings. For half an hour at a time throughout the day, she sat inside the tent, the 30.06 laid across her lap, listening. As Sharon would tell me years later, "I'd never felt so alone in all my life."

Vin and Grace arrived on August 11. Four days later, all six of us set out to tackle Peak 7775, the third-highest in the Igikpak region. The mountain was a bit remote, requiring us to cross a 5,400-foot pass, descend into a northern valley, and skirt two vestigial glaciers just to get to its foot. But we worked out a scrambling route that eschewed any terrain tough enough to call for a rope. I coaxed Sharon upward, believing that a first ascent of her own would reward her for the anxious vigils she had kept at base camp on August 6 and 9. We lagged almost two hours behind the others, but Sharon gamely plugged on, and at last we stood on the summit, all together, at 1:10 in the afternoon. At Vin's suggestion, we named the peak Sikspak, a pun blending the number of our party with the kind of Inupiaq suffix characteristically applied to high places (including, in our vicinity, Mounts Igikpak, Oyukak, Chitiok, and Papiok).

By the time we got back to camp, we had gained and lost 7,300 feet of altitude, as much as I had ever accomplished in a single day, let alone Sharon. As we recrossed the 5,400-foot pass, her knees were on the verge of collapse (they would take months to recover). Stifling her tears, she literally crawled the last few hundred yards to our tent. Yet of several first ascents in Alaska that Sharon would eventually make, Sikspak was the finest.

Our team never really cohered the way our chummy gang in the

Revelations had the year before, and no deep new friendships were forged in the western Brooks Range. Between Vin and me, in particular, a certain tension developed. I had first met him at Denali Pass, on our way down from McKinley in 1963, and admired his drive and enthusiasm. A short man, maybe five six, he was towered over by Grace, an anesthesiologist who was fifteen years older than he. Intensely competitive, Vin found it hard to accept the fact that Al, Chuck, and I had claimed Igikpak before he and Grace had even flown in.

Vin never became a good technical climber, but he was the strongest hiker and scrambler I had ever met. In consequence, he had become a consummate peak-bagger. Living in Anchorage, he had already, at the age of thirty-two, made more first ascents than anyone in Alaskan history. But most of Vin's peaks were little more challenging than the talus heaps that fringed Igikpak on the west and south. Unfazed by standards of quality, Vin had compiled an index card file of every climb ever made in the forty-ninth state, recording ascents in tiny, spidery handwriting. In Vin's procrustean system, a nondescript lump in the Chugach rated as much notice as, say, the magnificent Cassin route on the south face of McKinley. In the file, even Brad Washburn, every one of whose campaigns in Alaska from the 1930s to early 1950s had been a major achievement, occupied only both sides of a single card, as did I. Vin Hoeman himself was the sole three-card superstar.

Our disparate propensities emerged on August 18, when Vin and Grace announced that they wanted to set off on a week-long loop to the west, into Angayu Creek, to tackle Mounts Chitiok and Papiok. Without much trouble, after marathon hikes, they bagged these two glorified talus piles. We were reunited with the Hoemans only on the gravel bar at the head of the Noatak, where we awaited Morris's pickup. At base camp, we had spent only a single week with Vin and Grace.

Their peak-bagging loop thus avoided the best remaining challenge in the range, its second-highest peak, a satellite to Igikpak on the north, which we named Tupik Tower. On August 20, Chuck, Al, and I made a two-thirds-hearted attempt on this handsome spire, leaving Sharon for one more solo vigil at base camp. We found the rock on Tupik Tower's west ridge as loose and dangerous as Igikpak had been solid, and turned back after several dicey pitches. As far as I know, thirty-seven years later, the peak is still unclimbed.

Getting up Igikpak on the fourteenth day of the expedition had taken the pressure off our last two weeks in the Brooks Range. During most of those days, Sharon and I set off on aimless hikes near base camp, savoring the details of the gentle but infinitely lonely landscape. The mosquitoes had given up the ghost after August 10, and though each night the dark grew longer and each day the temperature imperceptibly dropped, we had entered that charmed month between the end of buggy summer and the onset of autumnal freeze-up. The yellow Arctic poppies wheeled heliotropically, their earnest blossoms following the sun. Swaths of Alaska cotton danced in the breeze. When it rained, the gray-green reindeer moss turned into a spongy carpet, but after a day or two of dry wind, it shriveled into a brittle vegetative coral that crunched audibly underfoot.

Near camp there was a major patch of blueberry bushes. Often barefoot, Sharon and I gathered bowlsful of the ripe fruit, which went deliciously with sugar and powdered milk. Our camp was at the headwaters of the Reed River. Somewhere hereabouts, in 1886 a government explorer had been guided by Eskimos to a hot spring, sacred to the Inupiaq. Despite days of searching, Sharon and I never found the hot spring. We found instead several deep pools flitting with trout. I had brought my fly rod, which I had scarcely unlimbered since boyhood, when my father still had the leisure to teach my brother Alan and me how to fish in the Roaring Fork and the inlet to Twin Lakes. Now I rediscovered the art of casting the fly so it landed gently enough not to spook the fish, and I hauled in quite a few trout, up to a foot in length, which, back at base camp, made a welcome substitute for glop. (There had been precious little opportunity to fish near base camp on the Shadows or the Revelation Glaciers.) One warm day, Sharon and I skinny-dipped in another pool on the upper Reed, then sunbathed for an hour, lolling on the soft tundra.

Most hauntingly, we discovered, about a mile from camp, a series of odd cairns stretching across the valley, seven in number, each built atop a small boulder. They were clearly Eskimo in origin, but what their purpose was, I had no idea. Months later, an anthropologist would suggest to me their function. The Inupiaq had once hunted caribou by driving them into brushwork traps. Cairns atop boulders simulated additional hunters, away from which the caribou would shy. Four men could thus pretend to be eleven, all the more efficiently to harry their prey toward the trap.

During these idyllic days of wandering near base camp, I fell in love with the Brooks Range. I would eventually return for seven more trips, not all of them climbing expeditions. And during those days, a quatrain from a half-forgotten poem—was it Auden?—kept running through my head, epitomizing the place:

> In the stream the silver grayling
>   Anticipate the dark;
> Upon a shore of granite
>   The lichens disembark.

Most valuable of all, Sharon and I got along better in the Arctic than we normally could in Denver. At ease in "my" mountains, I shucked off, as Sharon was the first to note, the constant, fretful impatience that I carried like a backpack with me through the slog of the school year. For a few healing weeks, I lived wholly in the present. Painful though our base camp partings were, as I headed off into the uncertainty of alpine risk and ambition, as she laid the rifle across her knees and prepared to face down the grizzlies that prowled the tundra, those moments gave an edge to our partnership that was impossible to hone in civilization. I had accepted by now that Sharon could never be an equal teammate on the rope. But there was a quieter joy in sharing with her one of the most beautiful places on earth, and despite her incessant apprehensions and the worry that she was holding up the rest of us, she responded to the wilderness—to the swiveling yellow poppies and the darting trout, to the rumble of tired distant thunder, to the moon sliding between silhouetted southern hills—at least as keenly as I did.

On August 26, Morris picked us up on the Noatak gravel bar and flew us back to Bettles in three trips. All too soon, Sharon and I were back in Denver, starting the fall term again. Another interminable off-season loomed.

Igikpak had been one of the best climbs of my life, and it had been intensely gratifying to lead the wildly exposed summit pitch, the crux of the whole ascent. Yet after the summer was over, puritan to the core, I could not shake the feeling that 1968 had been a softer year in the mountains than any of my previous five. Back in our bungalow on York Street, I brooded on the possibility that I had lost the fever pitch of fanaticism through which Don and I, a few years earlier, had hallucinated mountaineering immortality. There was no denying that something was different. As I had written in my diary on the next-to-last day of the expedition, "For the first time, I've begun to wonder if I haven't avoided more unusual experiences by coming back to Alaska every year for six straight. . . . Maybe next summer we'll go to Europe. Or I'll really write."

By now, at the age of twenty-five, I had a solid reputation in the American mountaineering scene. I had written articles for the *American Alpine Journal* four years running, I had given slide shows all over the country, and *The Mountain of My Fear* had been reviewed in the *New York Times*.

While still at Harvard, I had turned down invitations from more senior climbers to join them on expeditions to the Andes. After six straight years in Alaska, the obvious leap in my exploratory résumé would be an expedition to the Andes or the Himalaya. With such a transformation in mind, as early as the beginning of 1967 I had accepted an invitation to join an attempt on K2, the world's second-highest mountain, scheduled for the spring and summer of 1969.

Regarded today as the hardest and most dangerous of all the fourteen peaks in the world exceeding 8,000 meters (26,240 feet) in altitude, K2 had been climbed only once, by a massive Italian team in 1954. Since 1960, thanks to tensions between Pakistan (the country in which K2 stands) and China, the mountain had been closed to all foreign climbers.

The new initiative was the brainchild of Boyd Everett, Jr., a securities analyst for the Lehman Corporation in New York City. Nine years older than I, Everett had connections in high places that had allowed him to penetrate the barriers of U.S. and Pakistani bureaucracy.

During my undergraduate years, Boyd, a Harvard grad, had hovered on the outskirts of the HMC, often volunteering to pair up with novices on their first routes at the Gunks. We had, however, never quite taken the man seriously. For one thing, as a Wall Street stockbroker who sometimes showed up at the Uberfall (the center of Gunks social life) straight from the office, still wearing his suit and tie, Boyd seemed something of a dandy among our band of unwashed climbing bums. More important, though, he was a weak rock climber—as he was the first cheerily to admit. In his whole life, I doubt that he ever led a pitch harder than 5.5.

Boyd compensated for this shortcoming, not by bagging obscure peaks in the Chugach, as Vin Hoeman had, but by becoming the leader of expeditions on major peaks in Alaska and the Yukon that were—depending on your prejudice—either masterworks of logistics or freaks of equipment and personnel overkill. Between 1963 and 1966, Boyd led expeditions that succeeded on the east and west ridges of Mount Logan (19,850 feet), the northwest ridge of Mount Saint Elias (18,040 feet), the first ascent of King George Peak (12,300 feet), and the southeast spur on McKinley (20,320 feet). These were noteworthy accomplishments, but none had involved really difficult technical climbing. At a time when North Americans were starting to apply the fast-and-light alpine style to expeditionary mountains (as we had on the Angel in 1967), Boyd was still boasting in print about the many thousands of feet of fixed rope his teams had strung up low-angle snow ridges. The more fixed rope, he seemed to imply, the tougher the climb.

I had turned down invitations from Boyd to join two of these expeditions, but K2 seemed a real plum. By the summer of 1967, I was listed as one of eight "official organizers" of the projected 1969 assault. Among my duties was to pass confidential judgment on other climbers—some of them my friends—who had the temerity to apply for vacant slots on the K2 trip.

Boyd's criteria for filling out the team amounted to an elaborate rationale for his style of expeditioneering. In a letter to us organizers, he emphasized that the technical ability of a candidate, though useful, was secondary. "The most important thing," Boyd insisted, "is what kind of an expedition personality and character he has. Quite obviously no prima donnas are needed no matter how good they are technically." No one would be considered who had not previously climbed above 18,000 feet. (On Logan, McKinley, and Saint Elias, Boyd himself had four times pierced that arbitrary altitude barrier.)

"It is expected that all of the climbing team will be between the ages of twenty and forty," Boyd wrote in another memo. "Climbers who will be under twenty-five or over thirty-five in 1969, particularly the former, must have unusual qualifications to be eligible." Not coincidentally, Boyd himself would be thirty-five in 1969.

Boyd's own candid appraisals of candidates struck me as capricious and condescending. Of Pete Carman, who had been one of the primal forces on our 1963 Wickersham Wall expedition, he wrote, "Used to be a strong climber and good mountain man. Reported not to have been too strong on Mount Deborah this summer but impending marriage may have been a distraction." (In 1967, while the six of us were in the Revelation Mountains, Don Jensen had organized a second attempt on the east ridge of Deborah. Despite receiving an air-drop on the col between South Hess and Deborah that it had taken us two weeks to reach in 1964, despite throwing at the mountain one of the most talented parties ever to climb in Alaska, the 1967 team was stopped by hideous weather only a hundred feet higher than the high point Don and I had reached in 1964. Boyd's stricture on Pete was ridiculous. In 1967, Pete had been one of the strongest climbers on Deborah. And I knew that, faced with a challenge as technical as the east ridge, Boyd himself would have cowered in his tent rather than lead a single pitch on the terrifyingly steep and rotten schist that rose in that serpentine curl above the col.)

Another pair of candidates was Kim Schmitz and Jim Madsen, who, though only twenty years old, were fast becoming Yosemite legends. Already they had smashed the speed records on two great El Capitan routes, the Nose and the Dihedral Wall. The latter ascent, wrote Steve Roper, the definitive Yosemite historian, some years later, "left the Camp 4 regulars [i.e., the best rock climbers in America and possibly the world] speechless."

Boyd's judgment was somewhat cooler. "Climbed El Capitan (Nose Route) in record time last spring," he wrote of Schmitz and Madsen in a confidential note to us organizers. "No expedition experience. . . . I know nothing about them personally."

Madsen's own letter of application to Everett listed a mind-boggling résumé of ascents between the ages of fourteen and twenty that ranged from hard lines on Mount Rainier to new routes in winter in the Colorado Rockies, as well as record times on Yosemite classics. His last paragraph crystallized for me everything that was wrong with Everett's approach to assembling a K2 team:

> The list comprises only about one-tenth of all the climbs I've done. . . . Frankly, I dislike very much writing this type of letter to you. I'm neither proud or ashamed of what I've climbed and could give a damn what other people think. But apparently it is a necessity here for I want to be on this expedition and I want to be working on the hardest thing being done.

Whether this broadside put Boyd off or not, Madsen's application soon became moot. In October 1968, after a fierce storm in Yosemite, Schmitz and Madsen helicoptered to the top of El Cap to see if two friends, who had been caught by the storm high on the Dihedral Wall, were in trouble. Madsen anchored a rope and rappelled down the upper pitches of the wall to investigate more closely. As climbers routinely do, he tied a knot in the lower end of the rope to prevent his sliding off, but somehow the knot slipped through his multi-carabiner rappel rig. He fell 2,700 feet to his death. According to Schmitz, Madsen's last words were, "What the fuck?"

In their bivouac, Madsen's friends, hearing the sound of a falling body, assumed it was that of a deer. As they climbed on that morning, they discovered Madsen's eyeglasses, shattered on a ledge, but only when they topped out did they learn who it was who had taken the long plunge.

Everett's recruitment-by-gossip-and-innuendo stuck in my craw, so much so that I wrote him a letter complaining about the sort of back-stabbing and "counter-informing" his process threatened to foster. He wrote me back, vigorously defending his approach.

In the end, however, it was not my dissatisfaction with Boyd's leadership per se that led me to back out of the K2 expedition. It was that that kind of trip—a campaign by twenty to twenty-five climbers, most of us strangers to one another before the expedition, conducted in an anachronistic load-heavy, rope-fixing style—was anathema to my own mountaineering aesthetic. It was not by accident that, by the end of my string of thirteen straight expeditions, I could say that I had conceived and organized (or, in the case of McKinley, at least co-organized) every one of them, and that I came to prize the lightweight alpine style over the militaristic deployment of troops and matériel favored by the likes of Everett. Nor was it an accident that I never went on an expedition to the Andes or the Himalaya, confining my thirteen expeditions to Alaska and the Yukon.

In this respect, I was the true protégé of my mentor, Brad Washburn. Unquestionably the leader of the matchless Harvard Mountaineering Club gang in the early 1930s, Brad would never go on an expedition led by anyone else, nor would he, after some teenage forays in the Alps, climb anywhere but Alaska and the Yukon. Meanwhile his closest HMC buddies—Terris Moore, Adams Carter, Bob Bates, and Charlie Houston—would set off on expeditions to China, Nepal, Pakistan, Peru, and Ecuador. Bates and Houston, in fact, would be the co-leaders of the 1938 and 1953 American K2 expeditions.

By 1968, Everett had to face the likelihood that Pakistan would not, after all, grant permission for K2. It would not be until 1974, in fact, that the Karakoram would be reopened to foreign visitors, after a hiatus of fourteen years. Meanwhile, with a strong group of climbers already committed, Everett started casting about for another objective. In the end, he chose Dhaulagiri in Nepal, the world's sixth-highest mountain, first climbed by a Swiss team in 1960 and unrepeated since. Boyd made a last appeal to me to join the Dhaulagiri team, but by then I had put together a small group of my own to climb in the Arrigetch in the summer of 1969.

On April 29, 1969, only eight days after reaching base camp, six climbers and two Sherpas toiled up the lower slopes of Dhaulagiri, reconnoitering a new route they had chosen with their binoculars. They included a number of excellent alpinists, among them Dave Seidman, a Dartmouth graduate who had been one of four men to pioneer a stern new route on the south face of McKinley in 1967, and Lou Reichardt, who would go on to become one of America's most accomplished high-altitude mountaineers, as well as Vin Hoeman and Boyd Everett.

Suddenly the eight men heard a loud roar. Because an afternoon fog had descended on the mountain, they could only guess that an ice cliff had broken off above, triggering a big avalanche that was bearing down on them. With no place to hide, Reichardt dove face-first into a shallow hollow in the slope and covered his head. His back was pummeled with avalanche debris, but he was not seriously hurt. As I heard the story, the moment the chaos ceased, Reichardt got back to his feet and exclaimed, "Wow, that was close!"

No one answered him. The other seven men had been swept away and buried beneath tons of snow and ice blocks. Reichardt spent an hour frantically digging through the jumbled debris without finding a trace of his companions. Then, as he would write in the *American Alpine Journal*, "I made the loneliest of trips down the glacier and rock to the 12,000-foot acclimatization camp, shedding crampons, overboots, and finally even disbelief on the way."

One might think that such an experience would cure a young

man of climbing for good, but Reichardt went on to be the first American to climb K2 without oxygen in 1978, to spearhead the brilliant first ascent of the Kangshung Face on Everest in 1983, and to serve as president of the American Alpine Club.

In Denver, when I got the news from Dhaulagiri, my first reaction was shock and sorrow at the loss of Vin Hoeman and, yes, of Boyd Everett. But only instants later, I felt an almost nauseating wave of relief. Had I not turned down Boyd's invitation, resisted his last-minute blandishments, I would in all likelihood now be sharing his and Vin's icy tomb. During subsequent months, I began subconsciously to convert that relief into self-congratulation, as if my misgivings about Dhaulagiri had had as much to do with a wise appraisal of avalanche danger as with Everett's peculiar way of choosing a team.

There was, to be sure, no shortage of second-guessers about the accident, which remains the most deadly ever suffered by Americans in the Himalaya. The team's sirdar, or head Sherpa, Phu Dorje, was quoted as saying that Everett had consistently ignored his warnings about avalanche danger on the proposed route, ordering the sirdar back to the 12,000-foot camp when he would not shut up. "The leader's obstinacy and impatience," Dorje angrily asserted, "cost five Americans and two highly experienced Sherpas their lives."

Grace Hoeman was inconsolable. Though Vin was her third husband and they had been married only a little more than two years, he was the love of her life. On Alaskan first ascents, whether of talus heaps or no, they had tied their destinies and their happiness together.

It was characteristic of Grace, who had a paranoid streak at the best of times, that she had to blame Everett for the loss of Vin. It must have been Boyd who chose the route, who cajoled the others into risks they would not otherwise have taken. "It was good that Boyd didn't come back either," she wrote Sharon and me. "Yes, I am very bitter about it, since it was Boyd's doing that separated me from the man I loved far more than myself." The accident "borders on mass murder." Where was Vin's diary, which Grace presumed he must have left in base camp? Had it been "deliberately destroyed"?

Grace learned the real truth about Dhaulagiri in the cruelest of ways—from a letter from Vin that arrived weeks after his death. The missive revealed that the choice of route had been Vin's more than Boyd's. As they had started up the mountain, her ever-competitive husband had nursed a dark secret ambition: that his teammates would one by one give up the challenge, leaving him to go solo to the summit, in the fashion of Hermann Buhl on Nanga Parbat in 1953, whose astonishing deed had become mountaineering legend.

After the spring of 1969, Grace continued to climb, but some of her Anchorage friends concluded that she had stepped over an invisible line into reckless abandon, as though she no longer cared whether she lived or died. In April 1971, just two years after the Dhaulagiri catastrophe, Grace was swept with her ropemate to her death in an avalanche of her own, on an uninspiring peak in the Chugach Range.

Then in 1976, in the Tetons, Chuck Loucks, whom I considered one of the safest climbers I had ever roped up with, misjudged a tricky move on an easy lead, well above all the major difficulties on the long route. He slipped and fell more than a hundred feet, hit a ledge, and died in the arms of his belayer, a close friend who had been in the Arrigetch with Chuck in 1964.

In less than a decade after our idyllic, laid-back expedition to Mount Igikpak, half of our team of six had died in the mountains.

Our Arrigetch trip, planned for August, would be another expedition that I could share with Sharon. But once more, as if to compensate for the scaling down of ambition that the Brooks Range, in all its muted beauty, portended, I planned to climb in other mountains before heading north to Alaska.

During the school year of 1968–69, I visited Hank Abrons in Cleveland, where he was attending Case Western Reserve medical school. Hank had been the most experienced of our group of seven on the Wickersham Wall, but I had not climbed with him since 1963. Now Hank invited a new friend of his over, named Denny Eberl. I knew Denny by his excellent mountaineering reputation. The same age as I, a Dartmouth grad, Denny had been a member of Everett's successful teams on the west ridge of Mount Logan and the northwest ridge of Mount Saint Elias. He had also made the second ascent of the formidable north face of Mount Edith Cavell in the Canadian Rockies, and then, in 1967, with Dave Seidman and two others, Denny had pioneered the fierce new route on the south face of McKinley.

All three of us, Hank, Denny, and I, had been, in fact, among the eight "official organizers" of Everett's proposed K2 expedition. By the time we met in Cleveland, we had all three backed out of the fateful Dhaulagiri trip.

Hank had hinted that he and Denny had a secret project in mind for the summer of 1969, and after a couple of beers, Denny opened a manila envelope and laid a black-and-white photo on the table. "Look at this," he said conspiratorially. "The north face of Mount Temple."

From having seen other photos of it, I recognized the great face— a 4,500-foot cascade of snow and steep rock that was one of the most daunting precipices in the Canadian Rockies. I had never, however, climbed in that sprawling range.

"The only route that's been done is Greenwood's," Denny went on, "way over here on the right edge of the face." His finger traced the line. "This big snowfield is what Chouinard called the Dolphin. I want to go right up here." He indicated an obvious rib left of the Dolphin that snaked up the very center of the north face. "The direttissima. I know it'll be a classic route. What do you think?"

I was flattered to be invited, yet already, within an hour of meeting him, some instinct of wariness made me shrink away from Denny's intensity. "What about that hanging glacier on the summit?" I hedged.

"That's the first thing everybody says!" Denny spat in disgust. "I've been wanting to do Temple since 1962, but I couldn't get anybody to go. Anyway, I think that ice cliff ought to be stable. And I'm sure there's a way through it."

By the end of the evening, I had signed on the dotted line that floated invisibly through our conversation. A few weeks in the Canadian Rockies would make a good prelude to the Arrigetch. And if we could get up Temple . . . well, Denny was right. It was a beautiful line. The ascent would become a classic.

By the time Sharon and I arrived in Banff near the end of June, Hank and Denny had already endured a week of bad weather there. Like other climbing bums, we set up our tents illegally in a dank forest back of the Alpine Club of Canada headquarters, where by day we killed time with other mountaineers. Nobody was getting up anything. The guides said the snow-and-ice conditions up high were those of late spring.

Day after day we loitered on. On the campground picnic table, Hank cooked up hearty spaghetti glops accompanied by gourmet salads full of fresh vegetables. We hung out in Banff's smoky bars, drinking Labatt's Blue and playing shuffleboard. One evening we downed a few beers with Brian Greenwood, the legendary British expat who had authored the only route on Temple's north face and who was Banff's resident mountaineering genius. Denny was paranoid that someone would beat us to his "classic" line, so we said nothing to Greenwood about our plans, even while managing to steer the conversation toward Temple. I suspect the hard man guessed our game, for there was a certain twinkle in his eye as he described watching a gigantic avalanche pour off the hanging glacier near the top and plunge right down the middle of our proposed line.

Don Jensen also showed up in Banff, with his new wife, Joan. Having gotten his BA from Fresno State in 1967, Don was hard at work in grad school at University of Southern California. I had not climbed with Don since our washout of a week in the Palisades over Christmas 1965, just five months after Huntington. Having consulted with one another, Hank, Denny, and I invited Don along on Mount Temple, but I knew from the way he had glanced only diffidently at Denny's route photo that he would decline. That summer, Don's refuge was his mathematics, and while we were cooking glop or tossing a football, Don would ostentatiously cover his own picnic table with scraps of paper on which he had scribbled arcane theorems he felt it his duty to solve.

The charade reminded me of how Don had stayed home from the Gunks to make charts and diagrams before Deborah. I felt a mild vexation. I wanted to say, "Okay, Don, if you're not into climbing this summer, then why'd you come to Banff?"

Beneath the vexation lay an insoluble sadness. It was around Don and Don alone that, just six years earlier, I had wound my half of our double helix of destiny, had plotted a limitless future of unclimbed mountains all over the globe. As it turned out, I would never again climb with my erstwhile best friend, but for a single afternoon in 1971 when he visited me in the middle of a job-hunting foray. We drove out to Rattlesnake Gutter, a local crag I had discovered, did a couple of short top-rope climbs, and called it a day. In the end, I suspect, our characters were simply too different for our partnership to last.

Day after day in the Rockies, the weather stayed atrocious. When it was raining and 40 degrees in Banff, we knew it was snowing up high. More senior climbers frequenting the ACC clubhouse—they might have been in their mid-thirties—inveighed darkly, "After these storms, it'll take days before the peaks are in condition." Silently we dismissed these caveats as the conservative nattering of old farts.

By now, Sharon and I had spent ten days in Banff without even a good hike to show for it. Denny and Hank were well into their third week of waiting. There was no sign the weather was ever going to change. We began to give up all hope of Temple. Then, one morning, Denny suggested that we each take a hit of mescaline.

I had not sailed into the late 1960s as a complete naïf. Though the Beatles left me cold, I had bought all the records I could find of Jimi Hendrix: they rested on my shelf next to Schubert. I owned a pair of purple velvet bell bottoms. The following year, I would play an eager part in shutting down the DU campus in outrage over the bombing of Cambodia and the Kent State shootings. Already I had persuaded Sharon to withhold part of our income tax as protest against the Vietnam War.

About drugs, however, I was pretty much in the dark. I had been at Harvard when Timothy Leary was fired, but had no grasp of what the weird experiments he inflicted on his grad students were really about. In the Revelations, during storm days, Rick and Matt had smoked the occasional joint. I had not only refrained, but vocally expressed my disapproval. By 1969 I had smoked a joint or two myself, gagging so violently at the smoke in my lungs that I got almost no high from the weed.

Mescaline seemed like a huge next step. It took a good hour of Denny's persuading before Sharon and I agreed to swallow the little pills he passed out. (Hank, who had done mescaline once or twice before, decided not to do so now.) Denny had insisted that a rainy day in Banff was the perfect occasion for getting high: no jobs or classes to feel guilty about, no censorious family members within a thousand miles, endless free time on our hands. "It's like watching a movie," he advertised. "When you're straight, you only see what's going on in the center of the screen. When you're high, you pick up all the stuff that's happening on the edges."

I would take mescaline about twenty times during the next decade, without ever quite recapturing the profound transport of that first hallucinatory adventure. During the next twenty hours, I went through all the clichéd stages of the drug trip: from the first half-hour's "I don't feel it—nothing's happening" to the nonstop giggles, from fascination with the swirling wall patterns I had never noticed before to the paranoia on first encountering strangers that surely they knew just by looking in my eyes, from the munchies ten hours in to astonishment that I had actually finished a fifteen-word-long sentence that I had begun uttering a week ago.

Denny's metaphor seemed too trite for the revelations of mescaline. I was convinced that the drug not only redirected my attention to the edges of the screen, but that it heightened my perceptions. In the afternoon, we went to a live concert of Baroque music. In the middle of an interminable Telemann suite, I realized, for the first time ever, that I could hear the almost inaudible ping of the cellist placing her second finger on the D string a half-second before she drew her bow.

The deepest gift of mescaline, however, was its stretching of time. The passage of five minutes by my watch seemed as rich, as full of events, as a whole day in normal time. Only now that I was pharma-cologically liberated from their pall did I realize how the clock and the calendar tyrannized over my life. The slowing down of time itself seemed like a glimpse of immortality.

Then something terrible happened. The skies abruptly cleared. At 10:00 P.M., I could see Venus and the brightest stars in the west. The endless storm had ended.

Still tripping, Denny and I started frantically gathering our climb-ing gear, aided by the sober Hank. I tried to sleep, but the drug kept my mind racing until 5:00 A.M. In the morning, with no more than an hour's sleep each, Denny, Sharon, and I drove north with Hank out of Banff. We parked at the trailhead and hiked in to Lake Annette. The day was holding gloriously clear. There, above us, gleaming in the sun, was the gigantic north face of Temple. We rested through the afternoon, cooked dinner, and fell asleep early. Not early enough, however. The alarm went off at 2:00 A.M.

In the dark, we cooked Cream of Wheat as we put on our boots. My mind was screaming with the alpinist's eternal injunction: *Hurry up! Hurry up!*

The climb, we had figured, would take three days. Sharon would watch our progress today, hike out, return to Banff, then hike in to meet us three days later. Shivering with cold and anticipation, I kissed her goodbye as she lay in our double sleeping bag. The parting felt worse by far than our setting out for Igikpak had the year before. "Be careful," Sharon whispered.

It seems incredible to me now, but it was not until 2004 that, gaz-ing at an old piece of legal pad paper on which I had later sketched our route, I saw the date that we had started up Mount Temple and realized its significance. July 9, 1969. It was eight years to the day since Gabe had fallen to his death from the First Flatiron.

Had I noticed the coincidence at the time, however, I am sure it would not have made a difference. No mere calendrical superstition would have kept me—or Hank or Denny—from heading off into the all-but-lethal trap that awaited us on Temple.

At first, everything went perfectly. Hank elected to go in the middle the first day, allowing Denny and me to trade leads. Passing the lowest rock band with two moderate pitches, we entered a section of the face that, peering through binoculars, I had nicknamed the Black Groove. The rock was limestone, unfamiliar to my fingertips after four straight years in granite ranges, but reasonably solid. I had thought the climbing here would be hard, but to my delight it was so easy that we moved continuously. Every fifty yards or so, I pounded in a piton and clipped in—our only protection in case one of us fell. Moving continuously requires perfect teamwork, a cooperation I thought unlikely our trio would attain, since Denny and I had never climbed together. But now we flew upward like a perfectly oiled machine. We were already way ahead of schedule.

In an article I wrote two months later, I recorded my feelings during those early-morning hours: "This is it, this is the only thing like it. Rhythm, choice, and the clean haste of good climbing: This is what it means to be alive."

Far sooner than we expected, we reached a detached column of rock protruding from the rib. The Pillar, as we called it, required us to belay once more, but we dispatched it in three pitches no harder than 5.6. "It's going to be a classic," said Denny breathlessly, as I handed him the hardware. "I can feel it." Already we had climbed two-fifths of the face. We began to speculate that we might vanquish the great wall in only two days, and in the back of our minds lurked the wild possibility of knocking off Temple in a single day's marathon push.

We stopped on a small platform protruding from the rib for a quick lunch—candy bars, cheese and crackers, sausage, and raisins. All at once, I realized how tired I was, and Denny looked tired as well. Later I would understand that doing mescaline was like taking speed: the twenty-two-hour spell of nonstop stimulation required a day or two of rest and sleep to recover from. Had we not been tripping when the weather cleared, I doubt that we would have dashed so impetuously up to Lake Annette. Guilt over our self-indulgence had driven us prematurely onto the wall.

In only nine hours, we had climbed half the north face. Our lunch platform was the point we had planned for our first bivouac. As we had surged up the easy ground just behind us, I had actually worried that there wouldn't be enough hard climbing on the route. But now, the sun faded behind high clouds, and it started snowing lightly. A light breeze chilled us. The fear of getting caught in a storm washed away my overconfidence.

After lunch, we came to grips with the Black Bands, a series of short cliffs that we had long projected as the crux of the whole route. And here, the character of the north face changed radically. The first pitch was mine, and it was nasty: shattered prongs of rock barely frozen into the ice, reminiscent of the treacherous schist on Mount Deborah. At the top of the pitch, I wasted many minutes trying to get an anchor in that was sound enough to safeguard the next pitch.

Denny led on. Our lightning progress had dwindled to a pathetic crawl. After fifteen feet, Denny rounded a corner and went out of sight, leaving Hank and me to judge the difficulty by the inching out of rope. At long last, Denny yelled "Off belay!," then brought Hank up. With my hand on a carabiner, ready to dismantle my anchor, I waited for the signal for me to come up, gather the hardware from Denny, and lead on. But it didn't come. I waited and waited, stifling the urge to yell out "How's it going?" or "What's happening?"

Gradually I became aware that Denny's anchor must have been so poor that he had brought Hank up only so that he could climb on to a better stance. At last, after what seemed like more than an hour of standing in place, Hank called for me to climb. I swarmed up the slope, realizing what a gutsy lead Denny had made, for here the shattered rock was even looser and steeper than on my pitch.

Rejoining Hank, I shuddered at his ludicrous anchor, a single nylon sling draped over a spike of rock. I looked up. Denny was stranded only forty feet above, resting on minuscule holds. A big detached flake blocked his path. He was worried that climbing past, he would dislodge it and send it crashing down onto us. Now Denny and Hank started arguing about where to go. In Denny's voice, for the first time I heard a frantic tone.

At last he made the move, pulling as gently as possible on the detached flake, which miraculously stayed in place. Cursing as he climbed, Denny scrabbled upward, at last reaching the foot of the upper band. Hank and I each took tension as we came up second and third. Denny's lead, I realized, had been a brilliant one, unratable—for no number grade could embrace the perilous looseness of the fractured limestone.

On the "sharp end" of the rope again, I traversed left, looking for a weakness in the upper Black Band. It was about 3:00 P.M. The snow had stopped falling, and the sun had come back out: now it bathed the upper slopes of the mountain. As I searched for a climbable line, I noticed with alarm that small billows of snow—mini-avalanches—had started to pour down from above. Reckless with adrenaline, I lurched my way up the cliff, pulling loose stones that I flung behind me into the void. Trickles of meltwater were streaming down the rock, running up my sleeves, soaking my neck and chest. Somehow I made it up the cliff. Only a single last band, far more broken than the Black Bands we had conquered, stood between us and the huge, concave snow bowl that swooped upward toward the vertical ice cliff just below the summit.

But now I comprehended the trap. The concave bowl above us was loaded with new snow, piled there by the weeks of storm. The afternoon sun had warmed and melted the slopes, which were now hair-trigger ready to slide. The old farts at the Alpine Club clubhouse had been right, after all. We ought to have waited days for the Rockies to get in condition, for the slides to clear off the overloaded slopes and basins. Our impetuous haste had lured us into a desperate cul-de-sac, which only a renewed haste might allow us to escape.

The little slides began to run constantly. Underestimating the last broken band, we needed three pitches, not one, to surmount it.

An hour later, all three of us stood together at a good belay stance, just fifteen feet below the top of the band, which I prepared to lead. But those fifteen feet proved damnably hard. I was clinging to small holds, looking for the next one, when we heard a deep rumble that seemed to make the very mountain vibrate. The rumble crescendoed into a roar.

Suddenly a gigantic mass of wet snow plunged off the cliff, fifty yards to the left of us. I had seen massive avalanches on the Wickersham Wall, had ridden out a wind-slab avalanche with Rick Millikan in the Kichatnas, but none of those slides had prepared me for the terror of this sight. The most awful aspect of the avalanche was how the debris gathered speed as it plunged off the cliff, then smashed with a loud report on the ledge below. It looked more like tons of wet cement than snow.

Our smooth teamwork had fallen apart. "Maybe we ought to bivouac," I yelled, clinging to my holds.

"Bivouac? Where?" Denny shouted back.

"Let's go!" Hank interjected. "We've got to move!"

They were right: the fifteen-foot cliff was no refuge against a slide like the one we had just seen. I lunged upward, using the pick of my ice axe to snag a rock I couldn't otherwise reach. At last, I had gained the concave bowl. I started scrambling upward through thigh-deep snow, gasping for breath. I was almost out of energy, but Hank screamed at me, "Hurry up!"

A hundred and twenty feet up, I used the illusory safety of a pair of curling plumes, almost like mid-slope cornices, to kick a platform in the snow (no hope of a real anchor) and belay my teammates up. Denny had just left the ledge below the last cliff when another giant slide came down to the right of me, directly over the belay stance where the three of us had stood arguing.

Denny took over the lead, plowing on upward through the soggy thigh-deep snow. Once more he went out of sight. "How's it look?" we yelled every few minutes. Denny did not bother to answer.

When at last the rope came tight and I could start up, I discovered just how truly agonizing our situation was. The concave bowl was gigantic. The lip of the hanging glacier, toward which Denny slogged his feeble way, was still many hundreds of feet above. Avalanches were cutting loose all over the bowl, some starting at our level, some above us and to the right. Any one of them would have easily scoured us clean.

And then, in a split second, I saw the answer. To our left, a shallow gully marked the wake of the first huge avalanche. The slide had gouged the gully down to bare ice. Over there, I thought, there was little debris left to slide. To cross the gully without crampons would require a burst of inspired ballet on tiny chunks of rock frozen into the ice, but it would quickly deliver us to a break in the hanging glacier, beyond which we could wallow safely in the low-angle drifts of the summit snowfield. It was our chance to stay alive.

"Denny!" I yelled. "What about the chute on the left?"

Neither of my partners answered. "Denny!" I screamed louder. "Where the hell are you going?"

He looked down in annoyance. "For the ice cliff!" he yelled back.

"Damn it, Denny! That's six times as hard!"

"Shut up, Dave!" Hank rejoined from above. "It's Denny's lead. It's his decision."

Exhausted, Denny reached a small rock outcrop into which he hammered a single piton, then brought Hank and me up. By now, even the steps he was kicking in the 50-degree slope were breaking underfoot and starting little slides of their own.

As soon as I reached Denny, I lit into him. "You've got to be crazy! If we cross the chute, we're safe in five minutes."

"Cross the chute?" he yelled back. "It's ready to slide any moment. It would be suicide!"

"The stupidest thing we can do," Hank said, "is stand here and argue while some avalanche wipes us out."

For the first and only time in my climbing life, I thought seriously about unroping from my teammates. A solo dash across the polished gully seemed to me safer than pushing on upward toward inevitable doom. Denny's pale blue eyes blazed with fury. I recognized in them the fever of fanaticism—the very same passion I had carried onto Huntington and had inflicted upon Matt as we climbed on toward the summit after our near-fatal fall. Here, on his "classic" route on Temple, even faced with the likelihood of death, Denny still cared vitally about the perfect vector of the direttissima. He would play Russian roulette with the avalanches rather than spoil that line on the photo with a leftward escape.

"Hank," I said, trying to calm myself, "you have to decide. Which makes more sense?"

Hank slowly enumerated the pros and cons of each choice. It was absurd, I thought, to stand here volleying words like debaters, while everything was collapsing around us. Hank's parsing of our choices, however, came out slightly in favor of my escape route.

"I'm going on!" Denny abruptly proclaimed.

"Damn it, Denny! You're outvoted! We'll be off this in five minutes. Give me the hardware!"

At last Denny gave in. The look on his face was leaden with loss.

Crossing the polished gully, I performed one of the finest leads of my life, as adrenaline danced my feet from one tiny hold to the next and I pivoted over the pick of my ice axe. I had to give both Denny and Hank tension to get them across. When Hank joined me, he said, "You son of a bitch, you had a lot of nerve going across like that." I searched his face, hoping to hear ribald congratulation in his words, but Hank's eyes were as cold as Denny's. It did not matter. We were saved. I lay on my back in the nearly level snow and murmured, "Off belay."

We trudged on up the snowfield into the dark, crossed over the summit without even pausing, then, after midnight, found a ledge for our bivouac. Crammed sitting up, all three in the nylon sack, soaked to the skin, we tried to get comfortable enough to catch a little sleep. Hank, who was slightly less exhausted, babied Denny and me, cooking soup on his lap and melting snow for Tang and lemonade as we tried to restore our badly dehydrated bodies. Both Denny and I gagged on the warm soup and almost threw up.

Sometime before dawn, I woke to feel Denny shivering beside me. Of the three of us, he was the only one without a half-bag. Not sure whether he was asleep or awake, I put my arm around him, offering him not only warmth but a mute apology.

At Lake Annette, Sharon had watched us all day in binoculars. She had thrilled at our fast progress, but then the sky had dimmed with the brief snowstorm and she had lost sight of us. When it cleared again, she saw the avalanches starting to come down. They took so long to fall, she could hear the roar, locate the avalanche in the binoculars, then watch it thunder all the way to the base of the great wall. In that magnified view, she discerned the full violence of the cascades of cement-like snow.

And all that afternoon, she never again found our three tiny dots in the binoculars. Weeping with despair, Sharon thought that the chances were better than even that an avalanche had carried us to our deaths.

She could not face a night alone at Lake Annette. Shortly before dark, she hiked out, drove to Banff, and rented a cabin from the Alpine Club. Cautioned by me over the years never to send out a premature alarm, however, she told no one what she had seen on Temple. After a sleepless night, she drove back to the trailhead, then hiked back in to Lake Annette. There was no one there. She sat down, stunned with grief, on a bedrock slab.

The three of us had set off at dawn, clumping down the normal west-side route on Temple, which Denny and Hank had reconnoitered during their first days in Banff. Hank's knees were killing him. I could remember being so tired only once or twice in my life.

At last we skirted under the north face and approached Lake Annette. I saw Sharon sitting there just as she looked up to discover the three of us hobbling toward her.

In the moment before she ran into my arms, her face was frozen in a look of sharp astonishment. There was fear and reproach in that look, along with joy. As the morning had worn on, she told me later, she had debated with herself whether to hike over to the bottom of the face and start poking through the avalanche debris. Suddenly, there we were, moving, however slowly, intact and whole. It was as if we had returned from the dead. And in that moment, a ghost spoke in the back of her mind: *How many more times in my life can I go through this?*

EIGHT

Professor of Mountaineering

AFTER TEMPLE, THE ARRIGETCH AMOUNTED TO a bucolic anticlimax. Our team of five, including Sharon, ran into one of the coldest Brooks Range Augusts in recent memory. That meant that while the mosquitoes were extinguished early, we sat out a number of base camp snowstorms, watched ice plate the granite slabs we hoped to climb, and belayed in down jackets rather than T-shirts. During three weeks based in Arrigetch Creek, we made five first ascents, including that of the range's highest peak, which we called Caliban (our motif this summer being Shakespearean rather than biblical), but none was in a league with Igikpak.

We worried about early freeze-up, but got the best weather of our trip on a seven-day float down a hundred miles of the Alatna River that we undertook at the end of our expedition. That week of lazy drifting on the placid current, past groves of birch and willow expiring in a blaze of autumnal colors, hearing wolves howl in the distance, catching fat grayling in every other pool into which we tossed our lines, lingering past midnight around our gravel-bar campfires, furnished an idyll the likes of which I had never before enjoyed in Alaska. On September 2, right on schedule, Daryl Morris touched down on a prearranged sandbar to fly us out of the Brooks Range.

In the Arrigetch, we had suffered not even a dangerous moment, let alone a close call. And Sharon had learned to relax in these mountains as she never had beneath Igikpak. Though she climbed none of our five peaks (all of which were technical), she explored far more terrain, hiking with us to the heads of side valleys, scrambling across cirques to the bases of 2,000-foot walls, than she had in a month the year before. At Sharon's urging, we included a gold pan in our air-dropped supplies, and during slow days she and I spent many an hour panning fruitlessly for the gleaming sand in Arrigetch Creek.

I passed much of the expedition in an oddly contemplative mood. As on Igikpak, my teammates were solid climbers and congenial fellows, but I would develop no lasting friendships from among their company. In the middle of the trip, I read Graham Greene's *The End of the Affair*. The novel stunned me, as few books have before or since, both with the exquisite craft of Greene's prose and with the irreducible tragedy at the core of the story. And the book goaded me to a sense of shame about my own writerly efforts by the age of twenty-six.

In retrospect, that shame seems slightly ridiculous. I had already written two books that had been accepted by Vanguard. None of my colleagues in the DU writing program had had more than a few short stories or poems published in the little magazines. Thanks to the luck of having a subject as arcane but dramatic as mountaineering, I had all too easily tasted early success. Yet that summer in the Arrigetch, I began to wonder if my obsession with climbing was getting in the way of my ambition as a writer.

At twenty-six, I worried that I was getting old, that I had already let too many opportunities slip by. Our close call on Temple was still in my mind when I wrote in my diary on August 23,

> I have a certainty that there's plenty of time left to write those books—plenty, more than enough—if I just don't get killed or distracted. . . . No doubt the distraction is really the greater, the more pernicious danger. Piled up over months, years—the papers to be graded, the times it's easier to turn on the tube than think, the times I have to get out of doors and throw the football. . . .
>
> What this summer has told me is that I have to write. I've spent two years talking about the books I thought I was going

to write, to the point at which one of them has slid past the impulse . . . and lies in a kind of junk heap. I've got a lot to write, and I know I can make the time for it. There are always less important things to sacrifice. What could a twentieth or twenty-third Alaskan first ascent mean to me compared to the spark or seed of a good or even a great book?

Today, I have no recollection what those two failed books over which I agonized might have been about. But I can see how thoroughly I was my father's son. In the 1990s, several years after he had died of melanoma, Dad's journal from his first year of graduate school at Harvard turned up in my mother's housecleaning. The entries both shocked me and filled me with sorrow. At twenty-three, Dad had been the budding star of the astrophysics department, who would go on to plant the banner of his coronagraph above the highest town in the United States; but in the winter and spring of 1939, he scolded himself over and over, "I *must* work harder" ("must" triple-underlined), "I *must* learn my differential equations."

Back at DU in the fall of 1969, I began my own last year of graduate school. Sharon had earned her MA the previous spring, and was now working as a substitute teacher in the Denver public high school system. I had passed my language exams in Latin and French; I had more than enough course credits for the Ph.D.; I would soon sail through my oral comprehensive exam; all that remained was to write my dissertation. The main reason I had chosen DU in the first place was that there, instead of some intensive study of Crashaw's use of metonymy or sophistic argument for the rehabilitation of John Clare, I could produce a specimen of "creative writing" for my dissertation. Still half-convinced that books about mountaineering did not really count, I had a novel in mind as I sat down to write that autumn. It would be, I assumed, the first of several great works to flow from my pen.

This time it took me not nine days, not two months, to write a book, but a solid eight months from October through May. Determined to keep my imaginative fit intact from the impediments of criticism, I showed not a page of the book to my advisor, John Williams, before I was finished. *Shadwell* was, I thought, a work of satire in the eighteenth-century tradition. The name of my protagonist, Dennis Shadwell, conflated two now forgotten "scribblers" whom my beloved Swift and Pope had savagely pilloried.

In mid-May 1970, the moment I walked into the meeting called for my dissertation defense, I knew something was dreadfully wrong. The same professors who had invited Sharon and me over for dinner, with whom I had drunk pitchers at the Stadium Inn, would not look me in the eye. There was an excruciating silence in the room, before John Williams cleared his throat and declared a commencement of proceedings.

During the next two hours, I learned that the mentors who had taught me everything I knew about Elizabethan drama, about Middle English prosody, about Melville and Hawthorne and even Swift and Pope, shared the unanimous verdict that I had written an appallingly bad novel. Defiant to the end (as every thick-skinned writer must be), I would require another couple of years to recognize just how right that verdict was.

I have not tried to reread *Shadwell* in the last thirty years; I am not even sure I still have a copy. But the novel utterly dismayed my professors, some of whom had read and admired *The Mountain of My Fear*.

During the defense, those professors tried to be gentle with me. The consensus, however, was clear: *Shadwell* was not acceptable as a dissertation. But what was I to do? Take another semester—another year?—and try to fix what was wrong, or start over? By now, I had a teaching job lined up for the fall of 1970. In the musty room, sweating with discomfort and half-formed anger, I felt like a suspect trying to prove his innocence.

In the end, my DU professors let me slip through with my Ph.D., despite their withering appraisal of my dissertation. Unwilling to accept their verdict, I sent *Shadwell* off to Vanguard. In 1968, to celebrate the publication of *The Mountain of My Fear*, the kindly, eccentric head of the press, Evelyn Shrifte, had flown Sharon and me to New York for a week on the town, during which we attended the National

Book Awards, dined at Il Gattopardo with Joyce Carol Oates, and got front-row seats for a Supremes concert at the Copacabana. Now, in late 1970, Evelyn arranged a meeting in her office to render her verdict. With real regret, she told me that Vanguard would not be publishing my novel. She went on to murmur a few of the trade's homilies of rejection, invoking such words as "noncommercial" and "not sufficiently realized." But suddenly, she looked me in the eye and asked, "Do you know anybody like that man?"

I tried two or three other publishers before giving up. One editor was far blunter than Evelyn, writing me a one-line rejection slip that said something like, "There's nothing so much wrong with this, except that I couldn't get the slightest bit interested in any of the characters."

Today, I count it among my blessings that Shadwell was never published. And sometimes I muse that, but for the thoroughness of Ann Arbor's University Microfilms, the dreadfully bad (and potentially embarrassing) piece of book-length dreck that I wrote at twenty-six might have passed cleanly out of existence.

In the summer of 1970, as if I didn't know what else to do, I headed back to Alaska for the eighth straight year. On a last-minute whim, I joined Hank Abrons for a return to the Kichatna Spires in June, even though I suspected (after Huntington and the Revelations) that that was the worst month of all for climbing in the Alaska Range. On my first two-man expedition since Deborah, I had high ambitions: to climb Middle Triple Peak, second highest in the range, a fierce tower that promised to be as difficult as Kichatna Spire.

During twenty days, Hank and I climbed nothing. We were rusty from a sedentary winter, and correspondingly timid, though I doubt that in the best of shape we could have made a dent on Middle Triple, for every ridge and gully in the Kichatnas was booby-trapped with heavy loads of winter snow that were melting in the twenty-hour sun of June. After Temple, we knew better than to tempt fate on such terrain. We tried two minor peaks, turning back in the face of soggy cornices perched precariously on knife-edged granite, and never even set foot on Middle Triple. As I later wrote, in a rueful note for the *American Alpine Journal*, summing up our three-week washout, "The trip was a porridge of white-out, drizzling snow, and insincere patches of blue sky. . . . The snow conditions were consistently hideous, but probably typical for June."

Middle Triple was not climbed until 1977, when, in a dazzling effort, two young climbers tackled its hardest route, the 3,000-foot-high west face. In 1966, during our October escape from the Spires, we had shuddered as we became the first humans to walk beneath this near-vertical precipice, coated smooth from bottom to top with rime ice. The 1977 ascent was spearheaded by Charlie Porter, who in the late 1970s and early 1980s became a fugitive legend, putting up some of the hardest routes in North America (more than one of them solo) without ever deigning—such was his purist aesthetic—to celebrate his deeds in the curtest journal note or most casual public slide show.

Hank and I chose to hike out of the Kichatnas to Rainy Pass, thirty miles as the crow flies to the south, just as our party had in October 1966. In June flood, however, even the minor stream of Morris Creek was raging and unfordable. We had to detour six miles toward its headwaters before crossing on a snow bridge formed by avalanche runout. Half those six miles were a bushwhack through alder thickets, infuriating and exhausting with seventy-pound packs on our backs.

The last day, I marched on filled with dread, for I knew that the Happy River, a far more major watercourse than Morris Creek, ran athwart our path. The river had been named by the government surveyor J. E. Spurr, whose party had nearly drowned in it in 1898. We reached the banks only after a ten-hour push. The river defeated our first three attempts at different bends, when pounding waist-deep current and slippery cobbles underfoot threatened to upend us. Although I have never learned to swim, in those days I prided myself on being a good wader. On our fourth attempt, where the river braided out among island gravel bars, I barely made it across. Turning back to look at Hank, I saw that he seemed frozen on the last island.

He had already fallen flat on his face crossing a relatively minor stream, even before Morris Creek.

By now we had only one ice axe, which I knew could help stabilize Hank as he forded the last and worst channel. I threw the axe (after practicing with a stick), but it sailed over Hank's head. Eventually I was able to supply him with a stout willow branch. To quote my diary, "He came over, shaky but methodical. Then he'd made it. I don't care about the axe. We're safe now, that's what counts."

Our failure rankled, but there was something gratifying about having come to grips again with the magnificent Alaska Range, after two summers in the Brooks. Nothing soft about the Kichatnas.

By midnight that same day, Don Sheldon had flown us to Talkeetna. Hank and I threw our sleeping bags on the floor of his hangar, but we both found it hard to sleep. I had not been back to Talkeetna since our Huntington expedition. As I ended my diary the next morning,

The place is full of memories of 1965, all of them sad. Everything seemed so wonderful then, on the way in, and so bleak on the way out. Across the puddle-strewn airstrip is the schoolhouse, and beside it the baseball diamond where Matt and I played. But there's no looking back.

Only a week later, I had begun my summer's second expedition, also a two-man effort—or rather, a one-man, one-woman trip, for I had decided, rather than drag Sharon along on another climbing outing, to design an exploratory jaunt for just the two of us. During the previous year, I had grown enamored of the Klepper Faltboote I had bought—a German-made collapsible two-person kayak fabricated from a wooden frame and a rubber-and-canvas shell. We had used the Klepper on the Alatna River in 1969, effortlessly doubling the pace of our three teammates, who paddled a balky rubber raft. The Klepper was no good in rapids, but it was ideal for packing up and portaging or for flying as cargo into remote places.

For our objective, I had settled on the Tikchik Lakes in far western Alaska. On the map, the Tikchiks and the adjoining Wood River Lakes made an intriguing north-to-south stack of ten narrow but long bodies of water, most of them interconnected by short, swift outlets. Flying in by Grumman Goose from Dillingham, we were landed on floats at the western head of Lake Chauekuktuli.

During the next eighteen days, Sharon and I accomplished a leisurely traversal of Chauekuktuli and its southern neighbor, Lake Nuyakuk, each some thirty to forty miles long. No doubt my infatuation with the Klepper, like my pride in fording rivers, served as some kind of counterphobic compensation for not only never having learned how to swim, but for harboring a lifelong terror of water. On the lakes, we were the soul of caution, staying put in camp when a breeze stirred the surface into even moderate chop. Unlike the goal of a climbing expedition, the point of our Tikchik journey was not to arrive at any particular destination, but simply to absorb the lonely beauty of an unfamiliar wilderness.

During those eighteen days, we ran into only one other party, a group of veteran geologists ensconced in tents and a plywood shack near the outlet of Chauekuktuli. Surprised to see us, they cooked up a hearty roast pork for dinner, but wondered aloud why we hadn't chosen to abet our progress with an outboard motor. Aquatic neophytes, we did not voice our romantic conviction that the roar of a motor would have spoiled the splendid silence of the place.

The eastern ends of the great lakes lay in almost level tundra plains, but their western bays headed in a range of unexplored, unnamed mountains. A few were handsome, spiky peaks, but most could only be called talus lumps. Still, these were virgin summits, and I had planned several-day jaunts at the beginning and end of our boat trip to reconnoiter them and bag a few first ascents. But on our first such attempt, we ran smack into the worst alder thickets I had ever seen in Alaska. After an hour of fiendish bushwhacking that gained us less than half a mile, Sharon was in tears. In the end, we claimed only one summit, that of a nondescript mountain we named Detour Peak, and even that took us three days, as we fought our way through the alder to blessed timberline, then back again.

The Tikchiks, we quickly learned, were prime grizzly bear country. Ironically, we never saw a single bear during the eighteen days, but we ran across more grizzly tracks and piles of excrement (some quite fresh) than on all of my other Alaskan trips combined. In Fairbanks the previous year, I had met the seventy-year-old Adolph Murie, a famous biologist who, with his brother Olaus (by then deceased), had performed many epic treks through the Brooks Range, including a monumental winter journey by dogsled in 1922. Murie swore that guns were unnecessary and unsporting in grizzly country. In all his years in the north, he had had only one close call with Ursus horribilis, when he had won a sprint for a cabin door by a nose over an overzealous beast.

Under Murie's sway, I had left my borrowed 30.06 at home this year, relying on ammonia sprinkled around our food boxes to keep the bears at bay. The scat and tracks, however, unnerved Sharon, and even gave me a moment's pause when we packed up all our gear and food in one cache, the Klepper in another, and left them on the Chauekuktuli shore during our four-day loop among the mountains. Had a hungry bear torn our caches apart, we would have been in serious trouble.

Despite my determination to share a truly laid-back trip with Sharon, the intensity of the place had its impact. On several occasions, I left Sharon on shore while I bushwhacked back to get the Klepper to pick her up. As I wrote in my diary, "She's very nervous when I'm out of sight at all; and I must admit even I notice the effect. It's a wild, often gloomy place, and the two of us seem very alone in it." The mosquitoes were consistently dense, the alders unrelenting. We waited out one storm of wind and cold rain that didn't let up for seventy-two hours straight. Her fears made Sharon even more conservative than I, and we had several quarrels about whether the chop was mild enough to allow the launching of our kayak.

Yet the two-and-a-half-week trip on the Tikchiks turned into a sustained and matchless idyll. We saw few mammals, but the bird life was phenomenally rich: ducks and geese bobbing on the waves, eagles and hawks lumbering overhead, cliffs full of swallows, and flocks and rookeries thick with birds whose names I did not know. Between rainstorms, the sky was sometimes spangled with mackerel cirrus. On clear days, the surface of the still water paired the landscape with its inverted twin. Though my fly rod was ineffectual against the big lake trout and northern pike, we spent long minutes watching these monsters of the deep swim oblivious three feet beneath our boat.

Our idyll reached its peak during the last five days of the trip, when we made camp on a small island a hundred yards off the shore of Lake Nuyakuk. Convinced (no doubt fallaciously) that we were thus safe from all possible bear attacks, we relaxed into the perfection of our subarctic utopia. We spent our days boating leisurely into Nuyakuk's twin headwater cirques, Portage Arm and Mirror Bay, returning each afternoon to our cozy camp. The tent was pitched in a hollow of cushion-soft tundra. Smooth greenstone billows shelved from the island shore into deep, dark water. Of an evening, we would sit around a small fire of alder branches, cooking glop as we gazed at the darkening hills.

The emptiness of this wilderness of lakes, in which I could not pretend to be an expert, conspired with our lurking anxieties about bears and weather and waves to give the trip an edge—the very edge that escaped my existence in Denver, where I numbed myself with the domestic routines that marriage seemed to prescribe. Only years after it was over did Sharon and I begin to realize how special our Tikchik trip had been. There, I suspect, we grew as close as we would ever get, and for once, despite my impatience to bash through the alders and claim some of those distant summits to the west, I allowed myself for days at a time to loll in the haven of intimacy, and to receive the love that Sharon so unstintingly gave.

The third trip of my Alaskan summer was designed as pure lark, but it ended up setting in motion a rapprochement for which, more than three decades later, I am heartily grateful. The day after Sharon and I flew out to Dillingham, my father flew in, at the controls of a twin-engine Beech Baron he had bought a few years before. Too workaholic to allow himself an outright hobby, Dad had rationalized learning to fly the airplane as a business convenience. On puddle-jump jaunts to scientific meetings around the West, he had sometimes chartered a private plane rather than fly commercially. During one such flight, the pilot got violently ill and was barely able to land the craft at the nearest airstrip.

Dad decided that it made sense to learn how to handle the controls himself. And as soon as he started his lessons, he realized that he had a real knack as a pilot. He bought the Baron and used any excuse he could concoct to log hours in it—including taking each of his four children on short scenic flights over the Rockies.

A decade before, when my father's wangling of the Japanese abortion had saved Lisa and me from the purgatory of early parenthood, I had been too choked with shame to express any gratitude. At Harvard, as I became a serious climber, I did my best to ignore my parents' anguish over the risks I took—as when, after we had been reported missing and presumed dead on Mount McKinley, my HMC friends and I had turned the lurid newspaper report of Dad's telephone vigil into japes about the "Sun King."

It would not be until after his death in 1990 that I fully realized, from the comments of his closest friends, how proud my father had been of my accomplishments. He could brag about my books and climbs to his colleagues, but had trouble giving me an unironic pat on the back. I was aware instead of a competitive tension between us. In his office on the CU campus one day in 1967, I told him that Vanguard Press had accepted the first draft that Dad had told me I had no business sending off without extensive revision. He grinned eerily, stuck out his hand for me to shake, and said, "Congratulations, you beat me to it." Not until 1969 did he publish his own first book, a slender volume called *A View of Century 21*, cobbled together out of crystal-ball lectures on the future of science that he had delivered at Claremont College.

Yet during my DU years, Dad had responded warmly to the Brooks Range slide shows I had projected on the occasional weekend up in Boulder. Of that enthusiasm, and Dad's new airplane hobby, our 1970 lark was born.

With an outdoorsy friend from Boulder who was a professional pilot, Dad had flown the Baron up the Alaska Highway all the way to Dillingham. Now Sharon and I climbed aboard for a three-hour hop to Fairbanks, where we shopped for gear and groceries. From there, we headed north to Bettles. Dad parked his plane beside the airstrip, and Paul Shanahan—Daryl Morris's erstwhile assistant, who had taken over the air charter—winged us 120 miles west to Lake Selby, on which he made a deft landing on floats. During the next eight days, the four of us had no agenda but to fish, paddle the Klepper in aimless circles, photograph flowers, pick blueberries, and sit around the campfire on stools we made out of Blazo crates left by surveyors decades before.

At first, Dad found it difficult to relax, and unsettling to be cut off from the telephone that had, daily during the past thirty years, kept him in touch with his scientific duties. During those three decades, he had scarcely taken a vacation longer than a weekend. That July Dad was fifty-four, exactly twice my age. After his first years at Climax, when he had skied and hiked up 13-ers, he had gotten too busy to make exercise part of his life. Now he was a little overweight and completely out of shape, but I had reckoned with those shortcomings in the design of our trip. The brief hikes we took across the russet tundra were voyages of discovery for him, and building the campfire each evening (it was he who had taught me how, at Twin Lakes twenty years before) a welcome challenge.

That outing was the first of five Brooks Range trips my father and I would share between 1970 and 1977. After Selby, we camped, successively, on Lakes Omelaktavik, Alatna, Kurupa, and Shainin, for periods as long as two weeks, and never had to share the place with a single hiker or fisherman. In the back seat of the Klepper, I would paddle my father out to choice coves in each lake. He had never forgotten how to fish, and by adapting his fly rod to troll deep with a lure, he hooked countless specimens of the lake trout and pike that had baffled me in the Tikchiks.

Each year we assembled a different band, composed of his pilot companions and my climbing buddies (including Sharon, who went on the first two trips). On two of our larks, there were forest fires raging out of control far to the south: just as on Igikpak, the wind blew the sweet smoke all the way up to our treeless domain, blearing the sky with a pastel smog. For sport, we made a baseball out of tundra wound in duct tape and used a tentpole for a bat. A lefty, Dad would tap the plate, then aim the bat at the pitcher and waggle it in a threatening loop, just as he had seen Rabbit Maranville do at Braves Field during his boyhood.

Dad had taught me to watch for the rare green flash, which occurred when the sun set behind a distant skyline on a day graced by exceptionally pristine skies. The flash is caused by atmospheric dispersion, which separates the color of the sun into its spectrum of different hues, with green on top. I had seen the green flash perhaps a dozen times in my life, but on the Alatna Lakes in 1972, we saw it not once, but many times, at will, as we hiked up the hillside behind camp to replay the sunset.

With my climbing pals, I would set off up the surrounding valleys to bag first ascents of nameless talus lumps. On two such forays out of Shainin Lake in 1977, I made discoveries that would have gladdened the heart of Adolph Murie. The first, the interlocked antlers of a pair of buck caribou, covered with moss, the skulls intact. Here, decades ago, the rutting beasts, unable to disentangle, had starved to death. The assemblage looked fragile, but I couldn't pull the antlers apart.

The second, an undercut bank on the lakeshore where, three feet deep in the black soil, I found an astonishing collection of bones. For generations, this had evidently been an Inupiaq campsite, where the people had trapped and eaten caribou and bear.

Always, the midsummer light seduced us into staying up well past midnight. Sitting on our Blazo stools, we would brew up cup after cup of coffee or hot Tang. We ate the fish Dad caught until we were so sick of them that even Spam tasted great. Around our willow-twig campfires, in the words of Callimachus, "we tired the sun with talking as we sent him down the sky."

None of the conversations between my father and me plumbed the depths of the interpersonal, or delved back to the crises of my wayward adolescence. We never attained the ideal that my mother, in her cups, was wont to urge on us: "I think people should just level with each other." The talk was all about the expanding universe, or ranges elsewhere in Alaska I longed to explore, or bizarre characters we had met in conferences or classrooms. Yet it was all the better for its avoidance of the personal. Those weeks in the Brooks Range healed wounds that we scarcely remembered inflicting upon each other.

After 1977, we stopped going to Alaska together. On Shainin Lake, Dad was about to turn sixty-two, and he felt old. One or two of our hikes had badly worn him out. And after 1977, I began to lose my own passion for Alaska.

In March 1990, as my father lay on his deathbed on Bluebell Avenue, I had to leave Boulder (concurring, to the very end, with his unspoken dictum that no mere personal tragedy should get in the way of work) for Texas on a magazine assignment too important to pass up. The parting was excruciating. Dad was racked with nausea, dopey with painkillers. Fighting back tears, I told him, for the first time since the age of five or six, that I loved him. I kissed his forehead. I told him how much the trips in the Brooks Range had meant to me. "Maybe we can do another one," he mumbled. Those were the last words he ever spoke to me.

In the spring of 1970, with my doctorate almost in my pocket, I interviewed for teaching jobs back east. It was the beginning of the era of far too many newly minted Ph.D.'s competing for far too few assistant professorships. I had tryouts at Mount Holyoke and Middlebury, but ended up accepting a post at Hampshire College, an "experimental" college in Amherst, Massachusetts, scheduled to open its doors in the fall. Across a former apple orchard just three miles south of the campus my father had inhabited during the late 1930s, Hampshire's red-brick administration buildings and prefab modular dorms sprouted overnight.

The irony that had allowed me to get my first two books published now continued to work its unanticipated magic. Seven or eight years before, within the HMC, as we had neglected our studies in favor of weekends at the Gunks or Cathedral, as we shrugged off suggestions that we write senior theses, as we muddled through majors (like my mathematics) that we had lost interest in, we climbing bums were sure that our passion for *grand alpinisme* would prove disastrous for any careers we might later pursue. But climbing had given me the salable subjects of my first two books. Later, when I turned to freelance writing full-time, it would give me an expertise that helped me break into mainstream magazines. And now, in 1970, it landed me my job at Hampshire. The college's founders, wed to their experimental design, were not about to countenance the foofaraw of a traditional athletic program, with its varsity teams and stadiums. Instead, they went in search of a bona fide professor-type who could also devise an Outward Bound–style program in lieu of athletics. In 1970, there were very few Ph.D.'s in the country who had actually taught at Outward Bound, let alone led expeditions to Alaska.

In early September, Sharon and I packed all of our belongings into a U-Haul truck (driving the diminutive Saab off a loading dock into the cargo hold, then tying it down with climbing rope) and motored, over three boring days on the Interstate, 2,000 miles east to Massachusetts. There we sublet an Amherst College–owned house in the center of town from a dean on sabbatical leave in England. From our tiny bungalow in Denver, we had graduated to a Victorian mansion, surrounded by generous lawns and umbrageous copper beeches: the house had once belonged to Howard R. Garis, the creator of the Uncle Wiggily books.

With me pulling down the extravagant salary of $12,000 a year, Sharon felt relieved, for the first time in her adult life, from the need to get a job. She settled in to our ten-room mansion, read Thackeray and E. M. Forster, tried to write poetry, and started drinking sherry at 3:00 in the afternoon. Rather than lolling in unaccustomed luxury, however, she felt lonely and ill-at-ease in the rambling house, tiptoeing from room to room as though she were afraid of breaking some heirloom. Her discomfort was reinforced by monthly letters from the dean's wife telling her how to wash the sheets and store the china. By sometime in the winter, Sharon realized that she was on the brink of a major depression.

Meanwhile, I threw myself headlong into my new job. No institute of higher learning was ever launched on a more manic jag. That first year, Hampshire had only 250 students, but alternative education, riding the crest of late 1960s disdain for the Establishment, was so in vogue that our eight-to-one ratio of applicants to acceptances meant that in 1970, Hampshire was harder to get into than Harvard or Yale. Those 250 members of the elect brought to their first year of college a messianic zeal to change the world, but also, as it would take me a while to recognize, a sense of entitlement that we faculty were all but powerless to dampen.

Wearing my half-time hat as professor of literature, I taught courses in creative writing, autobiography, and something amorphously called "Man and Nature." As founder of the Outward Bound–style program— I named my new creation the Outdoors Program, or O.P.—I built a ropes course in the woods, concocted an orienteering race, belayed students as they rappelled off the library roof, and led hikes ranging from a moonlight traverse of the Holyoke Range to midwinter assaults on Mounts Madison and Adams. As a nod to traditional athletics, I bought a mess of bats, softballs, gloves, and footballs, and—reverting to the childhood tyrant of the vacant lot—organized idiosyncratic contests on available patches of campus lawn. The coed soccer team I put together played exuberant matches in an ad hoc league embracing other nearby hippie schools such as Goddard and Marlboro. (The Amherst College freshmen pulled their team off the field when we refused to exclude women from our starting eleven.) In an official O.P. van, I led a delegation to a march on Washington to protest the war—a deed that did not please the administration. Halfway through the year, I hired an Olympic-caliber kayaker to diversify our outdoor offerings.

At the heart of my O.P., of course, was climbing. The two local crags in favor were Chapel Ledge, near Ashfield, and Rose Ledge, farther north beside Route 2—both within forty minutes of school. During a typical week that first year, I was in the classroom five days. But I also led an afternoon or Saturday hike, as well as two afternoon top-rope trips to Rose or Chapel, and a Sunday trip to Ragged Mountain in Connecticut or even a whole weekend at the Gunks. These latter outings were nervous propositions, for, although four or five students had done a little rock climbing before college, I trusted none of them to lead. Yet that year I was so full of my own manic enthusiasm, I did not understand why, dragging myself home to Uncle Wiggily's mansion on Sunday night, I felt so exhausted that I could barely maintain a conversation with Sharon, who had waited all weekend for company.

Thanks to the O.P., for the first time since my senior year at Harvard, I was climbing regularly through the school year, not just during the summer. I was soon in terrific shape. Yet there were severe limitations to what kinds of routes I could tackle with my neophyte students. Eight-pitch climbs at Cannon Cliff—the sorts of challenges we had cut our eyeteeth on in the HMC—were clearly beyond the pale, as were even the standard routes at Cathedral and Whitehorse. My frustration was epitomized by a day at the Gunks. With a good athlete who I thought was perhaps the most talented of the student climbers, I started up a three-pitch climb in the Trapps. Midway up the second pitch, I pulled over a typical Gunks roof: it was only 5.6 in difficulty, but it was wildly exposed. The roof completely psyched out my student partner, who wore his arms out hanging from the lip, even while I screamed instructions at him. He was too heavy to haul, so in the end I lowered him back to the belay ledge, then rappelled off in disgust.

In October, however, I made a wonderful discovery. Through a gloomy, boggy defile just east of the funky little town of Montague, a seldom-used one-lane dirt road trundled along a brook. A few miles in, a dark cliff rose above the left-hand bank. The place was called Rattlesnake Gutter. The rock, I found out at once, was not nearly as solid as Chapel or Rose, but the crag towered a good 130 feet off the ground, the upper ninety feet relentlessly overhanging. Discreet inquiries revealed, to my astonishment, that the Gutter was untouched by climbers.

Greedy with the joy at having an undeveloped cliff to myself—and in overpopulated Massachusetts, no less—I began taking students there twice a week. The lower forty feet of Rattlesnake, less than vertical, crowned by a walk-off ledge, were ideally suited to top-rope climbing. Here I could easily supervise twenty beginners at once, on five different routes, and I put up lines of my own, up to hard 5.9 in difficulty, that no student could master. But I lusted after the upper cliff, which promised new routes tougher and steeper than anything this side of the Gunks. Twice I attacked its central line and obvious prize, a stern chimney atop a forty-foot aid ceiling, but I could not coax the game students who tried to second the ceiling over the lip. Both times I had to rappel off rather than finish the route.

I was terrified that word of my find would get out to the local climbing community. The Eastern Mountain Sports store in Amherst was a hangout for some of the best rock jocks in the Pioneer Valley, as the area was known, and the outing club at the gargantuan University of Massachusetts had a climbing program of its own. Each time I drove up to Rattlesnake Gutter, I crossed my fingers as a charm against the apparition of a gaggle of U Mass beginners swarming all over "my" cliff.

One day in March 1971, as I sat on the belay ledge presiding over my cadets, a bearded fellow walked out of the woods, then loitered at the base of the cliff. I sent Mike Ubell, a nerdy youngster with a gift for gab, down to check out the stranger. As soon as Mike had struggled up a 5.4 climb back to the ledge, I asked, "What does he want?"

"I think he'd like to try a climb," answered Mike, then added, "He's from U Mass."

"Oh, shit!" I groaned. Addressing my assembled troops, I ordered, "Don't even talk to the guy."

Mike, however, disobeyed the injunction. On next reappearing on the ledge, he blurted out, "Hey, this guy's climbed in Alaska. Mount Hunter or something."

A real mountaineer, I thought, not just some outing club busybody. I stood up, advanced to the lip of the ledge, where I could see the newcomer, and, summoning a tone of hollow magnanimity, called down, "You want to tie in and climb something?"

In a remarkably short time—two minutes, maximum—the stranger had gained the ledge. He wasn't even breathing hard. We introduced ourselves. Ed Ward was doing graduate work in the Education School at U Mass. He had nothing to do with the outing club.

"So you did Hunter, huh?" I queried.

"Nah." Shyly, he averted his eyes. "We didn't get up it."

"Which route?"

"The south ridge. Got stopped by an overhanging wall."

From Huntington, we had often stared at the savage southern defenses of its neighbor peak, the lordly Mount Hunter. By now, I knew, three expeditions, whose members included some of America's best alpinists, had been defeated on various buttresses on that side of the mountain.

I said, "We climbed Huntington in—"

"I know," Ed interrupted. "I read your book."

During the next hour, Ed climbed three or four top-rope routes, including one hard enough that, among our Hampshire crowd, only I had solved it. We also chatted about the big ranges. At twenty-seven, he was the same age as I. As well as Hunter, Ed had done battle among the sheer granite walls of the Cirque of the Unclimbables in Canada's Northwest Territories, and had made the third ascent of the east ridge of 19,850-foot Mount Logan, the second-highest peak in North America.

As we were packing up the ropes to head back to school, Ed ventured, "Have we got time to try something hard?"

I was a bit nonplussed. Hadn't my hardest line been hard enough? "What do you have in mind?"

Ed pointed at a satellite cliff below the Gutter proper, just above the stream, only forty feet high. Though it fiercely overhung, it was so grungy with moss and mud, I had never set up a rope on it. Now, with the students voyeuristically taking in the show, Ed belayed me on an improbable line. I got twenty-five feet up, wore out my arms hanging from a slimy ledge, and fell off three times. "Lower me!" I called. "It just doesn't go."

"Let me have a try," Ed insisted.

As he reached the crux from which I had fallen, I gave him what climbers would later call "the beta"—hold-by-hold advice: "The only hope is to get your left toe on the ledge, then—"

All of a sudden Ed was up, without a fall or even a serious hesitation. I was impressed. I thought I was in good shape, but this U Mass grad student, who lacked a regular climbing partner, had just blown my best effort out of the water.

During the next several months, stealing the odd afternoon from our school responsibilities, Ed and I made the first ascents of three of the finest routes on the full 130-foot cliff at Rattlesnake Gutter. On two of them, which we named Mayday and Dog Days, Ed freed the upper overhang with brilliant leads, perhaps 5.10 in difficulty, or almost as hard as anybody in New England was climbing in those days.

As I would quickly come to realize, Ed was one of the most competitive fellows I had ever met. At the same time, he was supremely modest. Like Charlie Porter, during his whole climbing career, Ed would never publish even the shortest journal note about his conquests. During the previous five years, since my senior year at Harvard, I had lacked a year-round climbing partner. Now that Ed and I had started tackling new routes together, I realized how much I had missed the joys of such a comradeship.

During that spring, we downed many a beer at my two favorite Amherst watering holes, the Drake and Chequers. During one such occasion, I unveiled a scheme that, if Ed took the bait, would change his life irrevocably. Little did I reckon how it would change mine as well.

With 300 more students due to arrive at Hampshire in the fall of 1971, the college would more than double in size. The administration had authorized me to hire a third staff member for the O.P. I had been casting about for a specialist in some other outdoor discipline to balance our kayaking-climbing thrust. But Ed was too good to ignore.

At Chequers one evening, I asked: would Ed consider taking the Hampshire job, even though it meant quitting the Ed School?

He frowned darkly, then went on to explain. Like many another climbing bum, Ed had floundered about for a vocational vector. In the early 1960s, he had dropped out of college to join the army, and had ended up serving in Vietnam. Once his stint was up, he had gone back to the University of Minnesota, earning his BA in Latin American history in 1969. The next year he had come to U Mass, then switched from history to the Education School. Bent on earning an M.Ed., he hoped to forge a career working in the outdoors with disadvantaged and troubled youths.

I was nothing if not skilled, however, in the art of persuasion. I cajoled and blandished on. I promised Ed that he could integrate his social concerns with an O.P. job—it was Outward Bound itself, after all, that had pioneered the programs that were jocularly dubbed "hoods in the woods." It was clear that Ed was living on a meager budget. Instead of scraping by on his U Mass teaching fellowship, I cruelly pointed out, he could earn a lucrative salary—all of $9,000 a year—in the employ of Hampshire College.

In the end, I suspect, our new partnership meant as much to Ed as it did to me. In mid-May, he caved in at last. And thanks to another scheme I had been hatching, Ed would start work not in the fall, but in a couple of weeks, as soon as school got out.

Contractually, I had my summer free to do what I wanted. But I had decided to lead a student trip to the Arrigetch Peaks. In my original conception, our team would have done little more than hike through that maze of granite towers, half of which were still unclimbed, with Sharon and me as avuncular guides. But once Ed and I had paired up, I thought I could turn the Brooks Range into an elementary school in the rudiments of mountaineering for my young charges, while sneaking off with my new partner to claim some of the tougher virgin summits.

There were minimal fringe benefits involved in taking students north. A grateful administration authorized our driving nearly 5,000 miles to and from Alaska in the O.P. van. And Ed, Sharon, and I received a $1,000 stipend for the effort, which did not even cover our personal expenses. It was not these perks that motivated me. Despite the frazzling marathon of my first year of teaching, in June 1971 I was still fired with the idealism in which Hampshire College had incubated. What finer educational deed could I perform than to share the place I loved best in the world with a handful of protégés?

Our party ultimately numbered ten: Ed, Sharon, and I as leaders, along with seven eighteen-year-olds. We arrived in Bettles in early June, planning to fly in to Takahula Lake and hike to the same base camp the 1964 party had occupied. But our pilot, Paul Shanahan, told us that Takahula was still covered with ice, while the Alatna River was raging over its banks. Approach by float plane was out of the question. Out of loyalty to me, Shanahan booked a helicopter and pilot and charged me only fixed-wing rates.

On June 9, Sharon and I headed in on the first flight. Free to choose our base camp almost at will, we settled on a generous tundra bench 600 feet above the valley floor, facing south. A snowbank-fed rivulet served as our water supply. The bench was backed by a long, forty-foot-tall cliff of impeccable granite—as perfect a *gymnasium* for teaching the students how to climb as we could have devised. During the next three weeks, I would revel in the most perfect base camp setting of any of my thirteen northern expeditions.

A team of ten, however, was three more than I had ever gone into the mountains with—several more, indeed, than I had vowed I would ever put up with in the great ranges. The logistics alone were hectic—cooking glop for ten, or, on a given day, making sure that everyone set out on a hike or scramble that was within his or her capabilities.

For me, the real rub, however, had to do with how those seven students apprehended the expedition. At twenty-eight, perhaps I should have been wise enough to anticipate the personal distress that I might incur by sharing a place and an endeavor that for me partook of the sacred with acolytes for whom it loomed only as a kind of curricular option.

Among the seven there stretched a broad spiritual spectrum. Nancy Lord, a thin, pretty hippie from New Hampshire, had a genuine pilgrim soul. The Arrigetch overwhelmed her and changed her life for good. After college, she would move to Alaska and become a commercial fisherwoman and nature writer. In a wistful essay she published in 2003, Nancy recalled the rapture that had suffused her that June more than three decades before:

> I climb to the top of a boulder and spread myself over its sun-warmed surface. It pleases me to think that I may be the first person ever to climb up and sit on top of that particular rock. . . . Everything about the entire valley and surrounding peaks, sky, and last, lost never-never land pleases me; if I had to construct an image of paradise, this would be it.

At the other end of the spectrum was a couple for whom, I gradually realized, the Arrigetch meant little more than one more exotic junket in their overprivileged lives: next year, camel-trekking in Morocco, perhaps, or a stint on an Israeli kibbutz. Call them Daniel and Alex. Around camp, they behaved as though they were the stars of some romantic comedy, kissing and making out, singing Peter, Paul and Mary tunes in unison, reading passages from Hermann Hesse out loud to each other.

Daniel had brought along an expensive camera and a battery of lenses. "Oh, Daniel," Alex would coo, framing a wildflower tableau with her fingers, "wouldn't that make a beautiful photo silkscreen?" Daniel would fire off half a roll.

On our practice cliff, Ed and I taught the students all kinds of rope- and piton-craft, and closely supervised their first shaky leads. We also split up to drag the students, in cumbersome teams of four and six, up a pair of easy peaks, the East and West Maidens, of which they thereby made the second ascents (the peaks having first been bagged by the 1964 party). A little learning, of course, is a dangerous thing. After ten days in the Arrigetch, the four most ambitious students (Daniel and Alex among them) thought they were ready to set off on major climbs by themselves. They sulked under Ed's and my interdiction, until, against our better judgment, we let them go off to tackle second ascents of easy peaks, while we fussed over their progress through binoculars. On a lump on the ridge we had named Tasmania, Daniel and Alex survived a sixteen-hour marathon, nearly three times as long as it had taken Ed and me to lead a student each up the unimpressive peak a week before.

On the tenth day of the trip, Ed and I finally got to go after a prize. In 1969, in the next valley north, I had hiked to the base of a phenomenal 2,000-foot wall that swept unbroken up to a needle of a summit: the cliff looked like something out of Yosemite Valley. The peak had been named Badile by the 1964 party, after its resemblance to a famous mountain in the Italian Alps, but those pioneers had not made an attempt on the peak. Now, on a chilly, windy day, Ed and I got up Badile, not by that intimidating north face, but by a much shorter, slightly devious route on the south and east. The summit was as sharp as it looked, too small for more than one of us to stand on at a time, yet Badile had been an easier climb than we expected.

The next peak on the ridge to the east, called Disneyland by the 1964 team, made up for it. Two weeks after Badile, as we approached the headwall on Disneyland, the rock got steeper and steeper. Having led a treacherous and difficult hand traverse, I belayed Ed to a stance so inadequate we both had to hang from slings. The vertical wall above looked unclimbable, so I suggested backing off. But, just as he had on the day we met at Rattlesnake Gutter, Ed said, "Let me have a try."

Only 200 feet below the summit of this striking peak, Ed dug deep into the reserves of nerve and skill that would make him, of all the close partners I had had or would have during my climbing career, the most dependable in the clutch. The crux pitch began with a twenty-foot-tall balanced flake so fragile that it vibrated under hand and foot. The only protection Ed could place was a sling looped over the top of the flake. Had the slice of stone come loose, the combined weight of plunging rock and leader would probably have ripped me from my anchor and sent us both to our deaths. Once off the flake, Ed inched his way up a desperate vertical chimney. After an hour's sublime effort, he had solved Disneyland.

Some years later, we received a heartily gratifying (if unintended) encomium on our climb, when two excellent American rock climbers tried to make the second ascent of Disneyland. Under the misapprehension that their south face route was a different line from ours, they reached the same crux flake and chimney, declared the risk unjustifiable, and rappelled off without reaching the summit.

On these two splendid first ascents—far harder than any of the five our party had claimed in 1969—Ed and I had indeed escaped the students to climb to our heart's content. Yet we received a strange reception on regaining base camp after each climb. Sharon, Nancy Lord, and two of the other students lavished congratulations on us. The other four of our tutees, however, who happened to be the most competitive of the group, barely acknowledged our success, and never asked any details about our adventures. It took me a while to realize that, having graduated from the kindergarten of our base camp top-rope cliff, those four (including Daniel and Alex) were full of a hubris that blinded them to the difference between the second ascent of West Maiden and the first ascent of Disneyland.

On Igikpak in 1968, Chuck Loucks had told me that his 1964 party had seen at once that the finest peak in all the Arrigetch was a slender pinnacle they had named Shot Tower. He and several teammates had hiked to its base, only to stand and stare. The peak, 1,100 feet from foot to summit, was as clean and soaring as the finest Chamonix aiguille. The only apparently thinkable route was the west ridge.

Now, from our tundra shelf base camp, Shot Tower stood outlined against the sky on the opposite side of the valley, with the west ridge in profile. Through binoculars, Ed and I studied it for many an hour. At last, on June 22, we set out to try it. Only Sharon accompanied us to the base, where she sat through half a day, shooting telephoto pictures as we dwindled into specks, then leaving us a precious full water bottle before she hiked back to camp in the late afternoon.

Setting off up the first pitch, both Ed and I were pessimistic. "You probably won't have to wait too long," I told Sharon. "We may back off right at the beginning."

Yet at once we laid our hands on granite more perfect than any we had found elsewhere in the Arrigetch. Trading leads, we followed a series of thin vertical cracks that accepted our pitons and nuts. The wall was so smooth that our belay stances were minimal: at one, I stood on top of our daypack, which was clipped to a pair of pitons. Six hours into the climb, we came to the Mushroom, an overhanging knob interrupting the west ridge, which we feared would stymie our progress. Instead, Ed led a delicate traverse to the left that circumvented the Mushroom. Mindful of Hinterstoisser's fatal error on the Eiger in 1936, we strung here the only fixed rope we had brought along, to allow us to reverse the pitch on the way down.

It was the summer solstice, the longest day of the year, and the temperature was oppressively warm, in the low 70s. In the afternoon, a violent lightning storm swept over the Arrigetch, a true rarity in the Arctic. Twelve pitches off the ground, intensely vulnerable, we wriggled down into a providential ten-foot-deep crevice and hid from the lightning bolts that singed the air around us. In the fissure we found a dirty cake of winter ice: with our piton hammers, we broke pieces of it loose and sucked on them, stuffing other pieces into our pair of almost depleted quart water bottles.

Binocular inspection before the climb had made it clear that the crux of the whole route lay near the top, where a blank vertical wall weirdly interrupted the ridge. I had held out hope that a thin crack on the left edge, actually looming over the sheer north face of the tower, would allow us a bypass. We reached the foot of the cliff around 9:00 in the evening. My bypass proved nonexistent. Worse, the sixty-foot wall actually overhung by a few degrees. The only possible line was a thin, bottoming-out snake of a crack that disappeared for four- and five-foot sections at a time.

We were already close to exhaustion after ten straight hours of hard climbing, and our tongues were furred with thirst. Doggedly, Ed started up the vestigial crack, aid-climbing with stirrups. We had only twenty-two pieces—pitons and nuts. Ed used every trick in the book to pound and slot them into the inadequate fissure—tying off knife blades with hero loops to minimize the torque, tapping nuts with his hammer to wedge them into grooves that threatened to spit them out.

Halfway up, he sighed, "We just don't have the pins to do it." But he kept trying.

A nut came out under his weight and Ed fell three feet. He scrambled back onto the rock. At one point he down-climbed to retrieve a nut and a piton he had aleady placed, so that he could reuse them above. Half as a joke, he had brought along a "cliff-hanger"—a piece of chrome-molybdenum bent like a coat hanger, used in Yosemite to hang on a wrinkle of rock while one drilled a bolt nearby. To surmount five feet of blank wall, Ed used the cliff-hanger twice, hanging from it in his stirrups. At last, almost whispering, he said, "I think it'll go." Ten minutes later, he was up.

To this day, I think of Ed's lead on Shot Tower as the finest single pitch I have ever had the privilege to second. On those sixty feet of granite, he had placed twenty-one of our twenty-two pieces, reusing the nut and the piton he had back-cleaned. All this, not on some friendly New England crag, where in a jam we might have called for help, but in the Arctic, more than a hundred miles from Bettles and our tenuous link with the outside world.

Two more easy pitches, and we stood on top of Shot Tower. It was a little before midnight. In the north, the sun hung low in the hazy sky, above the flat triangles of the Maidens. We felt as though we were alone in the universe.

The descent verged on nightmare, for we were so tired that it was all we could do to concentrate on setting up the rappels properly. We had to ration our hardware, lest we run out of pitons and nuts to anchor the last rappels. Finally, at 7:30 in the morning of July 23, after twenty-one straight hours of climbing, we stepped off Shot Tower and collapsed in the tundra, giggling with relief.

We guzzled the water Sharon had left for us. Then, hobbling like geriatrics, we stumped down to the valley floor below and back up the opposite hillside to base camp. We made frequent rest stops, at each of which we lapsed into hallucinatory trances of fitful sleep.

Shot Tower was the best climb I had done since Huntington. To this day, it remains the finest pure rock climb of my life. And though I had known Ed for only a few months, the perfect teamwork that we forged on that ascent grounded a friendship that, thirty-four years later, remains as strong as ever. In 2005, Ed and I still climb together.

On July 1, we packed up our base camp and headed for Takahula Lake. It took us three miserable days, bushwhacking in the unseasonable heat through the usual alder and willow thickets and the unusual hordes of mosquitoes. Carrying sixty-pound packs, the students tottered down-valley, taking more and longer rests than even Sharon thought possible.

With the lake now free of ice, Paul Shanahan was able to land on floats on July 4. From the start of our planning for the trip, I had wanted to end the journey with a full 150-mile paddle down the Alatna River to the Indian village of Allakaket. (We had done two thirds of the river trip in 1969, but I was disappointed by our arbitrary pickup on the sandbar as a conclusion to a month in the Brooks Range.) Now Shanahan brought in our boats as he ferried out our climbing gear. His flights gave the students the option to cut short the trip, skip the river, and fly straight to Bettles. Several of them, notably Daniel and Alex, seemed homesick. I was not surprised to witness these signs of crump among our charges, and I would have been happy to float the river with a reduced party. The competitive tension that had gripped our camp life from the beginning, however, now prevented even the most ambivalent students from hopping aboard Shanahan's Cessna. Changing her mind, Alex averred that the only appeal of the escape hatch had been "just the fun of flying in a small airplane."

In eight uneventful days, we ran the Alatna all the way to Allakaket. The river so teemed with mosquitoes that they emitted a constant drone from the willow stands on either bank, but we escaped the worst of their ravages by camping on windy gravel bars. At times the float approached an idyll, but I spent many an hour in the back seat of my Klepper brooding on what I had wrought by taking students to the Arrigetch.

In the summer of 1963, of course, I had taught Outward Bound in the Colorado Rockies. But despite my apprenticeship on the talus heaps of my native state, the Elk Range had never been sacred ground for me. Nor was Rattlesnake Gutter, however proprietary I felt about the crag I had discovered near Montague.

The Brooks range—Alaska itself—was different. As we drifted down the placid river, I could not escape the feeling that I had profaned something: if not the empty wilderness itself, at least my own love of it. By now, in their joined-at-the-hip self-infatuation, Daniel and Alex were rubbing everybody's nerves raw. Alex sulked and gobbled food; Daniel fawned over her like a high-strung purebred in a dog show.

The nadir of my disenchantment came on the first day on the river. Leading in the Klepper, Sharon and I drifted silently toward a pair of wolf cubs frolicking on the left bank. One black, the other brownish blond, they must have been only days old, for they were still wobbly on their feet. For long, enchanted moments, the cubs paid us no more notice than they might have a floating log. I turned slowly in my seat and saw the first raft come around the bend behind us. I put my finger to my lips, pleading for silence, but it was Daniel and Alex, singing some song at the tops of their lungs. The cubs fled into the bushes. Those are still the only wolves I have ever seen in the wild.

It was tempting to scapegoat Daniel and Alex, to blame their thrill-bagging dilettantism for all that seemed wrong with the expedition. But in reflective moments, I recognized that I had only myself to blame. At the core of my chagrin was an instinct, puritan as ever, that told me that getting paid to share what I loved most in life with rich-kid clients amounted to a kind of spiritual prostitution.

Of a more pragmatic mold, Ed suffered no such misgivings. Taking students into the wilderness was a job, no more, no less. It sure as hell beat serving as a private in Vietnam. And though Daniel and Alex grated on his nerves as much as they did on mine, he had no trouble separating that inconvenience from the joy of climbing Shot Tower.

On the Alatna, I vowed never again to take clients of any kind to Alaska. During the coming years, my qualms about getting paid to unleash Hampshire students on the outdoors only intensified.

Though I did not at first recognize the fact, it was the very act of teaching that came to me freighted with malaise. A year or two later, reading a magazine interview with Gore Vidal, I was cut to the quick by one of his characteristically snide throwaway lines, as Vidal dismissed the role of the college English professor as "teaching old poems to bored children."

In the fall of 1971, Sharon and I moved onto the campus, taking up residence in one of the modular dorms plopped among the birches of a long disused tract of former farmland. On either side of our apartment, student stereos blared at all hours. One of the reasons for our move was that Sharon, who had been unable to land a teaching job in the public schools of the Pioneer Valley (peopled by the densest glut of MAs and Ph.D.'s in the country), could now eke out a stipend as a "resident associate"—Hampshire-ese for dorm mother. But she quickly grew disillusioned with the job, whose duties included calling plumbers to fix students' backed-up toilets and separating drunken roommates who were at each other's throats.

The main reason for the move, however, was that I still passionately believed in the utopian ideals on which Hampshire seemed to be founded. From the start, even the faculty espoused such radically egalitarian mottos as "we're part of an experiment unprecedented in American education" and "we have as much to learn from you students as you do from us." It would take years to discover the flaws that were built into the very design of the college, or to stop blaming ourselves for the professorial burnout that inevitably ensued.

In 1974 or 1975, one particularly bright and iconoclastic student wrote his senior thesis on the intellectual origins of the college itself. What he found among the musty documents of the founders surprised and bemused everyone. Hampshire had actually been conceived as early as 1958, by a bunch of educators most of whom were ensconced at Amherst College. Gazing into their crystal ball, these pundits had deduced that the looming crisis in higher education would issue from the head-on collision of an expanding student body with a paucity of young Ph.D.'s. At Amherst, the student-to-faculty ratio had long been fixed at nine-to-one. To alleviate the crisis, the new institution the seers envisaged would somehow offer an "Amherst-quality" educational experience at a ratio of sixteen-to-one.

In 1958, there was thus no whiff of the experimental about the prodigal school that would sprout from the apple orchard as Hampshire College. But the planners dithered for a decade. By the time they got serious again, the late 1960s were in headlong career. At the last minute, to appeal to donors, the founders threw in every bell and whistle they could scrounge up among the screeds of academic radicals that were the fashion of the day.

From the original design, the only feature saved was the sixteen-to-one ratio of students to professors. Meanwhile, as Hampshire opened its doors in September 1970, we faculty members taught a full load of courses. Yet not only did we not give grades (issuing long-winded student evaluations in their stead), but course credits had no bearing on a student's progress. Rather we shepherded each pupil through self-designed programs called Divisions I, II, and III. These rites of passage were loosely modeled on the comps a Ph.D. candidate had to pass near the end of his sentence in graduate school, with as many as four or five professors sitting in judgment on a single student's body of work.

Hampshire was too hip to offer the faculty tenure. Instead, we came up for reappointment every three, four, or five years, and the committees that determined our future included students as full voting members. The school was also too hip to demand a fixed load of advisees for each teacher to supervise (sixteen being the logical number). The shirkers among the faculty saw a golden loophole here, advising as few students and serving on as few Division I, II, and III committees as they could get away with, while the rest of us bleeding-heart idealists took up their slack.

That first fall, Hampshire was not only the hardest college in the country to get into—it was also the most expensive. Small wonder that the place drew mostly rich kids, with a tiny smattering of minority students on scholarship.

Why did no one see coming what such an ill-considered design would inevitably produce? Having to beg and cajole to get a faculty member to serve as her advisor or Div III chairperson, a student for whom demanding things from her elders came naturally fared far better at Hampshire than a timid or courteous soul. And the faculty reappointment process turned (predictably) into a popularity contest. A number of my colleagues who were, in my view, intellectually hollow at the core, but who lavished praise on the feeblest student effort, snagged the longest possible reappointment terms after their grateful protégés sang their praises on judgment day. At the other extreme, I sat by in horror, dissenting to no avail, as a brilliant political scientist who had the bad timing to suffer a nervous breakdown and come out as gay right before his reappointment meeting got summarily canned. Even more painfully, an English teacher who was one of the few African-Americans on the faculty earned bad marks because he had the temerity to damn William Styron's *Confessions of Nat Turner* and because student after student testified that the man spoke so slowly in the classroom they found themselves hopelessly bored. (During the scarifying meeting at which we decided the professor's fate, with the man himself asked to leave the room, his closest friend on the faculty revealed that his colleague had cured a lifelong stutter by teaching himself to speak slowly and deliberately. No matter: the committee fired him anyway.)

Among a student body made up of rich kids who had won the eight-to-one admissions lottery, it was to be expected that there would be a full complement of Daniels and Alexes. What was more insidious was that Hampshire rewarded its students for wielding their entitlement, arrogance, and self-satisfaction. Harvard, too, had been full of entitled rich kids, but one of the place's saving graces (to an extreme that was a fault in reverse, inflicting cruel damage on students such as Don Jensen) was that a dumb comment or flawed term paper got smacked flat by a withering professorial put-down. At Hampshire, we professors risked our careers if we smacked anybody flat.

Meanwhile, the air was leaking fast out of the balloon of alternative colleges. By the mid-1970s, some of our experimental sisters, such as New College in Florida and Franconia in New Hampshire, had folded, while others were desperately retrenching. At Hampshire, the eight-to-one acceptance ratio quickly dwindled to two-to-one, and by 1975 we were accepting almost anyone who applied. The crazy hippies who had filled the first two classes were increasingly replaced by conservative drudges prepping for law and business school.

On the faculty, most of us were too close to the process to see what was going on. I myself was a true naïf. As the administration drifted to the right, hoping to keep the college afloat in a changed academic market, I stuck doggedly to my liberal guns. Yet the plunging morale of the place deadened everyone's spirits. To be sure, the manic high of the fall of 1970 could not have lasted long. But by 1975, like most of my colleagues, I was too depressed to look around me and recognize the dystopian swamp in which we were mired.

What kept me going was the passionate conviction that the mind and body could after all be seamlessly linked, that (in personal terms) I could be both a climber and a writer, and could offer that model to my students. At my second reappointment, accepting a promotion, I insisted that my official title be changed from Assistant Professor of Literature to Associate Professor of Literature and Mountaineering. The president grudgingly gave in to my whim.

Succumbing to the Hampshire zeitgeist, I myself was sometimes too easy on my students, particularly wannabe writers with mediocre gifts. Only after I took up writing as a full-time occupation did I recognize that facile encouragement of an aspiring author who lacked the talent, discipline, or bulldog temperament for the freelancer's way of life did him a disservice.

Thanks to that softness, and to my workaholic diligence, I became one of the more popular teachers at Hampshire. And the most popular course I ever taught (I would offer it during three different semesters over as many years) was called Literature of Great Expeditions. We read Hakluyt, Bernal Díaz, James Cook, John Wesley Powell, Apsley Cherry-Garrard, and others, but on weekends and afternoons I devised a series of mandatory field exercises designed to drive home the experiential reality of exploration. We bivouacked, thirty-five strong, tied in to the limbs of a giant maple tree on campus through a subfreezing night in late October. We made and ate nineteenth-century pemmican and jerky. We crossed the Connecticut River on a raft made only of available driftwood. In a forest on the west edge of campus, I organized a yeti hunt. Ed played the yeti, hiding beneath fallen leaves or in treetops, pelting his pursuers with acorns that, according to the rules of the contest, delivered fatal blows. The hunt was organized along military lines, à la Cook or Cortés. The generals (appointed by me) wore hard hats, barked orders, and executed insubordinates on the spot. After each field exercise, back in the classroom, we "processed" what insights we had gained into the ordeals of Scott at the South Pole or Frobisher on Baffin Island. The students loved the course, and I was in my element.

By 1973, with the college at its full enrollment of 1,200 students, we had expanded the O.P. to embrace not only two climbing teachers and a kayak instructor, but a naturalist who led botanical outings and a feminist from the U Mass Ed School who encouraged women to forge a noncompetitive rapport with the great outdoors. (We had discovered, to our disappointment, that while just as many women as men came out for our beginning kayaking and climbing trips, only men persisted long enough to become relatively skilled.)

With Ed on board full-time, increasingly I turned over to him the weekend trips to the Gunks or the ice gullies of Mount Washington. I whittled my own climbing outings down to afternoon top-rope trips to Chapel Ledge, Rose Ledge, and Rattlesnake Gutter. By pushing the hardest forty-foot routes at those diminutive crags, I stayed in good shape, but a certain staleness crept into the routine.

Having stuffed the typescript of Shadwell deep inside a cardboard box in my storeroom, I set out to write another book—a memoir about Lisa, which in the end would prove as unpublishable as my wretched dissertation novel. I tried to carve out a slot from 7:00 to 9:00 each morning for my writing, but then the School of Humanities and Arts would decree an early-morning meeting, or two of my colleagues could sit in judgment on some student's Div II progress only at 7:30 A.M., or (all too often) I was simply too tired or hungover to write. On the good days, just as I hit my stride, I would have to wrench myself away from my typewriter and head off to the classroom, where instead of writing, I pretended to teach students how to write.

I had gone off to Alaska again the previous two summers, extending my streak to eleven years straight, but nothing that I climbed in 1972 or 1973 was in the same ballpark with Shot Tower. In the former year, though I climbed with Ed in the Grenadier Range of Colorado's San Juan Mountains (where Don and I had made our first winter ascents in 1963), we tackled only moderate routes. Ed's 1973 summer was a complete bust. Having accepted a job teaching at the Northwest Outward Bound School in the Cascades of Washington state, on one of his first days in the field he went out for a morning jog, landed awkwardly as he skipped down a road cut, and broke his ankle. He was laid up for the rest of the summer.

By the fall of 1973, both Ed and I had turned thirty. At that point in life, we might well have let new routes in the great ranges slip away from our grasp, as many a former hard man of our acquaintance had already done. Teaching climbing to beginners was a classic way of avoiding "real" climbing, as I had seen as early as 1963 among my fellow instructors at Colorado Outward Bound. A mordant essay by the British climber and essayist Harold Drasdo, in which he categorized such a stratagem as "opting into a risk-free role," had haunted me ever since I had first read it around 1966.

Fortunately, an itch of discontent prickled beneath both Ed's skin and mine, and even more fortunately, over beers at Chequers and the Drake, we shared our feelings. At last, one gloomy November evening in a bar in South Hadley—if I could remember the name of that cozy pub, which no doubt is long defunct, I would hoist a glass to it today—we took the plunge. We pledged to each other to go back to Alaska together in the summer of 1974. We promised ourselves that we would attempt the most difficult climb of our lives. On the tabletop before us lay a Brad Washburn photo of the peak we had chosen—Mount Dickey, looming above the Ruth Gorge, up whose southeast face rose an achingly beautiful arrow of an arête, a full 5,000 feet from glacier to summit.

With luck, on Dickey we might succeed, as I had nine years before on Mount Huntington, in performing the hardest climb yet done anywhere in Alaska.

By that fall, I was serving on the board of directors of the American Alpine Club. The annual meeting, on the first weekend in December, would be held in Los Angeles. The Thursday before, I packed my suitcase and was halfway out the door on my way to the airport when I picked up the day's mail. There was a note from Adams Carter, editor of the *American Alpine Journal* and one of my former Harvard Mountaineering Club mentors.

> Dear Dave:
>   What a sad thing about Don Jenson. Will you be good enough to do the obituary in the AAJ for us? And apparently such a needless death. Bicycling you are so much out and vulnerable.

I dropped my suitcase and telephoned Ad. Even as I waited for him to answer, holding the note before my eyes, I red-penciled in my head the misspelling of Don's last name. Ad seemed surprised and even a bit ashamed that I had had to learn the doleful news from him.

"Where did it happen?" I asked. I was ashamed in turn to realize that I did not even know where Don was living. I had last seen him for a day or two in 1971 when he had dropped by Hampshire College, owner of a new Ph.D. from USC, as he toured the country looking for a teaching job. It was then that we had gone out to Rattlesnake Gutter and set up a couple of top-rope routes.

"Aberdeen," Ad answered.

"South Dakota?"

"No, Scotland. Wait, I'll get Joan's letter." Don, as I would later learn, had landed a post-graduate fellowship at the University of Aberdeen. He was on his way to work when the accident happened. The only explanation was a single sentence in the letter Joan had written Ad, knowing the *Journal* would publish an obituary. Joan's wording was as blank and formulaic as the most reticent death notice: "Don was killed instantly while bicycling on slippery roads."

Somehow I never managed to make direct contact with Joan. For thirty years thereafter, I had only that summary phrase in my head to conjure up Don's end. Gradually I convinced myself that Don had skidded out of control on wet pavement and crashed head-on into a stone wall. I even wondered if he had been in one of his funks, when, as I had seen during the first days on Deborah, he verged on the accident-prone.

Only in 2003, by a long-shot chance, did a letter from Joan, forwarded by my publisher, reach me. We began an e-mail correspondence. And only then did I learn more about what had happened that day in Scotland—though not even Joan really knew. As she wrote,

> Don was bicycling to work at the university on a frosty morning in Aberdeen and was hit by a truck. Killed instantly. Actually there are no more details—this is as much as I know. My father had to identify his body (for which I am ever grateful, and can only imagine how he must have felt) as I refused to look at Don dead, preferring to remember him as alive and vibrant.

On the airplane to Los Angeles, I sat in shock, staring uncomprehending at the Alpine Club treasurer's report and secretary's notes of the previous meeting. I got through the session of the board of directors, telling each of my colleagues, "I'm sorry if I'm not concentrating very well. I just learned about the death of Don Jensen. He was my best friend, you know—on McKinley and Deborah and Huntington with me." They murmured their condolences.

I spent the evening at the Santa Monica home of my high school buddy Paul. He had met Don once or twice, and he, too, offered his sympathy. Paul was in a mood to reminisce about our childhood in Boulder, but I needed to be alone. After Paul went to bed, I turned off the lights, put on a Schubert record I found among his shelves, and started drinking Scotch.

All at once I was weeping uncontrollably. Wakened, Paul stumbled out in the dark and put his hand on my shoulder. "I'm okay," I stammered. "Just leave me alone for now, Paul, please."

It was no accident that Don and I had drifted apart. In 1967, he had only half-invited me on his score-settling return to Deborah, and I had not tried to lure him to the Revelations. In Banff in 1969, Don could have joined us on Mount Temple, but instead he had taken refuge in his picnic-table-top equations. By 1973, I knew that Don and I would probably never again share an expedition. At best, we might have reunited for a week in the Alps or among his beloved Palisades.

And yet I wept inconsolably in the darkness of Paul's living room. The sadness that enveloped me was darker than anything I had felt after Gabe's or Ed Bernd's deaths. Dimly, I recognized that it was not simply the loss of Don that I was mourning. Like the young girl addressed in Gerard Manley Hopkins's famous poem, it was Margaret I grieved for, not "Goldengrove unleaving." I grieved for the loss of the limitless future Don and I had dreamed for ourselves at the age of twenty, for the climbs all over the globe that now we would never share, for the fading of the illusion of perfect friendship that we had glimpsed on the summit day on Huntington.

On the way back from Los Angeles, I stopped in Walnut Creek, east of San Francisco, to visit Don's parents. Don's father told me that their first inkling of the catastrophe had come when he had picked up the phone to hear Joan crying—crying so hard, in fact, that she could not get a word out, but had to hang up with the grim message undelivered. At last Joan's father, visiting in Scotland, had broken the news.

Don's father showed me the letter they had subsequently received from Joan. It contained the same blank, formulaic phrase as the letter to Ad Carter: "Don was killed instantly while bicycling on slippery roads." His parents were as mystified as I was as to the details of the accident.

Don's mother, who had fussed over me and fed me well on previous visits, was in a frame of mind that I had never before encountered in anyone. She seemed fully cognizant of Don's death, but then

I would overhear her, in the next room, ask her husband, "Is Dave here to go climbing with Don?" Though only in her sixties, she had already fallen victim to Alzheimer's disease. Holding my breath in disbelief, I heard Don's father scold her gently, then subside into stifled sobs of his own.

The unraveling of Don's family would prove the stuff of Greek tragedy. Not long after my visit, his mother died of her terrible malady. And a few years after that, Don's father learned that he had contracted an incurable cancer. A hunter all his life, he ended it with his own gun.

Yet in Los Angeles, the day after the American Alpine Club board meeting, I started talking to several climbing acquaintances about Ed's and my plans for Mount Dickey. We had decided that we needed a team of three for the assault. Lacking good friends in the East who we thought might be up to such a challenge, we had agreed that I would scout out the AAC gathering, which yearly brought together many of the finest climbers in the country, for a candidate to fill out our trio on Dickey.

The Ruth Glacier flows from the southeast buttresses of Mount McKinley some forty miles out to the tundra lowlands. Along the way, it carves an icy highway between stupendous granite peaks—most of them still unclimbed by 1974. Two northern sentinels of that colossal corridor—the Mooses Tooth on the east, Mount Dickey on the west—had been ascended by their easiest routes. But no one had even attempted any of the giant walls, ranging on average more than 4,000 feet in height, that loomed over the fiercely crevassed valley of the Ruth Gorge itself. Since the 1950s, Brad Washburn had taken dozens of stunning aerial photos of these walls. Climbers who perused them realized that they were beholding a subarctic Yosemite Valley, at twice the scale of its California rival. (Washburn himself had calculated that if the glacier were to melt, the full depth of the Gorge would reveal itself as a mind-boggling 8,000 feet.)

Ironically, the first explorer to traverse the Ruth Gorge was the infamous Dr. Frederick A. Cook in 1906, who temporarily conned his only partner, a Montana horsepacker named Edward Barrill, into agreeing to fake the first ascent of McKinley. It was Cook who named the glacier, after his daughter. The hoax was exploded as early as 1910, when Cook's former teammate Belmore Browne rediscovered the insignificant peak, less than 6,000 feet high and twenty miles southeast of the true summit of North America's highest mountain, on which Cook had photographed poor Barrill holding an American flag. It was these pictures that he would pass off in his book *To the Top of the Continent* as genuine McKinley summit photos. In the 1950s, Washburn and Adams Carter had duplicated those photos on "Fake Peak" so perfectly that rock features the size of a baseball could be recognized and compared. The full route by which Cook claimed to have gained the top of McKinley remains unclimbed today. And yet in 2005, there are still diehard believers who are convinced that Cook told the truth.

The southeast face of Mount Dickey seemed to Ed and me the most perfect of all the lines in the Washburn photos of the Ruth Gorge. Yet the slightly protruding arête, we were convinced, offered a reasonable—perhaps even a relatively safe—series of walls, ledges, and grooves up which we might weave our labyrinthine path. Everything depended on the quality of the granite, which on the nearby Mooses Tooth had been reported to range the full gamut from clean, sharp crack systems to a crumbly nightmare stuff likened to brown sugar.

Climbers guard the secrets of their upcoming projects as fiercely as divers do newly discovered shipwrecks. At the AAC meeting in Los Angeles, I did not walk up to prospective partners and start babbling about Mount Dickey. Instead, I felt them out with vague queries: "So, what have you got planned for next summer?" They tended to answer just as vaguely: "Oh, I don't know, maybe something up in the Bugaboos." It was the same coy game that Denny, Hank, and I had played with Brian Greenwood in the bar in Banff before Mount Temple.

It did not take long, however, to realize that one particular acquaintance was on the right wavelength. I had befriended Galen

Rowell at previous AAC meetings, but had never gone climbing with him. Three years older than I, at thirty-three, he was an integral part of the legendary Camp 4 crew at Yosemite, having put up bold new routes in the company of such luminary colleagues as Yvon Chouinard, Warren Harding, and Royal Robbins. I knew that Galen had recently come off two failed attempts on the Mooses Tooth, so he was conversant with the treacheries the Alaska Range could dish out. (Later, on Dickey, he would tell me that he had begun to wonder if he would ever reach any summit in the forty-ninth state.)

At some point that weekend, I pulled out the Washburn photo. Galen nodded sagely. He knew Dickey, it turned out, even better than I did, for on his second Mooses Tooth expedition, he had skied across the Ruth and actually laid his hands on the base of the southeast face. Eyeing the same route Ed and I had chosen, Galen had tried without success to talk several acquaintances into a Dickey expedition.

With that happy coincidence, our team was complete. Galen did not know Ed Ward even by reputation (few American climbers did, since Ed kept so modest a profile), but he took my word for my partner's strength and dependability. (After Dickey, in the journal *Ascent*, Galen would write, of belaying Ed on a crux pitch, "I felt I was watching a movie in which Gary Cooper was on my side.")

The son of highly educated Berkeley intellectuals, who were a concert musician and a professor of philosophy, Galen had thrice dropped out of UC Berkeley, supporting his climbing habit for years by running an auto repair shop. His professional ambition was to become one of the best outdoor photographers in the country, a campaign in which he would soon succeed. In 1974, as we left for Dickey, he had recently completed his first assignment for *National Geographic*, a first-person saga of a cutting-edge Yosemite climb that was a cover story.

By the time I flew back to Massachusetts, all that remained was to get in shape for such a challenge—to get, in fact, into the best climbing shape of my life. Both Ed and I had a constitutional aversion to working out in gyms, but now, in the spring of 1974, we pumped iron with a vengeance at the Amherst College weight room and ran five-and-a-quarter-minute miles around the indoor track. We made a pact to limit our intake of beer to three bottles a night per person. On student trips to the Gunks, we carved out at least an afternoon per weekend to pair up on hard routes by ourselves. And somehow we got free of our Outdoors Program duties long enough to put in a very long day scaling the eight-pitch Direct Direct route on Cannon Cliff, one of the most challenging climbs in the East.

By now I knew better than to venture into the Alaska Range in early June (as Hank and I had in the Kichatnas in 1970), when the tons of snow and ice accumulated during the long winter were sloughing off every wall in sight in a riot of avalanches. Instead, once the spring term came to a close, Ed and I headed out to Colorado, where we further honed our skills and acclimatized to altitude on the cliffs near Aspen and on Longs Peak. Fourteen years earlier, still an alpine innocent who had never tied in to a rope, I had paused at Chasm View on a hike up Longs and stared in awe across the most savage precipice I had ever seen—the Diamond, a thousand feet of dead-vertical granite capping the 2,000-foot-high east face. Now Ed and I rappelled off Chasm View, traversed the mossy and treacherous ledge called Broadway, and bivouacked at the foot of a route called D7. The next day we climbed this straightforward but dizzyingly exposed aid route. We bivouacked once more, then traversed over the summit and down the tourist route, hobbling out to the trailhead by late morning on the third day. At last we thought we were ready for Mount Dickey.

Sharon accompanied Ed and me to Colorado, although she would not head north with us for the big climb. Sensing how important this program of revitalization was to me, she did her best to be support-ive; she even tried to teach Ed and me some stretching routines she had learned in a yoga class. In unguarded moments, however, I became guiltily aware of just how frightening to her the prospect was of my plunging back, as some mountaineering writer had once put it, "to square one of risk and hardship." In certain looks on her face, I saw the dread with which she anticipated another month of waiting by the phone for the call that would deliver her from the constant fear that the worst might have happened.

By early July, Ed, Galen, and I were camped in Don Sheldon's hangar in Talkeetna, sorting out gear. This would be my fourth expedition, stretching back to the Wickersham Wall in 1963, on which Alaska's most famous bush pilot performed the flying and air-dropping. During those eleven years, Don had gone from being a hero of mine to becoming a friend. In 1965, as we had waited to fly in to Huntington, we had met Don's new wife, Roberta Reeve, a beautiful dark-haired woman who was the daughter of Bob Reeve, the most celebrated Alaskan bush pilot of his own era, the 1930s and 1940s. Don never talked about Roberta, but one day, as Matt Hale and I hung out near the school building just across the scruffy baseball diamond that adjoined the airstrip, the loquacious Mrs. Campbell, who apparently taught grades kindergarten through twelve, confided in us her take on the change wrought in Sheldon's life by marrying for the first time at age forty-three. "Campbell," Don had burst out one day, apropos of nothing, his boyish face unable to hide a goofy grin, "I never knew a man could be so happy."

In 1974, I heard through the grapevine that Sheldon had been stricken with stomach cancer. Writing to him in the spring to ask if he could fly us in to and out from Dickey, I had discreetly tried to ask about his health. It was not a subject he was wont to dwell on. He wrote me back, jauntily asserting that he had "escaped the hospital" to fly the heaviest roster of mountaineering clients ever in the summer of 1973.

I would learn later, from Roberta, that through the summer and fall of 1974, Don struggled against constant pain and nausea. Yet he never took a day off. During his incomparable career, Don had cracked up a hefty number of airplanes making landings where no one else ever had—"but I've never injured a passenger," he would often add. So that I could retrieve our base camp after Dickey, that summer Sheldon would once more land in a place no one else had ever attempted, on a short side arm of the Ruth Glacier. Six months later, still only fifty-three years old, he was dead.

A decade earlier, had we had the audacity to attempt a wall like the southeast face of Mount Dickey, we would have attacked it expedition-style, stringing fixed ropes up most of the pitches, establishing tent camps and food and gear depots, as we had on Huntington. But in 1974, the three of us agreed, it would be far more elegant to climb our prize alpine-style. In the Washburn photos, the first 1,000 feet, up a near-vertical buttress, promised the hardest climbing on the whole route. We expected lots of aid work there, like what Ed and I had tackled on the Diamond. We would compromise slightly, then, by fixing ropes on the first 800 or 900 feet of our route, returning to base camp after each effort. Then, with good weather, we would take four or five days' worth of food and go for broke up the route, bivouacking where we could.

The logistics of the attack, which Ed and I had puzzled out back in Amherst, had a certain elegance of their own, but also, we thought, ought to add a margin of safety to the out-on-a-limb proposition of a big-wall climb in Alaska. We would first climb Dickey by its easy, back side route on the west—the route pioneered by Washburn in 1955. Near the summit, we would plant a cache containing tent, sleeping bags, and extra food. We would also mark this route with willow wands. All this as insurance against the possibility of staggering to the top of the southeast face in a blizzard, on the verge of hypothermia and/or exhaustion, and facing a blind descent on a route unknown to us.

After laying that summit cache, we would circle all the way around Mount Dickey, climbing down an unexplored icefall to reach the arm of the Ruth Glacier, where we would set up base camp beneath our towering route. If all went well, three days later we would receive Sheldon's airdrop at that base camp. Then the rest would be up to us and to the mountain gods.

On July 10, Sheldon flew us in to the broad basin just north of the Ruth Gorge, today officially named the Don Sheldon Amphitheater. Taking advantage of a real estate loophole—a tiny square of glacial terrain inexplicably excluded from Denali National Park—Sheldon had purchased a nunatak. On this prong of stable rock poking out of the eternally flowing glacier, he had erected a small six-sided prefab cabin, paired with an adjoining outhouse. This bungalow in the middle of nowhere still serves today as a cozy jumping-off point for dozens of expeditions to the Ruth Gorge, Huntington, the Rooster Comb, and the southeast flanks of McKinley.

From the Mountain House, as Sheldon had dubbed his cabin, we set off in the penumbral light of 2:30 A.M. on July 11 to climb the back side of Mount Dickey. The steep snow slope was easy enough so that we could travel simultaneously, roped together at seventy-foot intervals. Ed and I wore snowshoes, Galen short skis. First on the rope, I was plodding along in a happy trance when I suddenly heard distant jabbering noises. Incredible—could there be another party on this obscure mountainside, and were they speaking Japanese?

I looked back to see Ed with his axe jammed to the hilt in the snow, a tight rope belayed around the shaft. It turned out that Galen had plunged through a snow bridge and fallen thirty feet unchecked into a hidden crevasse—the first such plunge of his life. The distant jabbering was Galen shouting his outrage and alarm at the top of his voice, his cries muffled by the glacier itself. Belayed by Ed with the other half of the rope, I crept up to the edge of the small hole in the featureless slope and peered in. Galen had landed on his feet; luckily, he was more scared than hurt. Before I could offer to haul his pack out, however, he seized his camera and fired off several shots of my head poking through the tiny skylight orifice, concern written on my face. It was an image he would later publish several times over.

Once Galen was restored to the surface, we resumed our winding trek up the mountain's west flank. Only a thousand feet below the summit, a storm moved in. Soon it was snowing hard, as we plodded upward in a total whiteout. Our schedule would not allow a second chance to lay the cache near the summit, so we pushed blindly on, at last reaching a level shelf on the summit ridge. We wrapped our precious belongings in a tarp and marked them with a long pole. We guessed we were only about a hundred feet below the invisible summit.

Now ensued a disagreement that could have had weighty consequences. Both Ed and Galen thought we were on the ridge leading north from the summit. I was dead certain that we stood instead on the west ridge. If we did not know exactly where on the mountain our cache lay, we would have little chance of finding it after we topped out from the big climb. We argued on as the blizzard raged around us. I was outvoted two to one, but I had always prided myself on a talent for orientation, and just before the whiteout had turned the world to a blur, I had taken a careful mental bearing on the summit. At last, through sheer pigheadedness, I battered down my partners' objections.

We descended through the storm, relying on the string of willow wands we had placed on the way up to keep us safely on the route. Camping at Pittock Pass, a col separating the Ruth from an unexplored branch of the Tokositna Glacier to the south, we collapsed in our tents. By morning the skies had cleared magnificently, the temperature had plunged, and there was not a whisper of wind. The rope we had simply flung to the ground the afternoon before had turned into a frozen snarl of perlon spaghetti, like some *objet trouvé*.

We tromped off south, crossing one more stretch of Alaskan wilderness that my teammates and I had the privilege to be the first ever to tread. All the training of the spring paid psychological dividends now: I felt supremely content to be where I was. The usual ambivalence of my first few days on an expedition was missing, thanks to the commitment Ed and I had forged in the Amherst College weight room and on Cannon and the Diamond.

Then we turned a corner and suddenly found ourselves above the icefall that led down to the Ruth Gorge. For the first time we saw the beetling 5,000-foot precipice of Dickey's south face, with our route at the far end, in daunting profile. All three of us uttered exclamations of awe and admiration.

Late on July 12, Sheldon delivered our base camp airdrop with his usual feather touch. Our only loss was a few ounces of powdered soup. Our tents pitched on a glacial shelf beside a meltwater rivulet and a scattering of comfortable boulders on which to lounge, we spent the first few days just taking in the hugeness of our surroundings. Through binoculars, we stared at the features of the wall, trying to divine whether the granite we beheld was clean slabs and corners or congealed brown sugar. Though it was July, avalanches spilled off the summit snowfield of Dickey and hurtled noisily down the vertical mile of space to the floor of our glacial arm. At our backs, less than two miles away, even more terrifying slides, triggered by fractured séracs, crashed down the sinister north wall of Mount Bradley—still unclimbed today and, as far as I know, unattempted.

On July 14, we finally came to grips with the thousand-foot buttress that rose abruptly out of the glacier, the rudely vertical commencement of our long, long route. We had expected to find hard aid-climbing here, but now, to our delight, the rock proved as solid as in our blithest dreams, and we were able to climb the three hardest pitches almost entirely free, at a difficulty ranging no higher than 5.8. My 130-foot lead, our sixth overall, was one of the most thrilling pitches I had ever put in anywhere: a balletic tiptoe up an 80-degree slab, with sharp crystals and nodules for tiny hand- and footholds.

At the end of eleven and a half hours of climbing, we had scaled the first 1,000 feet, fixing lines on 900 of them, and had placed a food-and-gear cache at our high point. We rappelled down the fixed ropes, all three of us at once, staying a pitch apart, before trudging back to base camp. So absorbed had we been in the puzzle of the route that during the whole fourteen-hour effort, we had paused only for a few bites of chocolate. Ecstatic at our progress, we nonetheless realized that we had solved only the lowest fifth of the 5,000-foot wall.

The plan now was to wait for good weather, then go for it— climbing alpine-style as fast as we could, bivouacking on ledges. The route, as we had ceaselessly studied it with our binoculars, promised to be an immensely complicated series of zigzags. We recognized the danger of actually getting lost on the wall—of being too close to the rock to know where we were on the route we had traced on our Washburn photo. A concomitant risk would be missing the ascent line if we had to rappel off if defeated by a storm or unclimbable terrain. Still, we hoped to tame the southeast wall in a single push of three to five days.

We waited for three days as uncertain weather wafted in and out of the Ruth Gorge. During that vigil, I felt the stirrings of malaise and even of fear, as I think Ed and Galen also did. As I wrote in my diary on July 15, "There is a current of tension running through the casual atmosphere [of base camp]. Dickey simply can't be taken lightly. It's so big."

It was in these moments of enforced leisure that I thought about Sharon, waiting in Colorado for news from Alaska. It was not simply that, as in previous years, I worried about her worrying about me. There, in the claustrophobic canyon on the side arm of the Ruth, with the hardest climb of my life looming over my future, I missed Sharon painfully. As a half-futile stab against that anxiety, I was writing my diary as an extended letter to her. Closing one entry, I wrote, "It's clearing off now (8:15). Probably we'll go tomorrow. Don't worry about us. Maybe by the next entry, we'll have climbed Dickey. Or come down for good, one way or another, victory or defeat."

On July 16, with the weather improving, I went for a solo two-hour walk, circling well out in front of our route to get the least foreshortened possible look at it. The glacier here was free enough from crevasses so that I could safely stroll about alone. But what I saw made me deeply pessimistic. "I was very discouraged," I wrote that afternoon, "by what the binoculars showed of the middle portion of the route. I now think we won't make it. Which, paradoxically, makes me more willing to go up on it in mediocre weather—fatalism, I suppose." My estimation of the middle section would prove to be prescient.

That evening, the sky cleared off completely. There was no putting it off. We got up at 3:30 A.M. on July 17, ate breakfast, and hurriedly packed. My nerves jangling, I had managed only two hours of fitful sleep.

We were on the rock by 5:45 A.M. With Galen going first, me second, and Ed third, we used mechanical ascenders, called Jumars, to sprint up the fixed lines. Ever since I had first Jumared on ropes left in place in the Kichatnas in 1966, I had been leery of the practice—and for good reason. In the great ranges, fixed ropes can easily be damaged by falling rocks or by winds rubbing them across sharp edges. And there is no way to detect that damage from below. In 1966, on an attempt on a new route on the North Face of the Eiger in winter, John

Harlin, perhaps the leading American alpinist of his day, had fallen 4,000 feet to his death when a fixed rope had broken under the weight of his body. Just minutes before, his British partner, a lighter man, had Jumared up the same rope, noticed a frayed segment, but neglected to warn Harlin.

Only two hours into the climb, on the eighth pitch, we came close to a serious accident. As Galen had Jumared up the line, he had not realized that he had shifted the position of the rope so that now it ran over a huge loose block. As soon as Galen got off the rope, I got on it. At once, forty feet above me, I heard the block creak and saw it shift. The rope itself was all that still held it in place. There was nothing to do but to Jumar gingerly toward the menacing stone. Just as I got to the block, it fell partway out of its niche. I held it tight with my shoulder, but it was too heavy to shove back into balance. Ed was Jumaring at least a hundred feet below me, oblivious to my predicament, but in the direct line of fall if I had to let the rock go. I yelled to Galen. He managed to rappel down the same line I was Jumaring on. Together, we wrestled the block back into its niche, then shifted the rope so that it lay clear of the troublesome stone.

Above our gear cache, we were on new ground. For pitch after pitch, though the route line was devious, the climbing stayed relatively easy. We had worked out a system so that, tying and untying from assorted ropes, each of us got to lead every third pitch. The leader climbed with a very light pack or, on the hardest pitches, with none at all. The second Jumared on the climbing rope, carrying a heavier pack. On the worst pitches, the third man carried his own pack as he Jumared and cleaned the pitch of the nuts and pitons the leader had placed; then he had to rappel down to pick up the leader's pack and Jumar with it back up to the belay stance. All of us hated the job of coming third, while we hungered for the heady play of leading a new pitch.

Since Galen had never climbed before with Ed or me, I had worried that it would take some time to smooth out our teamwork. Instead, that day we climbed with magical efficiency. At 10:30 P.M., we found a small ledge that would serve for our bivouac. In seventeen straight hours of serious climbing, without even stopping for a bite of chocolate or a swig of water, we had swarmed up twenty-seven pitches. None of us had ever before climbed anything like twenty-seven pitches in a single day! We were 3,000 feet off the glacier. We had already passed the halfway mark on our gargantuan wall.

We laid our uncoiled ropes out for sleeping mattresses and crawled into half-bags and down jackets. Despite my utter exhaustion, I had trouble falling asleep. As we had discovered during the first days of the expedition, Galen was a heavy snorer. Now, on our ledge, he was out like a light, snoring away as sonorously as he might have in a comfortable bed back home.

I managed four hours of sleep. When we woke, it was to a changed world. The few wispy clouds that we had noticed around midnight had coalesced into a solid fog bank that was slowly creeping up the Ruth Glacier toward us. The perfect weather had lasted only a day.

Over breakfast, we urgently discussed our options. The prudent course would have been to descend. But Galen pointed out what retreat would mean. To rappel twenty-seven pitches safely, we would have to use up at least two pieces on each anchor. Some fifty pitons and nuts—the bulk of our supply of hardware—would be sacrificed to the descent. As Galen put it, "If we go down now, our Alaskan climbing is finished for the year."

We decided to push on upward, hoping the storm would hold off for another day or two. Within an hour, a mist had risen from the glacier and enveloped us in whiteout. We were worn out from the previous day's effort, our limbs stiff and cramped, our hands puffy, the knuckles scraped raw. Yet we climbed on with a doggedness that had a ragged, almost panicky thread to it.

And now the middle section of the route that I had worried over through binoculars unfurled its treachery. During the previous several pitches, the rock had been slowly but steadily deteriorating from the perfect stuff on which we had cavorted on the initial buttress. By the beginning of our 31st pitch, the granite had turned to brown sugar, barely held in place by some geologic glue. Eighty feet up my lead, swallowed in fog, I could no longer see Galen belaying me. To make things worse, it had begun to snow. Half the holds I seized came loose in my hands, but I scuttled upward all the same. At the end of the pitch it took me twenty minutes to place five bad pitons that might together approximate one good anchor. "Are the ropes fixed?" came the impatient cry from below. "Wait a minute, god-damn it!" I yelled back.

The next pitch, our 32nd, was Galen's lead. Those 150 feet of inspired climbing, which would turn out to solve the crux of our route, amounted to one of the most dazzling performances I would ever witness in the mountains. There were no decent cracks, so Galen took his piton hammer and gouged out footholds in the rock itself, as if he were climbing ice, not granite. Twice or three times he drove pitons straight into the crumbly rock. A hundred and twenty feet out, he thought he was stymied. He could see a shallow ledge thirty feet above, but no way to get to it. As he later wrote in *Ascent*, "In another situation I might have given up. . . . I convinced myself that I couldn't downclimb the pitch and that thirty feet of sixty-five degree rock *had* to be possible. Up was the only way."

The ledge, which Galen somehow reached, looked like a dead end: above it the decomposed wall rose stern, crackless, and almost vertical. Perhaps two hours after Galen had started up the 32nd pitch, I arrived on his ledge, Jumaring third. The prospect was deeply alarming. "Where's Ed?" I blurted out.

Relying on his Yosemite bag of tricks, Galen had driven a single expansion bolt for anchor just above the fragile ledge. Through that bolt, he had lowered Ed to the right around a corner, in an irreversible pendulum maneuver that would cut us off for good from our line of ascent. The only hope, it seemed, was to swing rightward into a chimney system that might afford us an escape route upward.

But even Galen knew that his gambit was a desperate one. In *Ascent*, he later recaptured his stream-of-consciousness musings, as Ed dangled out of sight in terra incognita:

This isn't courageous. It's not even fun. It's stupid. I don't want to be here. Hey, all you phony forces out there: I don't believe in you, but I will if you just get me out of here. I'll admit it. Yes, I am a chickenshit. Just get me out of here. . . . It's a bad dream. It's got to be.

Then, out of nowhere, muffled by the intervening corner of cliff, Ed's cry reached our ears: "Perfect rock! It goes!"

By now, it was about 7:00 in the evening. The light snowfall had stopped, but a drizzling rain took its place, with the temperature just a degree or two above the freezing point. We guessed that we were about 700 feet below a band of snow that, gazing at the Washburn photo, we had named the Exit Ledge. That generous horizontal ramp promised not only a good bivouac site, but a traverse left to avoid the last perpendicular cliff. From the Exit Ledge, the summit rose only about 800 feet above, and that last slope looked as though it lay back at a reasonable angle.

It was now absolutely imperative to get to the Exit Ledge before the storm broke in all its fury. Perfect rock Ed had indeed found in our right-hand chimney system, but the climbing once more grew very hard. My 34th-pitch lead proved yet another crux, as I passed an over-hang on bad pitons—the hardest aid-climbing on the whole route—then was stumped only ten feet below a belay ledge. I tried aiding the short wall first with a cliff-hanger (that wrinkled piece of chrome-molybdenum Ed had used to solve his own crux on Shot Tower) and a razor-thin postage stamp of a piton called a rurp. Both broke loose under my weight and I fell, caught by a good nut just below. Finally I dispatched the wall by climbing it free, hard 5.8 on rain-slicked rock.

Around 8:00 P.M. we pulled ourselves at last onto the Exit Ledge. We had accomplished a fifteen-hour day even more grueling than the previous day's seventeen-hour marathon. We set up our bivouac in three adjoining nooks, none really adequate. I made a cramped cave out of two corners of rock and the tent fly we carried, managing to cook dinner for all three of us inside my lair. Galen found a coffin-shaped aperture in the cliff, crawled into it, and lay almost unmoving throughout the night. "If the rock had shifted half an inch," he told us in the morning, "I'd have never gotten out." Ed simply reclined on a flat rock, wrapped himself in a bivouac sack, held a mitten in front of his face, and managed to sleep. When I beheld him in the morning, I felt as though I was looking at a victim's body discovered by rescuers.

Had we been carrying the kind of bivouac gear we had used in the Revelations in 1967, we would not have survived that night. But in the last seven years, companies had begun to invent gear that would revolutionize big-range mountaineering and allow climbers to survive nights out in conditions that would have killed their predecessors. In our case, the critical items were half-bags and jackets filled with synthetic fiber rather than goose down, and outer parkas that were waterproof but allowed bodily condensation to evaporate.

Even so, we passed a terrible, almost sleepless night. The storm had not waited for us. In the morning, we were trapped in an all-out Alaskan blizzard, with wind up to fifty miles an hour, fine snow lashing our faces, the temperature between 15 and 20 degrees Fahrenheit. Going down was no longer an option. It was up and over the top or . . . well, there was no avoiding the logic . . . or die.

In theory, we had been prepared to go for the summit from the Exit Ledge even in a storm. But we had badly underestimated those last 800 feet of the mountain. Trying to go light (Galen would later characterize us as "carrying the lightest loads we had ever taken on a big wall"), reasoning that the route was essentially a rock climb, we had brought with us only a single ice axe and one set of crampons. The latter fit my boots, so I took the gear and led our rope of three the whole day on July 19.

We got off to a terrible start when Ed, trying to Jumar the rope we had fixed the evening before on our 41st pitch, had his ascenders slip on the iced-up rope, causing a ten-foot fall. We had to lead the pitch all over again. From the top of it, I headed upward on a leftward diagonal traverse. As we had suspected, the Exit Ledge marked the contact line between granite and an altogether different kind of rock: it proved now to be the same rotten black schist Don Jensen and I had battled on Mount Deborah a decade before.

Despite the storm and our inadequate gear, I was in my element. If there was one kind of climbing that I could pride myself on being truly expert at, it was this: what alpinists call mixed—snow, ice, and rock scrambled together in an unpredictable mélange. The slope varied between 45 and 60 degrees in steepness. It was almost impossible to hammer pitons into the fractured schist, but I placed what token protection I could. Most of the day, we traveled continuously; on the harder stretches, I chopped steps in the ice for my crampon-less partners and belayed them as they used the picks on their piton hammers in lieu of ice axes. Rime ice coated every ledge and corner of rock, and we soon had ice in our beards and hair. On one ledge, Ed abruptly commented, "I don't like this. It seems really dangerous." But what choice did we have?

Objectively, I recognize today that the climbing we did on that third day on Dickey's southeast face was some of the riskiest I ever performed. On the unbelayed pitches, had one of us slipped and fallen, he would most likely have pulled the other two off, after which there would have been only an infinitesimal chance that our plunge would have ended before the glacier floor, nearly 5,000 feet below. But on July 19, I felt not only supremely confident—I was awash in an exuberance that seemed transcendental. On the climb, I had kept the Washburn photo of our route crumpled up in my shirt pocket. Now, in this desert of mixed rock and snow, I kept pulling out the picture and correlating fins of schist and runnels of blue ice with the features Washburn's camera had captured from the airplane. I lost all track of time, and headed up and left toward the flat stretch of summit ridge (invisible in the storm) where, I was convinced, we had deposited our life-assuring cache nine days before.

After many rope-lengths of climbing, I emerged suddenly on level ground. It had to be the summit ridge. I dropped my pack, then belayed Ed and Galen up. The cache, I thought, ought to be just to the west of us. Still roped, I headed along the ridge. Almost at once, I found a green willow wand drooping out of the snow. Then, just beyond, right where it should have been, the tall pole marking our cache. Whooping with joy and relief, we pitched the tent, crawled inside, and brewed up pot after pot of soup and lemonade.

Three days later, Sheldon picked us up at the Mountain House. His first words to me, as I waddled through deep snow toward the cockpit of his Super Cub, were, "Congratulations for not getting yourselves killed on that thing."

In 1979, in their landmark book *Fifty Classic Climbs of North America*, Steve Roper and Allen Steck hailed our Dickey climb as "the first Grade VI rock climb in Alaska." In 2004, *Climbing* magazine saluted our deed as "at the time the hardest alpine route in North America." Galen, alas, would never read that encomium. Having become one of the most celebrated wilderness photographers in the world, he was killed, with his second wife, Barbara, in August 2002, in a private plane crash on a routine flight to his home in Bishop, California.

Our route on Dickey was not repeated for twenty-nine years, until a pair of very talented young American mountaineers, Steve House and Jeff Hollenbaugh, made the second ascent in September 2003. In previous seasons, House and Hollenbaugh had knocked off several other classic routes in the Alaska Range in times that were radically shorter than the first ascenders had required. Heading up Dickey, they expected to make comparable hash of our three-day climb, but in the end, their second ascent proved almost a carbon copy of ours. It took them just as long to climb the route, which they, too, finished in an all-out storm. Climbing on their second day up into the brown-sugar wasteland of Galen's and my 31st and 32nd pitches, they were sure that the route could not possibly go there. Wasting several hours on an ill-advised pendulum, they finally headed up into the really bad rock, where they found Galen's pitons still driven straight into the granite, and the single bolt he had placed above the crumbly ledge. The pair tested the twenty-nine-year-old bolt, then lowered off it themselves to reach the chimney system where Ed had found the perfect rock that allowed us to escape our trap.

House and Hollenbaugh were magnanimous in praise of our ascent. In the *American Alpine Journal* in 2004, Hollenbaugh wrote, "Their climbing this route in only three days in 1974 was an amazing achievement. Twenty-nine years after, we did little to improve on the style and time of the first ascent."

Such kudos, three decades after the most difficult climb of my life, fill me with a bursting pride that no glowing book review or literary award has ever bestowed. And in late July 1974, as I headed back to Colorado with Dickey under my belt, I was brimming with a deep sense of fulfillment.

Yet for all the longing with which, during my glum, fatalistic days on the Ruth Glacier, I had looked forward to seeing Sharon again, I have today no clear memory of our reunion. And in September, as I headed back to Hampshire College for my fifth year of professorship, I was not at all sure just what Dickey had meant. I had an amorphous feeling that the great climb had changed my life in some lasting way, but if I had had to articulate how, I would have been at a loss for words.

NINE

Backing Off

FROM THE FALL OF 1974 ON, STRIVING TO MAIN-
tain the illusion that it was still an elite institution of higher education, Hampshire drifted slowly but relentlessly to the right. "Publish
or perish," which in 1970 we faculty had sneered at as a relic of the
dark ages of benign neglect of the actual teaching process, became a
stern criterion on the reappointment checklist. Having published my
two early mountaineering narratives, as well as having for years con-
tributed reviews of nature and adventure books to the *Washington Post*,
I suffered no frowns of disapproval from the deans, who began to
monitor the impact of our academic meteors on the dead moons of
the scholarly journals. But one of my best friends in the School of
Humanities and Arts, who happened to be not only a popular but a
good and very hardworking history-and-lit teacher, was put on a year
of humiliating probation, during which he was expected to crank out
critiques elucidating certain unvisited corners of, say, the role of trade
unions in the Spanish Civil War or the early novels of John Dos Passos.

One consequence of this rightward slippage was that the Outdoors Program began to be subtly marginalized. No one could com-
plain that the O.P. was not popular. On opening day each autumn,
under the banner we unfurled over the library steps that read "What
Is the Outdoors Program?," a throng would gather. One blithe September afternoon, after my opening address, Ed and I hauled off some
fifty first-year students (the term "freshmen" having been a sexist
no-no at Hampshire since 1970) to Rattlesnake Gutter for a top-rope
outing. But it became harder and harder to convince the administra-

tion that a yeti hunt in the woods really had anything important to contribute to a student's Div III project.

I struggled, to little avail, to win for my O.P. colleagues some kind of token adjunct faculty status (most of them had graduate work or even MA degrees under their belts). In 1974, stressed out by my schizophrenic job as half-time lit prof and half-time O.P. director, I tried to persuade the president of the college to transfer the latter post to Ed. I ticked off my buddy's skills and diligences, none of which the president denied. Ed, moreover, was full-time O.P., far more in touch with its daily doings than I. Yet there was a chill in the presidential office. Finally I said, "What's the problem?"

The man shrugged his shoulders, then answered, "Somehow I just can't see Ed Ward showing up in his greasy down jacket at a budget meeting and making an effective case for the Outdoors Program."

I was speechless. My down jacket was every bit as greasy as Ed's, but apparently the president saw only the Ph.D. sewn on its sleeve.

Like the administration, by 1974–75 the student body had become far more conservative than the band of if-it-feels-good-do-it hippies who had launched the school in 1970. But in the meantime, climbing, kayaking, and other outdoor "sports" were riding a nation-wide vogue. The nerdiness epitomized by our early-1960s Harvard Mountaineering Club gang, sneaking off to the Gunks in our blue jeans to perform our arcane rituals on the rock, had been supplanted by the coolness of lycra-clad studs and babes gliding up overhangs in Patagonia and North Face ads.

Hampshire was one of a small handful of colleges in the country where an eighteen-year-old could learn to kayak or climb under the aegis of teachers who were in effect professionals at those disciplines. Eric Evans, our kayaking instructor, was in the middle of a seven-year run as national champion in slalom white water; in the 1972 Munich Olympics, he finished seventh in the sport. Thus by 1974, a certain number of high school students were choosing to attend Hampshire because of the O.P., which had acquired a modest reputation that spread from coast to coast.

Among the hundreds of tutees with whom Ed and I assaulted the cliffs of New England and the Gunks over the nine years we taught at Hampshire (eight years, in Ed's case), about a dozen eventually developed into first-rate climbers. Only one, however, would become a lifelong partner on the rope with both of us, sharing ascents long after our Hampshire days were over.

In the spring of his junior year in high school, a somewhat naïve but limitlessly curious kid from Corvallis, Oregon, toured the East Coast, shopping for colleges. "Fresh off the turnip truck," as he would describe his then self two decades later, he found Harvard—the school his father, a graduate of its medical school, had hoped to steer him toward—snobbish and chilly. Amherst College seemed a kindred slough of elitism, but while he was visiting that campus, someone suggested that he check out the hippie school three miles down the road to the south. As the kid walked up the long, curving driveway to Hampshire College, the first person who crossed his path was a pretty young woman wearing a see-through blouse. In that instant, the college choice was made.

At eighteen, Jon Krakauer was a wiry, sharp-featured youth with a tangled crown of curly brown hair. Tightly strung and oppositional by temperament, he challenged authority at every hand, and had a hunger for experience and knowledge that I had scarcely ever witnessed in another student. Jon's father had been a mountaineer of the peak-bagging ilk, dragging his son halfway up a 10,358-foot mountain called South Sister, in the Cascade Range, before the terrified eight-year-old burst into tears and begged retreat. The Krakauer family, moreover, were close friends of the Unsoeld family, destined for both mountaineering glory and tragedy. A charismatic and mercurial professor of religion and ordained minister, Willi Unsoeld gained lasting fame in 1963 by completing the dazzling traverse of Mount Everest by the first ascent of its west ridge with his close friend Tom Hornbein. Both men survived an ill-equipped bivouac at 28,000 feet on the South Col route—the highest night out ever spent to that date anywhere in the world—but the vigil cost Unsoeld nearly all his toes.

Undaunted, he went back to the Himalaya in 1976 to try a new route on 25,645-foot Nanda Devi. On that expedition, Unsoeld's daughter Devi, whom Willi had named after the mountain he thought the most beautiful on earth, and who had been Jon Krakauer's childhood chum, died of peritonitis in her father's arms. In 1987, Willi himself was killed in an avalanche on Mount Rainier.

Jon had done some climbing before he came to college, but his adolescent passion was for ski racing. Then, at fourteen, in the middle of a race, he took a really bad fall and suffered spiral tib-fib fractures of both legs. His father, waiting at the resort at the base of the hill, heard Jon's screams of pain from thousands of feet above, over all the din of lift machinery and tourist buzz.

Thanks to that mishap, Jon's legs grew shorter than normal and slightly bowlegged, and by eighteen he stood only a mite over five eight. Though the catastrophic tumble soured him on ski racing, he turned to climbing as an equally nerve-racking substitute.

From his first weeks at Hampshire, Ed and I took notice of Jon's skill and ambition. And we liked the lad. His intensity somehow failed to preclude a keen sense of humor, and he had not a pretentious bone (broken or not) in his body. Unlike other hotshot rock climbers in the O.P., Jon not only hankered to lead Roseland, a classic 5.9 at the Gunks, but he wanted to know everything that Ed and I knew about Jim McCarthy, the brilliant bohemian who had put up the route way back in 1960. As soon as we became friends, Jon started borrowing books from my fairly ample mountaineering library, devouring each tome like a youngster with a new comic book. (This, in an era when young climbers on the whole were woefully uninterested in the history of their pastime.)

Borrowing a back-page feature from the quirky journal Summit, Ed and I put up a bulletin board outside our office dominated by the rubric "Know Your Mountains." Each week we posted a photo of some cynosure from the greater ranges, inviting our students to thumbtack their guesses as to its identity. Other students hazarded conjectures that were usually wildly off the mark, but Jon aced most of our quizzes. In the barely decipherable hieroglyphs of his printed scrawl, half capitals, half lower case (somehow Jon had never mastered cursive writing), he would triumphantly proclaim "Snowpatch Spire, east face" or "Mount Asgard, Baffin Island."

Jon's enthusiasm and frenetic energy won Ed and me over. He was the first student we fully trusted to teach other students the rudiments of our craft. When the college finally built a gymnasium, Jon, under Ed's light-handed supervision, served as the architect of the first indoor climbing wall ever constructed in the East, as he sawed blocks of wood into esoteric shapes (fabricated hand- and footholds) that he bolted to the interstices between the cinder blocks just beyond the out-of-bounds line of the basketball court. In his third year, Ed and I appointed Jon the leader of a students-only January mini-expedition to the Gore Range of Colorado. It was a credit to the then twenty-year-old's judgment that his group reached virtually no summits during their ten days in the mountains, for freakish conditions had turned the range into a death-trap maze of avalanches ready to cut loose on the flimsiest pretext.

Unlike myself and most of my Harvard Mountaineering Club cronies in the early 1960s, who had accepted our social geekiness as a given, Jon, who had considered himself a geek in high school, cut a rather dashing figure at Hampshire. From the start, he had no shortage of girlfriends, and among the hard-core O.P. crowd, Ed's and my favoritism of Jon earned him some envy.

By the fall of 1973, Sharon had had enough of playing dorm mother, I of trying to read with stereos blaring through the cardboard-thin walls, so we moved off-campus, renting a spacious split-level house on Bay Road, about a mile east of the college, nestled under the leafy lumps of the Holyoke Range. At some point I invited Jon to move into a spare basement room, for which he coughed up forty bucks a month. Soon we became not only mentor and protégé, but drinking buddies, heading in Jon's perpetually crippled VW bus into Amherst to down pitchers at the Drake (the Massachusetts drinking age then being eighteen). Over our beers, we talked endlessly not only about climbing, but about life itself. During these lubricated tête-à-têtes, Jon's lingering ingenuousness merged with his intense curiosity. "What's it like to be married?" he would blurt out. Or, "Dave, what do you do when you're going out with one girl but you're really attracted to another one?"

No entitled rich kid, Jon headed home to Corvallis after his first year of college, where he whiled away the summer in such glamorous precincts as a tarpaper factory, saving up dough to pay Hampshire's exorbitant tuition fees. In the winter of 1973–74, however, infected by Ed's and my preparations for Mount Dickey, Jon decided to prosecute an Alaskan expedition of his own. Inspired by my lyrical tales of the Arrigetch peaks, he gathered six acquaintances (five of them fellow Hampshire students) and headed off to Bettles in late June. During three weeks based in the same valley that Ed, Sharon, and I had chosen in 1971, Jon's team made six ascents, knocking off the last three major challenges in that compact range—peaks named by their predecessors Xanadu, Melting Tower, and Arthur Emmons. On all three of these difficult climbs, Jon was the driving force.

Back at Hampshire for his third year, Jon had succumbed to the full-blown fever of mountaineering fanaticism, just as I had at his age. For the summer of 1975, still treading in his mentor's footsteps, he planned a serious expedition to the Kichatna Spires. That would take place in July. What to do with June?

Over one of those pitchers at the Drake, Jon and I agreed to spend three weeks in early June in a little-known region of Canada's Yukon Territory, called the Tombstone Range. A small explosion of startling monolithic towers embedded in the otherwise dreary Ogilvie Mountains, rising from the headwaters of the north fork of the Klondike River, only 2 degrees south of the Arctic Circle, the Tombstones promised a wilderness as lonely and stark as the most ascetic explorer could wish.

Only one party had ever climbed there, and their brief note in the Canadian Alpine Journal sang the praises of "Bugaboo-style granite." The few published pictures made these handsome spires look like a cross between the Bugaboos and the Arrigetch. The pioneer party had made no dent in the range's finest unclimbed peaks.

Yet in the spring of 1975, on sabbatical leave from Hampshire, which I wasted sitting at home on Bay Road trying to write another novel, I was far from the mountaineering mood of the year before, when Ed and I had trained so diligently for Dickey. For Jon, the Tombstones would serve as a warm-up for the sterner challenges of the Kichatnas. I hoped only for a short, mellow expedition, something comparable to our 1969 foray into the Arrigetch, an outing with some good climbing but with only minimal risk to life and limb.

A mere four years before, fed up with Daniel's and Alex's recitations of Hermann Hesse, I had vowed never again to take Hampshire students to my beloved Far North. But Jon was different. And for companionship as well as logistical help, we invited a classmate of Jon's, a likable and laid-back fellow named Mark Fagan. Mark dabbled as a climber, and in the Tombstones he would be content to hike, scramble, or rope up with the two of us to bag the easier first ascents.

I was proud of the throwback, minimalist style of our expedition. The three of us would forgo airplane support, packing gear and food for three weeks in from the Dempster Highway, a forlorn dirt haul road that bisects the Yukon from south to north. At the end of the trip, we would hitchhike back to Dawson City, the nearest outpost of civilization. Should we get into trouble, we would have to get ourselves out: we carried no radio, and only Sharon and a handful of friends had even a vague idea where we were.

I already knew that June was a bad month to climb in Alaska and the Yukon, but it was the only span that fit both Jon's and my schedules. Sure enough, the hike in turned out to be one of the most brutal backpacking ordeals I had ever undergone. The landscape lay choked in snow. Only three miles off the Dempster Highway, we managed to cross the Klondike River on an ice pan that fortuitously bridged the river's angry brown flood. For the rest of the trip, we were haunted by the thought that, on the hike out, with the ice pans broken up or melted out, we might find ourselves trapped on the wrong side of an unfordable river.

The late-spring snow was so wet and soft that when we tried to wade through it, we sank waist-deep in slush. Jon and Mark had brought skis, I snowshoes, but even with these aids, the going was desperate. I was in just as good shape as my partners, but snowshoes didn't work as well in the muck as skis. As my bearpaws kept plunging even through broken track, I couldn't keep up with the youngsters, and on one hideous four-mile carry, I fell down ten times, a personal record. Each time, to get back onto my feet, I had to roll onto all fours, jerk my monstrous pack back in place, carefully plant one snowshoe, and perform the second half of a deep knee bend, all the while teetering on the edge of another fall.

Because of the weight of our gear, we had to double-pack—carry one load forward, hike back with an empty pack, then retrace the route with the second load. During the eleven-hour day on which we finally reached our base camp ("one of the truly hardest hiking days I've ever had anywhere," I wrote in my diary), we thus traveled twelve miles to win a forward progress of only four. As if this were not tribulation enough, during most of the first week, a cold rain fell incessantly, and fog shrouded the mountains so tight that we couldn't even fantasize about routes.

That summer I was thirty-two, Jon twenty-one. The eleven-year gap in our ages had everything to do with a tension that hung over our trip from the first day on. The two finest peaks in the range, as we knew beforehand from maps and pictures, were Tombstone and Monolith, both untouched by the previous party. I hoped to get up one or both of them by the easiest route, but Jon was determined to tackle a big wall on each—even though nothing he had yet done in life, even in the Arrigetch, qualified as a certifiable big wall.

Despite the arduous grind of our hike in, at base camp Jon was electrified with manic ambition. He wanted to bomb off at once toward the two prize mountains and have at them. I wanted to test our wings—and the quality of the rock, which looked, as I had grumpily remarked, nothing like the Bugaboos—on some less serious first ascent. The hike in had suggested to me that we would need skis and snowshoes simply to approach the ridges and faces we hoped to climb. Despite his sunny disposition and sly sense of humor, Mark was powerless to mediate between Jon's and my disparate goals.

Finally, Jon agreed to put aside his craving for Monolith and Tombstone—both still ten miles away to the west—while we reconnoitered the nearest objective that could legitimately be called a big wall, albeit a smallish one. This was the east face of Little Tombstone, which rose in a parabolic arc, steepening steadily toward the top of its 1,200-foot expanse.

On June 3, Jon and I hiked into the cirque at the base of the climb to check it out. "The route looks messy and wet in the lower, easier half," I wrote in my diary, "but clean and nice on the nearly vertical wall itself." With binoculars, we spotted a series of thin crack systems that might accommodate our pitons and nuts and connect the dotted line from base to summit. Once on top, we could scramble down the gentler west face of the mountain. As I stared at the route, for the first time during the expedition I felt the reawakening of the old urge. I wanted to be up there, doing battle again not only with implacable ice and rock, but with my own hopes and fears. As it had during my twenties, the tedium of the school year just behind me sloughed away. Once more, a steep wall of obscure rock and snow that had never felt the touch of human hand was begging me to explore it.

Then it rained and snowed for twenty hours straight. We vegetated in our tent at Divide Lake. Our conversations died insipidly, and the few books we had brought—Barth's The Sot-weed Factor, Pirsig's Zen and the Art of Motorcycle Maintenance, Faulkner's The Town—offered no escape from the doldrums.

At last, on the morning of June 5, the skies cleared. Jon and I didn't get onto the climb until 11:30 A.M., but at such a latitude in June, when it never gets truly dark even at midnight, there is no penalty for a late start. Unroped, Jon and I started scrambling up the mossy ledges at the foot of the wall. The going was easy, but it soon grew treacherous. The moss, soaking wet in places, ground loose beneath our climbing shoes from the rock beneath; in other spots, it was still frozen, and we slipped when we placed a toe or a heel on what looked like a good green foothold. Two hundred feet up, we stopped to rope up, then started belaying.

Now came that potent moment—like the disheartening thud in

1964 when Don and I had first kicked our boots into the rotten black schist of the east ridge of Mount Deborah—when we discovered the true quality of the rock in a range no one knew much about. To Jon and me, the Tombstones suddenly revealed their true nature. Not only was every crack seamed with slimy moss, so that we had to scrape away loose dirt and vegetation to drive home a piton, but the rock itself was patently inferior to the granite of the Bugaboos. This stuff was not so much rotten as exfoliated: instead of abounding in deep, clean-cut fissures (like the Bugaboos), it burgeoned with hollow flakes and plated slabs, the equivalent in stone of the skin of an onion, each thin layer unstably covering the next. When one of us drove a piton sideways into a crack beneath a flake, it rang not clear and musical, but with a dull thump. The danger was that driving the piton could pry the whole flake loose and send it plummeting toward the belayer below.

As I brought Jon up to the top of the second pitch, a big snowslide suddenly poured down the couloir to our left, only twenty feet away. Here was another consequence of our too-early arrival, for summit snowfields all over the Tombstone Range were loaded with the same wet slush through which we had waded to base camp, and all it took was a little sun to set the stuff in motion.

We had anticipated this hazard, but, peering through our binoculars two days before, had convinced ourselves that the face itself lay out of the line of any substantial slides. The avalanches sloughing loose from just below the top, we rationalized, ought to funnel into the couloirs right and left of the wall. So much for theory. As Jon led our fifth pitch, we heard a roaring sound above. I jerked my head up in time to see perhaps half a ton of snow blocks appear in midair. Jon had traversed right, and so was out of the fall line, but as I shrank tight to the wall and hunched my shoulders, the debris crashed and bounced straight over my head. Only a few particles of rock and a fine spray of snow hit me, but glimmerings of Mount Temple rattled my brain.

Jon, who had never been so close to an avalanche before, was momentarily unnerved, but he finished the pitch and brought me up. By 4:30 in the afternoon, we had reached the big ledge halfway up the east face. We had been climbing for five hours without a break.

Above us, the rock turned vertical or overhanging. We ate a hasty lunch and took stock.

I'd had enough. "Let's get off this thing, Jon," I said, "before one of those slides takes us out. Besides, this first pitch off the ledge looks really nasty."

But Jon's ambition was rekindled. "Let me just take a crack at it," he pleaded. Reluctantly, I gave in.

The pitch was indeed a nasty one. It began in an ugly, cavelike hollow, festooned with loose, downward-pointing prongs, virtual granite stalactites. There was no hope of climbing it free: Jon would have to go on aid, dangling short nylon stirrups from whatever pitons he could drive into the shallow cracks between the prongs.

Like the skilled carpenter he would become after college, Jon nailed his way out of the cave. He had to drive each piton with gingerly care, pounding it only deep enough to take his weight, for a more vigorous effort ran the risk of prying loose flakes and prongs that might collapse on him. After quite a while, Jon reached the lip of the cave and passed out of sight above me.

The sun had long since wheeled west behind the bulk of Little Tombstone. I stood on snow as the rope inched out, shivering with cold. At first I actually hoped Jon would fail, so that we could succumb to my instinct and back off this perplexing wall. But at last he was ninety feet out. I heard him call, "Off belay!" It had taken him a full two and a half hours to gain those ninety feet. Now I had no choice but to follow.

As I Jumared up the rope, removing the pitons, I realized that Jon's feat had been a brilliant one—one of the finest aid leads I had ever witnessed. The whole pitch overhung by a few degrees, and the placements of most of the pitons Jon had relied on were cunning in the extreme. At the belay stance, Jon handed me the gear. It was my turn.

This 7th pitch, though slightly easier than Jon's, turned out to be the hardest aid lead I had ever accomplished. The angle of the wall relented to just less than vertical, but the crack I followed was so poor that I had to hang from two or three bad pitons in a row, then make a free move on sketchy holds to get to the next point of aid. Yet the difficulty of the climbing absorbed me. For the first time on the expedition, my ambivalence vanished. I was happy; I was climbing well; I wanted this first ascent as badly as Jon did.

Immersed in the trance of our craft, we each led another slow, difficult pitch. Dusky midnight came and went. In the cold, the snowslides had ceased their mischief. Back at base camp, Mark was no doubt sound asleep. In the distance, we heard the mournful wail of a wolf. We must, I realized with a dawning excitement, be getting near the top of the wall.

At 3:00 A.M., I turned a corner to the left, still hanging in my stirrups, and saw a joyous sight. The wall abruptly lay back to an angle of only 50 degrees. And there was the top, a mere forty feet above me! We were home free.

Then I took a second look, and felt my joy crumble. Ten feet above, the last flake offered the most dubious of cracks for a piton. Above that, the rock was devoid of even the shallowest groove. I would have to climb those last forty feet virtually without protection. The low angle meant that it should go, a matter of spidering up on nubbins and flat-soled friction. It didn't look that hard . . . or did it?

I was close to exhaustion. We had been climbing for almost sixteen hours straight, with only a twenty-minute lunch break half a day ago. I moved up and hammered an angle piton behind the last flake. It gripped even more poorly than I had thought it would: I could perhaps have pulled it out with one hand.

I yelled down to Jon, out of sight below. "We're forty feet from the top! It really lies back here, but it's unprotectable." I hesitated. "Do you feel like leading it?"

"Sure!" came back Jon's hearty cry.

I retreated to the brow of the wall, where I had placed my last good piton. I drove three more into the same crack, clipped in to this anchor, then hung a nylon belay seat from the pitons. As I brought Jon up, I sat in the belay seat sideways to the nearly vertical wall, facing right, my feet dangling loose over the void.

"I see what you mean," Jon said, as he joined me and gazed at the blank but low-angled slab above. We sorted our hardware. Just at that moment, the sun rose in the northeast. As Jon started to climb, I fed the rope through a carabiner attached to the left-hand-most piton.

He moved carefully past the bad flake, then onto new ground. As I watched, a mixture of dread and hope surged like an alternating current through my veins. Jon's toes sought the tiny wrinkles and knobs that gave him purchase. He was moving calmly, with precision and grace.

Now he was twenty feet above me. Only twenty feet to go. "It's thin," Jon said quietly—shorthand for tricky and delicate.

Jon lifted his left leg with deliberation and placed his toe on a nubbin at waist level. He gathered himself before shifting his weight slowly to the left foot. And then the nubbin broke.

Grabbing at nothing, he slid feet first, then started to bounce. He passed just behind me on the left, then flew into the abyss. Whipping downward, the rope plucked the bad piton out from behind the flake above like a toothpick.

I knew exactly what I had to do, but my brain screamed a silent injunction: *Hang on! Hang on!*

The rope came tight in a violent jerk. My left hand was pulled into the carabiner and ground hard against the granite, but I held fast with my right. I must have closed my eyes, for when I dared to look, I saw Jon twenty-five feet below me, hanging sideways against the wall. "Thanks for stopping me!" he yelled. As he had bounced off the wall and flown through the air just left of my belay, he had turned upside down, and for an instantaneous moment of terror imagined falling headfirst out of his harness.

Now Jon got out his Jumars and climbed the rope back up to me, where I clipped him to my anchor. "How's your hand?" he asked breathlessly.

I looked at it for the first time. The back of my hand was bleeding, and deep gouges scarred the knuckles where the rope had ground them against the rock, but as yet I felt little pain. "It's all right," I said.

"Man, I had it made! Let me give it another—"

Had I been in the frame of mind I was on Huntington ten years before, at the apogee of my own obsession, I would have agreed at once, or even offered to take the lead. But I had passed that point for good. Getting up Little Tombstone was not the most important thing in my life.

"No," I interrupted Jon. "We've got to back off."

"Dave! Twenty feet! We can do it."

"We can't risk another fall here."

We argued for five minutes or so. A decade before, I had talked a dubious Matt into pushing upward after we had fallen seventy-five feet together. Now I was not going to be talked by Jon into climbing on up into the trap of the last forty feet of the east face.

Passionately though he argued, Jon had been badly scared by his plunge. In my fifteen years of climbing, I had never caught a leader fall from my belay anchor alone—let alone from a hanging belay. Jon would never again suffer such a fall in a career that now spans more than three decades of ascents all over the world.

At last, Jon acquiesced. I would like to think that he gave in partly because he respected my judgment, the wisdom I had gleaned in the eleven more years of climbing I had under my belt than he did. And today, I think we made the right decision. As far as I know, the east face of Little Tombstone is still unclimbed.

I set up the first rappel from my hanging belay. With the decision to back off, Jon seemed to slump into a dispirited torpor, which alarmed me. I knew by now that descending a mountain was far more dangerous than climbing up one. If ever we had to be sharp, it was in setting up these rappels.

So, as we crept down our ropes into the sunny brilliance of our second fine day in a row, I assumed a fussy, hypervigilant role. Twice I improved anchors that Jon had set up, adding an extra piton or nut. I double-checked his rappel setup, and insisted that he check mine. Once, just as he got on the rope, he pulled loose a heavy block that struck him in the thigh. He screamed with pain, then kneaded the bruise with his fingers.

My gouged and bloody left hand swelled so fat that it felt as clumsy as if I were wearing a mitten. I willed myself to concentrate. Yet the lead of defeat hung heavy on my tongue too. We both realized that, as we used up most of our hardware getting off the climb, we had not only failed on Little Tombstone, but would leave ourselves with too little gear to attempt any other serious routes in the two weeks ahead. Jon's dreams of big walls on Tombstone and Monolith were evaporating in our retreat. And somewhere during that stodgy spiral toward earth, I realized that this would probably be my last real expedition.

The rappels were dangerous and tricky. It was hard to find good anchors, and most of ours ended up being hanging ones. As we slid down the rope, it constantly snagged on blocks above, threatening to pull them loose.

At 7:30 in the morning of June 6, we stepped off the east wall onto a grassy alp, then pulled the ropes down for the last time. We had been climbing for twenty hours straight. We took off our rock shoes, wiggling our toes wantonly in the brisk air. There was still not a breath of wind, not a sound in our universe. We were too tired to eat or even drink. Lying back on the grass, each of us fell asleep for two or three minutes at a time. "Oh, man," said Jon, then left his sentence hanging.

It was good to be alive.

We spent another thirteen days in the Tombstones, making three easy first ascents: one a walk-up, the other two (with Mark) requiring only several roped pitches apiece. Yet when we passed beneath the towering north face of Monolith, staring up at its features, I could almost hear Jon's silent wail of deprivation. On our last possible climbing day, we had to turn back halfway up a middling-hard peak because of the paucity of our hardware and truly grungy moss over rotten rock.

Yet in the wake of our defeat on (and narrow escape from) Little Tombstone, a kind of serenity descended on our three-man universe. Despite the bad weather (cold rain and fog on more than half the days), as we poked around side valleys farther west, we felt the privilege of explorers treading ground that almost surely no one else had ever walked. A faint generational tension still hovered in the air. Having had to backpack all our food in from the Dempster Highway, we were on tight rations, requiring a discipline of which the two twenty-one-year-olds were not always capable. We stacked our food along the inside wall of our four-man tent. I positioned my sleeping bag next to it, so that I could bat away the clutching paws of the youngsters whenever they got the munchies.

On June 18, we completed the hike out. Fording the Klondike, which had hung like a sword over our expedition, proved a piece of cake, a knee-deep wade where the river braided wide over gravel.

In Dawson City, Jon and Mark each ate eighteen straight ice cream cones. Then Jon somehow got involved in a serious poker game, where he promptly blew forty dollars of the precious nest egg he had saved up for the Kichatnas.

Two weeks later, flying with his two partners from Talkeetna, Jon found the Kichatnas completely socked in. On impulse, they changed their objective to the Ruth Gorge, where their pilot, Cliff Hudson, put them down on July 4. They turned their attention to the Mooses Tooth, the fierce and beautiful mountain that looms directly across the head of the Gorge from Mount Dickey. In a marathon thirty-three-hour push ranging through parts of three calendar days (they were hallucinating car horns and flashing lights by the time they made their last rappels), the trio made the second ascent of the storied mountain, by a new route—an elegant arrow of an ice runnel that tops out just below the summit on the west. The Ham and Eggs Couloir, as Jon's team named their route, has by now become a classic test piece in the Alaska Range.

That summer, Jon was just starting to come into his own as one of the outstanding mountaineers of his generation. The culmination of his early career would come in 1977, when he pulled off an astounding climb on the Devils Thumb, an equally storied mountain on the Alaska-Canada border, hiking alone in from and out to the ocean, wending his way through a series of perilous icefalls on the Baird Glacier, and soloing a new route on the mountain's southeast face. (That ascent Jon would later chronicle in both *Eiger Dreams* and *Into the Wild*.)

When Jon married Linda Moore in 1980, he capitulated to her

understandable anxiety about the whole business and agreed to quit mountaineering. (A climber of modest ambition herself when Jon met her, Linda broke her arm bouldering and soon turned her back on the pastime.) For four years, Jon kept his promise, but the itch was too strong not to scratch. Living at the time in Seattle, Jon started sneaking off to nearby crags the way other men visit their mistresses. A confrontation ensued. To Linda's credit, she recognized just how vital mountaineering was to Jon's very soul, and relented on the marital bargain—even though in subsequent years she agonized (just as Sharon had agonized over me) when Jon was away for months at a time attempting the North Face of the Eiger, succeeding on Cerro Torre in Patagonia (often called the world's hardest mountain), and making first ascents of soaring granite aiguilles in the Queen Maud Land region of Antarctica.

The nadir of Linda's anxiety came during several weeks in 1996, when Jon, on assignment for *Outside* magazine, got caught up in the worst disaster in the history of Mount Everest, when fifteen climbers died, including four members of Jon's team, led by Rob Hall, who himself perished high on the South Col route. From that terrible tragedy Jon reaped a lasting depression, the deepest of his life. But out of the debacle he wove *Into Thin Air*, not only one of the best-selling, but also one of the best books ever written about mountaineering.

At Hampshire, Jon had indeed been my faithful protégé. Curiously, however, in college Jon had absolutely no ambition to be a writer. After graduating, still following in his mentor's footsteps, he moved to Boulder; for a brief period, he even lived in a room my parents lent him in our house on Bluebell Avenue. Like many another climbing bum, Jon took a series of construction jobs, a métier in which, according to time-honored tradition, you can throw down your tool belt and head off for some distant range at a moment's notice and not jeopardize your standing in the trade.

Today, at fifty-one, Jon is still climbing exceedingly well, leading 5.11 regularly and bagging the occasional 5.12, though for the most part he has turned his back on the greater (and more dangerous) ranges. From his house in Boulder, he routinely drives to Estes Park, hikes in to the base of the east face of Longs Peak, climbs a hard route on the Diamond, descends and hikes out, then drives back to Boulder in considerably less than a single day. To accomplish the same deed in 1974, on the Diamond's easiest route, Ed and I had required an effort extending over three grueling days.

Back at Hampshire for my sixth year of teaching, I knew that my life had turned a corner. The potentially catastrophic leader fall Jon had taken only twenty feet below the top of Little Tombstone had catalyzed misgivings that I'd harbored for years. During the expedition, I had often regarded Jon as a slightly reckless, overly impulsive climber, however brilliant and driven. Sometimes I scolded him in the privacy of my diary, as in this entry on June 12: "One period of minor hostility with Jon on the way down [from one of our easy later climbs], over my unwillingness to consider seriously a truly ridiculous possible route on Monolith: a steep couloir, overhanging at top, with a huge icicle right at the top and a fully iced vertical chimney above that. I think he's into some subtle kind of machismo thing. He gets his mind on a route and raves about it."

Yet when I reread those passages today, I hear a subtext—the sorrow that I had lost the all-consuming fanaticism that climbing at the highest level requires, and that had seemed to give my life meaning and shape for thirteen years. At twenty-one, I, too, had been a reckless and impulsive climber, and had gotten away with it. Jon, at twenty-one, was plunging into that magical obsession from which I, at thirty-two, had begun to step away.

Sometimes, unable to sleep in the wee hours, I would dwell on the close calls I had undergone in the mountains, numbering them, rating them by relative "closeness." The closest of all had been Matt's and my fall on Huntington. One should not lightly use the word "miracle," but ever since that July day in 1965, I have so regarded the luck of our rope snagging on the knuckle-sized nubbin of rock and sparing Matt and me a 4,500-foot fall to our deaths. But there were too many other close calls: the tent buried in snow on the Deborah col as

Don and I slept oblivious; his bad crevasse fall on the Gillam Glacier later on the expedition; the rocks bouncing over our tents low on the Wickersham Wall; the tons of falling rocks that just missed us on our third day in the Revelations; the hypothermic desperation of our climb closing the loop of the Butterfly Traverse; the avalanches that could so easily have swept us off Temple; the avalanche Rick Millikan and I had ridden out in the Kichatnas; the last storm day on Dickey, with only my crampons and ice axe to see us through. Those and yet others, some not so close, some whose closeness it was impossible to gauge. And now, Jon's fall on Little Tombstone. Not to mention the three fatal accidents by the time I was twenty-two . . .

In the summer of 1976, for the first time in fourteen years, I did not return to Alaska or the Yukon. There was no expedition for me. As I had suspected during our slow, battered descent from Little Tombstone, I was done for good with serious mountain expedition-eering. Yet if by 1976 I could no longer say that climbing was the most important thing in life, I had no idea what might take its place. It seems a measure of my anomie that summer that today, I cannot for the life of me remember what I did do between June and August 1976.

In 1977, on a trip with Jon to the Bighorn Range in Wyoming, I participated in my last serious first ascent—a wonderful, 1,000-foot route on an unnamed peak, splendid climbing on compact granite. We carried no pitons, relying only on nuts for protection. Jon deftly led the crux move at the very top of our 11th and last pitch. On the summit, I let out a cheer of unadulterated joy.

As a Hampshire professor, I was well along the road to burnout. Within the Outdoors Program, I turned over to Ed virtually all the more ambitious climbing trips, the weekends at the Gunks and Can-non, the ice climbing clinics on Mount Washington. Ed was begin-ning to taste burnout himself, but of a far more puritanical (and far less self-indulgent) stamp than I, he flogged himself onward to redoubled efforts. During an O.P. staff retreat, as, encouraged by the feminist we had hired from the U Mass Ed School, we agonized out loud over our own "personal development," Ed crossly interrupted, "This is all very well and good, but our students have needs." Ed was like Boxer, the brainwashed horse in *Animal Farm*, berating himself over and over again, "I will work harder!" In 1977, he led the most ambitious O.P. climbing trip ever, to Yosemite Valley over spring vacation, where, among other ascents, he and the most gifted of his students climbed the daunting Salathé Wall on El Capitan.

Meanwhile, I rounded up the beginning and intermediate climbers and trudged off again and again to Rattlesnake Gutter, Rose Ledge, and Chapel Ledge. By now the top-rope climbs were as familiar to me as the characters on a typewriter keyboard: in the lingo of our trade, I had them wired. Competitive to the end, I still derived a wan pleasure from effortlessly cruising a forty-foot route that the best of the intermediate students couldn't get up. But there were days when I actually hoped it would rain on the way to Rattlesnake, so that rather than go climbing, we could stop off instead at a funky little watering hole in Leverett, drink a few beers, and shoot pool.

By the late 1970s, Ed and I took a fierce pride in the fact that, despite shepherding our students through adventures as ambitious as Yosemite and the Arrigetch, none of our charges had suffered an injury more serious than a sprained ankle. Yet during those years, in the course of routine O.P. trips, both Ed and I each narrowly avoided an absurd accident that, but for the canny application of an instinctive last-second act of vigilance, could have killed us. At the Gunks in the very first Hampshire autumn of 1970, I led the initial pitch of a short classic called Layback. That pitch took me up a chimney, left on a traverse beneath a ceiling, then straight up the layback itself to a good ledge. In those days, the climb was rated only 5.3; with the Harvard Mountaineering Club, I had taken beginners up it many times. But the initial moves in the chimney are actually quite hard, and today the climb is rated 5.5.

In any event, now neither of the beginners on my rope could solve the first moves, despite my efforts to haul them upward with tension. In impetuous disgust, I doubled the rope and got into a body rappel, not bothering to use the harness and carabiner brake-bar setup that by 1970 had become the norm. As I slid down the rope, I cleaned the pitch of the protection I had placed on the lead. This required me to swing awkwardly right under the ceiling and reach far to remove the nuts I had placed. The last piece, a big metal hexcentric attached to the rope with a sling and a 'biner, I could barely dislodge, and in doing so, I fumbled it, and saw it drop down the chimney almost to the ground. No problem: I would finish the rappel, then scramble up and retrieve the chockstone.

What I failed to notice—could not, indeed, have noticed—was that as the chockstone fell, it got caught in a twist of the climbing rope and freakishly lodged itself in a crack only a few feet off the ground, forming a de facto anchor squeezing the lower end of the rope as tightly as if I had tied it off to a tree. As I swung back left to resume my rappel, the tight rope suddenly thwarted my pendulum. Because I was in a body rappel, I was flung upside down, head over heels, three quarters of the way through an involuntary skin-the-cat of the sort I used to perform on door jambs as a party trick.

I had no idea what had gone wrong, but instinct roared in my brain, *Hang on with the left hand!* Forty feet below me, the beginners screamed in terror. I managed to stop the skin-the-cat only inches short of being thrown completely free of the rappel rope. Helmetless, falling headfirst toward the boulders at the base of the cliff, I would probably have broken my neck.

Many years later, at the end of an afternoon outing at Chapel Ledge, Ed was taking down the top ropes he had strung all over the diminutive cliff. In those days, on the local crags, we tied the top end of the rope to a tree, then had the belayer slide a figure-eight loop over his head, sit near the edge of the cliff, and safeguard the climber from above. At Chapel, there was one longish, easy climb, an inside corner about eighty feet high. Priding himself on efficiency, Ed routinely used the rope hung on that climb as his personal escalator, zipping down it (also on a body rappel) to set up or retrieve ropes on lower ledges.

That day, Ed had asked his assistant instructor to take down some of the other ropes. What she had managed to do, however, on the eighty-foot escalator, was untie the bowline knot attaching the top end to the tree; but then, distracted by some other chore, she had left the rope circling the tree so that it looked as though it were still tied in. On the edge of the cliff, the rope in its S-curve around his body, Ed started to lean back on rappel. But he glanced at the anchor tree, and something didn't look right. Only then did he discover his assistant's insidious mistake. Had he gotten on rappel, he would have pulled the rope with him and fallen backward, unchecked, those eighty feet to the ground.

More than a few expert climbers have died in such nonsensical accidents. The irony their friends inevitably murmur over is the obvious one: "To think that after all his expeditions to the great ranges, he would buy the farm on an easy scramble up to the base of a climb, on a short rappel at a dinky local crag, on a route he could have soloed in the dark . . ." If Ed's and my near-misses at the Gunks and Chapel carried any message, it was an equally facile one: climbing is always dangerous, even at the trivial level. In the course of hundreds of outings stretched over eight or nine years, the odds were reasonably high that Ed or I might make one small but lethal mistake.

Today, a quarter-century after we left Hampshire, Ed and I still banter over our perfect safety record. Of a fatalistic disposition, Ed will say, "Man, we were lucky to get away with what we did in the O.P."

"No, Ed," I argue back, "we were careful."

In 1978, however, during fourteen agonizing hours through a winter night in Utah, I thought there was a fair chance that a student on one of my O.P. trips had died, and if he had, most of the blame would have justly fallen on me.

Hampshire practiced the January term, a one-month hiatus between fall and spring semesters during which each student took a single intensive course. In theory, we faculty got every other January off, but like everything else at Hampshire, this was a standard honored in the breach, with the shirkers counting on a paid vacation, the workaholics such as Ed toiling hard through every January term "because the students have needs."

For me, the path of least commitment would have been to fob off a "creative writing" course that met three or four times a week on campus. But in January 1971, I led ten students on a ten-day trip to

the San Juan Range in southwestern Colorado. This giddy and successful jaunt became, thanks to the wizardry of one of the students,
who put together a slide show–cum–musical score that regaled the
whole college, one of the high points of Hampshire's collective first
year. Today, when I think back on how, with only Sharon as a
co-leader, I got nine of the ten students—complete beginners—to the
summit of Mount Sneffels, via a far from trivial couloir up which I
fixed a couple of ropes and spotted the pupils on the hard moves, I am
inclined to shudder in agreement with Ed's verdict that we were lucky
to get away without a serious accident.

That trip set a mold. In January of 1972, 1974, and 1976, I led
three more Colorado mountaineering trips, to the Sangre de Cristo
and Elk Ranges. Each was a major undertaking: the students driving a
Hampshire van 2,000 miles each way, the buying and packaging of
supplies for a mini-expedition, the drive to the trailhead and the arduous two-day hike in to base camp. They were journeys fraught with
potential danger, too, in the form of frostbite, hypothermia, and avalanche. I will agree with Ed, moreover, that we were lax in 1975 in
allowing a student-led trip to the Gore Range, where the avalanche
conditions were the worst of any of those five Januarys, and where we
were just plain lucky to have as sound a mountaineer as Jon Krakauer
in charge.

As with everything else at Hampshire for me, slowly but steadily
the fun went out of it. I evolved from a hearty and companionable
leader in 1971 to a cranky sourpuss in 1976. Yet for a while, in 1978,
I thought I had found a way to refresh the January term, by exploring
a wilderness that I didn't already know like the back of my hand. That
trip to Utah, the most ambitious of my five January O.P. jaunts, also
had much to do with my personal drift away from climbing.

An older student in the O.P., named Kirk Olsen, who had skillfully
led a number of hiking trips, had fallen under the spell of the canyons
of the Southwest. Offering to co-lead our 1978 January trip, he talked
me into heading for the Maze district of Canyonlands National Park in
Utah, rather than the high peaks of Colorado. And he also talked me
into an eighteen-day foray, not the mere ten-day sojourn that I had

stamped as the norm. (In the end, with our van snowed in far down a dirt road that it took a grader three days to plow, our trip stretched across twenty-one days, a longer span than my Mount Dickey expedition.)

At once the intricacy of the canyons, the route-finding puzzles they posed, and above all the presence of rock art and ruins left by the Anasazi and Fremont peoples more than 700 years ago, galvanized my mountain-jaded spirit. The Maze trip would furnish a turning point in my life. In the 1980s, I would start exploring the canyons with a vengeance. Since then, I have made more than a hundred trips to Utah, New Mexico, and Arizona, chiefly in quest of backcountry ruins and rock art, and I've written three books and many articles about the Native Americans who left their mark on that incomparable landscape. Today, it is not the ranges of my once-beloved Alaska, but the canyons of the Southwest, and especially of southern Utah, that constitute my favorite place on earth.

The 1978 January term trip might have turned into a happy lark, but for two things. At the age of thirty-four, I could no longer abide the chitchat of eighteen-year-olds. Camped in the curl of a little-explored sandstone defile, with the brilliant constellations wheeling overhead, how could they jabber on about their favorite TV shows, about the intrigues within their modules, as we named their coed dorm suites? (Today, I would cut the students some slack, recognizing that their patter was probably a nervous reaction to the utter alienness of the Maze, into which even the park rangers were nonplussed that college kids would venture in the dead of winter.)

On my last Colorado January trip in 1976, a ski traverse of a non-descript sector of the Elk Range, I had felt no urge to go off and bag summits on my own. But in the Maze, I was afire with the yen to explore, to follow each twisting side canyon to its cul-de-sac end, rather than tend to my plodding and timid students. The gulf between me and them was thus more acute than it had ever been.

The other factor was the presence on the trip of the single most defiant, reckless, and—the word, I believe, is appropriate—socio-pathic student I had ever encountered. In a piece I published in Out-

side in 1984, "Burnout in the Maze," I called this fellow Brian, as I will name him here. During the first nine days of the trip, he violated every rule I laid down. Slipping away from camp, Brian would solo clumsily up some loose, hazardous chimney around the corner, until I found him and ordered him down. When I parked the students on a slab in dense fog while I scouted the route ahead, I returned to find that Brian had wandered off on his own into the mist. Then, on the tenth night, I overheard him whisper urgently to his tent-mate, fifteen feet away from my sleepless vigil: "Let's cut loose from these pansy mothers and do our own expedition. We can take a tent and just go."

I resolved then and there on the only appropriate response. In the morning, Kirk would hike Brian back to the van, drive out to Green River, and put him on a bus back to Hampshire. I had never before kicked a student off a trip, but if ever there was a reason to do so, it was now.

Instead, I let Kirk talk me out of the punishment. Give Brian another chance, he pleaded. We'll both keep an eye on him.

Kirk was all too aware of my restless dissatisfaction, my need to flee the students for at least one day of exploring at my own pace. And so I made the pivotal mistake. I let Kirk persuade me that I could take that day off. It seemed at first a safe decision. It was solo day (an Outward Bound invention): we assigned each student a nook or alcove where he or she would spend twenty-four hours alone, staying put but bathing in the elixir of wilderness solitude. To ensure safety, each student would remove a stone or a stick from a cairn every several hours, which Kirk, making the rounds, could observe without intruding on the student's isolation. At the last minute, Brian announced that he would stay in camp with Kirk, rather than do a solo. I was puzzled by this uncharacteristic decision, but left camp at dawn convinced that it made my truancy all the more harmless.

During the next ten enchanted hours, I made a twenty-five-mile loop, scrambling out of the Maze all the way south to the near edge of the Fins, then back by another branch of canyon. Along the way, I discovered the Harvest Panel, one of the eeriest and most masterly pictograph galleries in all the Southwest. As I trudged back to camp just before dusk, I was awash with happiness. Kirk was feeding sticks to the fire.

"Where's Brian?" I asked.

Kirk had an odd look on his face. "He's taking a walking solo."

"What the hell is a walking solo?"

"He headed down Horse Canyon a couple of hours ago. He said he'd be back by sunset."

"Oh, Jesus."

I was exhausted, but we loaded up our packs with emergency supplies and set off in the direction Brian had taken. There was a full moon, and we found we could track our fugitive without the aid of headlamps. But as the hours passed, his footsteps degenerated from a steady march to a weaving stagger. We found his pack, discarded, an almost full water bottle inside. At regular intervals, we called Brian's name as loud as we could, hearing only the mocking canyon echo of our cries in response.

It was close to midnight when we tracked Brian's steps to the foot of the canyon wall on the west, where they ended. As I had feared, the incompetent climber had set off to climb. In the dark, I scrambled up 300 feet, calling Brian's name, but it was a risky business.

Numb with a sense of doom, I rejoined Kirk. "Back to camp," I said. "We'll try again in the morning."

I got two hours of fitful sleep, Kirk none at all. At first light, as we headed back down Horse Canyon, I was convinced that the odds were better than even that Brian was dead. After two miles, we rounded a bend—and there he was, stumbling toward us. As we closed the distance, I saw that his face was ravaged with fear, and that he was bleeding from one arm.

"Is this the right direction?" were his first words.

"Come on," I answered, and started back toward camp.

The story Brian later told me made little sense. The day was so pleasant, he said, he had discarded his pack. The temptation to climb the western wall was overwhelming. The sun had set almost without his noticing it. In the dark, easy rock had turned hard. He could go up but not down. He spent the night in a small cave, shivering with cold.

He never heard us calling his name. In the morning, on the descent, he fell off a small cliff and banged up his arm. By the time Kirk and I found him, Brian was so disoriented he had no idea whether our camp lay up-canyon or down.

The next day, the snow started falling—snow that would have frozen Brian to death in his bivouac—and it didn't stop for three days. Climbing out of the Maze, on the crux section, where we had followed an ancient Anasazi hand-and-toe trail, I had to scrape the snow off each hidden sandstone indentation and belay each student toward the canyon rim. By the time, a day later, that we regained our van, we were plowing through thigh-deep snow. And on that last grim march, I promised myself, *This is it. Let the Kirks of the world lead student trips.* I was done with the whole business. The exploring I would spend the rest of my life pursuing would be with friends, not clients, for the sheer fun of it, not for a job.

I expected to feel a certain sorrow at this new resolve. Instead, I sensed only relief. Just before reaching the van, I glanced back at Brian. He remained as much as ever an enigma, but some light had gone out of his eyes. During his suicidal solo into the dark, I wondered, had he realized after all that life was worth living? There was no way to ask him, and no way, I suspected, that he could answer.

During the nine years that I taught at Hampshire, the student who came to the college with the most mountaineering experience under his belt was not Jon Krakauer, but Tim Rouner, a gangly, curly-haired six-foot-five youth who had grown up in New Hampshire and in Wayland, a Boston suburb. Arriving in the fall of 1976, just after Jon had graduated, Tim had already done a good bit of rock climbing and put up some very hard new ice routes in New England with his older brother by two years, Rainsford, then a Harvard student. Tim was an appealing, earnest, poetically minded hippie, loping across the campus barefoot even in winter. For all his climbing, he was no hard man, wearing instead a sensitive soul on his sleeve. Like Jon, Tim in his first year suffered no shortage of attention from Hampshire women.

By that point, within the Outdoors Program, I had relegated myself to the top-rope trips to the nearby crags. I don't think I ever climbed with Tim. But he had read my Alaskan books, regarded me as a mountaineering guru, and asked me to critique his poetry. Unmistakably a rich kid from a privileged background, Tim did not come with the built-in entitlement of so many of his classmates. He approached me for advice and criticism with a deferential courtesy, and his gratitude for whatever I tossed back was so effusive that it made me slightly uncomfortable.

At Hampshire, it was Ed, along with two or three of the other best student climbers, with whom Tim paired up on weekend climbs. In the spring of 1977, Tim went on Ed's Yosemite trip, where the two of them made the three-day ascent of the Salathé Wall, in conditions bad enough that a climber above them, having fallen and broken his leg, had to be winched off El Cap by helicopter in a dramatic rescue.

It was curious, then, that in May, Tim chose me rather than Ed to ask for advice on the most important decision of his young life. With Rainsford and an experienced older climber named Peter Cole, Tim was planning an expedition to Alaska. Rainsford and Peter had climbed together in the Canadian Rockies, the Tetons, and the Sierras, and both had done routes on El Capitan in Yosemite. This would be, however, Tim's first expedition to the greater ranges. Their objective was as serious a climb as could be found in the Far North—the untouched 6,500-foot northwest face of Devils Thumb, on the Alaska-Yukon border.

That very month, Jon Krakauer was in the midst of his extraordinary solo expedition to Devils Thumb. Jon had had his eye on the same face, but after passing beneath the great wall and watching avalanches pour off it, he had circled halfway around the peak before claiming his solo new route on the opposite side of the mountain. I knew the northwest face from maps and photographs. It was obvious that the colossal precipice was on the verge of assuming that most cherished of mantles among mountain objectives, a Last Great Problem. But by 1977, though a number of fine mountaineers besides Jon had had their eye on the northwest face, no one had actually set foot on it.

Tim's question for me was a simple one. Did I think he was ready for such a challenge?

I did not answer right away. There were factors to weigh on the minus side. Tim was only eighteen, with little or no big-mountain experience. As a first expedition, the northwest face of Devils Thumb was at least as ambitious an undertaking for its day as if Don Jensen and I, more than a decade before, had set out for the west face of Huntington without having tackled McKinley and Deborah beforehand.

Yet on the plus side were Tim's and Rainsford's fine ice routes in New England, and Tim's gutsy performance just two months before with Ed on the Salathé. Rainsford's and Peter Cole's much greater experience ought to serve as insurance against Tim's greenness. Finally, I remembered the grumpy forewarnings of the Harvard Mountaineering Club mentors when Don and I had been twenty-one years old, and despite what had happened to us on Deborah, I was glad I had ignored those cautious caveats.

I told Tim I thought he was ready for the Devils Thumb, a good enough climber to attempt its northwest face. He grinned broadly. My imprimatur seemed to have burst some inner dam of doubt.

At the beginning of August, the trio helicoptered from Petersburg, Alaska, into the Witches Cauldron, an ominously named stagnant glacial arm of the Baird Glacier directly beneath the great face. On August 2, Tim and Rainsford climbed the first two pitches and fixed ropes on them. The next day, with the weather holding good, they began their alpine-style climb.

Above the fixed pitches, the going suddenly got easy. Peter Cole raced ahead, scrambling unroped, with Rainsford second, Tim trailing third. The terrain got a bit trickier, mixed ice and rock, the latter a shattered diorite that was often unstable underfoot, but to make such progress so effortlessly was heady stuff. Within a matter of only hours, Peter Cole had reached a point almost a third of the way up the great face. Shortly before, Rainsford had wondered aloud whether they shouldn't rope up. Cole had urged just another pitch; then they would pause to reassess.

As Cole led on out of sight, Rainsford stopped to wait for his younger brother. But Tim didn't come. The minutes crept by. Rainsford called Tim's name, but there was no answer. He started rappelling back down. Several hundred feet lower, he saw a subtle sign in the snow, one with terrible implications. It was a sitzmark in the slope, the kind made by a skier who loses his balance—or by a falling climber.

Spurred by adrenaline, Rainsford descended to the lip of an ice cliff. Out of hardware for rappel anchors, he used his hammer to pound his ice axe deep into the slope as an improvised anchor, then strung a shaky rappel over the cliff. Once clear of the lip, he saw Tim sprawled on a ledge below. It was obvious that he was dead.

When Rainsford reached his brother's body, he found it still warm. He cradled Tim in his arms and screamed curses into the void.

No one would ever know exactly what had gone wrong. Perhaps a falling stone had hit Tim and caused the fall, or a broken crampon had made him slip (one of his crampons was missing when Rainsford reached Tim), or snow balling under his crampons had made him skitter loose. It would later occur to me to wonder if, lagging behind his more experienced companions, intimidated by their unroped sprint on such a gargantuan face, Tim had hurried to catch up and simply made a misstep. On our last day on Dickey, there were plenty of places where one false step by any of the three of us could have pulled us all, roped together but unattached to the mountain, off the face and into the final plunge.

On Devils Thumb, Peter Cole had waited for an hour at the high point before descending on his own rope, using up his portion of the hardware for rappel anchors. After he joined Rainsford on the ledge, the two men wrapped Tim's body in a sleeping bag and moved it to a nook protected from falling rocks and ice. Then they climbed several sideways pitches to a safer refuge, where they bivouacked that night, before descending in the morning. They had no radio (nor would a radio from the Witches Cauldron have worked to contact anyone outside), so they had to endure an agonizing ten-day wait before hiking down to the seacoast and a predetermined rendezvous with their pilot. Rainsford spent much of that time gathering rocks to pile up as a kind of monumental cairn to mark his brother's passing.

In late summer, Ed and I were stunned by the news from Devils Thumb. I had expected failure on the formidable route for the three New England climbers, not a fatal accident. At the memorial service in Wellesley, we met Tim's parents and siblings (including Rainsford) for the first time.

The Rouner family embraced the tragedy of Tim's demise in a fashion that struck me as the polar opposite of that of Ed Bernd's parents in 1965. Leroy and Rita knew everything about climbing and had encouraged their two sons' campaigns against crags and mountains, even though it meant living with a constant anxiety tingling in their nerves. In his boyish enthusiasm, Tim had talked his father—a good athlete who had rowed on the legendary Harvard crew—into trying out the sport. At Quincy Quarries, Tim had dragged a terrified Leroy up a thirty-foot top-rope climb; later, he had even coaxed his father up a bona fide four-pitch route at Cathedral Ledge in New Hampshire.

A Congregational minister and professor of philosophy at Boston University, Leroy had been in India, where earlier in life he had done missionary work, when Tim had died. The interminable journey back to Boston was a predictable nightmare, but almost as soon as he got home, he headed for Petersburg, Alaska, where Rita and Rainsford were waiting. Father, mother, and surviving son flew by helicopter into the mountains and landed on the ice of the Witches Cauldron, just so the parents could see the magnificent wall that had taken Tim's life. There, Leroy refused to view Devils Thumb as a place of evil. Staring up at the huge precipice, he said to Rita, "I can see why these guys wanted to come."

From the glacier, Rita chose a flat, sharp-edged, sizable chunk of diorite to serve as a headstone for Tim's grave in New Hampshire. The pilot carried the rock out in a cargo net slung below his helicopter. Earlier, a crack mountain rescue team, using another helicopter, had retrieved Tim's body from the mountain.

In the makeshift Petersburg mortuary, Leroy, Rita, and Rainsford had their last moments with Tim, whose body had been laid out naked on a bare table under a bright light. This potentially traumatic encounter seemed to serve a therapeutic purpose for the Rouners. As Leroy later wrote:

> He seemed to have waited for us. The body of a nineteen-year-old boy/man in great physical shape is a beautiful thing anyway. He had a fractured skull, a broken neck, and a broken leg, but he didn't look busted up.

In Seattle, Tim's body was cremated. The Rouners carried the urn back east, where, in a second ceremony at the family home, High Meadow Farm, near North Sandwich, New Hampshire, Tim's ashes were laid to rest and the headstone was erected. A throng of climbing buddies, college friends, and relatives joyously celebrated the life of a gifted youth who had died at nineteen.

Because of the part I had played in encouraging Tim to participate in the expedition, I harbored a certain burden of guilt that autumn. And the sheer waste of Tim's life plagued me. Was it worth it, after all, the whole dangerous game of mountaineering?

My response was to try to be as supportive of the family as I could. I had long conversations with Rainsford and Leroy. Over the next decade, Rainsford would struggle to write a book about Tim. Years after Devils Thumb, wandering into the reading room at Harvard's Widener Library, I would occasionally find Rainsford staring at a pile of papers scattered about him, pen in hand. Whatever became of that book, I have no idea.

Both Rainsford and Peter Cole continued to climb after Devils Thumb, sharing a trip to Tuolumne Meadows above Yosemite, though in the 1980s Rainsford's mountain activity dwindled to almost nothing, as he got involved in volunteer work in Palestine refugee camps. Today, at fifty-three, Cole is the proprietor of a successful adventure photography business, and he still climbs at a high level. As he told me in 2004, "I wouldn't know where to turn if I didn't have climbing in my life. I mean, I like riding my bicycle, but it's just a means to an end"—i.e., the foot of the cliff.

In 1989, Leroy published his own meditation on Tim's death, a slender volume called *The Long Way Home*. A moving chronicle of the journey from India to Petersburg and back to Wayland and New Hampshire, it is more about Leroy himself, about the metaphysical agon the accident had inflicted upon his instinctively loving and optimistic spirit, than about who Tim was. Though published twelve years after Tim's death, the book comes to no easy resolution. It is instead an extended inquiry into God's ways to man, full of indissoluble anger and pain.

All the Rouners, including Tim, believed in God, but a God, I suspect, profoundly different from the Creator in whom Ed Bernd's parents placed their fatalistic faith, as they pondered the possibility that by killing their son on Mount Huntington He was saving Ed from a worse death in Vietnam. Yet as I witnessed the impact of the tragedy on the Rouner family, I wondered whether their open embracing of the truth, their refusal to blame climbing itself for their loss, their dogged faith in a loving God, did them much more good than the Bernds' superstitious preservation of Ed's bedroom as a cluttered shrine, exactly the way he had left it in the wee hours of the damp June morning in 1965.

It is a commonplace that the death of a child often tears a family apart. I could see the strains between Leroy and Rita before my eyes that autumn, and between Rainsford and his two younger siblings, Jonathan and Christina, who were not interested in climbing at all. In *The Long Way Home*, Leroy summarizes the brief course of couples therapy he and Rita entered into, having acknowledged the marital problems Tim's death had provoked. The counselors, themselves a couple, subscribed to a peculiar (and to my mind, idiotic) offshoot of Freudianism that holds that there is no such thing as an accident. Instead, the therapists proposed, Tim's death might have been an unconscious suicide, in response to conflict between his parents that the nineteen-year-old had already detected.

Outraged, Leroy refused to continue the sessions, yet that refusal only further angered and upset his wife.

It was Rita with whom I briefly became closest among the Rouner family. I helped her publish several poignant poems she had written about Tim in Climbing magazine. To me, she freely acknowledged the ruptures torn in the family fabric by Tim's disappearance. Those tensions were epitomized by a trivial yet deeply symbolic moment in the late fall of 1977. Rita and Jonathan were in the living room of their Wayland house. Two years younger than Tim, four years younger than Rainsford, Jonathan had veered far from their example. He was no hippie, but a conservative, well-dressed preppie. He was more interested in basketball than the outdoors. He had declined his father's request to fly to Petersburg to see the mountain and Tim's body laid out on the mortuary table.

Rita went to the window, where she caught sight of a long V of geese flying south across the dimming sky. "Jonathan, come see the geese!" she had exclaimed. But Jonathan grunted a demurral, not bothering to stir from the couch. Rita burst into tears, then—hating herself later for the cruelty of the stab, but unable to smother it—cried out, "Oh, Jonathan, Timmy would have looked at the geese!"

As for the northwest face of Devils Thumb, twenty-seven years later it remains a Last Great Problem—perhaps the Last Great Problem in North America. Since the ill-starred first attempt in 1977, the 6,500-foot precipice has repulsed thirteen further attacks, including several by parties that included some of the top climbers in the world. No team has even reached the halfway point on the wall. And in 2003, the face claimed two more victims, expert Canadian alpinists who were presumably avalanched off their route. Their bodies were never found.

In the first decade of the twenty-first century, a motto of our craft has it that nothing is unclimbable. But in articles in the 2003 American Alpine Journal and a 2004 issue of Rock and Ice, experienced climbers (one a survivor of a 1982 attempt on the precipice) postulate that if there is an unclimbable wall anywhere on the continent, it may be the northwest face of Devils Thumb. The argument is not simply that the difficulties are too severe: it is that a fiendish combination of weather, snowfall, rotten rock, and the shape of the wall mean that it is never "in

condition"—i.e., stable enough to climb without constant bombardment by falling stones and avalanches. As one veteran of the face jauntily puts it, "If someone succeeds, it's just a failed suicide attempt."

In the 1930s, much the same rhetoric was attached to the North
Face of the Eiger in Switzerland, the most dangerous wall in the Alps,
which killed eight of its first ten suitors. Today, the 1938 conquerors
of the Nordwand—Heinrich Harrer, Anderl Heckmair, Ludwig Vörg,
and Fritz Kasparek—are enshrined in the pantheon of alpine achievement. Almost nobody remembers the first two climbers who dared
attempt the face, a pair of young men from Munich named Max Sedl-
mayer and Karl Mehringer, even though a perch on the wall, the Death
Bivouac, commemorates their demise.

Today, outside of the small circle of friends who knew him and
partners who roped up with him, the climbing world knows nothing
of Tim Rouner. He died before his genius could make a lasting mark,
though guidebooks to New England ice still list him and Rainsford in
the fine print of first ascents of classic pitches. Perhaps because the
accident struck so early on the expedition, before the trio had really
made much of a dent in the great face, the attempt of Tim, Rainsford,
and Peter Cole—so daring, so far ahead of its time—gets short shrift
in the chronicle of Devils Thumb. In the articles in the *American Alpine
Journal* and *Rock and Ice*, the death of Tim Rouner is relegated to a virtual footnote.

TEN

The Unexamined
Life

VIRTUALLY NO MOUNTAIN CLIMBERS QUIT OVER-
night, turning their backs for good on the pastime that fueled the
primes of their lives. The cardinal exception is the Italian Walter Bonatti, one of the greatest mountaineers in history. Beginning as a
teenager in the Alps shortly after the Second World War, Bonatti went
on, from 1951 to 1965, to forge a matchless record of visionary
ascents. His solo *direttissima* on the west face of the Petit Dru above
Chamonix in 1955 has been called by big-wall expert Doug Scott
"probably the most important single climbing feat ever to take place
in mountaineering." Bonatti's 1958 first ascent of Gasherbrum IV in
Pakistan, with teammate Carlo Mauri, raised the standard for climbs
in the Karakoram and Himalaya to a whole new level.

At age twenty-four, Bonatti was the strongest member of the massive 1954 Italian team that made the first ascent of K2, the world's
second-highest mountain. He returned from that expedition embittered, after the teammates who reached the summit (and to whom
Bonatti had ferried the crucial oxygen bottles) forced him to undergo
what was then the highest open bivouac ever attempted, at 26,500
feet. Bonatti knew his share of mountain tragedy, as well, twice surviving violent summer storms on Mont Blanc that took the lives of
teammates and accidental companions whom he did all that it was in
his power to save.

In 1965, on the hundredth anniversary of its first ascent, Bonatti put up a new route, solo, in winter, on the treacherous north face of the Matterhorn, a deed that electrified the climbing world. Then, at age thirty-five, he walked away from mountaineering. Becoming a photojournalist for the magazine *Epoca*, he turned to other realms of adventure—deserts, rivers, jungles—sometimes on daring solo jaunts. But he never went back to alpinism. When I interviewed Bonatti for a magazine article in 2003, I found that, at age seventy-three, he harbored not the slightest regret about quitting cold at the peak of his career. But for his continuing embitterment over what had happened on K2, he seemed a man completely at peace with himself and the world. He was, in his own word, *realizzato,* "fulfilled."

I know of a few (but only a few) instances of climbers quitting abruptly after witnessing the death of a best friend. In the late 1950s and early 1960s, Washington state native Ed Cooper was one of the best big-wall climbers in America. Then, in 1964, as Cooper and his inseparable partner, Jim Baldwin, backed off a route in Yosemite in the dark, something went wrong with a procedure that that pair of veterans normally had down pat. (Speculation had it that Baldwin, with a heavy haul bag hanging from his waist, reached a generous ledge and got off rappel—only to have the haul bag roll off the ledge and pull him to his death.) Cooper stopped climbing and became a top-notch wilderness photographer.

Peter Gillman is one of Britain's leading mountaineering journalists, the author of countless articles and a dozen-odd books, including (with his wife, Leni) *The Wildest Dream*, the definitive biography of George Leigh Mallory. A few years ago, Gillman told me that he had climbed enthusiastically as a young man, until one day, on a British crag, his partner had fallen leading a steep pitch. Gillman had caught the fall, but his teammate dangled free in space under an overhang. In those days, before the invention of climbing harnesses that attach you to the rope by the waist and both upper legs, all of us used "swami belts"—simple lengths of nylon tubing wrapped three times around the waist and tied in a solid knot. With Gillman powerless to lower his partner to any saving ledge, he had to stand frozen in his belay while his good friend was slowly suffocated to death by his swami belt. That was enough for Gillman, who quit climbing on the spot—but retained for decades thereafter the keenest curiosity about mountaineering.

The norm, however, is to keep climbing after the death of a close friend and partner, as Rainsford Rouner did after Tim's death on Devils Thumb, as I did after the fatal accidents of Gabe Lee and Ed Bernd. And the normal trajectory of a climber's career after the age of thirty or thirty-five is a gradual tapering off, as one's skills and ambitions dwindle, and as other things in life (marriage, children, jobs) rear their important heads.

For some reason, climbers as a breed are particularly susceptible to guilt over what ought to be a natural scaling down with age. The most eloquent expression of a good climber's anticipating and accepting the decline of his talent and appetite that I know of comes in the last paragraph of Lionel Terray's *Conquistadors of the Useless*, written just a few days before the great French mountaineer's fortieth birthday:

> My own scope must now go back down the scale. My strength and my courage will not cease to diminish. It will not be long before the Alps once again become the terrible mountains of my youth, and if truly no stone, no tower of ice, no crevasse lies somewhere in wait for me, the day will come when, old and tired, I find peace among the animals and flowers. The wheel will have turned full circle: I will be at last the simple peasant that once, as a child, I dreamed of becoming.

But Terray could not live up to his own elegiac valediction. In his early forties, he charged off on expeditions to the east peak of Chacraraju in the Andes, to Nilgiri in Nepal, and to Huntington in Alaska. And indeed, a stone lay in wait for him, in the form of his fatal fall from the route in his backyard Vercors in 1965.

Because I have written so much over the years about mountaineering, new acquaintances frequently ask me, "Do you still climb?" My pat answer is, "Yeah, but not like I used to." If my inquisitor persists with a "Why not?," I usually say, "It's simply too hard—and too scary—to keep it up unless you stay in great shape."

If the acquaintance still wants to know more about my choice to become a casual, part-time climber, often I will go on, "You know, I've found other kinds of adventures"—usually I'm thinking of those Anasazi canyons in the Southwest—"that fulfill me the way climbing used to. And writing itself is as all-involving as mountaineering used to be." Yet every time I utter these formulas, an imp whispers in my ear, "Bullshit, Roberts." For I know that nothing else that I have done in life has matched the adamantine intensity of the tightrope walks between life and death that I performed in the mountains in my twenties and early thirties.

Underlying each such exchange with an inquisitor is a messy, squeamish sense of guilt. And when I stop to think about it, that guilt puzzles me. Why should I, at sixty-two, feel guilty for not climbing as well as I did at twenty-two on Huntington, or at thirty-one on Dickey?

An analogy with professional sports may be apt. I doubt that Hank Aaron, at seventy-one, agonizes regularly over the fact he can no longer turn on a ninety-five-mile-an-hour fastball and jack it over the left-field fence, or that Larry Bird, a mere forty-eight, rues the fate that no longer has him launching three-pointers as he falls out of bounds. Pro sports, to be sure, can be cruel. Most athletes are washed up by their early thirties, left (as few climbers are) to wonder what to do with the rest of their lives. The sports pages are full of sad tales of once great stars who don't know when to hang up their spikes. But at least in pro football or major league baseball there comes an unambiguous divide, when the team to which a player has given his heart and soul drops him from its roster and no other squad will pick up his contract. At the local crag, for better or for worse, no avuncular figure will walk up to you, look you in the eye, and say, "Roberts, I hate to break it to you this way, but it's time you turned in your hardware."

My guilty reaction to tapering off as a climber may be a bit extreme, but it's far from abnormal among aging mountaineers. A few old friends of mine, some of whom quit climbing altogether for ten or fifteen years, have taken it up again in their fifties or sixties, and profess to get as much of a kick out of doing "mellow" rock climbs at safe cliffs as they did from the hairier exploits of their youth. Since Jon Krakauer's and my fine new route in the Bighorns in 1977 (my last serious first ascent), I've gone out climbing at least twice a year every year. At Red Rocks, just west of Las Vegas, my three oldest climbing buddies—Jon, Ed Ward, and Matt Hale—along with two other longtime pals, both named Chris, have organized climbing reunions five or six times since 1995. In July 2004, all six of us spent two weeks climbing in the Dolomites of Italy. These have been halcyon outings, furnishing some of the happiest moments of my last decade. On some of these trips, I've gotten back into decent enough shape to climb 5.9—child's play for today's young rock jocks, but about as hard as anybody was climbing when I started in the early 1960s.

Yet always on the cliffs, I feel an ineradicable ambivalence, as I never do setting off down a canyon in southern Utah. I am reminded of a conversation I had decades ago with Bill Buckingham, who in his day had been a bold pioneer in Alaska, in the Logan Mountains of Canada's Northwest Territories, in the Tetons and the Wind Rivers. At the time I was nearing forty, and Bill was a few years older. Drinking beer in his Boston apartment, we were talking about the tribulations of getting back on the cliffs after a layoff of several months. "It's no fun," I said, "getting scared out of your mind on 5.7."

Bill grinned and took a swig. "How about scared out of your mind on 5.3?"

Ed and I both left Hampshire in 1979. He moved to Colorado to attend business school at Denver University, earning his MBA, then transported himself back east, eventually settling down in Northampton, Massachusetts. During the past two decades, he has served as a business analyst and computer specialist for a series of defense firms, banks, and insurance companies. Today, married, with a son (his only offspring) in college, Ed works for Babson Capital, a Springfield-based asset management company.

If Ed's chosen métier lies not quite so close to his heart's desire as mine does, during the last quarter-century he has gone through sporadic fits of renewed climbing passion, during which he has whipped himself into form and gone off to Yosemite or the Diamond with Jon Krakauer. In the Dolomites in 2004, Ed was in great shape, climbing 5.11 to my 5.9 at the same age.

I managed to exit Hampshire on a paid sabbatical for the spring term and with a summer NEH fellowship at Stanford in hand, a kind of nest egg of cash and time to see me through the launch of what I hoped would become a full-time career as a freelance writer. At Stanford, I took a rejuvenating seminar for college teachers under the legendary English critic Ian Watt, author of *The Rise of the Novel*, while I happily researched the Victorian Arctic in the stacks of Green Library.

During our Hampshire years, Sharon had wisely given up the search for a job teaching high school English. Volunteering at Northampton State Hospital, a mental institution full of hard cases, she discovered a talent for therapy. Eventually she earned a Ph.D. in psychiatric social work from Smith College.

In 1979, Sharon got a job at the prestigious but troubled McLean Hospital in Belmont, Massachusetts, where she would spend sixteen years before resigning to take up full-time private practice. In the fall of 1979, then, we moved to Cambridge, where we have lived ever since.

Although Sharon was on the fence about the question, I had been sure since the day we married in 1967 that I didn't want kids. No doubt the dolors of my own childhood and adolescence went into that gut-level decision (I remain an admirer of Philip Larkin's most famous poem, the scabrous "This Be the Verse"—"They fuck you up, your mum and dad./ They may not mean to, but they do"). Even if those Boulder years could not be held accountable, my lifelong horror of the domestic would have clinched the case against furnishing the apartment with young 'uns.

At Hampshire, my salary had slowly crept upward to the princely stipend of just under $20,000 a year. During my first two years of freelancing, I earned only about $7,000 a year. Sharon helped me out, but for long, lonely months at the typewriter in 1979 and 1980 I lived with a constant hum of anxiety as to whether I had ruined my life.

It would take me several years to recognize that I was doing everything wrong, freelance-wise. I was writing articles on spec and sending them to magazines that would never have published anything in such genres. I made no effort to head down to New York City to cultivate editors. The queries that I sent off, I suspect, were full of jaunty promises that thinly veiled my quiet desperation.

And my Ph.D. and nine years of teaching now served me ill. For all my Hampshire burnout, I had become an academic at heart. This came home to me one day in what I still think of as the best rejection letter I have ever received. Fresh from my Stanford summer, I wrote a short piece spun off my Arctic research that I titled "The Myth of the Fat Eskimo." My clever hypothesis was that British explorers in the nineteenth century had projected an image onto the Eskimos they found in the Canadian Arctic—that of the fat, cheerful, childlike, "greasy" naïf—that was completely at odds with physiological and cultural reality. I contrasted that stereotype to the kindred Victorian projection onto the African Negro—the dark-souled, cunning, treacherous, lustful savage. I came up with an ingenious explanation for the difference: that of all the lands explored by the British during the heyday of Empire, the Arctic was the only terrain in which (unlike the Danes in Greenland) they never hoped to settle.

Mike Curtis, an editor at *Atlantic Monthly*, who was one of the few important contacts I had made, sent my piece back with his one-line note: "This is a marvelous answer to a question no one has asked."

During those fretful months in my Cambridge apartment, not having gone out climbing for months, I had the leisure and the psychic distance to contemplate what mountaineering had meant to my life. In particular, I reviewed the shock of those three early fatal accidents in which I had participated, and my choice to keep climbing afterward. I had written about Ed Bernd's death in *The Mountain of My Fear*, but never a word about Gabe Lee's or Doody's and Merrihue's. The result of my ruminations was the essay eventually titled "Moments of Doubt."

I typed up my meditation and sent it off, unsolicited and with only a brief cover letter, to *Outside*, the mainstream magazine I was then most eager to break into. A junior editor found it on the slush pile, read it, and recommended it to the editor-in-chief, John Rasmus.

Twenty-five years and two other magazines later, Rasmus (currently at the helm of *National Geographic Adventure*) swears that "Moments of Doubt" is still the only piece he ever retrieved from the slush pile. As I mentioned earlier, that essay remains my best-known magazine article. It furnished the title for my first collection of mountaineering pieces, and it has been anthologized a number of times. Despite (or because of) my unflinching recitations of the three deadly accidents, "Moments of Doubt" struck a sympathetic nerve with all kinds of readers, whether or not they were themselves risk-takers: 99 percent of the responses to it that have reached my ears have been laudatory.

At heart, the essay was a justification for the climbing life. The piece ends thus:

> Some of the worst moments of my life have taken place in the mountains. Not only the days alone in the tent on Huntington after Ed had vanished—quieter moments as well, embedded in uneventful expeditions. Trying to sleep the last few hours before a predawn start on a big climb, my mind stiff with dread, as I hugged my all-too-obviously fragile self with my own arms—until the scared kid inside my sleeping bag began to pray for bad weather and another day's reprieve. But nowhere else on earth, not even in the harbors of reciprocal love, have I felt pure happiness take hold of me and shake me like a puppy, compelling me, and the conspirators I had arrived there with, to stand on some perch of rock or snow, the uncertain struggle below us, and bawl our pagan vaunts to the very sky. It was worth it then.

Yet within months of the publication of "Moments of Doubt" in December 1980, I would be furnished with a poignant reminder of just what our wanton play in the great ranges had cost certain others. The *Reader's Digest* picked up the piece, and as it was being prepared for publication in 1981, I got a call from a fact-checker (the *Digest* being famous for its assiduity in ensuring that what the author wrote was really true). In "Moments of Doubt," I had recounted the painful and apparently fruitless weekend in Philadelphia in August 1965, when I had tried to explain to Ed's parents how he had died and what a "great accomplishment" he had performed on Huntington. Now the fact-checker told me that he was required to call Mr. and Mrs. Bernd to verify that meeting.

My heart sank. "Do you really have to?" I pleaded. I had lost touch with Ed's parents more than a decade before, when Mr. Bernd's trickle of complaints about the insurance companies' refusal to pay off without proof of death had dried up. It was now sixteen years since Ed's death, but I remembered the bedroom shrine.

I realized that when my piece appeared in *Reader's Digest*, with its circulation of millions, it would inevitably come to the attention of the Bernds, as its publication in the relatively specialized *Outside* had not guaranteed. "All right, but prepare yourself," I warned the fact-checker. "I wouldn't be surprised if they were still in mourning."

"You know," he answered, "I trained in the ministry. I think I can handle this."

He called me back a couple of days later, sounding deeply shaken. "You were right," he said. "It's as if it happened yesterday." There was a pause. "But they say you never came to Philadelphia."

I was stunned. According to the fact-checker, Mr. Bernd had said, "No, Dave never came to visit us after the accident." There was no animosity in his tone. "Wait a second. I'll check with my wife," he had added. Mrs. Bernd had likewise averred that there had been no such visit. Yet both parents swore that Matt, Ed, and I had spent the night in their Philadelphia home on our way up to Alaska—while in reality we had stopped for at most two hours in the middle of the night, munching on Mrs. Bernd's sandwiches, with all three of us itching to get back on the road.

At the age of thirty-seven, I could comprehend how memory reshaped traumatic events, stretching our dutiful June visit into a full night of good sleep in real beds, repressing altogether the agony of my foolish mission in August. But that two separate individuals, married

or not, could collaborate in such a mnemonic rewrite of the past flab-
bergasted me—and pierced me with a fresh sadness for the Bernds'
suffering.

"We can't publish that part of the piece unless you can prove you
went there," the fact-checker went on. I urged him to call Matt Hale—
for, after Don Jensen's death in the bicycle accident in Scotland in
1973, he was now the only other survivor of our team of four. Matt
told the fact-checker, "I can't *prove* Dave visited the Bernds, but he told
me all about it." Matt himself had paid a visit—equally unconsoling
to the parents, as he remembered—in the fall of his senior year at
Harvard. In the end, the *Digest* let my passage stand. I never heard again
from Mr. and Mrs. Bernd.

After the gloom of my last years at Hampshire, despite my meager
income as a freelancer, I felt reborn in my new life as a writer. In
1980, an editor friend serving as my agent landed me a contract for a
book about explorers who had faked their greatest deeds. The advance
was a whopping seven thousand dollars. When Sierra Club Books
published *Great Exploration Hoaxes* in 1982, I finally had a third book in
print to trump the three that languished in my closet.

Sometime during this heady span, I visited Jon Krakauer, who was
living in Seattle with Linda. During the long weekend I would spend
with Jon, I had but a single agenda—to pound home the idea that he
should lay down his carpenter's hammer and try freelancing himself for
a living. By 1981, at the age of twenty-seven, Jon had published nothing
more than climbing articles in the *American Alpine Journal, Climbing,* and the
English journal *Mountain.* But these were well-wrought pieces, and
besides, I had known ever since his last year in college—when he had
written a fascinating (if uneven) eighty-page meditation on that ascent
and on climbing in general—that Jon had what it took to be a writer.

In Seattle, I was relentless, but Jon was just as relentless in return.
There was no way he could fool the world of editors, he insisted, passing himself off as a "real" writer: they would see through the sham
from the start. The most stubborn of friends and partners, Jon had
almost never allowed me to talk him into anything—except, perhaps,
backing off Little Tombstone after his 45-foot fall. Now Linda joined

in, ganging up with me on Jon, for she knew how unhappy he was continuing to pound nails as a means of gainful employment. In the middle of his voluntary four-year sabbatical from climbing, he had little in fact in life that gave him joy.

At the end of two straight days of haggling, Jon gave in—provisionally. He agreed to try writing full-time, but only as a six-month experiment. If it failed, he would go back to construction. In the fall of 1983, he set out dubiously on his new course.

The assignments trickled in, but for a while, Jon was convinced that too much of the work he was getting was hand-me-downs from me, as I steered my own editors in his direction. For me, whatever else the tribulations, writing had always come easily. For Jon, the process was (and still is) an unalloyed agony. He could sit for three days in front of the typewriter (later the computer screen) and not complete an initial paragraph. To avoid the freighted moment of committing the first words to paper, Jon would dash off to the library or the bookstore to do more "research." Only after he underwent this ritual of mental self-flagellation would the dam break and the prose pour out, sometimes in a flood that kept him up all night.

By 1985, Jon was at last making a living as a writer. But he shared none of my enthusiasm for our métier as the best of all possible jobs. About that time, over the telephone, he initiated an exchange that we would remember and repeat many times afterward. "If I ever won the lottery," Jon said, "I'd quit writing."

"Not me," I rejoined. "If I won the lottery, I'd really start to write."

In the middle of another phone call around 1985, suddenly fed up with my rose-tinted take on our way of life, Jon burst out, "Dave, you don't get it. I'm thirty-one years old, I'm working my ass off, and I'm making less money than I would flipping burgers at McDonald's."

In 1982, John Rasmus assigned me to write a profile of Reinhold Messner for *Outside* magazine. The scuttlebutt was that the thirty-seven-year-old climber from the German-speaking South Tirol had become the strongest high-altitude mountaineer in the world. Five years before, with the Austrian Peter Habeler, Messner had climbed Pakistan's Hidden Peak—Gasherbrum I—in only three days, the first alpine-style ascent of an 8,000-meter peak ever performed. In 1978, Messner and Habeler had become the first men to climb Everest without bottled oxygen. Two years later, Messner climbed Everest solo, without oxygen, by a new route—a feat eventually judged by many to be the single finest deed in mountaineering history. Four years after my interview with Messner, he became the first man to reach the summit of all fourteen 8,000-meter peaks.

I spent but a single hour in Messner's Munich apartment, the maximum he would grant a journalist. I found the man intense, gruff, and unforthcoming—until he discovered that I was a climber myself, after which he opened up a bit. Despite the shining deeds they had performed together, Messner had recently quarreled with Habeler, in no small part because the latter had written his own book about Everest, with several passages that cast the South Tirolean in a less than heroic light. By 1982, the feud between the two great climbers and former friends looked irresolvable.

The joint profile I published in Outside, a cover story, provoked a certain buzz. Rasmus assigned me to interview other leading climbers and adventurers. Eventually I wrote profiles of John Roskelley, the top American Himalayan climber of his day; Catherine Destivelle, considered the best woman climber in the world in the 1980s; Lynn Hill, the American who would inherit Destivelle's mantle; Ed Viesturs, who by now has climbed thirteen of the fourteen 8,000-ers (all but Annapurna) and who will almost surely be the first American to achieve that feat; as well as a number of other men and women who were pushing the limits of the possible on sheer cliffs and in remote ranges.

I found that I had a knack for writing profiles, a skill at digging beneath my subject's well-prepared facade. The trick came naturally to me of taking careful mental notes of the unguarded remarks that slipped out over the second beer, when I'd packed up my tape recorder and closed my notebook and the subject assumed the official interview was over. Profile-writing is intrinsically a hostile act, for if you succeed (as in Lillian Ross's legendary tour of Abercrombie &

Fitch with Papa Hemingway for *The New Yorker*), you reveal not only aspects of the subject's character of which he or she is unaware, but glimmerings that the subject would just as soon the world never knew about. Roskelley, for example, was initially furious with my profile in *Outside* and called me up to let me know so in blistering terms. But after a number of his close friends told him, "Sorry, John, Roberts's got you pegged," he had the magnanimity to seek me out for a drink and an apology.

Those profiles served another, more personal purpose. In the crazy-house mirrors those hard men and women held up, I saw my own erstwhile obsession with climbing reflected in distorted but recognizable images. It had required the waning of my own fanaticism to awaken an anthropologist's curiosity about the whole business of climbing. The process had begun before I wrote for *Outside*, in the 1970s, when Allen Steck and Steve Roper, the editors of the sporadic (and often marvelous) journal *Ascent*, had hired me as a kind of littérateur-in-residence to pen, in successive years, sardonic surveys of the climbing journals of the U.S. and Britain, of the best expedition narratives ever written, and of the failings and rare successes of climbers' autobiographies.

Along with the expected quota of raging egomaniacs among top climbers, I discovered a few genuine nice guys, among them Peter Habeler and Ed Viesturs. Yet all my subjects had in common an intensity and a self-preoccupation that—though clearly functional in the third bivouac on the Eiger or above 26,000 feet on Everest—seemed more than faintly disturbing in a person one might choose as a friend rather than as a hero. If the narcissism of many of the spoiled rich kids I had taught at Hampshire had helped to sour me on academe, now the abundant narcissism I found in the makeup of climbing stars nudged to a new level my latent skepticism about the mountaineering life.

In my own case, I had concluded, climbing made a very poor model for how to get through "normal" life. I found that gloomy premise reinforced as I researched my profiles. One of my most interesting subjects, and by far the most poignant, was a youth named Hugh Herr. In January 1982, still in high school, this seventeen-year-old, with a close friend, climbed Pinnacle Gully on Mount Washington, got disoriented in a blizzard, and blundered by mistake into the Great Gulf rather than down the usual descent route to the Harvard cabin. Four days later, rescuers found the two boys huddled beneath a boulder, on the verge of death. The rescue effort had already turned costly when veteran climber Albert Dow was killed in an avalanche while out searching for the lost youths.

Both Hugh and his friend had suffered severe frostbite. In the end, doctors could not save Hugh's feet and lower legs, both of which were amputated six inches below the knees.

I clamped on to this story not simply to chronicle another tragedy in the mountains, but after hearing the news that, only months later, Hugh was back into climbing, using artificial feet. When I met the kid at his home in Lancaster, Pennsylvania, I liked him at once. He was shy, polite, deferential, and full of regret that his fuck-up in the mountains had cost a rescuer his life. At the same time, in his own way, Hugh was as fanatical about climbing as Reinhold Messner. It was astonishing that, at eighteen, with inflexible wooden blobs for feet, he was leading 5.11 pitches and the occasional 5.12 at the Gunks. But I thought I was witnessing the most extreme case of full-blown denial I had ever come across, for Hugh had jauntily nicknamed himself "the mechanical boy," and actually claimed that, by switching wooden feet he had machined himself, adapting the shape of his appendages to a given route, he actually had an unfair advantage over climbers with real feet.

Hugh's upbeat demeanor filled me with dismay. I quoted an older climbing friend of mine: "What's the poor guy going to do when he's twenty-five and doesn't want to lead 5.11 any more?" And Hugh's sorrowing father, who seemed to me to have the right take: "You have to remember, he can climb a whole lot better than he can walk. That's a lot of crap, that it's an advantage not to have feet." I ended my piece by wishing the boy well.

More than two decades later, the Hugh Herr story has a surprise ending, and a happy one. Hugh's interest in climbing indeed dwindled while he was still in his twenties. But although when I interviewed him he planned not to attend college, he ended up going to MIT, where he earned a master's degree, and to Harvard for his Ph.D. Hugh's life work has been the design of revolutionary prostheses for amputee athletes. His genius for design has made a profound difference in this nascent field. I can think of no finer example in mountaineering of a climber turning personal catastrophe into a contribution to the general good of humankind.

The question we climbers are always asked by nonclimbing friends, by the media, by the stranger we happen to sit next to on the plane, is "Why? Why do you do it?" I was never able to formulate a coherent answer myself, nor did I ever come across one uttered by any of my profile subjects or in the pages of the memoirs and narratives penned by even the most articulate of mountaineers. Often we throw up our hands in frustration, as if to signify, "If you've never tried it, you'll never understand."

The most famous answer, of course, is Mallory's. In 1923, in the midst of a discouraging and exhausting lecture tour of the United States, as he tried to raise funds for the 1924 expedition on which he would vanish, the umpteenth journalist asked him, "Why do you want to climb Mount Everest?" "Because it is there," Mallory snapped back. Ever since, commentators and biographers have debated whether Mallory's rejoinder was an irritable non sequitur flung out to silence a tiresome inquisitor, or a brilliant spontaneous apothegm— or both.

There is a kernel of profundity in Mallory's four-word answer. Between 1890 and 1912, some of the toughest and bravest explorers in the world risked and sometimes lost their lives trying to "discover" the North and South Poles—featureless blanks of pack ice and glacier, respectively, defined by the arbitrary inclination of the earth's axis, and thereby known to exist even though no one had ever seen them. The Poles had to be reached simply because they were there.

For me, the closest utterance to an acceptable answer to the eternal question comes from an unlikely source. In a documentary film, Vladimir Nabokov was once asked why butterfly hunting was his deepest passion, taking precedence even over writing. The activity,

Nabokov answered, was "a way of rebelling against the void fore and aft." For a good atheist like myself, climbing at its best seemed to serve that very function, however cryptic the formula sounds.

"Why do you climb?" is, after all, a perfectly reasonable question. It betrays the average non-risk-taker's incredulity that anyone would expose himself to such hardship and danger for so apparently ephemeral and intangible a reward. It can be paraphrased in the more negative version, "You've got to be crazy to go climbing!"

During our Harvard Mountaineering Club days, we acolytes gleefully repeated an anecdote that had reached our ears. After the 1963 American Everest extravaganza, Dan Doody, who had been a member of the expedition, albeit a disgruntled one, appeared on some television show. The host asked him the eternal question. Whatever Doody answered, it must have been inadequate, for now the host frowned shrewdly and bored in: "Have you ever had a death wish?"

"Yes," answered Dan, to the host's surprise.

"When?"

"The only time I worked a nine-to-five job."

Why is it so hard for climbers to explain why they climb? From Victorian days onward, climbing writers have spilled flagons of ink shaping transparently lame answers. The view from the summit clearly has little to do with the climbing urge, or else we could get the same high upon alighting from a cable car. Strenuous exercise in pristine nature can be achieved without the risk of life and limb. Lasting friendships can be forged without leader falls.

The compulsively introspective Messner, who has written more than forty books, goes on and on about climbing as a path to self-discovery. Only by undergoing the most extreme ordeals in the mountains, he writes repeatedly, can he plumb the inner depths of his being. The only trouble is, he never bothers to tell us just what he found in those depths.

If you could have asked a sixteenth-century Spanish conquistador why he was risking his life to set out for the New World, he would have had a ready answer. "To find gold and silver and claim land and become rich as I never could in Spain." A megalomaniac leader such as Cortés or Pizarro would have added, "To win eternal glory and fame." The Dominican and Franciscan friars who accompanied those perilous *entradas* would have had equally ready explanations: "To save the benighted souls of the heathen savages."

Lionel Terray's autobiography, as previously mentioned, is titled in English *Conquistadors of the Useless*. (A literal translation of *Les Conquérants de l'Inutile* would have been *Conquerors of the Useless*. On the other hand, *conquistador* is simply Spanish for "conqueror.") There is a point to be made here. Climbers by and large shy away from the journalistic cliché of "conquering" a mountain. Only in its American edition was Sir John Hunt's account of the first ascent of the world's highest mountain titled *The Conquest of Everest*. Hunt's properly British title was *The Ascent of Everest*. In a genuine apothegm, Mallory weighed in on this question: "Have we vanquished an enemy? None but ourselves."

A concomitant myth to which good mountaineers have flaccidly subscribed over the years is that there is nothing competitive about climbing—or that the only competition going on is between an athlete and his limits, or a cragsman and the rock he treads. This is pure nonsense. As Sandy Campbell, the first kayaking instructor we hired for the Hampshire Outdoors Program, told me in 1971, "I thought kayakers were the most competitive people I knew, until I met climbers."

There is, alas, no getting around the fact that climbing has always been intimately tied up with fame and glory, with the dark urge to triumph over rivals, with the greedy ego gratification of being recognized as the best. In the early 1960s in the U.S., when climbing was still so arcane a pastime that nobody outside our ingrown groups cared a whit what we were doing, recognition still counted for everything. If and when, at the Gunks, a demigod such as Jim McCarthy or Art Gran bothered to throw a crumb to Matt or me—"Hey, nice job getting up the Maria Direct"—we burst with pride and nursed the compliment for weeks.

Dennis Gray, a British climber who started in the late 1940s, offers a lovely vignette of this sort of scene in his autobiography, *Rope Boy*. At the age of twelve, on a Boy Scout outing, Gray arrives with his troop at the foot of a diminutive crag called Hangingstones Quarry.

A tall, athletic, white-haired man was balanced on what appeared to me a vertical holdless face. Nonchalantly he pulled a handkerchief out of his trouser pocket and blew his nose. . . . He began to move upwards, and . . . his agility, grace of movement, control, and, above all, the setting high above ground, with no apparent safety devices, sent a thrill through my young body such as I had never before experienced. . . . One of the group whispered to a newcomer, "It's Dolphin!"

Arthur Dolphin was one of the top British climbers of his day, and, as the performance with the handkerchief made clear, he reveled in his onlookers' recognition of that status. In that moment, Dennis Gray determined to become a climber.

During the last twenty years, the myth that climbing is noncompetitive has fallen by the wayside, for two reasons in particular. Never have the grade ratings that measure the difficulties of routes been more assiduously worried over, with rock jocks spending sleepless nights trying to determine whether their latest creations should be deemed 5.14a's or only 5.13d's. The hard-core journals solemnly debate which forty-foot-long wrinkle in Oregon or southern France may be the hardest pure rock climb in the world at any given moment. Further complicating the matter is a whole lexicon of new jargon to stamp the style in which a climb is performed, ranging from "hang-dog" through "pinkpoint" through "redpoint" to "on-sight."

The other development that turned climbing overtly rivalrous was the invention of the climbing competition in the early 1980s. Originally held on local crags, but now almost entirely on artificial walls, and usually indoors, these meets pit some of the best rock climbers in the world head-to-head against one another on fiendish routes whose holds are made of fiberglass and polyurethane. The "comps" come complete with official juries, codices of rules, time clocks, isolation chambers where candidates await their turns (so as not to benefit from observing their predecessors' mistakes), audiences cheering from the bleachers, and trophies and cash for the winners. By the early 1990s, an international World Cup totaled up the finishes from seven or eight sanctioned comps to crown a men's and a women's world champion—just like Grand Prix race car driving.

In 1988, on assignment for *Outside*, I covered the first international competition ever held in the U.S., at Snowbird in Utah. Arriving as a grumpy skeptic, ready to slather the comp with scorn, I ended up standing on my feet cheering wildly with the rest of the crowd as the wiry Frenchman Patrick Edlinger, last on the wall, became the only competitor to "flash" the desperate route, claiming victory as he slapped the highest hold.

Yet climbing has not suddenly turned competitive during the last two decades. It has always been thus. The first ascent of the Matterhorn in 1865—then the Last Great Problem of the Alps—devolved into a race between Edward Whymper's English team with Swiss guides and another party simultaneously attacking the mountain from the other side, led by the Italian Jean-Antoine Carrel. On the summit, seeing the tiny dots of the Italian team struggling below him to the south, Whymper and his partners shouted themselves hoarse and rolled rocks off the summit (at no small peril to the Italians) as they gloated over their victory.

Are we climbers, then, akin to the conquistadors of the sixteenth and seventeenth centuries? From a modern perspective, the conquistadors seem a particularly nasty bunch. If you read the letters columns of journals such as *Climbing* and *Rock and Ice*, you might well conclude that climbers, too, are a nasty bunch, as they fire bitchy salvos across each other's bows over such apparently harmless deeds as chiseling holds, placing bolts on rappel, and claiming a redpoint that was really pink. There are still crags in the U.S., like the Gunks, that have a mellow, friendly ambience. But there are other climbing areas where the invidious vibes so pollute the air that you feel almost as though you ought to present credentials or a badge before daring to rope up.

If narcissism runs rampant among top climbers, one might answer that the same could be said of high achievers in many walks of life—pro athletes, CEOs of major corporations, writers themselves. In mountaineering, however, the narcissism all too often goes hand-in-hand with a disturbing coldness, an absence of compassion. The Scot

Dougal Haston was one of the finest mountaineers in the world in the 1960s and 1970s, completing, among other great routes, the south face of Annapurna and the southwest face of Everest. In his autobiography, In High Places, Haston ponders the great game of risk and produces a chilling formula: "If anything goes wrong it will be a fight to the end. If your training is good enough, survival is there; if not nature claims its forfeit."

In the world of a Dougal Haston, there is little room for the softer emotions. A single sentence in In High Places acknowledges Haston's domestic life: "One other significant event that year—I finally married my girl-friend Annie." Haston's biographer reveals that his publisher had to twist the climber's arm to get him to mention Annie at all.

Nor, in the end, could Haston live up to his own recipe for survival. Out for a casual morning ski run behind his house in Leysin, Switzerland, in 1977, he was killed in an avalanche.

In order to continue to tiptoe among the appalling land mines of big-range mountaineering, hard men have always taken refuge in rationalizations such as Haston's. In 1997, when I interviewed Ed Viesturs, I mentioned to him a rigorous German study that concluded that on any given expedition to an 8,000-meter peak, a climber stands a 1-in-34 chance of dying. By that point, Ed had been on seventeen such expeditions. He had come very close to dying on K2 in 1992, and in May 1996 he had climbed past the bodies of his good friends Rob Hall and Scott Fischer, ace guides who had frozen to death just a week earlier, in the Everest debacle chronicled in Jon Krakauer's Into Thin Air. A simple probability equation allowed me to calculate that, according to the German formula, Ed had so far accrued a 40 percent chance of dying.

He looked at me agog. "That's ridiculous," he said. Ed's argument was that he was a far more skilled and careful climber than the average member of an expedition to an 8,000-er, so the formula didn't apply to him. I pointed out, "Yeah, but that statistic counts chubbers who just go from base camp to Camp I. You're always going for the summit without oxygen." Ed was unconvinced. I asked him what chance he thought he'd actually run of dying in the Himalaya. "One in a hundred," he said. "No, not even that much." "But Ed," I protested, "you nearly died on K2."

In the summer of 2004, I updated my Viesturs account. By then, he had gone on thirteen more expeditions to 8,000-meter peaks. He had climbed Everest six times, once as the star of David Breashears's IMAX film. According to my probability formula, he had now rung up a solid 60 percent chance of dying. I told him so. "That's ridiculous," he said again. "I just don't buy it."

In 1999, I collaborated with Conrad Anker on a book called The Lost Explorer, about his finding Mallory's body high on the north side of Everest. The great loss in Anker's climbing career had been the death of his best friend and mentor, Mugs Stump, in 1992, when a sérac collapsed on him while he was guiding two clients on the South Buttress of McKinley. In order to keep climbing at the highest level, Conrad concluded that guiding clients on big mountains was too dangerous, and he resolved never to do so again himself. When I gently suggested that this sounded like a rationalization, Conrad argued its logic till he was breathless.

Just a month after our collaboration, Conrad and his now best friend, Alex Lowe, were caught in a huge avalanche on Shishapangma in Nepal. Seeing it coming from far above, Conrad had instinctively run to the right, Alex down and to the left. The avalanche pummeled Conrad, carrying him down the slope and breaking his shoulder; but it buried Lowe (and a third teammate) so completely the party was never able to find their bodies.

Conrad is too modest a man to claim that his instinctive dash to the right was informed by a higher wisdom than Alex's. (Magazine articles had just begun referring to Lowe as perhaps the best mountaineer in the world.) But now Conrad concluded that 8,000-meter peaks were too dangerous: in the future, he'd limit himself to 7,000-meter peaks.

It is natural that climbers need to believe that there's a reason they didn't get killed, that they can actually control the risk. When Doody and Merrihue fell to their deaths out of Pinnacle Gully, I believed in my guts that I had not been blown out of my steps on the same climb in the same wind the day before because I was in better training than those veterans. Today, I view that smug recipe as pure rationalization. Few of us climbers can really accept the role of sheer luck in our survival.

From the late eighteenth century on, mountaineering has boasted as rich a literature as any other field of adventurous endeavor. Yet climbers are notoriously inarticulate, even mute, about why they do what they do, and about how they respond to the deaths of others. Hermann Buhl, the great Austrian climber who made the first ascent of Nanga Parbat solo in 1953, was one of the heroes of my youth, and his memoir, *Lonely Challenge*, served as one of the bibles of my apprenticeship.

Rereading the book recently, I was taken aback by a scene in the second chapter, titled "A Lesson from Death." At the age of fifteen, in 1940, Buhl roped up with a companion named Sepp Fuchs to try a long route in the Wetterstein Alps. High on the wall, they saw a solitary figure scrambling toward the base, then starting to solo up the same route. When the two lads were 700 feet off the ground, the soloist caught up with them. Buhl and Fuchs offered him a rope, but the stranger declined and charged ahead out of sight.

Ten or twenty minutes later,

We were startled by a clattering sound. Falling stones? We ducked close into the rock, waiting for the hail of stones which never came. Instead, a dark, heavy object—rather long, like a sack full of something—sailed past through thin air. I recognized it suddenly as a human body—that of the lone climber! A cold chill ran down my spine. It was flying straight at Sepp, clinging to the wall below me. Bound to knock him off, I thought, and gripped the rope more tightly than ever. But the lifeless body missed my friend by a couple of feet and went hurtling out into the void.

Completely unnerved, the two youths managed to finish the climb and scramble down the back side. At the foot of the wall, they found others attending to the dead climber; someone laid a wreath of larches over his body.

Buhl's initial reaction was the human one. "For days and weeks after this fearful experience I was so shaken that I could not bear the sight of my mountaineering equipment. For a time I thought I should give up my climbing career, which had hardly even begun." But of course, the Austrian did not quit climbing, even though nightmares of falling bodies plagued his sleep for weeks. Instead, he absorbed the "lesson" of the chapter's title.

What was that lesson? The last line of the chapter hits the page with a bathetic thud: "What I had learned was that climbing can be a dangerous business and that it can lead to a sudden end."

Buhl himself died on Chogolisa in the Karakoram in 1957, when a cornice broke beneath his feet and he plunged into the abyss. His body has never been found.

Especially in my first years in Alaska, I would have said that what drove me to climb was the inexhaustible thrill of going where no one else had ever been. A similar note is struck by Alfred Mummery, the greatest British climber of his day, in the lyrical last chapter of his classic work, *My Climbs in the Alps and Caucasus*. Assessing "the pleasures and penalties of mountaineering," Mummery asserts,

> The true mountaineer is a wanderer, and by a wanderer I do not mean a man who expends his whole time in travelling to and fro in the mountains on the exact tracks of his predecessors—much as a bicyclist rushes along the turnpike roads of England—but I mean a man who loves to be where no human being has been before, who delights in gripping rocks that have never previously felt the touch of human fingers, or in hewing his way up ice-filled gullies whose grim shadows have been sacred to the mists and avalanches since "earth rose out of chaos."

Mummery's credo cost him his life, when with two porters he vanished on Nanga Parbat in 1895, on the first attempt ever made on any 8,000-meter peak.

For me, on deeper reflection, the wanderer explanation does not really hold up. In July 1965, had I been plunked down not on the Tokositna Glacier, but on some barren stretch of tundra on the Arctic Slope north of the Brooks Range—terrain every bit as unknown and untrodden as the west face of Huntington—I would not have set forth in the exploratory ecstasy I felt those first days on the granite of our great wall.

"Why do you climb?" may be a question that does not admit of a rational answer. In the works of two British climbers, utterly opposite in temperament, I find a more compelling "explanation" of our pastime than I do in the writings of Mummery or Messner or even Mallory.

The Scot Tom Patey was one of the outstanding British climbers of the 1950s and 1960s, a specialist in steep ice routes. He was also a balladeer and essayist of no small talent. After his untimely death in a rappelling accident in 1970, his widow, Betty, collected his poems and articles and published them in a book called One Man's Mountains, which mountaineers have treasured ever since.

Patey does not agonize over the question of why we climb. He takes our fanatic avocation as a given. Yet for Patey, the whole business remains fundamentally absurd, a modern-day tilting at windmills. The only suitable stance from which to write about it, then, is the satiric.

In perhaps his finest piece, called "A Short Walk with Whillans" (the title an allusion to Eric Newby's A Short Walk in the Hindu Kush, a delightful memoir about amateurs getting in over their heads among the mountains of Afghanistan), Patey plays straight man to his partner Don Whillans on a failed attempt on the Eiger Nordwand. Whillans himself was one of the great British mountaineers of the twentieth century, the author of countless "desperates" at home, summiteer with Dougal Haston on the brilliant campaign against the south face of Annapurna in 1970, at the time the hardest route climbed in the Himalaya. Hard-drinking, chain-smoking, abrasive, and strictly out for himself, Whillans had a fatalistic streak that, in the hands of Patey, turns into a kind of black comedy that manages to illuminate the addictive insanity of playing the climbing game for keeps.

Thus, on their own retreat from the face, turned back by barrages of rockfall, Whillans and Patey run into a pair of Japanese climbers heading upward. The whole encounter, as rendered by Patey, replete with Whillans's shameless ethnic baiting, gets to the heart of our absurdly perilous (or perilously absurd?) endeavor:

> "God Almighty," [Whillans] said (or words to that effect), "Japs! Come and see for yourself!"
>
> Sure enough, there they were. Two identical little men in identical climbing uniforms, sitting side by side underneath an overhang. They had been crouching there for an hour, waiting for the bombardment to slacken. . . .
>
> "You—Japs?" grunted Don. It seemed an unnecessary question.
>
> "Yes, yes," they grinned happily, displaying a full set of teeth. "We are Japanese."
>
> "Going—up," queried Whillans. He pointed meaningfully at the grey holocaust sweeping down from the White Spider.
>
> "Yes, yes," they chorused in unison. "Up. Always upwards. First Japanese Ascent."
>
> "You—may—be—going—up—Mate," said Whillans, giving every syllable unnecessary emphasis, "but—a—lot—'igher—than—you—think!"
>
> They did not know what to make of this, so they wrung his hand several times, and thanked him profusely for the advice.
>
> "'Appy little pair!" said Don. "I don't imagine we'll ever see them again."

The other climbing writer who seems to me almost accidentally to get to the core of the climbing impulse is John Menlove Edwards, whose own life was unmistakably tragic. With Colin Kirkus, Edwards was one of the two finest British rock climbers of the 1930s. His technique was a paradox. To onlookers, he seemed to be struggling clumsily on the lead, starting and stopping, fidgeting and improvising, with no trace of the graceful fluidity of, say, George Mallory two decades before. Yet Edwards would get up wet, grimy cracks and slabs in north Wales that no other climbers could follow.

Edwards became a professional psychiatrist, one who by all accounts gave such attentive care to his clients that he worked therapeutic wonders. Yet his highest ambitions were theoretical. Rejecting Freud, Adler, and Jung out of hand, he sought a kind of unified field theory that would explain all human behavior. According to his biographer, Jim Perrin, Edwards believed "that the will could be trained to control the nervous and muscular systems of the body, and also the sub-conscious and instinctual parts of the mind." When his rather dotty ideas were dismissed by his peers in the profession, Edwards suffered a profound sense of failure in his life's work.

By the age of twenty, Edwards knew and in large part accepted the fact that he was homosexual, in an era when British law still proscribed all homoerotic behavior. His great heartbreak came at the age of twenty-five when he fell in love with Wilfrid Noyce, a handsome seventeen-year-old schoolboy who soon became Edwards's protégé on the rock. The two men had a brief affair, but the essentially heterosexual Noyce broke it off. On Scafell in England's Lake District in 1937, Noyce took a horrendous 180-foot leader fall: only a piece of expert belaying by Edwards kept him from hitting the ground and killing himself. As it was, Noyce lay unconscious for three days in the hospital. Perrin credits Edwards's ceaseless bedside vigil for pulling Noyce through.

Noyce would go on to be one of Britain's leading mountaineers, a principal player in the 1953 first ascent of Everest. His memoir of that expedition, South Col, is a better book than Sir John Hunt's official chronicle, The Ascent of Everest. In 1962, the forty-four-year-old Noyce was killed with his much younger partner Robin Smith in a roped fall in the Russian Pamirs. Smith was not only one of the leading British climbers of his generation, but showed promise of becoming one of its finest climbing writers as well. Teammates suspected that the by then less-skilled Noyce, who all his life had inclined toward the accident-prone, probably fell and pulled Smith to his death.

Edwards's own last decade and a half were unremittingly bleak. Along with professional failure, he veered toward insanity. He diagnosed himself as schizophrenic, although in today's terms he would much more likely be seen as bipolar, swinging between moods of black despair and bursts of manic energy. He not only climbed routes virtually no one else could get up at the time, but he periodically set out on solo, midwinter open-boat rowing expeditions on the high seas. His seven-day round-trip jaunt from the coast of Scotland to the Isle of Harris in the Outer Hebrides, in December 1935, would give the finest boatmen today serious pause.

Always a reckless driver, Edwards, on a motorcycle, collided in 1957 with a boy riding a bicycle. Edwards suffered a broken arm, but the boy died beside him in the hospital. Shortly thereafter, as he tried to sharpen a sickle with his arm still in a cast, Edwards sliced off the back of his hand, severing tendons and removing several knuckles. Meanwhile, his mental state was spiraling into a whirlpool of despair. In February 1958, Edwards committed suicide by swallowing potassium cyanide—an excruciating way to die.

Like Patey, in his writing Edwards never analyzes the sources of the climbing impulse. Rather than playing it as mock-heroic comedy, however, Edwards regards climbing as something he cannot help doing. It is a kind of disease—"brief symptoms," he self-observes, not entirely tongue-in-cheek, in an account of one of his early climbs, "of some psycho-neurotic tendency."

Edwards's writing, which he took very seriously, is opaque, contorted, and private. At its most lucid, however, he becomes the consummate exponent of the dark side of climbing—of doubt, fear, futility. Thus, in a Gerard Manley Hopkins–like stanza in one of his best poems, he apostrophizes the rock itself:

> You rock, you heaviness a man can clasp,
> You steady buttress-block for hold,
> You, frozen roughly to the touch:
> Yet what can you?

One of Edwards's most haunting passages—a great, frenetic single sentence—is about an experience all climbers have had, but few have written about: being too nervous and off-form even to get started on a route:

> Look at yourself I said, and do you know what this is, that it is schizophrenia, the split mind: I know but I do not care what I said: it is stupid: what could you do if you did get ten feet higher up, the rocks have not started yet to become difficult, take yourself off from this cliff: oh, this climbing, that involves an effort, on every move the holes [sic] to be spotted and often there are none, then every limb placed, the body set into the one suitable position found but with trouble, then with the whole organism great force must be exerted, before anything happens, and this is to be done while the brain is occupied sick and stiff with its fears: and now you have been doing this for well over an hour and a half and the strain must be telling: get down therefore.

If one read only the books and articles of climbers themselves, full of celebrations of great deeds and narrow scrapes in the mountains, one might never suspect that the choice to risk life and limb had any moral consequences whatsoever. (As mentioned earlier, I read my first mountaineering books, starting around the age of twelve, as escape literature, on a par with the Hardy Boys.)

On the descent from the first ascent of the Matterhorn, after rolling the rocks off the south side to vaunt their triumph over Jean-Antoine Carrel's Italian party, Edward Whymper's team of seven roped up all seven together. Today, that would be regarded as a grievous mistake, but by the standards of the day—and given the vast discrepancies in talent among Whymper's companions, ranging from professional Swiss guides to Englishmen who were little more than strong hikers—it was not an altogether foolish decision. Whymper came last.

Then one of the least experienced climbers slipped and fell. He knocked the guide just below him off his feet, starting a lethal chain reaction. Whymper tried to brace himself by gripping the nearest rocks. Soon four men were plunging down the steep face of the most difficult mountain in the Alps. The rope came tight between the fourth and fifth men—and suddenly broke.

Whymper and his two fellow survivors, the guides Peter Taugwalder père et fils, watched in horror as their comrades fell and bounced 4,000 feet to a certain death. Completely unstrung by the accident, the Taugwalders would never have made it off the mountain themselves had not a hypervigilant Whymper shepherded them down.

The Matterhorn disaster remains the most famous accident in mountaineering history. (No less an artist than Gustave Doré etched an engraving of the fateful moment.) Back in England, Britain's finest mountaineer faced intense criticism. The hue and cry were no doubt exacerbated by the fact that one of the victims was a nobleman, Lord Francis Douglas. The rumor circulated that Whymper had cut the rope to save his own neck. Queen Victoria sought advice from her retainers as to whether the sport of mountaineering ought to be outlawed altogether.

Prominent spokesmen, such as Alfred Wills, then president of the Alpine Club, sprang to Whymper's defense. But much of the rhetoric of outrage took the tone of an editorial in the London *Times* on July 27, 1865:

> What is the use of scaling precipitous rocks, and being for half an hour at the top of the terrestrial globe? There is use in the feats of sailors, of steeple-climbers, vane-cleaners, chimney sweepers, lovers, and other adventurous professions. A man may be content to die in such a cause, for it is his life's battle. But in the few short moments a member of the Alpine Club has to survey his life when he finds himself slipping, he has but a sorry account to give of himself. What is he doing there, and what right has he to throw away the gift of life and ten thousand golden opportunities in an emulation which he shares only with skylarks, apes, cats, and squirrels?

Whymper himself was deeply embittered by the opprobrium heaped on his head. Strictly speaking, he was not, as the phrase often has it, "hounded out of England," but in later life, he ventured far afield to pursue his mountain craft, making first ascents in the Andes in the 1880s. It is not by happenstance that Whymper's grave lies in Chamonix, where he died in 1911, rather than on his native soil.

The stirring last paragraph of Whymper's classic book, *The Ascent of the Matterhorn*, amounts to as succinct and eloquent a summation of Mummery's "pleasures and penalties" as can be found in our literature:

> There have been joys too great to be described in words, and there have been griefs upon which I have not dared to dwell; and with those in mind I say, Climb if you will, but remember that courage and strength are nought without prudence, and that a momentary negligence may destroy the happiness of a lifetime. Do nothing in haste; look well to each step; and from the beginning think what may be the end.

But even before my own mountaineering tailed off in the late 1970s, I found the doubters more interesting than the celebrators. Such lyrical evocations of the joys of mountaineering as William O. Douglas's *Of Men and Mountains* or even Gaston Rébuffat's *Starlight and Storm* (which I briefly embraced, at age twenty, as a credo of my alpine faith) end up seeming to me intellectually flaccid.

No comment has struck me more forcefully than one I read in an interview with writer Sebastian Junger in 1997. As Junger's *The Perfect Storm* and Jon Krakauer's *Into Thin Air* bounced back and forth in first and second place on the *New York Times* nonfiction best-seller list, Junger found himself annoyed that he was lumped with Krakauer as an "adventure writer." The commercial fishermen who died in the millennial tempest Junger wrote about were not seeking an adventure (as the affluent clients who came to grief on Everest were), they were trying to make a living.

Underscoring this point in the interview, Junger drew a further distinction, between what he called courage and heroism. Climbing

Everest, Junger asserted, takes all kinds of courage, but it should not be called heroic. The writer then offered an apothegmatic formula: "Heroism is courage in the service of others."

In a subsequent essay, called "Colter's Way," Junger amplified his gripe. Dan Osman, a daredevil solo climber who had invented a new "sport"—that of jumping off cliffs attached to an anchor only with his climbing rope—had recently killed himself in Yosemite, attempting a record 1,000-foot jump, when the rope broke. Junger compared Osman to roughnecks working oil rigs—also a perilous "pastime."

> Oddly . . . it's the mountaineers who are heaped with glory, not the roughnecks. . . . A roughneck who gets crushed tripping pipe or a fire fighter who dies in a burning building has, in some ways, died a heroic death. But Dan Osman did not; he died because he voluntarily gambled with his life and lost. That makes him brave—unspeakably brave—but nothing more. Was his life worth the last jump? Undoubtedly not. Was his life worth living without those jumps? Apparently not.

Junger's cardinal perception stunned me into self-reassessment. For all that mountaineering had meant to me personally, what good had all those first ascents in Alaska done anyone else?

In 2004 I talked this over with Junger (whom I had gotten to know when we were both contributing editors at *Men's Journal*) over the telephone. "Don't get me wrong," he said. "I'm in awe of climbers and other risk-takers like Osman. I can't imagine—physically or psychologically—doing what they do. But it says a lot about America that the people who died in a fishing boat got lumped in with 'adventurers.'

"I started out writing fiction, back in those days when everybody wanted to be Raymond Carver. That's why I switched to nonfiction. My fiction wasn't going to change anything in the world. I honestly believe that by writing about folks like those fishermen, I can change things for the better."

Yet over the years, as I gnawed on the bone of Junger's trenchant but tidy distinction between courage and heroism, I came to see that it was relativistically bound by time and culture. Who really could define, for all ages and all peoples, the meaning of "in the service of others"? In 2003–04, I wrote a book about the Pueblo Revolt of 1680, the lightning-strike rebellion by an alliance of Puebloans that drove the Spanish out of New Mexico for twelve years. No figures in that pageant seemed to me more thoroughly evil than the most severe of the Franciscan friars, who sought converts by the hundreds among the "pagan savages," who punished the Puebloans who continued to prac- tice their own kachina religion with torture and even execution. Yet every one of those friars was utterly convinced that he was doing the highest good. It took no small courage to be a friar in seventeenth- century New Mexico. Twenty-one Franciscans were put to death by the Puebloans on the single day on which the Revolt erupted. The priests were willing to take such risks because there was no more noble work on earth than bringing Christ into the hearts of unbeliev- ers. Here, from the Spanish point of view at the time, was courage in the service of others, in spades.

Ever since I had first read Richard Hakluyt's *Voyages*, I had been struck by a profound irony that hovered about the Renaissance expe- ditions chronicled in the dry first-person accounts Hakluyt gathered. Some historian has estimated that on any given voyage to the New World in the sixteenth or early seventeenth centuries, a sailor stood a 1-in-3 chance of not coming back alive. (That makes Himalayan mountaineering seem as safe as a sandbox in comparison!) Hakluyt's writers indeed make frequent reference to the "adventurers." The term consistently applies, however, not to the sailors who went to sea, but to the financiers in London and Bristol who bankrolled the expe- ditions. In Renaissance terms, it was they who took the real risks.

After my freelance writing became a viable way to make a living, in 1982, I had the privilege of participating in all kinds of nonclimbing adventures, either on assignment for magazines or as research for books. Skiing up Snaefellsjökull in Iceland with Jon Krakauer in win- ter; prowling through newly discovered caves in Belize in which the

Maya had performed human sacrifices in the ninth century; hiking up 20,000-foot Quehuar in the Andes to excavate Inca mummies sacrificed in the fifteenth century; spending ten days among the endangered Suyá people (who number only 180) in Brazil's Mato Grosso, a tribe that has been visited by fewer than twenty Westerners; seeking out undiscovered Aboriginal rock art in northern Australia; retracing the World War I front in the Dolomites of Italy; finding 2,000-year-old vestiges of the myrrh and frankincense trail in eastern Yemen; exploring the uninhabited coast of Edgeøya in Svalbard, teeming with polar bears, in quest of a Russian survival epic from the eighteenth century; trying to determine the fate of the visionary vagabond of the Southwest, Everett Ruess, who was murdered in 1934; rediscovering lost Apache camps in the Sierra Madre of northern Mexico; even getting stranded in China during the Tiananmen Square massacre in 1989—these are among the many happy or provocative adventures in which I have taken part during the last twenty-three years.

Have such exploits, though, genuinely replaced mountaineering in my life? It would be dishonest to say yes. Even the hairiest of those trips—rafting New Guinea's Tua-Purare rapids, an aerial bombardment of rocks by defenders of sacred tombs in Mali—have never come close to the sustained razor-edge tension of expeditions such as Huntington and Dickey. Ironically, the closest call I've had in the last quarter-century—a very close call indeed—came suddenly, in the midst of an otherwise uneventful day, in 1996 in Mexico's Copper Canyon. On assignment for Smithsonian, in a minivan, along with a photographer and two young American hitchhikers we had just picked up, I was being chauffeured by Carlos, a twenty-four-year-old tour guide out of Chihuahua City, on a narrow dirt road winding down a steep canyon toward the ex-mining town of Batopilas.

We had been on the lookout for Tarahumara Indians in native garb, and now one such fellow appeared, hiking up the road toward a festival. We crept past him at ten miles an hour. Carlos stared just a little too long in the rearview mirror—and drove off the road on the inside bend of a hairpin. I yelled, "Carlos, what are you doing?," but it was too late. The heavy vehicle plunged sideways, tilting to 45 degrees, skidding toward the void. Later I would see that the slope below us yawned 400 feet to the river, the first forty feet overhanging. In that careening instant, I thought, *Christ, this is it, we're dead.* And then the car stopped, teetering within inches of the plunge. We piled out of the uphill doors. Shortly I discovered that the right rear tire, scraping a groove through the roadside dirt, had collided with the upper edge of an old stone wall buried there, the vestiges of the donkey track that had preceded the road. Like a crack gymnast on dismount, the vehicle had stuck the landing on six inches of unmortared stone wall.

Two hours later, my hands were still trembling. Eventually, however, we went on with the journey and the assignment. What, in the long run, stood I to learn from that fluky escape? Never to let myself be driven by a twenty-four-year-old, no matter how cautious and responsible Carlos had seemed in the previous days? Never to drive down steep canyons? Never to leave the safety of my bed? (The stern injunction of a medieval Icelandic poem offers faint comfort: "Who travels widely needs his wits about him./The stupid should stay at home.")

No, the adventures of my writing career have not replaced the passion for mountaineering that waned in my mid-thirties. But they have given me something mountaineering never did.

Like most climbers, I had become a culturally insensitive and incurious traveler. When Sharon talked me into spending January of 1973 in England and Scotland, at first I sneered, "What are we going to do there? Look at cathedrals?" (I ended up enthralled with the cathedrals of Salisbury, Winchester, York, Wells, and half a dozen other medieval towns.) As mentioned before, at the age of thirty-eight I had never been to Europe. By now I've made well over a hundred trips to the Continent, most of them on assignment.

I needed, I think, to lose my monomaniacal passion for mountain walls to discover an interest in other peoples. The pattern is characteristic of hard-core climbers. It is no accident that in so many classic Himalayan expedition narratives, the porters are reduced to faceless "coolies," at first grinning cheerfully under their monstrous loads, then predictably going on strike, before the liaison officer harangues them back to their duties. Even among the Sherpas who perform so much of the real mountaineering on Himalayan peaks (and who take a disproportionate percentage of the risks), few emerge from those books as fully rounded characters.

For me today, the ideal adventure combines difficult travel of my own devising into the heart of a cultural mystery in a remote place. In my beloved Southwest, it is not the canyons themselves, however beautiful, that set the hook of my fascination: it is the imperishable enigma of the Anasazi (and Mogollon and Fremont) ruins and rock art that I keep finding in the strangest places.

During glum, reflective moments, I have sometimes brooded on the question of what mountaineering cost me, rather than what it gave me. To be sure, climbing bestowed on me, in the persons of Matt Hale, Ed Ward, and Jon Krakauer, the three most important and lasting friendships of my adult life. But what other friendships have I let wither and die, because nothing so dramatic as mountaineering ever bound me to those others?

In my narcissism, what opportunities for love and compassion have I let slip through my fingers? Whom might I have helped or comforted, had my own "needs" not come first? In particular—and these are dark and scary waters for me—I wonder whether I might have been a better husband to Sharon had I not been such a fanatic climber. And a better son to my parents.

Whatever the traumas that ensued from Lisa's pregnancy when we were seventeen, I did, I think, make my peace with my father before his death in 1990, and with my mother, who is still going strong at eighty-seven. No matter what kinds of failings I might wish, at my most self-serving, to impute to their parenting, I never had reason to doubt that they were proud of me, loved me, and wanted the best for me. Not every child can say as much.

Yet still, forty-four years after Lisa's abortion, I find it onerous to return to Bluebell Avenue, even for a short visit. My three siblings somehow sidestepped the miasma of familial ambivalence that assails me on every trip to Boulder. All three left home for college, grad school, or jobs, but all three eventually returned to Boulder to live. Alan's house stands only a block from where we grew up; Jon's (or

Jonny's, as I still think of my younger brother), only about a mile away. My sister, Jenny, moved in with my mother in 1997 to take care of her, only to have the roles reversed when she fell ill with emphysema hideously exacerbated by a rare protein deficiency that runs in our family (and that we discovered only with her illness). Jenny died in March 2004, at age fifty-seven. Even during her last illness, I could not rid myself of the regressive panic that settles upon my spirit every time I walk through the door on Bluebell Avenue. At the moment of her death, I was on assignment in New Mexico.

Sometimes, during an author interview, I will throw out the pat claim that writing has taken the place of mountaineering in my life. And each time, I know that this is a fib.

I am, I would like to think, the most compulsive writer I know. But compulsion is different from fanaticism. At home in Cambridge, I write every day. Yet that act is shot through not so much with the satisfaction of achievement, but with guilt at not achieving more. (My father at Harvard, with his differential equations . . .) If I write 2,000 words in the morning, I feel guilty for knocking off in the afternoon. In the 1980s, when I took every assignment I could get my hands on, thus often working on two or even three pieces at once, as I wrote one article I would feel guilty for not writing the other one at the same time.

When I finish a book after more than a year of effort—in that supposedly cathartic moment of putting the last words on the computer screen—I do not even feel relief, let alone satisfaction or joy. Instead, a bleak fog settles over my spirit: *Now what will I do?*

No, for me writing is not at all a substitute for climbing. Instead of taking on the shape of a daring ascent, veering wildly between hope and fear, writing a book is like some endless backpacking trip. To be sure, there were good views along the way, but at the end of the trail, I throw the heavy burden of my journey to the ground and sit there, mired in ambivalence. Usually I can muster a feeble satisfaction at having completed a difficult task, and done it well. But I never feel the slightest urge—as I have on many a mountain summit—to throw my arms into the air and shout with joy.

If I have wondered what mountaineering cost me, that itself is a narcissist's dilemma. Why not ask myself instead what my climbing cost others? For the leaden agony on the faces of Ed Bernd's parents in their sticky Philadelphia apartment in August, the dawning horror on Sandy Merrihue's face as she walked into the basin of Huntington Ravine, are still before my eyes.

Joe Tasker and Peter Boardman were among the cream of the British Himalayan crop in the 1970s and early 1980s, pioneering gutsy alpine routes without Sherpa support on such fierce peaks as Changabang, Kongur, and Dunagiri. In 1983, they disappeared together high on Everest's unclimbed northeast ridge.

Both men were also excellent writers. The Boardman-Tasker Prize, the most prestigious plum in mountaineering literature, honors their legacy. A few years after their disappearance, however, Maria Coffey, who had been Tasker's girlfriend for years before his death, made an unprecedented contribution to that literature. In *Fragile Edge*, Coffey, who had never been a serious climber herself, writes her side of the story, about waiting at home and worrying, about living with a man she loves, but who loves mountains more than her. The memoir is candid and unblinking, for Coffey had to come to terms with a packet of recent love letters she found in a trunk of Tasker's belongings, addressed to a woman Coffey scarcely knew existed.

In 2003, Coffey published *Where the Mountain Casts Its Shadow*, a rumination that carries her angle of approach to a more general plane, as she interviews dozens of survivors wounded by the losses of their hard men—mostly wives and girlfriends, but also children looking back from adulthood. The book is painful to read, but raises questions about the morality of risk-taking that have seldom before been asked in print.

Boardman and Tasker first climbed together on their brilliant two-man ascent of the west wall of Changabang in 1976. Each man wrote a good book about that expedition. Near the end of the trip, with the ascent safely tucked in their pockets, the two men underwent an encounter that must have been harrowing in the extreme, and that had haunted me ever since I read the two men's books.

Visiting the base camp of an Italian expedition on a neighboring peak, Boardman and Tasker find an American woman sitting silently in the tent. Her name is Ruth Erb. She is, it turns out, a member of a team trying to climb Dunagiri. As Boardman recounts the tale in *The Shining Mountain*, he wonders to himself: "Why was the woman next to us the only American here? Where were the others?" At last Erb speaks, in a soft voice:

> "We had an accident," she said.
> "I'm sorry to hear that," said Joe. "Was anybody hurt?"
> "Yes, four of us were killed three days ago. I'm the only one left."
> Slowly her words penetrated our bemused confusion of fatigue and elation. I winced as if I had been slapped in the face. Had we heard correctly? Her voice seemed so calm, so measured, it seemed to belie the content of her words.
> "Was anyone related to you?" asked Joe.
> "Yes, my husband."

In the end, Boardman and Tasker volunteer to climb to the bodies of the four victims, who had fallen to their deaths high on Dunagiri, to bury them in a crevasse and retrieve personal belongings—a deed of humanity apparently beyond the nerve or willingness of the Italians. At the site of the accident, Boardman fights back tears, and Tasker comforts him. They carry out the grim interment in ice. There is an awkward exchange:

> "I suppose we ought to say a prayer or something," I said.
> We had never discussed religion or beliefs before.
> "We'll stop for some moments," said Joe.

This vivid vignette necessarily gives us only a glimpse of the unspeakable ordeal Ruth Erb had endured. Ever since first reading *The*

Shining Mountain, some twenty-five years ago, I had fantasized about what it must have been like for Erb to live with her tragedy—both there on the glacier, and in the years to come. A curt note in the *American Alpine Journal* recorded the details of the catastrophe. As far as I know, Ruth Erb never wrote about that expedition gone wrong. The deepest griefs, perhaps, inevitably remain private ones.

V. S. Pritchett once said that a writer stops living at twenty-five, then devotes the rest of his years to writing about the first twenty-five. An exaggeration, one hopes: yet one of the consolations of growing older is the process of sifting through the past, seeking clues that one was too busy to notice as they flew by.

I had written about Ed Bernd's death a number of times: in three separate journal articles, in *The Mountain of My Fear,* and in "Moments of Doubt." Every time I gave my Huntington slide show, I had to retell the accident in the night, and its harrowing aftermath.

I had, however, no slide show from the First Flatiron. "Moments of Doubt" was the only time I had written about Gabe Lee. In some sense, he had remained a secret.

Seven or eight years ago—more than a decade and a half after "Moments of Doubt"—I realized that no matter how vivid my memory of Gabe's fall was, I had never really gotten to know Gabe as a person. I realized further that I had no clear idea how Gabe's death had affected the friends and relatives who had cared about him more than I did.

Brooding upon that long-ago event, I was seized with the impulse to rediscover Gabe, to wade into the ripples that must still be spreading outward from his demise. In the year 2000, I finally acted on that urge.

Thirty-nine years after Gabe's death, I was able to identify only two people still living in Boulder who had been close to him. One—a friend of my mother's—was Betty Evans, the widow of John Evans, who had been in the passenger seat in the car crash south of Houston that had killed Gabe's father. John Evans had been Gabe Sr.'s good friend and personal lawyer; in the crash, he had broken both shoulders, which healed only after a long stay in the hospital.

My mother reported that Betty would be glad to talk to me when I came to Boulder. But as the date approached, she changed her mind. The mere prospect of an interview with me, my mother reported, had stirred up the agonies of 1961 to the point that Betty was suffering sleepless nights. Eventually Betty wrote me a kind, apologetic note, explaining that she felt she could not bear to talk of Gabe.

Thus I received my first jolt, in the discovery that there are kinds of sorrow and pain that do not go away, even after nearly four decades. I began to wonder if I was getting in over my head.

My mother's other friend—call her Katherine—had been the Lees' live-in housekeeper for several years during Gabe's adolescence. I knew that, after Gabe's death, Katherine had refused ever again to set foot in my parents' house, but I attributed her avoidance to a kind of superstition.

My mother gave me Katherine's address. I wrote her, asking for a meeting, and offering, if she wanted it, a detailed explanation of how the accident had happened. Instead of responding, Katherine called my mother, who then called me, unsettled by the vehemence of the former housekeeper's reaction. Katherine, it seems, was furious with me for having had the nerve to ask that we might meet. In a voice charged with emotion, she told my mother that she would not talk to me, would not even answer my letter. As for my replaying the accident, Katherine already knew what had happened. She claimed that at her urging I had come by to explain Gabe's fall the day after the memorial service. (I have no recollection of having done so.) After all the years of dwelling upon what I said, she had reduced the accident to a simple scenario. I had thrown the rope down to Gabe. She knew enough about climbing to know you should never do that. The leader, the person on top, was the one responsible.

Clearly, then, Katherine blamed me for Gabe's death. She was offended by my intention eventually to write, as I had promised in my letter, "a testament of regret and apology to [Gabe's] loved ones, for holding life too cheap at eighteen." If I wanted peace of mind, Katherine scolded my mother, I should pray.

Katherine's anger stung me. I knew it was futile to make another overture. I had to accept the fact that she would live out the rest of her days convinced of the truth of an utterly garbled version of what had unfolded on the fifth pitch that July day in 1961. And I was stunned to imagine Katherine having lived all those years, not with Betty Evans's pain, but in a smoldering rage against me.

By the time I arrived in Boulder in May 2000, then, I was discouraged, and not a little daunted by the passions my search had already stirred up. I scarcely knew where to start.

I decided to pay a visit to the high school. As I walked through the front door of the stolid flagstone building (erected in 1937)—an odd cross between art deco and Midwestern gothic—I realized it was the first time I had been inside Boulder High since I had graduated a month before Gabe's fall. There in the foyer, unchanged by time, stood the dusty trophy cases, hallowing forgotten athletic battles. To the left, the dark auditorium, on whose stage every day during last period I had sat in the cello section while we mangled Mendelssohn's Hebrides Overture and Beethoven's Fifth.

Even the musty smell of the hallways was the same. Suddenly I was washed by a wave of Proustian remembrance—but in place of wistful longing, I felt only a shudder of relief at having escaped the confines of this asylum.

I found the principal's office, explained that I was an alumnus, promised vaguely that I intended to write something about my high school days, and was granted free run of the place. In the library I found my senior yearbook, *Odaroloc* (Colorado spelled backward). I had long since misplaced or thrown out my own copy. Leafing through its pages, I was plunged back into 1961. Dressed like Santa, there was Donna Akers, Miss Merry Christmas, forever radiant and virginal at eighteen. There was handsome, brooding Jim Lackey, all-conference end. Sly, sharp-witted Lynn Kuykendall, who would stay in Boulder and become a lawyer, was Most Likely to Succeed. Dewy-eyed Sharon Shackleford was the Best All-Around Senior. Hulking Darryl

Craft and voluptuous Janice Farrow won Best Smiles. As if those were not laurels enough, Craft was voted Cub Sweetheart, Farrow Homecoming Queen. There was my buddy Paul, the smirking Class Clown. I was startled to find my own portrait staring out of *Odaroloc*, as Boy of the Month for November. (Was it my straight-A average that had won me the nod? The reward was lunch at the Boulder Elks Club four Wednesdays in a row.)

And there were Gabe and I on the tennis team, posed with rackets in hand before the net. In lieu of a uniform, I seemed to be wearing Bermuda shorts. Gabe stood on the far right, his shy smile fixed on his face. We had finished the season five and two, losing to Aurora and Sterling, good for third place in the conference—a hell of a lot better than Jim Lackey's football Panthers had done, at one and nine (with five shutouts), or the basketball team, which finished two and sixteen.

On a nearby page, I was surprised to see Gabe, the same shy smile in place, wielding a 3-wood as part of the golf team. I had forgotten that Gabe even played golf. He was flanked by a promising sophomore named Hale Irwin.

Those hours spent inside Boulder High brought my senior year flooding back, in all its insipid detail. But I was no closer to rediscovering Gabe than when I had set out on my quest.

From Boulder, I drove to Estes Park to visit a legendary boot repairer and character named Steve Komito. In high school I had climbed once or twice with Komito, who was three years older than I, but I hadn't seen him since. A friend, however, had told me that Komito had been one of the rescuers on the scene below the First Flatiron.

While I talked to him, Komito slaved away in his cluttered shop, packing up rehabilitated boots to mail back to their owners. I asked him if he still climbed. He answered with a line I knew he must have used before: "Nowadays I only do easy climbs with pretty women, or pretty climbs with easy women."

Komito remembered getting the call from a fellow Rescue Grouper, driving to the Bluebell Canyon shelter, and running up the trail to the base of the Flatiron. "The first person I saw was you," he said, "sitting on the ground, your head in your hands, crying. Gabe was not far away, with the rope all tangled about him.

"None of us dared to touch his body, until a fat policeman arrived, out of breath. He turned Gabe over. There was a huge, gaping hole in his skull. The sight sickened me awfully, but the policeman just said, 'Well, he's for sure dead.' I helped carry the body out, but I don't remember that very well.

"I couldn't imagine a kid going through what you went through and ever climbing again. It was several weeks before I myself could climb again. Then I heard about you on Huntington in '65, and I thought, 'My God, he got back into it.'"

Prompted by my visit home, my brother Alan handed me another disturbing piece of the puzzle. He recalled that the day after the accident, I had recruited him to hike back up to the Flatiron with me to retrieve my daypack. There we were surprised to find the blood-stained rope in a snarled heap.

Not only did I coil up the rope to carry home, but, Alan insisted, I spent some time explaining to my brother how climbing worked, showed him a few bouldering moves, and urged him to take up the pastime himself. "You said," Alan remembered, "that not to go ahead and climb again would be to admit that you hadn't carefully weighed the risks beforehand. But you had weighed the risks, and you knew what had happened was part of the game."

I have absolutely no memory of that fool's errand on July 10, or of my behavior at the scene of the accident, but I am sure Alan's vignette is true to life. Could there be a better textbook example of denial (at the time) and repression (in the years afterward)? Squirming with shame at the callous eighteen-year-old Alan had dredged up, I plucked a corroborating detail out of the muddle of my memory.

For months after Gabe's death, I remembered, I had kept the rope coiled up on a shelf in my father's woodworking shop, adjacent to my childhood bedroom. I believe that I even harbored the fantasy of washing the blood out of the rope and using it again, before my father convinced me to throw it away.

Through Betty Evans, I got in touch with Gabe's sister, Marian, who lived in Seattle. She had been fifteen at the time of her brother's death. In response to my note, Marian sent me a heartfelt, two-page handwritten epistle that delivered another jolt. Marian, I learned, had been waiting thirty-nine years for me to get in touch with her. A friend in Seattle had tipped her off to "Moments of Doubt" after it had appeared in the December 1980 issue of *Outside*. She had read the piece in a breathless rush, hungry for resolution, only to end up dismayed. "I must say," she wrote, "I felt you had little regard for my family's feelings." Yet that dismay was now tempered by my overture: "David—I am grateful you have the courage to contact us."

In Seattle, for seven hours straight Marian and I talked, first in a quiet, seaside park, then, toward evening, in a waterfront restaurant. By the end, we were both wrung dry.

One of the questions that had pricked me during the previous few years was what had happened to Gabe's mother when all three children were young. As my rendezvous with Marian had approached, I began to fear that the answer would involve matters dark and dysfunctional.

Now, with extraordinary candor, Marian detailed an estrangement between her parents, a divorce, and a fierce custody battle that played itself out in a scenario more lurid than any I could have invented. The breach had climaxed in 1953, when Gabe was ten, Martin nine, Marian seven. Their mother had left Boulder, and the children had had little contact with her during the next seven years. In 1960, however, just months before their father's death, their mother had moved back to Boulder. Martin and Marian had refused to speak to her, but Gabe was in the process of attempting a rapprochement.

I had not even remembered what Gabe Sr. had done for a living. His income, Marian told me, came from the family business in Texas, buying and leasing oil rights. He was also a passionate private pilot. "Dad was kind of a misfit," Marian mused. "He loved his family, but he was a loner, like Saint-Exupéry. The only time he was happy was when he was flying."

Marian recalled the day the children learned of their father's death in Texas. "It just sucked the life out of us. We knew it had really happened, but we didn't want to see Dad's body. Gabe didn't cry. I may have cried—I can't remember. The three of us never sat down and talked to each other." A tremor came into Marian's voice. "If Gabe were alive today, we would get together and talk about it.

"Mom came to Dad's funeral. She came up to me with her arms open, crying. I turned and got into the limousine."

After the funeral, Gabe's aunt, who lived on a farm outside Boulder, assumed legal charge of the children. "She hired a series of people to take care of us," Marian said. "None of them worked out."

The brunt of Marian's revelations was to overwhelm me with a new awareness of the burden Gabe had carried around with him after March 1961, of the turmoil he was keeping barely in check when, on his return to school, he had brushed aside my feeble words of consolation, blurting out, "That's okay. When can we go climbing?"

At eighteen, I was too obtuse, as well as too inexperienced, to apprehend the link between Gabe's loss and the way he climbed after March. I simply thought he had suddenly become more skillful and nervier on rock. Only years later did I begin to wonder whether Gabe's newfound skill had been born of desperation. I would never believe he was suicidal: the "No! Oh, no!" that rang out as his last words was proof of that. Yet there is a fine line in climbing between the bold and the self-destructive.

Marian concurred. "I can believe Gabe took more risks after Dad's death. I thought he was distracted, disturbed—it was as if he had something clamped to his back. I had the feeling that he knew he wasn't going to make it—to take care of Martin and me, go off to college. It was more than he could bear."

The sun was westering over Puget Sound, as we sat side-by-side on a metal bench. Thoughtless in their late-spring play, kids cavorted a few yards away. Now Marian recalled July 9. "The birthday party was at my aunt's. I remember her standing in the kitchen, on the telephone. She listened for a minute, then cried out, 'Oh, my God, no! No! No! No!'

"Win Kinsley, who was a friend of our family, came out and sat with Martin and me and started telling jokes. I know he meant well, but . . . Later the Kinsleys took us to Wisconsin for the summer—to play around in the water and forget everything."

Marian was taken out of Boulder High and sent to a private school in Steamboat Springs, then to a school in Switzerland. "I remember a school assembly where they sang 'Climb Every Mountain,' from *The Sound of Music*. It was supposed to be inspirational, but it reduced me to tears."

Gabe's funeral was in Houston, where he was buried beside his father. (All these years, I had assumed Gabe's grave lay in Boulder.) Since 1961, Marian had never visited the cemetery. "I believe in an afterlife," she told me. "I believe Dad and Gabe are both somewhere, and something is stopping them from coming through. I went to a spiritualist church in San Francisco once, where they contact the dead. It didn't work.

"They're in those graves in Houston. Their bones are all broken up. I think of that often when I'm going to sleep. That isn't really them, though."

Gradually over the years, Marian accepted her losses and got on with life. Then she came upon "Moments of Doubt."

On our park bench facing west over the ocean, we had already been talking for hours. Marian's voice possessed an extraordinary range of feeling: by turns, she had sounded rueful, amused, bitter, hopeful, and stricken. Several times her eyes had watered. Now, as she narrowed her gaze in a glare, she turned on me the full force of the anguish and resentment my essay had provoked.

She began by paraphrasing several lines from the piece, which read: "'Attached to the memory of our day on the First Flatiron was not only fear, but guilt and embarrassment. . . . [T]he humiliation . . . lingered with me in the shape of a crime or a moral error, like getting a girl pregnant.'

"When I read this," Marian spat, "I wanted to vomit. David! I lost a father. I lost a brother. How could you compare this to something so trivial as getting a girl pregnant?"

I was speechless. I thought about telling Marian about Lisa, but kept my silence. "It was not a sign of someone who's thought about guilt," Marian went on. "I think it was a sort of literary thing. I was really hurt and angry."

She looked away, out across the water, then continued in a subdued voice: "You really did it. It had sort of healed over, but you opened the wound. You gouged it open. For weeks, I walked around in a daze. I would reread your piece and cry.

"I wished you had come to us and said, 'I want to talk to you about what happened before I write about Gabe.'"

There was nothing I could do but hear Marian out. In the aftermath of reading my essay, she had dug out her old copy of the *Daily Camera* clipping. In it, a number of witnesses were identified: the Rescue Group chairman, the Mountain Park patrolman who claimed he had tried to warn us off the cliff, two members of the crew who had helped find the body. For months, she had tried to contact these men by mail, seeking a further explanation of exactly how the accident had happened.

"Why didn't you write to me?" I asked.

"I was gathering ammunition against you."

Because she had never climbed, Marian had not understood my account in "Moments of Doubt" of the snafus that had led up to Gabe's fall. Yet images from my essay haunted her for years. "When I read about him taking the lifeline off and wrapping it all around him," she said, "it broke my heart. It's as if he had made a cocoon and he couldn't get out of it. Like his sarcophagus."

Half an hour later, Marian consented to my replaying the fifth pitch in all its dolorous detail. I used my pad and pen to sketch our positions, the mechanics of the rope, the lay of the cliff. When I was done, I said, "To me, the accident wasn't anybody's fault. It was just terribly bad luck—the rope getting stuck under that downward-pointing prong. Even to this day, I'm not sure what we should have done differently."

From the look on her face, I knew Marian wasn't buying it. "Do you still need to blame someone?" I asked.

"Yes."

"Who?"

She took a slow breath. "I blame you thirty percent, I blame Gabe thirty percent, and I blame God thirty percent. Maybe the other ten percent is luck."

Yet mixed in with Marian's anger was a certain compassion for me. "Maybe now that you're thinking about Gabe again, it will help you to unveil that secret in you—how you dealt with it, and how you didn't deal with it. You're harboring some deep sadness, just as we are."

Marian had given me her brother Martin's address. From Seattle, I flew to San Francisco, then drove to Berkeley. Martin greeted me at the door of an attractive 1930s house he had renovated, a few blocks south of the campus.

He proved as even-tempered as Marian was volatile. Nor, it seemed, had he nursed a resentment against me all these years. I was surprised to learn that Martin, too, had climbed, though never with Gabe: his own partner was a classmate from France.

There were odd divergences between Martin's memories and his sister's. "I was the one who drove you two up to Bluebell Canyon," he said. "I wanted to use the car that day." According to Martin, the news came to him not at the birthday party at his aunt's, but as he walked home from his French friend's house. "I heard a siren. There was a crowd of people outside our house. A neighbor told me about the accident. I walked off, lost in my own fog. I needed to sit down and take it in, but Win Kinsley tried to keep me from wandering off—we got in his car and drove somewhere. He wanted to reassure me that it was okay to break down and cry."

As a climber, Martin knew at once that the *Daily Camera* reporter had gotten the accident all wrong. "Yet there was always this mystery. Why did you unrope? I figured it must have been an impulsive thing. I was caught up primarily in the horror of Gabe's falling off the cliff.

"It was a tumultuous time for him. There were a lot of scary things going on in his life, but he wasn't suicidal."

We talked through dinner, drinking red wine. Martin himself exuded a philosophical calm. "Gabe and I weren't close, but down the road . . . What would he have become? I wish I'd known him."

That last phrase resonated for me. Not "known him better"— known him, period. In the camouflage of his reticence, Gabe had eluded us all.

"Did he ever have a girlfriend?" I asked.

"Not that I knew about."

In a fashion quite different from Marian's, Martin, too, had been shaken by reading "Moments of Doubt." "I never cried about Gabe's death until I read your piece," he confessed. "Basically, I cried in empathy for his last moments."

The biggest surprise for me was Martin's reaction to his father's death. "It came as a shock," he said, "but also as a kind of release. He was an overbearing son of a bitch. I wanted his approval and love, but if I brought him my best report card, he was ho-hum about it. He didn't have the capacity to get into his emotions—except anger."

Then, out of nowhere, Martin proffered a revelation that twisted deeper the knife of my guilt. "I think Gabe had pretty much given up on our father in disgust. He would never be Gabe's role model, never be someone to give praise and affection.

"I always thought Gabe looked up to you. I know he admired you, as a tennis player, a student, a climber, a person. Maybe that had something to do with his taking chances."

The pivotal moment on the First Flatiron had come when, as we stewed in the ambiguity of our predicament, Gabe had called out, "I think I can climb down to it!" In her perceptiveness, Marian had nailed me on the point, explaining why she had blamed me all these years. "Shit," she had said bitterly, "you let him do the dirty work."

By now, I had speculated for decades that Gabe's sudden discovery of skill and nerve on rock had been linked to his despair. But before that moment at Martin's table, it had never occurred to me that one reason Gabe might have volunteered to lead us out of danger was the desire to impress me, to win the approval his father could not give.

Before I had left Boulder in May 2000, Jon Krakauer had suggested that we reclimb the route on the First Flatiron together. Somehow, the idea had never occurred to me. What better way, though, to rediscover what had happened in 1961?

Perusing Richard Rossiter's guidebook, *Rock Climbing the Flatirons*, I was bewildered as to just which line Gabe and I had chosen. Rossiter's topos indicated fully ten different routes on the left side of the First, ranging in difficulty from 5.4 to 5.9. Only one of them had been put in before 1961, and it meandered about so much I was sure it was not Gabe's and my itinerary.

In the middle of the night before our outing, I was on the verge of calling it off. Despite taking sleeping pills at midnight and 2:30 A.M., I lay wide awake well past 3:00. It was not that I feared the difficulty of the climb: as far as I could remember, nothing Gabe or I had scaled that day had been harder than 5.6 (unless it was that unseen slab where he had slipped), and Jon was in the best rock-climbing shape of his life. It was rather that the prospect of retracing that fatal line spooked me, as if to do so were to taunt the very Furies who thirty-nine years before had chosen that same precipice on which to demonstrate their pitiless severity.

By morning, groggy after three hours of fitful sleep, I had decided to hike up to the base and make my decision there. It was a sunny, breezy day, not unlike that Sunday in July so long ago. Despite my apprehensiveness, the beauty of the mesa with its grasses, lush and green after a wet April, seduced me back to a certain tranquillity.

At the foot of the cliff, I could not remember where Gabe and I had started. The chief feature I recalled was the left-facing corner that had stretched for hundreds of vertical feet, gradually nudging us left. Jon and I chose the most prominent such dihedral and started up.

Nothing quite clicked, though I could see plainly why our soft-iron knife blades had been useless on this terrain. Placing wired stoppers and cams in shallow grooves, Jon was able to get in good protection. Because our rope was 200 feet long—fifty feet longer than my GoldLine in 1961—Jon's and my belay stances would not have coincided with Gabe's and mine.

Suddenly, in the second half of our third pitch, 450 feet up, as I surmounted a bulge, I was assailed with déjà vu—or with a sensation even more electric, for it was no mere illusion that I had been here before. I stood beside the bucket-shaped depression in which I had wedged my body to belay Gabe. Above me arched the inside corner that Gabe had followed; eighty feet up I saw the overhang that had bent his course leftward.

By sheer happenstance, Jon had eschewed the corner in favor of a sequence of small holds on the face to the left. As I approached his belay, I shouted, "This is it! This is our fifth pitch!" And when I joined him, I saw, only three feet above his head, a downward-pointing flake. I made one more move and seized the flake with my left hand. "This is the goddamned prong!"

My feelings were in contradictory riot. I felt a wild exultation, as though I had solved a problem that had afflicted my life. At the same time, my nerves danced in a jittery angst, and in the back of my throat, I tasted a residue of the nausea that had wrenched me here so long ago. I explored the prong that had caused all the trouble, sliding my fingers beneath it, probing the groove that was just the right width to pinch shut on a $\frac{3}{8}$-inch rope.

I felt almost as though Gabe were with us—though even as I tried to picture him arriving here, freeing the rope, draping it over his shoulder, and starting up, the image dissolved in my mind.

Jon led the next, short pitch as well, and as he moved smoothly upward, placing a pair of pieces in folded cavities of sandstone, I was acutely aware that he was moving across the very ground where Gabe had lost his purchase on the world. When I came up second, I held my breath as I made the delicate step where I guessed Gabe must have come off. It was the hardest move on the route.

Jon's belay was on the same generous, rounded shelf where I had sat down to wait for Gabe. As he tied me in to the anchor, I asked, "How would you have felt soloing that?"

"It would be scary," he said. "It's not that hard—maybe 5.6—but there's nothing positive there." No horns to wrap one's fingers around, no clean-cut ledges to seize.

For fifteen minutes we stood there as I stared around me. Hanging off my anchor, I could see the other ledge below and to the left, from which Gabe had set out to free the snag.

"What should we have done?" I asked Jon. "After all the experience we've had since, what would we do now in that situation?"

Jon did not answer at once, so I said, "When all's said and done, we should have sat here and yelled for help."

"You couldn't do that, wait for a rescue. You wouldn't do it today."

"Since it's so easy above here, we could have just left the rope and soloed up."

"You couldn't do that, either. You don't leave your rope on a climb."

There was a further puzzlement. Ten feet farther left on Gabe's belay ledge, a pine sprouted out of a crack, its girth sufficient that I knew the tree had been there in 1961. Could Gabe not have tied his end of the rope to that tree, then tried to improvise a diagonal rappel to the slab?

"You know how it is," Jon countered. "You're in a bind, it's not clear what to do, you make a snap decision. We've all done that a hundred times."

In my head, I heard Gabe's words again: *I think I can climb down to it!*

Half an hour later, we were setting up the rappel from the summit off the overhanging back side of the Flatiron. And when my feet touched the ground, I tasted the same grateful relief I had known at the end of every climb of my life, as well as something else: a draught of catharsis, laced with enduring sorrow.

For me, climbing was always about transcendence. In the spell that risk and fear, barely tamed by skill and nerve, cast over me, I found a blissful escape from the petty pace of normal life, from the death-by-banality of Boulder High and Bluebell Avenue.

I had first sought that transcendence with Lisa—only to have her pregnancy and abortion turn our love to ashes. Burdened with secret humiliation, I turned to Gabe and to rock climbing.

Yet in the hectic impatience I have carried with me throughout life, in the fact that lasting contentment has eluded me all these years, I would judge that in the long run, my quest for transcendence failed. If so, the failure was rooted first in Gabe's death, and then four years later, in Ed Bernd's. Those two fatal plunges must have branded my unconscious with the lesson that ascent was inextricably woven up with hubris, that to attempt transcendence was to have one's wings melt off in the sun. And thus, that the petty pace was what life was ultimately about. One must learn to live with what Freud called "ordinary human unhappiness."

I would guess also that, in the depths of a quandary that promised to be long-lasting, whose intricate hopelessness at eighteen I could not even glimpse, Gabe, too, sought transcendence on the rocks. That impulse cost him his life—along with bad luck, or the Furies, or whatever we call the fate that made his shoe slip from its wrinkle of sandstone.

"Why do you climb?" was the question I had sought to confront in "Moments of Doubt," recast in the form, "Is it worth the risk?" The answer I would offer now is different from the one I proclaimed in 1980. I would even say that the question is meaningless, for if it pretends to embrace the loss of Gabe, it has no way of reckoning the grief of Marian, the stoic truce of Martin.

The morning after my seven-hour meeting with Marian in Seattle, we had planned a wrap-up session before I left town. On the phone, however, we agreed to take a rain check. Marian confessed to an utter exhaustion in the wake of our exchange.

"Me, too," I said. "The whole thing yesterday stirred up stuff I hardly knew was there."

"I know," said Marian. There was a pause. "I think you're still trying to figure out what the secret is."

Today, at age sixty-two, I am far prouder of my best climbs in Alaska than of anything else I have done in life. And there, on those unexplored precipices, I tasted the most piercing moments of joy I would ever be granted—our forty quiet minutes on the summit of Mount

Huntington, with the sun coming up in the northeast over Deborah; the breathless moment in the middle of the night as Ed solved the crux pitch on Shot Tower; the last pitches in the blizzard on Mount Dickey, as, leading with our only ice axe and crampons, I knew I had found the way out of the maze of the great wall. Those, and countless other smaller moments spread over more than four decades, each suffused with its own starburst of joy.

In the human heart, however, there are nobler feelings than pride. And there are more important things in life than joy.

Acknowledgments

In contemplating and then writing this memoir of a life in climbing, I owe a debt of gratitude to every friend with whom I ever roped up. In particular, the many partners on my thirteen expeditions to Alaska and the Yukon gave me the happiest days I ever spent in the mountains. Of that number, three have remained the closest friends of my adult life: Matt Hale, Ed Ward, and Jon Krakauer. During the last decade, those three, along with our mutual buddies Chris Gulick and Chris Wejchert, have kept me climbing, albeit at a far more "mellow" level than in my tigerish youth. In various permutations during different years, our Gang of Six has assembled quite a few times at Red Rocks in Nevada, as well as once in the Italian Dolomites, where the climbing we have done together was merely the centerpiece of a week or two of imperishable hanging out and reminiscing.

Other mountaineers with whom I've done little or no climbing aided me greatly by opening their lives and feelings to me as a magazine writer. From their obsessions and sensibilities, so different from my own, I learned more about the climbing life than I could have simply by reflecting on my own alpine campaigns. Several of them, including Ed Viesturs and Conrad Anker, have remained good friends long after the assignment that brought us together.

If it is possible to be grateful to an organization, as opposed to its individual members, I owe much to the Harvard Mountaineering Club, whose raucous camaraderie and high ambition turned an ambivalent freshman into a serious climber. My debt to the HMC includes the wisdom and support of the club's elders, such as Adams Carter and Bradford Washburn. It was Brad who turned my HMC generation toward unclimbed challenges in Alaska.

In October 2004, by the sheerest of coincidences, a piece of my mountaineering past came full circle to intersect with the present. On a magazine assignment in New Mexico, I met John Burcham, a photographer's assistant. Burcham had climbed extensively in Alaska and knew of my ascents there. The day we met, he told me that a friend of his in Flagstaff, Arizona, had found a "very old crampon" on our route on Mount Huntington a few years before. The friend, Dan Foster, had brought the crampon home as a relic from the pioneers.

At once the wild supposition came to me: could that piece of gear be the crampon Matt Hale had stopped to tighten on July 29, 1965, leading to our roped fall together and miraculous deliverance by the nubbin, the closest call of both our lives (see p. 135)? After the New Mexico trip, Burcham mailed me a photograph of Foster's artifact. The rusty old crampon was made by Stubai; it was one of the first models to incorporate fang-like frontpoints; and its owner had replaced the original leather straps with white cloth straps. Thirty-nine years after our climb, however, neither Matt nor I could remember what crampons we had worn on Huntington. The second ascent of our route had taken place only in 1975, but after that, the route had been climbed fairly often. Could the crampon belong to some later party?

I took the photo with me when I visited Matt for Thanksgiving. We clicked through his Huntington slide show, hoping desperately for a close-up of one of Matt's crampon-clad feet—and there it was, a single picture I had shot as Matt climbed a few feet above me. The crampon was a perfect match, white cloth straps and all.

I talked to Foster over the phone, then shyly asked him if Matt and I could buy the crampon back from him. Instead, he offered to give it to us. In exchange, I would send him a first edition copy of The Mountain of My Fear, inscribed by both Matt and me.

Foster recounted finding the object in 1997. High on our west face route, he and his partners had endured a miserable bivouac in a storm that prevented their reaching the summit. Rappelling down our route the next day, they came to the anchor just above the Nose, the fierce overhang Matt had led on July 26. "Right next to the anchor," Foster told me, "there was something sticking out of the snow. I said,

'What's that?' then pulled it loose. I knew right away it was from the early era of front points. I thought it was a neat piece of history."

Foster and I figured out that the crampon must have fallen about two hundred feet from where Matt's footsteps had broken loose. At the time, Matt and I had assumed the footgear must have plunged all the way down the west face; I don't think we even looked for it, even though its loss worked a severe handicap into the rest of our trip. Instead, apparently, the crampon's points had caught on the slope, while perhaps sloughing snow had covered it. There the object had rested for thirty-two years, until Foster had stumbled upon it.

Foster had carried the crampon all the way back to Flagstaff, where he mounted it on the wall of his home. "Anybody who would listen," he said to me, "I would tell him all about it."

The crampon now hangs on Matt's wall in Alexandria, Virginia, a makeshift shrine to the single piece of gear in all our climbing days that came closest to serving as the fulcrum between life and death. For the rediscovery and generous return of that lost object, then, Matt and I extend our heartiest gratitude to John Burcham, and especially to Dan Foster.

Jon Krakauer, Matt Hale, Ed Ward, Rick Millikan, Sharon Roberts, and Susan Robertson read parts or all of my manuscript, correcting (in the case of my climbing pals) my errors of memory, as well as offering many canny suggestions. I am grateful also to Sebastian Junger for his profound distinction between courage and heroism, and for amplifying his thoughts on this critical question over the telephone. And there is no way that I can reckon my debt to John Rasmus, currently editor-in-chief of *National Geographic Adventure*, but also my editor at two previous magazines over the past twenty-five years, as well as the person who did the most to launch my freelance career, by rescuing "Moments of Doubt" from the slush pile in 1980.

My faithful agent, Stuart Krichevsky, believed in this book from the start and championed it once it was finished in exemplary fashion. His two expert assistants, Shana Cohen and Liz Coen, performed many a useful chore along the way. I feel a special warmth for Liz, who read the book chapter by chapter as I sent it in, and was kind enough to tell me how much it moved her.

At Simon & Schuster, assistant editor Johanna Li, Associate Director of Copyediting Gypsy da Silva, and copy editor Fred Chase performed their usual wizardry. With this volume, I have had the good fortune to work with one of the best editors in the business, Bob Bender, on no fewer than nine books dating back to 1993. It was Bob who, in a single piece of advice in his office a few years ago, turned my failed attempt at a very different kind of memoir into what has been the most emotionally intense and yet personally involving piece of writing I have ever done.

I am happy to say that my childhood chum Paul—by now, the only friend from Uni Hill, Baseline Junior High, or Boulder High with whom I am still in regular touch—chats with me over the phone several times a year and makes sure that we meet for coffee or beer whenever our paths cross.

The ethics of client-therapist confidentiality make me hesitate to record another acknowledgment in print. But I would be remiss not to credit the skills and empathy of Dr. George Fishman, my psychotherapist for several years just before I started work on this book, for excavating from my unconscious much of what there may be of self-understanding in these pages.

I feel deeply grateful to Gabe Lee's brother, Martin, and sister, Marian, for agreeing to talk to me thirty-nine years after I failed to talk to them after Gabe's death, and for being so honest in opening my eyes to the pain that long-ago tragedy inflicted upon them and still inflicts.

I will never find adequate words to thank my wife, Sharon Roberts, for the huge role she has played in my forging a plausible identity as a grown-up. Her love over the years, and her unflinching support for my climbing even when it scared her silly, have been incomparable gifts.

And finally, I owe a similarly incalculable debt to my mother, Janet Roberts, eighty-seven years old as this book is published, for never ceasing to care for the arrogant, alienated adolescent who left home for good at age eighteen. That she still loves me, despite all my faults and neurotic quirks, I have never doubted; and that she reads nearly everything I write is more than a wayward son has the right to expect.

Glossary

Note: Terms in **boldface** are defined elsewhere in the Glossary.

5.6, 5.8, etc. Rock climbs are rated by pure difficulty on a scale that (in the United States) now runs from 5.1 to 5.15. The rating of any given **pitch** is by subjective consensus of the various athletes who have climbed that pitch.

The history of grade ratings is something of a taxonomic comedy. Grade 5 originally meant "requiring rope and **protection,** but not direct **aid.**" (Grade 6 was for direct aid.) It was not until the late 1950s that climbers gave in to the self-evident need to subdivide the grade with decimal points, distinguishing a 5.3 route from a 5.6. The founders of this system assumed that no climb harder than 5.9 would ever be performed. The invention of 5.10 was an intellectual breakthrough that drowned out a chorus of conservative dissent. Today, the hardest climbs, at 5.15, are unimaginably more difficult than any 5.10 route.

aid-climbing. Any climbing on terrain too difficult to be tackled by means of hands and feet alone. In aid climbing, one attaches **stirrups** directly to pieces of **protection,** then climbs the stirrups rather than the rock itself.

aiguille. A sharp tower on a mountain ridge. See *gendarme.*

alpine-style. The technique of going light and fast on a big mountain, eschewing **fixed ropes,** established camps, and **load carries.** Considered better form than the slower, more gear-intensive traditional **expedition-style.**

anchor (noun). Any combination of **pitons, nuts, cams, ice screws,** and the like that secures a stance from which a climber **belays** his partner. The anchor can also be used as a **rappel** station. To anchor (verb) is to set up an anchor.

arête. A sharp, steep ridge.

bearpaw. A kind of snowshoe, smaller than normal, and oval, without an upturned toe or a tail. Better adapted to mountaineering than the traditional trail snowshoe.

belay (verb and noun). To secure one's partner by feeding the rope in or out as he climbs, with the shock of a potential fall absorbed either by a mechanical device attached to one's **waist harness,** or by passing the rope around one's back. "On belay!" is a signal called out by the belayer to indicate that he is ready to belay. "Off belay!" is the climber's signal that he has gained a stance and anchored himself to the cliff, and thus no longer needs the security of his partner's belay; the call is acknowledged by the belayer's "Belay off!"

belay seat. A nylon device, shaped like a miniature hammock, in which one sits, supporting all his weight, in a **hanging belay.**

big wall. Jargon: any cliff with more than about a thousand feet of vertical relief between base and summit.

bivouac (verb and noun). To spend the night on a mountain, (usually) without sleeping bag or tent. A bivouac tent or bivvy tent, however, is a lightweight, minimalist structure with barely enough room for two recumbent climbers. A bivouac sack, used in lieu of a bivouac tent, is simply a nylon sleeve big enough to accommodate two or three climbers; it serves mainly to keep the bivouackers relatively dry.

bolt, expansion bolt. A small, nail-like device drilled directly into the rock with a hammer. Used for **protection** or **anchor** only when no **pitons, nuts,** or **cams** can be placed.

bottoming-out. Characteristic of a crack too shallow to accept **pitons, nuts,** or **cams.**

boulder problem. A challenging route on a boulder, the top of which is usually no more than twenty feet off the ground. By "going bouldering," a climber hones his technique for longer climbs. Today, however, bouldering has become an end in itself.

cairn. A pile of rocks stacked to mark a trailless route.

cam, camming device. A kind of **nut** that can be flexed by a trigger handle to expand or contract in size. An ingenious device, invented by Ray Jardine in 1973, that has revolutionized climbing, because it works in cracks that refuse to accept **nuts.**

carabiner, 'biner. An oval snap-link made of light but strong metal, used to attach the rope to any piece of **protection** or part of an **anchor.**

chimney. A **chute** or fissure in a rock cliff broad enough to enter with one's body, but narrow enough to allow one to touch both walls. To chimney (verb) is to climb such a fissure by opposing pressure, usually feet or knees on one wall, rear end on the other, and hands alternating walls as one inches upward.

chockstone. Either a stone naturally wedged between the walls of a **chimney** or a vertical fissure, or a metal **nut** wedged in a crack to serve as a point of **protection.** Before British climbers started using machined nuts in this fashion, they often carried pocketfuls of pebbles and small stones on the **lead,** to be used as "chockstones" safeguarding the **pitch.**

chute. A narrow **couloir** or gully.

cirque. A basin formed by steep cliffs and peaks at the head of a valley.

clean, back-clean. To remove **protection** as one seconds a **pitch.** The leader back-cleans part of his own pitch to reuse his gear higher on the pitch.

climbing continuously, moving continuously. The technique of two or more climbers who, though roped up and placing the occasional piece of **protection,** do not belay each other but climb simultaneously. Used primarily on easy but dangerous **technical** terrain.

clip, unclip. To attach or detach a **carabiner** from a piece of **protection** or a rope.

clove hitch. An easily adjustable knot used to tie the climber's rope to an **anchor.**

col. A narrow mountain pass, usually between steep **couloirs** and/or sharp ridges.

cornice. A curling plume of snow and ice, formed by strong recurrent winds, that overhangs the leeward face of the mountain. Especially treacherous, for a cornice can be mistaken for the ridge crest itself, and one all too easily breaks through its insubstantial crust and plunges down the wall beneath. A double cornice is a rare but fiendish phenomenon, caused by winds so intense yet shifting that cornices form that overhang both sides of the ridge.

couloir. A steep snow gully, usually found high on a mountain.

crack system. A long series of connecting vertical cracks that thus indicates a feasible route on a rock wall.

crampons. Sets of metal spikes strapped to the bottoms of one's boots to enable climbing or hiking on ice and hard snow.

crevasse. A major crack or fissure in the surface of a glacier created by the glacier's flow over steep or uneven ground. Crevasses are typically narrow at the surface, but bulge to greater widths below. A hidden crevasse is one rendered all but invisible (and thus treacherous) after storms build a thin bridge of snow that closes the surface crack and disguises the crevasse's very existence.

crevice. A narrow, deep fissure in bedrock, to be distinguished from **crevasse.**

crump (verb and noun). Slang (possibly unique to the Harvard Mountaineering Club): to back out of a climb or trip prematurely; to get psyched out (and become correspondingly unambitious) by the danger of a climb or by foul weather.

crux. Jargon: the single hardest move on a pitch, or for the critical section of a longer route that, once climbed, turns uncertainty to success.

dihedral. A vertical corner in a rock cliff formed by adjoining walls that partially face each other. Also known as an inside corner.

direttissima. The most direct possible route on a mountain face. There is no equivalent word in English.

double-packing. Making two successive **load carries** over the same ground.

Ensolite. Closed-cell foam rubber, used mainly for sleeping pads, replacing the air mattress.

expedition-style. The traditional means of climbing a big mountain, involving stocked tent camps, **load carries,** and **fixed ropes.** See **alpine-style**.

fixed rope. A thin rope attached to **anchors** and left in place on a mountain pitch to facilitate subsequent **load carries.** The key to **expedition-style** ascents.

flake, detached flake. A thin but sizeable piece of rock, often barely attached to the mountain wall and thus in danger of being pulled loose by the climber.

flash. Jargon: to climb a route from bottom to top without a fall or hanging from any **protection** on one's first try.

frost feathers. Grotesquely intricate tendrils and "feathers" of snow, brewed up in storms, that adhere to steep, even vertical cliffs. Akin to **rime ice.**

gendarme. A steep tower of rock, usually found on a mountain ridge. See **aiguille.**

glissade (verb and noun). To slide under control down a steep snow or **scree** slope, usually by digging the edges of one's boots into the slope and slipping sideways like a skier.

go. Jargon: capable of being climbed. If a leader says, "I think it'll go," he means that he believes he can climb the pitch or stretch of ground ahead of him.

GoldLine. A twisted, three-ply nylon rope, standard gear in the 1960s and 1970s.

Grade VI. To be distinguished from the different grading system of individual pitches, such as **5.6, 5.8,** etc. Long climbs on big mountains are given a comprehensive rating of overall difficulty, ranging today from Grade I to Grade VII. During the 1960s and 1970s, Grade VI was the hardest rating, thus in some sense stamping a climb as a stellar feat.

half bag. A lightweight sleeping bag that covers only one's legs and midsection, often used in **bivouacs.**

half hitch. A knot used simply to back up another knot, preventing the end of the rope from working loose. The first half of a square or granny knot.

hanging belay. A belay position on ground too steep or smooth for the belayer to sit down or stand on his feet. Instead, he dangles a **belay seat** from his **anchor** and sits in that.

hardware. Collective term for a climber's various pieces of **protection,** ranging from **pitons** to **cams** to **ice screws** and the like.

headwall. A sizeable cliff found near the top of a mountain face.

hero loop. A small nylon **sling** used to attach the rope to a **piton** driven only partway home in a crack. By cinching the loop around the blade, rather than **clipping** in to the eye of the piton, one reduces the torque on the piton in a potential fall.

"hexcentric." A large **nut,** shaped like a piece of hexagonal tubing, used in wide cracks.

ice axe. One of the mountaineer's most essential pieces of gear. In its classic form, it consists of a metal head with adze on one side and sharpened pick on the other, a two-and-a-half-foot long shaft of wood or metal, and a sharpened metal point on the end of the shaft. Used for chopping steps in ice and snow, for **belaying,** for **self-arrests** in a fall or avalanche, for probing for hidden **crevasses,** and simply for balance (wielded like a cane) while hiking.

ice dagger, Icelite. A barbed, pointed section of L-bar aluminum, usually about two feet long, used for **protection** and **anchors** in ice or snow that is too soft or hollow for an **ice screw** and too hard for a **snow picket.** Invented by Don Jensen in 1964 for our Mount Deborah expedition.

icefall. A steep, extremely crevassed section of a glacier where the ice flows over contorted ground.

icefield. A glacier or icecap in a mountain range.

ice screw. A kind of **piton** for hard ice, threaded like a screw, rotated home as one hammers it directly into the ice.

in condition. Of snow and ice on a mountain: melted, refrozen, and stabilized sufficiently to be safe to climb.

inside corner. See **dihedral.**

Jumar (noun and verb). Brand name of the most popular mechanical ascender, used to climb ropes fixed in place, introduced in the late 1960s. A metal device that grips the rope under a downward pull, but slides easily upward, the Jumar replaced the **prusik.**

lead (verb). To climb a pitch first on the rope. A **lead** (noun) is a pitch so climbed.

line. Route on a rock wall or mountain.

load carry. A ferry of supplies across a part of the mountain or of the approach route that has previously been climbed or traversed.

Marwa "coat-hanger." A brand of ice screw, popular in the 1960s, with a very thin shaft, since discredited as unsafe.

massif. A continuous segment of a larger mountain range.

mixed ground. Terrain on a mountain where rock is mixed homogeneously with ice and snow.

moraine. Any ridge or mound of **talus** and gravel deposited by a flowing glacier.

mummy bag. A sleeping bag tapered at head and foot to fit the shape of the human body.

"nail." Slang: to pound in **pitons** on one's way up an **aid-climb.**

névé line. The line on a glacier in any given season where snow gives way to bare ice. A function of temperature and weather.

nunatak. A small outcropping where the bedrock beneath a glacier breaks the surface, forming a stony island in the surrounding sea of snow and ice.

nut. A less impactful alternative to the **piton.** A nut is an odd-shaped piece of metal, attached to a **sling** or wire, and slotted into a crack in the rock so that it holds under a downward pull. So named because the first such devices used by British climbers in the 1950s were actual machined nuts threaded with nylon **slings** to serve as **protection.**

overhand loop, overhand knot. The simplest of knots for making a loop in a rope, an over and under with a doubled hank.

parachute cord. A very thin nylon cord, used mainly for repairs and for tying equipment onto a pack frame.

peak-bagger. An epithet, slightly pejorative, for a climber more interested in reaching the most possible summits than in **technical** challenges.

perlon. A kind of nylon rope, with core and sheath design, rather than woven. Largely replaced **GoldLine.**

piece. Slang: any item of **hardware.**

pin. Slang: **piton.**

pitch. A rope-length, or partial rope-length; the terrain climbed by the leader before he stops to **anchor** and **belay.**

piton. A metal spike driven into a crack in the rock, used either as part of an **anchor** or to shorten the leader's potential fall. The piton has an eye through which it is attached by a **carabiner** to the free-running rope. An angle piton is a V-shaped spike used for especially wide cracks. A fixed piton is a piton left in place on a climb for the use of future parties, rather than removed by the **second.**

posthole. To plunge without snowshoes into deep, soft snow, up to at least the knee with each step.

prong. A small, protruding horn of rock.

protection. A collective term for all the **pitons, nuts,** and **cams** placed by the leader to shorten a potential fall.

prusik (verb and noun). To climb a rope by means of a pair of **slings** tied to the rope with a knot that grips under a downward pull, but can be loosened and slid up the rope. Before the invention of mechanical ascenders such as **Jumars,** prusiking was the only technique for climbing ropes fixed in place.

put up. Jargon: to make the first ascent (of a route on a cliff).

rappel (verb and noun). To descend a cliff by sliding down the rope, which is doubled and attached at the midpoint to an **anchor.** From the bottom of the rappel, the climber retrieves the rope by pulling one end, so that it slides through the anchoring **slings** or **carabiners** and comes loose. A body rappel (originally the only kind) is set up by running the rope between one's legs, across one hip, diagonally across the chest, over the opposite shoulder, and down the back to the hand, which is held even with the hip. The friction created by this S-shaped configuration allows the rappeler to control the pace of his descent with one hand.

rib. A shallow, protruding ridge on a face. See **arête.**

rime, rime ice. A coating of glazed ice that forms on vertical and even overhanging cliffs, plastered there by storms and winds. See also **frost feathers.**

roof. On a rock route, a section so overhanging that it juts out like a roof over one's head.

rope drag. Inordinate friction on the belay rope resulting from too many and too sharp zigs and zags as it passes from one piece of **protection** to the next.

rope up. To tie in with a partner or partners preparatory to climbing on **technical** ground.

scree. Very small stones massed in large quantities. A scree slope is a mountain shoulder or gully made up almost entirely of scree. See **talus.**

second (verb and noun). To follow a pitch led by one's partner, secured with a belay from above.

self-arrest. To stop oneself in a fall or an avalanche by lying face-down on top of one's ice axe to dig the pick into the slope.

sérac. A plume, tower, or lump of ice on the surface of a glacier or mountain slope. Particularly dangerous because it can collapse without warning.

"Slack!" The opposite of **"Up rope!"** A command to the belayer to give out rope to the climber to enable him to move more freely.

sling. A loop of nylon webbing, used for many different tasks, in particular for lengthening the distance between the piece of **protection** and the **carabiner** to minimize **rope drag.**

snow picket. A section of T-bar aluminum, usually three to five feet long, used for **protection** and **anchors** in snow too soft or loose for **ice daggers** or **ice screws.**

solo (verb and noun). To climb without a partner and (usually) without a rope or any means of self-protection. A fall while soloing is usually fatal.

spindrift. Very fine snow borne on the air, either in blowing storms or in the pummeling cloud driven ahead of an avalanche.

spot (verb and noun). As in gymnastics, to secure a person only a few feet above the spotter by raising one's arms and hoping to "catch" him if he falls off.

stirrup. A small ladder made of nylon webbing, with three or four foot loops, used to stand in when **aid-climbing.**

stopper. A particularly thin, tapering **nut.**

swami belt. A piece of nylon tubing looped three times around the climber's waist and tied tight, to which the climbing rope is then affixed. In vogue briefly during the late 1960s and 1970s, the swami belt had advantages over the traditional technique of tying in directly to the rope, but it was quickly superseded by the **waist harness.**

talus. Massed stones larger than **scree.** In the climber's sardonic epithet, a talus pile or talus heap is a peak made up almost entirely of talus and thus a boring hike.

technical, technical climbing. Any climbing difficult enough to require a rope and **protection.**

tension. A hard pull on the rope by the belayer to help his **second** up terrain he is having trouble climbing under his own power.

tent fly. A waterproof outer roof to cover a tent during storms. Manufactured to fit the tent nowadays, but in the early 1960s climbers made tent flies out of large squares of plastic sheeting.

thrutch (verb). Jargon: to climb in a ragged, half-out-of-control fashion.

top-rope (verb and noun). To belay a climber from above, rendering falls harmless. Top-rope climbing on small cliffs allows one to push one's skills to the limit.

topo. A detailed sketch of a route on a mountain.

topo maps. Extremely detailed maps with contour lines indicated, made in this country by the United States Geological Survey. Indispensable for exploring.

traverse (verb and noun). To climb a **pitch** by moving sideways or diagonally upward. Also, to cross a mountain or even a range by ascending one side and descending the opposite side.

"Up rope!" A command, usually by the **second** to his belayer, to pull in loose slack in the rope and thus reduce the length of any fall. See **"Slack!"**

verglas. A thin skin of ice overlying rock.

voie normale. The "normal," or easiest, route on a mountain, usually that of the first ascent.

waist harness, harness. A device, invented in the 1970s, worn around the waist and upper thighs, to which the climbing rope is tied. Compared to the earlier practice of tying the rope directly around one's waist or to a **swami belt,** the harness distributes the load (and the shock of a fall) in a far more comfortable—and ultimately, far safer—fashion.

whiteout. A weather condition in which fog, mist, or snowstorm renders visibility almost nil. A setup for getting lost in the mountains.

willow wands. Thin wooden dowels, usually painted green, stuck upright in the surface of a glacier every few dozen yards apart, to mark a trail and ensure route-finding in storms and **whiteouts.**

windslab. Plates of frozen snow poorly attached to softer snow beneath, the precipitating agent in windslab avalanches.

Index

About the Author

David Roberts has been called "a dean of modern adventure writing."
He is the author of seventeen books on mountaineering, adventure,
and the history of the American Southwest. His essays and articles
have appeared in *National Geographic*, *National Geographic Adventure*, *Smithsonian*, and *The Atlantic Monthly*, among other publications. He lives in Cambridge, Massachusetts.